THE S. MARK TAPER FOUNDATION

IMPRINT IN JEWISH STUDIES

BY THIS ENDOWMENT

THE S. MARK TAPER FOUNDATION SUPPORTS

THE APPRECIATION AND UNDERSTANDING

OF THE RICHNESS AND DIVERSITY OF

JEWISH LIFE AND CULTURE

The publisher gratefully acknowledges the generous support of the Jewish Studies Endowment Fund of the University of California Press Foundation, which was established by a major gift from the S. Mark Taper Foundation.

The publisher also acknowledges financial assistance provided by the Columbia University Institute for Israel and Jewish Studies.

Foreigners and Their Food

Foreigners and Their Food

Constructing Otherness in Jewish, Christian, and Islamic Law

David M. Freidenreich

UNIVERSITY OF CALIFORNIA PRESS
Berkeley   Los Angeles   London

University of California Press, one of the most distinguished university presses in the United States, enriches lives around the world by advancing scholarship in the humanities, social sciences, and natural sciences. Its activities are supported by the UC Press Foundation and by philanthropic contributions from individuals and institutions. For more information, visit www.ucpress.edu.

University of California Press
Berkeley and Los Angeles, California

University of California Press, Ltd.
London, England

Library of Congress Cataloging-in-Publication Data

Freidenreich, David M., 1977–.
Foreigners and their food : constructing otherness in Jewish, Christian, and Islamic law / David M. Freidenreich.
p. cm.
Includes bibliographical references and index.
ISBN 978-0-520-25321-6 (cloth, alk. paper)
1. Food—Religious aspects—Comparative studies. 2. Identification (Religion)—Comparative studies. 3. Religions—Relations. 4. Jews—Dietary laws. 5. Muslims—Dietary laws. 6. Food—Religious aspects—Christianity. I. Title.
BL65.F65F74 2011
201'.5—dc22 2011006099

Manufactured in the United States of America

20 19 18 17 16 15 14 13 12 11
10 9 8 7 6 5 4 3 2 1

In keeping with its commitment to support environmentally responsible and sustainable printing practices, UC Press has printed this book on Cascades Enviro 100, a 100% post consumer waste, recycled, de-inked fiber. FSC recycled certified and processed chlorine free. It is acid free, Ecologo certified, and manufactured by BioGas energy.

To all those with whom I have shared meals
and, especially, to Sara

CONTENTS

ILLUSTRATIONS

PREFACE

I love food. I enjoy eating but, even more, I love preparing food and sharing it with others. Many of my fondest memories and formative experiences are associated with meals, and my closest relationships have become so in part through the regular sharing of food. I have been fortunate enough to grow up and live in committed, supportive Jewish communities, and many of my meals have taken place within these circles. I have also been blessed with opportunities to share food with Christians and Muslims in settings ranging from relaxed Shabbat dinners at my home to intense conversations in an Arab classmate's dorm room over baklava and Iraqi coffee (not to be confused with the identical substance called "Turkish" coffee). This study is an exploration of a topic about which I am passionate: interaction with foreigners over food.

I should make clear from the start that I proudly practice what many of the authorities whom I study preach against. Although I am an ordained rabbi and consider myself an observant Jew, I eat food prepared by non-Jews and I share meals with non-Jews despite traditional norms prohibiting such activities. I disagree on principle with one of the primary motivations underlying the laws which I study. Religious authorities articulate foreign food restrictions as a means of thwarting efforts to establish connections across traditional boundaries, efforts that I believe are deeply enriching and vitally important. This study, somewhat subversively, demonstrates the connectedness of efforts by religious authorities to disconnect from one another, and it also demonstrates the value of making connections between their attitudes toward each other.

This book is not, however, a platform for my arguments in favor of commensality with religious outsiders. I am interested in understanding and explaining why the authorities I study articulate the restrictions they do, how these restrictions have developed over time, and how they relate to their counterparts in other religious traditions. The sources I examine continue to influence attitudes toward foreigners into the modern period and even the present day. If we are to understand one another better, with or without the sharing of food, we need to understand these sources on their own terms.

The bias I bring to this study manifests itself in the comparative approach I employ when interpreting religious texts. This approach is contrary to—yet complements—the traditional method of understanding such texts on the basis of sources found within the tradition's own canon and, in historically oriented circles, on the basis of the context in which these canonical texts were produced. This study is premised on the conviction that understanding sources from multiple traditions helps us understand the norms of any single tradition more clearly. I believe that the results of this study demonstrate the validity of its premise.

This book has been a challenge to write not only because it explores a broad and diverse array of sources—Jewish, Christian, and Islamic texts from their scriptural foundations through the Middle Ages—but also because it is intended for a broad and diverse array of readers. I imagine my audience to consist of individuals knowledgeable about some facets of the material I address but unfamiliar with most: students and scholars of Judaism, of Christianity, or of Islam with minimal background in other religious traditions, as well as students and scholars of comparative religion, law, and food studies with minimal exposure to premodern religious ideas and texts. My goal has been to write in a manner that is simultaneously accessible to all readers, including nonacademics, and sophisticated enough to engage the interest of experts. I have endeavored to keep citations and technical discussions to a minimum; in many instances, I refer readers interested in the more detailed discussion of a particular subject matter to articles that I have written for specialists. There will, however, no doubt be times when a reader feels that the discussion found this book is either unduly detailed or unnecessarily elementary, and I beg this reader's indulgence. As the bishop Stephen of Tournai (d. 1203) wrote in the introduction to a treatise intended both for lawyers and theologians, "If you invite two guests to dinner, you will not serve the same fare to those who demand opposite things. With the one asking for what the other scorns, will you not vary the dishes, lest either you throw the dining room into confusion or offend the diners?"[1] The value of bringing diverse readers to a common intellectual table, I believe, warrants the efforts to appeal to diverse tastes.

This book has its origins in my dissertation but has been thoroughly revised since then.[2] "Rewritten" may be a better description of the process, as I have spent more time "revising" than I devoted to writing that work. Nearly everything of value from the dissertation now appears either in this book or in one of the articles I have written since 2006, and anyone who cares to consult the dissertation should exercise caution: that work contains some ideas which I have since reconsidered and far too many errors. The process of rewriting-revising has been aided in countless ways by the comments, feedback, and insights of mentors, colleagues, and students with whom I have shared ideas and draft chapters, but I alone am responsible for what errors and faulty arguments remain.

I am grateful to the members of my dissertation committee—Michael Cook, David Weiss Halivni, Robert Somerville, Burton Visotzky, and Neguin Yavari—for their feedback on the dissertation and suggestions for future improvement. My colleagues and students at the University of Pennsylvania and its Center for Advanced Judaic Studies, Franklin & Marshall College, and Colby College have offered unfailing assistance and feedback, and I am thankful for the support provided by these three institutions and by their respective librarians. Harriet Freidenreich, Sara Kahn Troster, Jane Menton, John Turner, and Colby students in my spring 2010 seminar, "Food and Religious Identity," read and provided helpful comments on the entire manuscript; Samuel Klausner, Guy Stroumsa, and Sarah Stroumsa offered feedback on individual parts of this work. Jordan Rosenblum has provided especially valuable responses to my work in his book,[3] in his comments on my draft manuscript, and in numerous shared meals and conversations. I am grateful to Jordan for exemplifying the spirit of collegiality in pursuit of greater understanding.

I am pleased to acknowledge once more the financial assistance provided by Columbia University, the Jewish Theological Seminary, the Memorial Foundation for Jewish Culture, the Maurice and Marilyn Cohen Doctoral Dissertation Fellowship in Jewish Studies of the National Foundation for Jewish Culture, and the Mrs. Giles Whiting Foundation Fellowship during the years in which I worked on the dissertation. The Columbia University Institute for Israel and Jewish Studies generously provided a subvention to support the publication of this book, and I am thankful to Michael Stanislawski both for offering this assistance and for drawing my work to the attention of Stan Holwitz at the University of California Press. I am grateful to Stan and to the many other editors at the Press with whom I have had the pleasure to work.

Most of all, I wish to express my deepest gratitude to my wife, Sara Kahn Troster, for her comments, criticism, and advice, for constantly supporting me in all of my endeavors, and especially for the sharing of our lives—and our food.

NOTES ON STYLE AND ABBREVIATIONS

This work analyzes multiple independent sets of literature, each with its own community of academic researchers and its own standards for transliterations, abbreviations, and the like. I have made an effort to balance deference to the differing stylistic norms associated with specific disciplines and the advantages afforded by a uniform style applicable to Jewish, Christian, and Islamic sources alike. I follow the common practice of anglicizing the names of Biblical and Christian books and figures, but present the names of Rabbinic and Islamic books and figures in transliteration, in keeping with the standards employed by most Islamicists and many scholars of Rabbinic Judaism. Thus, rather inconsistently: Ishmael (Abraham's son, in the context of the Hebrew Bible), Ismāʿīl (the same person, in the context of the Qur'an), Yishmaʿel (a second-century Rabbinic Sage who shares his name with this biblical figure). When referring to the books revered as scripture by Jews and Christians alike, I generally employ the neutral, language-based term *Hebrew Bible* rather than the ideologically freighted terms *Tanakh* or *Old Testament*; I employ the latter term when its specifically Christian implication is intended.

All titles of books, including works of scripture, are italicized. My departure from the common convention of not italicizing names of Biblical books is due to a desire both for consistency (so as not to privilege one particular scriptural canon) and for clarity (so as to distinguish between *Daniel,* the book, and its protagonist, Daniel). Collections containing discrete units are not italicized. Thus: Hebrew Bible, Torah, *Genesis;* New Testament, *Acts;* Mishnah *Ḥullin;* Qur'an, *Sūrat al-Māʾidah.* Translations of the Hebrew Bible are based on the New Jewish Publication Society translation, while those of the New Testament are based on the New Revised Standard Version; in both cases, however, I have made occasional emendations in consultation with the standard critical editions. Translations of the Qur'an are based on those of Arberry, Dawood, Fakhry, and Paret in consultation with the standard Egyptian text, to which all citations refer. When not otherwise noted, all other translations are original.

I employ an amalgamated system for the transliteration of Semitic languages based on the standard Hebrew language guide of the *Encyclopaedia Judaica* and the Arabic transliteration system of the *Encyclopaedia of Islam* (with the customary alterations to that system). I use full diacritics in transliteratons of Syriac and Arabic terms except when those terms have entered into English parlance (e.g., Qur'an, not Qur'ān). Scholars will be able to recognize the original equivalents of my transliterations immediately even though they themselves might transliterate differently. In citations, colons separate a volume number from all other numbers, while periods separate sections from subsections, including the numbers of chapters and verses.

I have attempted to keep abbreviations to a minimum for the benefit of readers who are not familiar with the sources or conventions of a particular tradition or scholarly field. The abbreviations I do employ within the body of this work (besides the standard abbreviations for Biblical books) are as follows:

A.Z.	*'Avodah Zarah* (when referring to the *Mishneh Torah: Hilkhot 'Avodah Zarah*)
b.	son of
B.	Bavli (Babylonian Talmud)
c. (cc.)	canon(s), chapter(s) (the terms are interchangable in many Latin sources)
C.	*Causa* (a major section in the second part of Gratian's *Decretum*)
d.	death date
D.	*Distinctio* (a major section in the first or third part of the *Decretum*)
Ḥul.	*Ḥullin* (when referring to the Toseftan tractate: *Sheḥitat Ḥullin*)
Jub.	*Jubilees*
LORD	the four-letter Hebrew name of God (Yahweh)
LSJ	Liddell, Scott, and Jones, *A Greek-English Lexicon*
LXX	Septuagint (the Greek translation of the Hebrew Bible ascribed to seventy scholars)
M.	Mishnah
M.A.	*Hilkhot Ma'akhalot Asurot*, a section of the *Mishneh Torah*
NRSV	New Revised Standard Version translation of the Christian Bible and Apocrypha
OLD	*Oxford Latin Dictionary*
q.	*quaestio* (a subsection in the second part of Gratian's *Decretum*)
Q.	Qur'an

r.	regnal dates, or: recto
R.	Rabbi, or: Rav
Sh.	*Shabbat*
T.	Tosefta
v. (vv.)	verse(s), or: verso
Y.	Yerushalmi (Palestinian Talmud)
YD	*Yoreh De'ah,* a section of the *Arba'ah Ṭurim* and the *Shulḥan 'Arukh*
=	the identical passage in another version of the same source
//	a parallel appearance of the same or similar material in a separate source
§	a numbered subunit of text not otherwise identified

PART ONE

Introduction

Imagining Otherness

Something there is that doesn't love a wall,
That sends the frozen-ground-swell under it,
And spills the upper boulders in the sun;
And makes gaps even two can pass abreast.
The work of hunters is another thing:
I have come after them and made repair
Where they have left not one stone on a stone,
But they would have the rabbit out of hiding,
To please the yelping dogs. The gaps I mean,
No one has seen them made or heard them made,
But at spring mending-time we find them there.
I let my neighbor know beyond the hill;
And on a day we meet to walk the line
And set the wall between us once again.
We keep the wall between us as we go.
To each the boulders that have fallen to each.
And some are loaves and some so nearly balls
We have to use a spell to make them balance:
"Stay where you are until our backs are turned!"
We wear our fingers rough with handling them.
Oh, just another kind of out-door game,
One on a side. It comes to little more:
There where it is we do not need the wall:
He is all pine and I am apple orchard.
My apple trees will never get across
And eat the cones under his pines, I tell him.
He only says, "Good fences make good neighbors."
Spring is the mischief in me, and I wonder
If I could put a notion in his head:
"Why do they make good neighbors? Isn't it
Where there are cows? But here there are no cows.
Before I built a wall I'd ask to know
What I was walling in or walling out,

And to whom I was like to give offense.
Something there is that doesn't love a wall,
That wants it down." I could say "Elves" to him,
But it's not elves exactly, and I'd rather
He said it for himself. I see him there
Bringing a stone grasped firmly by the top
In each hand, like an old-stone savage armed.
He moves in darkness as it seems to me,
Not of woods only and the shade of trees.
He will not go behind his father's saying,
And he likes having thought of it so well
He says again, "Good fences make good neighbors."

ROBERT FROST, "MENDING WALL"

1

Good Fences Make Good Neighbors

A priest, a minister, and a rabbi walk into a bar. The bartender says, "What is this, a joke?"

Complete the joke as you will, the punch line that interests me is already implicit in the first sentence. Priest–minister–rabbi jokes are clichés in early twenty-first-century American culture, and there is nothing especially surprising or funny about the fact that these members of the clergy would walk into a bar together—the punch line comes as that scenario unfolds. Until recently, however, the scenario itself would have been inconceivable, for a host of reasons. This study focuses on one of those reasons: the bar.

Allow me to change the venue of this encounter from a bar to a restaurant so that an imam can join in on the joke. If our religious figures adhered to all of the dietary restrictions found in the classical sources of their respective traditions, their efforts to go out for dinner might prove quite comic. The imam, if a Sunni, would have no difficulty: if he did not want simply to order vegetarian, he could make a case for eating most meat dishes served at this (presumably Christian-operated) restaurant. A Shiʿi, however, might find himself eating an undressed salad at his own table. The rabbi would likely order a salad as well, although for different reasons than his Shiʿi counterpart. The two Christians might be willing to eat everything on the menu so long as the cooks aren't Jewish, yet they, like the Shiʿi, would demand a separate table (perhaps tables?) as well. Under such circumstances, it seems unlikely that these members of diverse religious communities would bother walking into a restaurant together in the first place. At a certain level, that's precisely the point.

An anthropological textbook succinctly expresses the reality we often take for granted: "Probably in every society to offer food (and sometimes drink) is to offer love, affection, and friendship. To accept proffered food is to acknowledge and accept the feelings expressed and to reciprocate them." The acts of sharing and exchanging food thus establish and reinforce a sense of commonality, of community. The converse is true as well: "To fail to offer food in a context in which it is expected culturally is to express anger or hostility. Equally, to reject proffered food is to reject an offer of love or friendship, to express hostility toward the giver."[1] Refusal to share or exchange food is a profound expression of the notion that the would-be participants in such interaction are, to a significant degree, different one from the other. Injunctions demanding such evidently hostile behavior toward certain classes of people convey powerfully the message that the divide between Us and Them ought not be bridged. These injunctions, moreover, construct the otherness of those classified as Them so as to more fully articulate the identity of Us.

Through the exploration of Jewish, Christian, and Islamic norms regarding food prepared by religious foreigners and the act of eating with such outsiders, this study illuminates the ways in which ancient and medieval scholars conceptualize the identities of Us and Them, as well as the broader social order which both subsets of humanity populate.[2] Regulations governing other people's food relate directly to the border lines demarcating religious communities, and advocates of such regulations embrace the proverb at the core of Robert Frost's "Mending Wall": "Good fences make good neighbors." By examining the classifications of foreigners and of foodstuffs embedded in these regulations, this study reveals several distinct definitions of what constitutes "good fences" and engages the insistent question of Frost's speaker: "*Why* do they make good neighbors?" In the process, this work also offers a model for the classificatory activity of contemporary academic scholars of religion.

FOREIGN FOOD RESTRICTIONS AND IMAGINED IDENTITIES

Food is not merely a source of vital nutrients. Because of its central role in human life and its practically infinite diversity, food also serves as a powerful medium for the expression and transmission of culture and, more specifically, of communal identity. Indeed, many of the choices individuals make regarding which food to eat and which food to avoid relate to their senses of identity. As Claude Fischler observes, humans are omnivores, biologically speaking, yet every culture classifies certain edible items as unacceptable in a civilized diet. "Human beings mark their membership of a culture or a group by asserting the specificity of what they eat, or more precisely—but it amounts to the same thing—by defining the otherness, the difference of others" who make different choices about what one should eat.[3] Indeed, individuals and communities frequently identify themselves, or are caricatured by others, in terms of their dietary practices; among Fischler's examples, the English call the French "Frogs" while the French depict the English as "Roastbeefs." By their implicitly reciprocal nature—They eat food *x* but We do not—these metonymic characterizations reflect Our perceptions of both Our identity and Theirs. Because these identity markers depend on the existence of a significant difference between the food practices of insiders and outsiders, however, they raise the uncomfortable possibility that the distinction between these groups could collapse: if insiders eat food *x*, might We become Them?[4] Willful abstention from foods associated (accurately or inaccurately) with a particular foreign community expresses the conviction that the distinction between Us and Them must remain intact. Thus, for example, some Americans who supported the 2003 Iraq War, which France opposed, chose to avoid consuming French wine and to rename the foodstuff commonly called "French fries."

Not all choices about food, however, serve to mark a distinctive communal identity or are understood in terms of that function. A parent telling a young child, "We don't eat worms," is not enculturating the child into a particular community. The statement by that parent, "We don't eat frogs," could convey the same generic message—some foods are unfit for consumption by civilized people—but it could also convey the message, "We are not French." A statement about Our food practices is only a marker of communal identity when accompanied, explicitly or implicitly, by a contrast with Their food practices. (A statement about Their food practices usually implies a contrast with Our own: the English do not characterize the French as "Fish," even though per capita consumption of fish is surely higher in France than that of frogs, because the English eat fish too.)

This caveat to the identity-marking function of food practices also applies to religiously inspired practices of avoiding certain foodstuffs. Although ingredient-based religious food restrictions have certainly marked the identity of their adherents in various times and places, this function is not intrinsic to these laws but depends instead on the difference between insiders and outsiders which these laws may or may not establish. To cite an example from the Hebrew Bible, the statement "We do not eat the meat of pigs" is, on its own, no more a statement of identity than "We do not eat the meat of vultures" or "We do not eat the meat of rock badgers," other animals on the Biblical list of forbidden species.[5] The pork taboo only marks its adherents as distinctive within the context of other people who regularly eat pork, and it only constitutes a marker of communal boundaries in the minds of those who contrast one group's refusal to eat pork with another group's willingness to eat it. Ingredient-based food restrictions classify foodstuffs—the meat of some animal species is permitted, but that of pigs and rock badgers, among others, is not—without necessarily classifying people in the process. For that reason, the function of these restrictions as identity markers that distinguish Us from Them is indirect and only latent: it may not be active at any given time nor intended by any given legislator or interpreter.[6] Thus, from the perspective of American Jews and Muslims, abstention from pork constitutes a significant marker of identity but abstention from the meat of vultures does not.[7]

There are, however, two types of religious food restrictions that manifestly and directly contribute to the formation and maintenance of a communal identity because they address not only foodstuffs but also the distinction between Us and Them. *Commensality-based regulations* prohibit the sharing of meals with certain people—think racially segregated lunch counters or middle school cafeteria cliques—and *preparer-based regulations* prohibit eating food made by certain people. By regulating food-related interaction across the border separating two groups, commensality-based and preparer-based food restrictions establish and reaffirm the distinct identities of each group while ascribing authority to a particular conception regarding the place of these groups within the broader social order. Some commensality-based and preparer-based restrictions regulate interaction over food with certain classes of co-religionists, prohibiting, for example, shared meals with heretics or consumption of food prepared by those who do not subscribe to sectarian norms. This study focuses on laws regulating the involvement of religious outsiders in preparing or sharing food. These "foreign food restrictions," as I call them for ease of reference, prohibit eating otherwise unproblematic food specifically because of the role played in its preparation or consumption by someone who adheres to a religion other than one's own.[8] Discussions of foreign food restrictions reflect the ideas of religious scholars about the systems of classification which these restrictions reinforce, systems that underpin conceptions of communal identity and of the ordered world itself. Food, as Claude Lévi-Strauss famously observed, is not merely good to eat but also "good to think," and foreign food restrictions are especially good for thinking about foreigners and the relationship between Us and Them.[9]

Social scientists have long recognized the significant role which commensality plays in the classification of interpersonal relationships and, consequently, in the formation of group identity and a sense of the proper social order. In the words of William Robertson Smith, a late nineteenth-century Orientalist, "those who eat and drink together are by this very act tied to one another by a bond of friendship and mutual obligation. . . . Commensality can be thought of (1) as confirming or even (2) as constituting kinship in a very real sense."[10] Claude Grignon, writing over a century later, emphasizes the converse of this observation, namely the significant function that excluding outsiders from shared meals plays in defining the limits of one's group and strengthening the bonds that unite insiders.[11] Mary Douglas, in turn, demonstrates the ways in which norms regarding suitable dining partners reflect patterns of social relations and ideas about "different degrees of hierarchy, inclusion and exclusion, boundaries and transactions across the boundaries. Like sex, the taking of food has a social component, as well as a biological one."[12] Prohibitions of commensality with foreigners, like the closely related prohibition of engaging in sexual relations with such individuals, constitute fences intended to preserve communal cohesiveness by "walling in" insiders and "walling out" outsiders. The authors of these restrictions focus on the importance of distinguishing between Us and Them and, in many cases, segregating the members of these groups. For that reason, they do not share the concern of Frost's speaker regarding "whom I was like to give offense" by erecting such walls.

Prohibitions against eating food prepared by outsiders not only impede social intercourse with foreigners but also, symbolically, prevent adherents of these restrictions from internalizing "foreign" attributes. Such injunctions reflect the notion that prepared foodstuffs embody the identity of their preparers. Lévi-Strauss distinguishes between the "raw" and the "cooked"; the latter, a reference to foods that have been subjected to "cultural transformation," symbolically embodies culture itself.[13] Fischler presents the act of food preparation as a symbolic means of assimilating natural ingredients into human culture before literally incorporating them into the human body. "'Raw' food is fraught with danger, a 'wildness' that is tamed by culinary treatment. Once marked in this way, it is seen as less dangerous. It can safely take its place on the plate and then in the eater's body."[14] "Cooked" food, however, can be fraught with its own form of danger: through preparation by an outsider, food can be seen to take on certain essentially foreign characteristics which the insider would then ingest. Some of the preparer-based foreign food restrictions we will encounter are based solely on the fact that a foreigner participated in the preparation process, while others specifically prohibit food which foreigners have prepared in the context of a religious ritual, such as an idolatrous sacrifice. (Self-respecting participants in such a sacrifice would never call it "idolatrous," but we will not see the world through their eyes in this study.)

Foreign food restrictions based on the foreignness of the preparer differ qualitatively from restrictions based on the idolatrous manner of the food's preparation. The former *mark* certain food and certain food preparers as Them—We may not eat Their food because They are not Us—but this marker says nothing about the identities of Us and Them beyond the fact that these identities are distinct. The latter, in contrast, convey a specific message about these identities: whereas They worship idols, We worship God alone and therefore abstain from all food associated with idolatry. Foreign food restrictions like the prohibition against consuming food sacrificed to idols not only mark the otherness of foreigners but also *define* the identity of those others (They are idolaters) and of Ourselves (We are monotheists). Embedded in such a definition is an evaluative judgment: We are superior to Them because We possess a positive attribute which They lack or because They possess a negative attribute from which We are free. Restrictions that convey content about the identity of others and thus ascribe different value to different groups can also be used to classify foreigners in greater detail: We, as monotheists, may not eat group A's food because They are idolaters, but We may eat group B's food, even though They are not Us, because They, like Us, do not worship idols. In this format, foreign food restrictions not only define but also *relativize* the otherness of foreigners by expressing the notion that members of group B are less inferior—indeed, less foreign—to Us than members of group A.

By marking, defining, or relativizing the otherness of foreigners, foreign food restrictions construct powerful and nuanced distinctions between Us and Them; these various types of distinctions contribute in significant ways to communal conceptions of both otherness and self-identity. Different types of distinctions, however, demand different kinds of restrictions. These restrictions, moreover, may limit access to desirable foodstuffs or result in undesirable social repercussions. It is no wonder, then, that over time boulders spill off these walls, at times leaving "gaps even two can pass abreast." The authors and heroes of religious texts, like the figures in Frost's poem, periodically mend these walls or decry the acts of those who wantonly breach them. In other contexts, however, we will see that these custodians of the tradition are sometimes themselves the hunters who

> have left not one stone on a stone,
> But they would have the rabbit out of hiding,
> To please the yelping dogs.

I mean by this analogy that religious scholars sometimes reconfigure or even dismantle traditional food fences in the service of their own agendas, classificatory and otherwise.

Because discussions of foreign food restrictions express particular systems of classifying insiders and outsiders, they reveal the ways in which their participants imagine their own communities, other religious communities in their midst, and the broader social order in which these communities are embedded. I use the term *imagination* in the same manner as Benedict Anderson, whose definition of modern nations as "imagined communities" both limited in scope and sovereign in nature applies well to premodern religions.[15] Such a community "is *imagined* because the members of even the smallest nation [or, I would add, religious tradition] will never know most of their fellow-members, meet them, or even hear of them, yet in the minds of each lives the image of their communion. . . . In fact, all communities larger than primordial villages of face-to-face contact (and perhaps even these) are imagined. Communities are to be distinguished, not by their falsity/genuineness, but by the style in which they are imagined."[16]

A major finding of the present study is that Jews, Christians, and Muslims have imagined their respective communities in qualitatively different "styles." The different methods members of these communities employ when classifying humanity reflect these differences in self-identification. Frost's speaker and his neighbor can only erect a shared wall because both of them embrace the same notions of ownership and acknowledge the validity of the same property line; they employ the same style of thought in conceptualizing their real estate claims. The religious elites who are the subjects of this study, in contrast, often do not construct their walls in the same places as do their counterparts from other religious communities. They draw incongruent border lines around their respective communities and establish different kinds of barriers along these borders because they imagine the proper social order in fundamentally different ways.

Anderson's work demonstrates the considerable degree to which the image of a particular group's "communion"—and its mirror-image, reflecting the group's lack of communion with foreigners—is shaped by the ideas of the educated elites who undertake to speak on the group's behalf. The elites who speak on behalf of a religious community, like their nation-oriented counterparts, are keenly aware of the boundaries surrounding their community and the presence of others beyond these bounds. They seek to disseminate ideas about Us and Them within their community through its institutions of education and enculturation.[17] These elites, moreover, take for granted the sovereignty of their community's religious tradition, which is to say the sovereign authority of the sacred texts at the core of the community's educational curriculum. By extension, religious authority rests in the hands of the very elites whose education qualifies them to interpret these sources properly and enables them to produce texts later incorporated into the curriculum.

We can, therefore, speak of both these texts and these interpreters as religious authorities. The ideas of these authorities about communal borders and food-related interaction across such lines contribute in significant ways to the imagined identity of their religious communities and, thus, to the ways members of these communities imagine otherness. By expressing these ideas and their underlying systems of classification within the traditional curricula, educated elites construct the notions of communal identity which future generations of scholars internalize. To the extent that these notions assume the quality of objective facts that shape the behaviors of community members, they have an even greater impact on the community's collective self-understanding: as Jordan D. Rosenblum puts it, "*texts prescribe practices; practices index identity.*"[18] Religious ideas regarding a community's identity and boundaries, however, are embedded in scholarly texts, so their diffusion among nonscholars often remains limited. Here, the parallel between modern nations and premodern religious communities begins to break down, as modern governments possess far more powerful means of communicating and imposing their classificatory systems upon society than do premodern religious authorities.

Tzvi Abusch, describing the Code of Hammurabi, explains that "the code is not binding and does not necessarily reflect actual practice; it is, however, a literary and intellectual construct that gives expression to legal thinking and moral values."[19] The same may be said regarding most of the works we will examine in this study: they do not reveal the extent to which foreign food restrictions were followed within any given community, let alone the degree to which the broader public internalized elite ideas regarding foreigners. They do, however, capture the ideas and thought processes that underlie these restrictions. For that reason, this study of texts about foreign food restrictions is a history not of social reality but rather of intellectual imagination.

The concept of imagination helps us appreciate the intellectual and inventive nature of the communal identities and boundaries which religious authorities express, in part, through foreign food restrictions. It also helps us understand the nature of the concerns about interaction with foreigners that underlie many of these restrictions. François Hartog, among others, has demonstrated the degree to which portrayals of foreigners reflect the imaginations of their authors rather than the reality they ostensibly depict. As such, these portrayals function not as windows onto a foreign landscape but rather as mirrors reflecting and intensifying the manner in which their authors understand their own community and its place within the broader social order.[20] It will become clear that the foreigners addressed by foreign food restrictions are frequently products of such imaginative activity, much as the neighbor in "Mending Wall" becomes "an old-stone savage armed" in the mischievous and increasingly mean-spirited imagination of the speaker. Indeed, one might even say regarding this speaker and his religious counterparts that walls and their classificatory foundations themselves foster vicious stereotypes about those on the other side of the divide. This is a further reason why foreign food restrictions are both unreliable as sources of social history and especially valuable as data through which to explore the intellectual activity of religious authorities as they construct the otherness of religious foreigners.

What interests me in studying texts about foreign food restrictions is neither "law in action," how laws function in society, nor merely "law in books," but rather what William Ewald calls "law in minds," the context of ideas upon which scholars of the law call when they formulate and interpret the rules found in legal literature.[21] This context is considerably narrower than the full panoply of religious ideas, so a history of normative ideas can only reflect one facet of religious attitudes toward communal identity and the otherness of foreigners. I have not, however, restricted myself to the study of legal literature in the strict sense of that term because religious authorities engage in normative discourse within other literary genres as well.

CONTEXTS AND COMPARISONS

Ewald defines the field he calls "comparative jurisprudence," in contrast to comparative law as commonly taught in American law schools, as the study of law produced in a culture other than one's own for the purpose of understanding how participants in that culture's legal system think about their own law.

> When we study a foreign legal system, the principal thing to grasp is not the external aspects—say, the sociological statistics about judges or the economic functioning of the rules or even the details of the black-letter doctrines—but rather what might be

> called the "cognitive structure" of the legal system. Recall that our goal is to be able to communicate with the foreign jurists; and communication requires not just that we observe their external behavior, but that we come to understand their style of thought and the reasons for which they act: that we regard them as conscious agents. We must therefore seek to embed the black-letter rules within a web of beliefs, ideals, choices, desires, interests, justifications, principles, techniques, reasons, and assumptions. The hope is that, in this way, we will come to understand the legal system from within and be able to think about it as a foreigner thinks.[22]

Law, as Ewald approaches it, is a conscious mental activity whose practitioners seek correct answers to legal questions within the framework of their system of norms. In order to understand the answers which foreign jurists provide, one must be able to think like a foreign jurist, a skill that depends on familiarity with the intellectual context of these jurists.[23] Indeed, familiarity with this context can often help us not only to understand the statements of foreign jurists but also to account for why they offer one answer to a particular question rather than another.

The present work of comparative jurisprudence examines ancient and medieval foreign food restrictions so as to understand the styles of thought which Jewish, Christian, and Islamic authorities employ when classifying foreigners and foodstuffs and, thus, to gain insights into the styles in which these authorities imagine the identities of their own communities. This study, however, is comparative in more ways than the one that gives "comparative jurisprudence" its title. Ewald calls his approach "comparative" because attention to similarity and difference is implicit when a law student from one culture analyzes law produced in another. In addition to this implicit act of comparison, I seek explicitly to account for similarities and differences between the distinct legal cultures associated with Judaism, Christianity, and Islam. I also seek to understand similarities and differences within the legal culture of individual religious traditions across different time periods, geographic regions, and schools of thought.

To accomplish these tasks, I construct what might be called horizontal, vertical, and diagonal comparisons among the foreign food restrictions which I analyze. By "horizontal," I mean comparisons that address norms articulated within the context of a single time period or cultural milieu, such as the ancient Hellenistic world or the medieval Islamic Near East. By "vertical," I mean comparisons that address norms articulated in different time periods within a single intellectual tradition, such as norms found in the Bible, the writings of Church Fathers, and the works of medieval Christian authorities. Synchronic and diachronic comparisons of these sorts are commonplace, even within scholarship that is not self-consciously comparative, because they reflect the fact that religious authorities both root themselves in a particular intellectual tradition and live in a specific historical and cultural environment. We should bear in mind, however, that vertical and horizontal comparisons sometimes involve norms associated with more than one religious community.

The intellectual patrimonies of Judaism, Christianity, and Islam include sources that predate the formation of these traditions (e.g., the Christian "Old Testament"), and religious authorities often interpret their own tradition within a cultural milieu shaped in significant ways by members of another religious community (e.g., rabbis in the "Islamic" Near East).

Less commonplace is the use of "diagonal" comparisons—those addressing norms that share neither a common intellectual tradition nor a common cultural milieu (e.g., Rabbinic norms originating in the ancient Hellenistic world and medieval Islamic norms). Diagonal comparisons are artificial in the sense that the relationship between the comparands would not exist had the comparativist not imagined it. Jonathan Z. Smith, however, observes that the same may be said regarding all comparisons.

> There is nothing "natural" about the enterprise of comparison. Similarity and difference are not "given." They are the result of mental operations. In this sense, *all comparisons are properly analogical* and fall under J. S. Mill's dictum, "If we have the slightest reason to suppose any real connection between . . . A and B, the argument is no longer one of analogy." In the case of the study of religion, as in any disciplined inquiry, comparison, in its strongest form, brings differences together within the space of the scholar's mind for the scholar's own intellectual reasons. It is the scholar who makes their cohabitation—their "sameness"—possible, not "natural" affinities or processes of history.[24]

Even seemingly "natural" comparisons, such as those between two texts from the same tradition or the same cultural and historical context, are the products of scholarly imagination. Comparisons that involve data from multiple traditions, locations, and time periods, diagonal or otherwise, serve to broaden the interpretive context associated with any given norm and thus enable us better to understand that norm and its authors.

I often use comparisons to generate hypotheses, viewing one comparand through the lens provided by another so as to see it from a perspective I might not otherwise have considered.[25] Because no explanatory weight rests on such an act of comparison, the artificiality of the relationship between its comparands is irrelevant. I frequently construct vertical or horizontal comparisons rather than diagonal comparisons to limit the degree of difference between the comparands, but the comparison of texts that, from most perspectives, stem from quite different contexts can provide especially valuable insights. By placing the analysis of disparate texts between the covers of a single volume, moreover, I implicitly invite readers to draw their own lines of comparison and adopt a variety of perspectives into our subject matter.

I also employ comparison as the basis for constructing generic categories within the class of texts I have brought together under the title "foreign food restrictions."

Taxonomy, like the acts of comparison that contribute to it, is an act of imagination that enables us to better understand specific norms by placing them in cohabitation with other norms as exemplars of generic categories. The application of multiple overlapping taxonomic criteria—religious tradition, time period, geographic region, type of food restriction, and style of classifying foreigners, to name only a few—yields greater insight into these norms.[26] This practice also serves to highlight the imagined nature of the resulting categories: because sources grouped together in one system of classification are separate in another, we are constantly reminded that there is no single "right" way to classify the data set under examination. This reminder is especially useful while studying the imagination-driven categories used by Jewish, Christian, and Islamic authorities to define Us and Them, categories that are easily taken for granted.

The imagined nature of the relationships I construct through comparison should not obscure the fact that actual relationships also exist among many of the works I study. At the broadest level, Judaism, Christianity, and Islam are all monotheistic religions that revere the traditions (if not the text) of the Hebrew Bible. All three religions, moreover, draw on elements of the common Near Eastern culture out of which they emerged and on the intellectual heritage of Greek philosophy. The same cultural and intellectual currents often affected religious authorities active in the same region irrespective of their traditional affiliation. These common factors contribute in significant ways to the formation and development of ideas about foreign food restrictions within all three traditions. Most specifically, the educational curriculum at the core of each tradition ensures that each tradition's authorities know the same foundational texts and ideas. One can often find sufficient evidence to demonstrate a given scholar's familiarity with the works of his predecessors and, sometimes, those of his contemporaries as well. Evidence for historical relationships among texts about foreign food restrictions allows us to trace the evolution of ideas about classification systems and communal identities. The insights gleaned from our comparative endeavors, moreover, further our ability to understand both specific conceptions of foreign food restrictions and the phenomenon of foreign food restrictions as a whole.

AN OVERVIEW OF THIS STUDY

Shaye J. D. Cohen, in his study of the boundaries that members of the educated Jewish elite created around their community, concludes as follows: "Jewishness, the conscious affirmation of the qualities that make Jews Jews, presumes a contrast between Us and Them. The Jews constitute an Us; all the rest of humanity, or, in Jewish language, the nations of the world, the gentiles, constitute a Them. Between Us and Them is a line, a boundary, drawn not in sand or stone but in the mind. The line is no less real for being imaginary, since both Us and Them agree that it exists. Although there is a boundary that separates the two, it is crossable and not always distinct."[27] The nature of the imagined boundary and the degree to which religious authorities tolerate its permeability reflect an aspect of the way those who speak on behalf of their communities define "Jewishness," "Christianness," and "Muslimness." This study examines the evolving conceptions of Us, Them, and the broader social order reflected in foreign food restrictions. The present chapter has laid out both the significance of the work's subject matter and the methods of comparison it employs.

Chapter 2, on food restrictions in the Hebrew Bible, introduces several themes that will recur throughout this study: the association of dietary practices with a distinctive communal identity, the anathematization of idolatry, notions regarding the proper method of slaughtering an animal, and conceptions of impurity. Discussion of the Hebrew Bible appears in part I of this study, the introductory unit, for two related reasons. The texts of the Hebrew Bible are foundational for both Judaism and Christianity—and also for Islam, albeit in a very different manner and to a much more limited extent—but they are not properly speaking the products of these religious communities. As Cohen makes clear, "Judaism" as a religious identity first develops within the Hellenistic world of the final centuries before the Common Era, after the composition of almost all of the Hebrew Bible; Christianity and Islam, of course, develop even later.[28] The second, and more important, reason for treating Biblical texts as prefatory is that these texts—with the telling exception of a work from the Hellenistic era, *Daniel*—contain no foreign food restrictions. Indeed, I will argue that pre-Hellenistic Biblical texts, in contrast to later interpretations of those texts, do not imagine Israelite food practices in contradistinction to those of non-Israelites. This conception of Biblical dietary laws emerges in tandem with the development, during the Hellenistic era, of a conception of Jewishness that is not purely ethnic. Chapter 2 illustrates an understanding of dietary laws different from that embraced by most of the Jewish, Christian, and Islamic authorities whose ideas we will explore subsequently. This chapter thus offers a valuable contrast to later discussions of foreign food restrictions.

The core of this study consists of three parts, one each for Jewish, Christian, and Islamic sources. Each part comprises three chapters that analyze the development of ideas regarding foreign food restrictions from their origins through their formalization in legal literature. Chapter 3 examines the reasons why foreign food restrictions develop among some Jewish elites within the Hellenistic world but not others, while chapters 4 and 5 consider what happens to these restrictions when subjected to Rabbinic analysis and presentation. Chapter 6 examines the ways in which New Testament passages about food restrictions, particularly foreign food restrictions, reflect an effort by early Christ-believers to create a unified community that spans the border between Jews and gentiles. Chapters 7 and 8 explore the ways in which those who speak for Christianity in its first millennium use foreign food restrictions to establish new borders around their religious community so as to exclude both idolatrous gentiles and, especially, Jews. Chapter 9 analyzes the roles that discourse about foreigners and food restrictions plays in the Qur'an. In chapters 10 and 11, we will examine the ways in which Sunni and Shi'i authorities employ discourse about food associated with foreigners to express distinctive conceptions regarding the nature of Judaism and Christianity and, more importantly, of Islam itself.

In addition to its focus on sources associated with a single religious tradition, each of the core units of this study discusses a specific factor that shapes discourse about foreigners and their food in all three traditions. Part II, particularly chapters 4–5, uses Rabbinic literature as a means of exploring the influence of the mode of thinking known as scholasticism on discourse about foreign food restrictions. Part III, specifically chapter 8, examines the impact on such discourse of conceptions regarding impurity, using Christian portrayals of Jews as the primary exemplar of this phenomenon. In part IV, chapter 11 considers the use of scripture in discourse about foreigners and food restrictions; this analysis draws both on instances of Qur'anic exegesis and also examples of Biblical exegesis encountered in prior chapters. The case studies that comprise the final part of this study (chapters 12–14) reflect the impact of these three factors—scholasticism, conceptions of impurity, and the use of scripture—on medieval discourse about foreign food restrictions.

Part V examines five cases in which medieval Jewish, Christian, and Islamic authorities apply traditional foreign food restrictions to adherents of fellow "Abrahamic" traditions. Chapter 12 considers Islamic and Christian discourse about meat that Jews refuse to eat; in chapter 13, we examine Islamic and Christian discourse about one another's food. Chapter 14 is devoted to the subject of Jewish conceptions of Muslims and Christians, as reflected in regulations governing wine associated with gentiles. These case studies highlight the importance that medieval authorities ascribe to their respective approaches to classifying humanity. They also show how distinctively Jewish, Christian, and Islamic styles of thought on this subject result in divergent responses to questions about the application of foreign food restrictions to contemporary foreigners. Chapter 12 begins with a discussion of the relationship between ideas about foreigners and the manners in which Jewish, Christian, and Islamic authorities imagine their own communities. Chapter 14 concludes by reflecting on the implications of this bond between attitudes toward Them and conceptions of Our own identity, both for the academic description of these ideas and for contemporary efforts at improving relations between different religious communities.

The present study demonstrates that Jewish, Christian, and Islamic foreign food restrictions rest upon different systems of classifying humanity, what Ewald might call distinct "styles of thought" particular to each religious community. In general, Jewish foreign food restrictions *mark the otherness* of non-Jews as "not Us" without drawing distinctions among gentiles. Christian foreign food restrictions *define the otherness* of certain non-Christians, distinguishing between gentile non-Christians, who are merely "not Us," and Jews, who are emphatically "anti-Us." Islamic foreign food restrictions—in ways that differ significantly between Sunnis and Shi'is—*relativize the otherness* of non-Muslims as "like Us" and "unlike Us." These differences in how Jewish, Christian, Sunni, and Shi'i authorities think about outsiders reflect what Anderson calls the distinct "styles" in which these authorities imagine their own communities.

The orientation of the three central parts of this study toward change over time within a single tradition foregrounds the task of historical and cultural contextualization. In this manner, I seek to avoid three pitfalls often found in works of comparative religion, summarized by Barbara Holdrege as (1) insufficient attention to differences, (2) insufficient attention to changes over time, and (3) insufficient attention to original context. Holdrege, in her comparative study of Hindu and Jewish conceptions of scripture, addresses these critiques by interpreting Hindu and Jewish sources independently, turning to comparative analysis only after thorough contextual analysis and reserving consideration of the significance of her comparative findings until her conclusion.[29]

The structure of Holdrege's work resembles a wedding cake: layers of tradition-specific cake, one on top of the other, some comparative icing between them, more cake and more icing, and finally smiling figurines on top representing the relationship between Jewish and Hindu sources. Although this structure is both effective and methodologically neat, it would be unduly artificial for the present study. I have chosen instead to blend comparison into each unit in a manner that more accurately reflects the integration of comparison at every stage of my own research and writing. The comparative content of this work increases as the study progresses and its readers encounter a wider range of sources for themselves, but early chapters are occasionally enriched with comparative observations and insights derived from the subject matter of later chapters, especially when comparison played a major role in shaping my own understanding of the sources I present. The end result of this structure is something more closely resembling a marble cake than a layered wedding cake, although perhaps a better metaphor—and one that would be acceptable to all of the religious authorities we left in that restaurant—is a salad, lightly tossed.

2

"A People Made Holy to the Lord"

Meals, Meat, and the Nature of Israel's Holiness in the Hebrew Bible

Recounting Joseph's meal with his brothers in Egypt, *Genesis* goes out of its way to describe the unusual seating arrangements: "They served [Joseph] by himself, and [his brothers] by themselves, and the Egyptians who ate with him by themselves; for the Egyptians could not dine with the Hebrews, since that would be an abomination to the Egyptians" (*Gen.* 43.32). The narrator also makes a point of noting that while Joseph served as Potiphar's personal attendant, Potiphar left all of his possessions in Joseph's care "except for the food which [Potiphar] ate" (39.6). The Egyptians, we are told, adhere to commensality-based and, it would seem, preparer-based foreign food restrictions. The fact that the narrator felt the need to describe these practices and explain the former in terms of a peculiarly Egyptian form of abhorrence suggests that it was not common among Israelites to exclude foreigners from their tables or prevent foreign servants from handling Israelite food.[1] Indeed, with the exception of *Daniel,* the latest work included in the Jewish scriptural canon, the books that comprise the Hebrew Bible neither advocate for foreign food restrictions nor encourage Israelites (or their successors, the Jews) to maintain an arm's-length distance from their neighbors in matters related to food.[2]

Viewed through the lens of this study's exploration of foreign food restrictions, the Hebrew Bible's nonchalant attitude toward the food of foreigners is striking and demands explanation. The Hebrew Bible, after all, emphasizes the distinction between Us and Them and the superiority of Israelite religion over all others, as do those who later speak on behalf of Judaism, Christianity, and Islam. Biblical texts that address dietary laws, moreover, consistently associate these regulations with Israel's distinctive identity. Because Israelites are holy, these texts declare, they must adhere to various norms regarding the consumption of flesh from formerly living creatures.[3] Why, then, do these texts fail to prohibit the consumption of meat prepared by non-Israelites or, for that matter, the practice of eating with non-Israelites? The silence of Biblical law in this respect becomes even more perplexing when we examine narrative references to instances in which Israelites consume food associated with foreigners. This chapter surveys such references before turning its attention to our central question; it concludes with a brief discussion of impurity, a concept whose significance to the present study will become apparent in subsequent chapters.

THE FOOD OF FOREIGNERS IN BIBLICAL NARRATIVES

The acts of offering and sharing food constitute central components of the rituals that establish relations between individuals and peoples within ancient Near Eastern culture,[4] and the Hebrew Bible portrays its heroes as active participants in that culture without any condemnation of their behavior. Abram accepts bread and wine from Melchizedek, King of Salem (*Gen.* 14.18); Isaac makes a feast for the Philistines Abimelech and Phicol (*Gen.* 26.30); Jacob shares meals with his Aramean kinsmen (*Gen.* 31.46, 54); Moses' Midianite father-in-law breaks bread with Aaron and the elders of Israel (*Exod.* 18.12)—these incidents are all examples of covenant meals involving preparation of food by foreigners or commensality with non-Israelites. Similarly, Joshua and the Israelite elders raise no objection to accepting bread and wine offered by foreigners interested in establishing a covenant with the Israelites, so long as these foreigners are not among the peoples with whom covenants are forbidden (*Josh.* 9). Among the reported incidents of commensality not associated with covenants, Samson drinks with Philistines at his wedding banquets (*Judg.* 14) and Elisha regularly eats at the home of a Shunamite woman (2 *Kings* 4.8).[5]

Indeed, *Deuteronomy* reports that God directly enjoins the Israelites to accept food from foreign peoples during their journey through the wilderness. Referring to Israel's impending travels through the territory of Esau's descendants, God states, "What food you eat you shall obtain from them for money; similarly, the water you drink you shall procure for money" (*Deut.* 2.6). Israelites should allow themselves to depend upon the local population for their provisions, and God has no objection to Israelite consumption of the food provided by these "kinsmen" (2.4). The permissibility of such behavior, however, evidently does not stem from the relationship between the descendents of Jacob and the descendents of Esau, as Moses makes the same offer to purchase food and water from the Amorite King Sihon of Heshbon (2.28). Eating the food of foreigners is simply not a problem in *Deuteronomy;* quite the contrary, refusal by the Ammonites and Moabites to offer the Israelites food and water on their journey constitutes an unforgivable expression of hostility (*Deut.* 23.4–7).

In the many references to feasting and drinking in *Esther,* a relatively late work within the Hebrew Biblical canon, one finds no indication that either the heroine of this story or its narrator sees anything wrong with Jewish participation in Persian banquets or Jewish consumption of Persian food and alcohol.[6] Esther is furnished with "her cosmetics and her food rations" upon her arrival at the Persian palace (*Esther* 2.9);[7] although these rations presumably came from the royal stores, there is no indication that Esther refused them. Indeed, Esther herself hosts two wine feasts involving non-Jews in order to forestall Haman's plot (5.6, 7.1). Adele Berlin states that the lack of any reference to the observance of dietary laws or other rituals "marks *Esther* as being different from other biblical and apocryphal works."[8] Esther's acceptance of food from a foreign king, however, has a precedent within biblical literature: King Jehoiachin of Judah, taken into Babylonian captivity, also received a daily allotment of food from King Evil-merodach of Babylon (*2 Kings* 25.29–30 // *Jer.* 52.33–34).[9] The lack of concern within *Esther* regarding non-Jewish food does indeed stand out in contrast to the tenor of Jewish works from the Hellenistic period of Jewish history, including the Greek version of *Esther* and the Biblical *Daniel*, but this nonchalance is unsurprising when viewed from the perspective of earlier and roughly contemporaneous Biblical texts.

One might expect to find concern about the food of gentiles in *Ezra* and *Nehemiah*, works associated with two Persian-appointed leaders of the Jewish community reestablished in Judea in the fifth century B.C.E.[10] These works, after all, express concern about interaction between Jews and members of the surrounding peoples and, without precedent, prohibit all intermarriage.[11] Although *Ezra* and *Nehemiah* seek to establish a firm boundary separating Jews from gentiles, neither indicates that Jewish food practices ought to function as boundary markers, let alone as walls that segregate Jews from foreigners. Nehemiah prevails upon his people to refrain from buying foodstuffs from gentiles on the Sabbath or holy days (*Neh.* 10.32, 13.16–17), but he raises no objection to acquiring food prepared by gentiles on other days. We will see in subsequent chapters that religious authorities regularly forbid food-related social intercourse with foreigners as a means of preventing sexual intercourse, thus furthering a particular vision of the proper social order. *Ezra*, *Nehemiah*, and earlier Biblical works that address the issue of sex with foreigners, in contrast, articulate no such prohibitions.

Even Biblical passages that associate the food of foreigners with the worship of foreign deities and illicit sexuality, two of the most heinous crimes in the Bible, lack explicit prohibitions targeting the act of commensality. God instructs the Israelites not to grant covenants to the inhabitants of the Promised Land, "for they will whore after their gods and sacrifice to their gods, and they will invite you, and you will eat of their sacrifices, and you will take wives from among their daughters for your sons, and their daughters will whore after their gods and will cause your sons to whore after their gods" (*Exod.* 34.15–16). The primary message of this passage is that Israelites must take care to avoid the worship of other deities (v. 14); for that reason, no vassal covenant may be granted to the peoples dwelling in the land and their worship sites must be destroyed (vv. 12–13). The reason toleration of these peoples is so dangerous is that their continued worship of foreign deities will inevitably result in Israelite worship of those deities through a process involving Israelite consumption of sacrificial food prepared by foreigners and sexual intercourse with foreign women.

A related narrative in *Numbers* reports that just such a process occurred during Israel's journey through the wilderness. "While Israel was staying at Shittim, the people profaned themselves by whoring with the Moabite women, who invited the people to the sacrifices for their gods. The people ate, and they worshipped their gods, and Israel attached itself to Baal-peor. And the LORD was incensed with Israel" (*Num.* 25.1–3). As the Psalmist puts it, "They attached themselves to Baal-peor, ate the sacrifices of the dead" (*Ps.* 106.28); the poetic structure of this verse emphasizes the central role played by the act of eating in the Israelites' attachment to idolatry. In the *Exodus* and *Numbers* passages, the act of eating foreign sacrificial food marks the point of no return on the path to worshipping foreign gods; in *Numbers,* such behavior is also associated with harlotry.[12]

Israelites themselves may not offer sacrifices to beings other than God (*Exod.* 22.19; cf. *Deut.* 32.17, *Lev.* 17.7). One may readily infer from these passages, along with others that emphasize the importance of Israel's exclusive relationship with its God, that Biblical texts frown upon the consumption of food which foreigners have sacrificed to their deities.[13] None, however, prohibits such behavior or condemns it directly. Even as the *Exodus* and *Numbers* passages recognize the danger associated with the food of foreigners, their condemnation falls solely on the worship of foreign gods, behavior that, in these passages, is not synonymous with consuming sacrificial food. There is nothing in the Hebrew Bible comparable in its directness or forcefulness to the New Testament's injunction to abstain "from what has been offered to idols" (*Acts* 15.29) or the Qur'an's prohibition of eating "that over which [a name] other than God's has been invoked" (Q. 2.173, cf. 5.3, 6.145, 16.115; see also M. *Ḥul.* 2.8). The definition of communal identity in terms of fidelity to one God alone is common to the Bible and post-Biblical religions, but only the latter anathematize those who consume meat associated with idolatry and employ abstention from food offered to idols as a mark of monotheistic identity. The absence from the Hebrew Bible of a prohibition against eating meat prepared by a non-Israelite is especially surprising given the fact that many ancient Near Eastern cultures understood the act of animal slaughter to bear inherent sacral significance.[14]

We return, then, to our initial question about the nonchalance of the Hebrew Bible with respect to food associated with foreigners, but now its urgency is greater. Why do the Hebrew Bible's dietary laws fail to prohibit the consumption of meat prepared by non-Israelites or, for that matter, commensality with non-Israelites, even though Biblical texts acknowledge an association between the food of foreigners, sexual intercourse with non-Israelites, and idolatry itself?

ISRAEL'S HOLINESS AND THE HEBREW BIBLE'S DIETARY LAWS

The most familiar of the Biblical dietary laws, the regulations governing consumption of meat from various animal species, appear in *Leviticus* 11.1–23 and *Deuteronomy* 14.3–20. These passages of the Torah, which seem to be independent expansions of a common precursor,[15] classify the meat of quadrupeds (four-footed animals such as sheep, antelopes, rock badgers, and pigs), water creatures, birds, and insects as permitted or prohibited for consumption in nonsacrificial contexts. Both lists are presently situated within literary contexts that emphasize Israel's holiness, which is to say its distinctive status among the nations as God's partner in an exclusive relationship. As the verse preceding *Deuteronomy*'s version declares, "you are a people made holy to the LORD your God: the LORD your God chose you from among all other peoples on earth to be His treasured people" (*Deut.* 14.2; cf. 14.21). Similarly, the presentation of dietary laws in *Leviticus* 11 concludes with God's declaration that "I the LORD am the one who brought you up from the land of Egypt to be your God: you shall be holy, for I am holy" (*Lev.* 11.45). Adherence to the regulations governing permitted and prohibited meat, these contexts indicate, constitutes an expression of Israel's holiness.

Absent from Biblical passages regarding these dietary laws, however, is any suggestion that the norms enjoined upon Israelites stand in opposition to non-Israelite practices. As we observed in chapter 1, the identity-defining function of dietary choices stems entirely from the establishment of such a contrast: statements like "We do not eat the meat of rock badgers" mark Us as different from Them only if We associate Them with the consumption of such meat, yet no such association appears in Biblical literature.[16] Although some Bronze Age and Iron Age finds attest to the limited consumption of pork, we should bear in mind that no text in the Hebrew Bible singles out the pig for special condemnation as a food associated with foreigners.[17] In terms of Biblical rhetoric, the pork taboo is indistinguishable from the prohibition against eating the meat of rock badgers, a foodstuff that was surely not a significant component of the non-Israelite diet, either calorically or symbolically.[18] Archeological evidence, moreover, indicates, not only that meat itself was an insignificant caloric component of the ancient Near Eastern diet,[19] but also that the vast majority of meat consumed in Canaan and its environs is permissible according to Biblical law. As Walter Houston observes, adherence to the norms expressed in the Torah "required no sharp changes in habitual dietary and cultic practices general in the land and its environs at least since the beginning of the Middle Bronze Age."[20] Neither Biblical rhetoric nor archeological evidence, therefore, suggests that adherence to the norms regarding permitted and prohibited meat would have sufficed to identify a person living in ancient Canaan as an Israelite.

Many scholars have nevertheless argued that Biblical dietary laws are intended to segregate Israelites from foreigners at meal times. In the words of Erhard S. Gerstenberger, "Anyone who intends to keep the taboos decreed by Yahweh regarding impure animals can obviously no longer have contact with those of different faiths, or, for example, dine with them at the same table. This enjoined purity cuts off any association with people who do not hold to the same divine commandment."[21] The fact that Israelites and their Jewish descendants are picky eaters naturally impedes interaction with those who make different dietary choices. This latent function of the Bible's ingredient-based laws became increasingly significant, both for adherents of these laws and for their interpreters, when Jews came to live amid populations that did not share the same cultural norms regarding suitable foodstuffs. There is, however, no basis for attributing a segregative purpose to the dietary laws in their Biblical context. After all, neither *Leviticus* nor *Deuteronomy* ascribes a social motivation to its regulations governing permitted and prohibited meat, and we have seen that Biblical texts consistently describe food-related interaction with foreigners without expressing any qualms about such behavior.

Biblical dietary laws, moreover, do not prevent Israelites from consuming the meat of permissible animals killed by non-Israelites, much less nonmeat foodstuffs prepared by foreigners. Both *Leviticus* and *Deuteronomy* regulate the preparation of meat in the context of addressing the prohibition against consuming blood, a prohibition that refers not to the practice of drinking blood but rather that of eating meat from which the blood has not been drained.[22] Because violation of this norm ranks alongside murder, idolatry, and illicit sexual activity as a cardinal offense within the Biblical system of morality (see, for example, *Ezek.* 33.25–26), the method by which one must prepare meat so as to remove its blood is of particular importance. No Biblical text, however, presents the prohibition against consuming blood in contrast to non-Israelite practice, whether by suggesting that non-Israelites consume "bloody meat" or by instructing Israelites to avoid meat prepared by foreigners. Quite the contrary, *Genesis* 9.3–6 declares that the blood taboo is incumbent upon all humanity and *Leviticus* 17.10–14 requires the *ger*, a non-Israelite member of Israelite society, to drain the blood from animals he intends to eat in the same manner enjoined upon Israelites.[23] Both *Leviticus* and *Deuteronomy* permit the consumption of meat from animals killed in nonsacral contexts so long as its blood has been properly drained, and neither expresses concern about who performs the requisite acts of preparation, the concern we would most expect from laws designed to segregate Us from Them.[24]

The segregationist argument rests primarily on the concluding passage of *Leviticus* 20, which appears to contrast Israelite dietary practices with those of the prior inhabitants of Canaan. A careful reading of this passage, however, belies such an interpretation.

> [20.22] You shall faithfully observe all My laws and all My regulations, lest the land into which I bring you to settle spew you out. [23] You shall not follow the practices

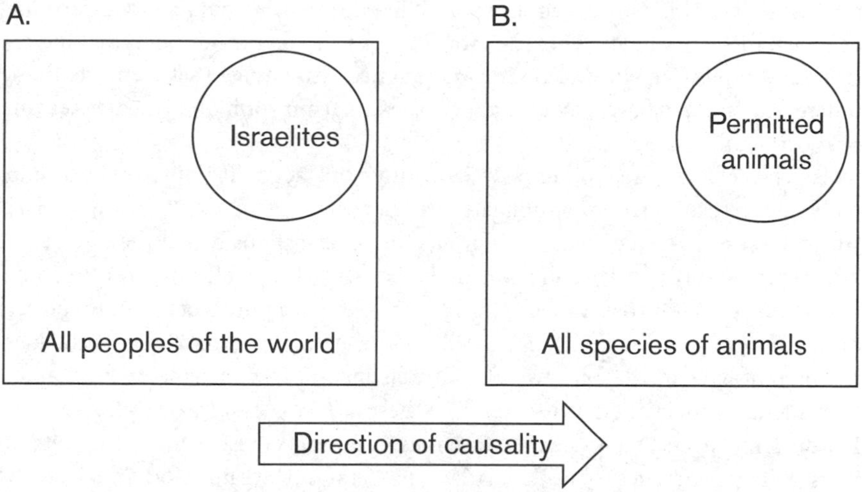

FIGURE 1. ISRAELITE DISTINCTIVENESS AND ISRAELITE DIETARY RESTRICTIONS. Just as God has distinguished Israel from among all peoples of the world (A), so must Israel distinguish permitted animals from among all species (B).

> of the nation that I am driving out before you. For it is because they did all these things that I abhorred them [24a] and said to you: You shall possess their land, for I will give it to you to possess, a land flowing with milk and honey. [24b] I the LORD am your God who has set you apart from other peoples. [25] So you shall set apart the pure quadruped from the impure, the impure bird from the pure. You shall not draw abomination upon yourselves through quadruped or bird or anything with which the ground is alive, which I have set apart for you as impure. [26] You shall be holy to Me, for I the LORD am holy, and I have set you apart from other peoples to be Mine.

The initial verses of this passage require Israelites to follow God's laws and forbid adopting the practices of the peoples of Canaan. Because of their cultic and sexual offenses, detailed in the previous verses and also in *Leviticus* 18, God declares that "the land became impure; and I called it to account for its iniquity, and the land spewed out its inhabitants" (18.25). Israelites must avoid the abhorrent practices associated with the Canaanites if they wish to avoid sharing the same fate. In *Leviticus* 20.22–24a, then, God enjoins Israelites to act differently from the prior inhabitants of the Promised Land while highlighting the difference between divine norms and the practices ascribed to non-Israelites. In verses 25–26, however, the focus shifts: Israelites are to act similarly to God, making distinctions among animals just as God has made distinctions among peoples (see figure 1). In Jacob Milgrom's words, "as God has restricted his choice of the nations to Israel, so must Israel restrict its choice of edible animals to the few sanctioned by God."[25] Whereas the first half of this passage contrasts Israelite norms with putative non-Israelite behavior, the second half compares Israelite norms to divine behavior, making no reference to non-Israelites or their food practices. The hinge that connects these differently-oriented halves is verse 24b: "I the LORD am your God who has set you apart from other peoples."

Israel is set apart from other peoples through the fact of its unique relationship with God, a relationship that obligates Israelites to observe God's laws and classificatory systems. Israel acknowledges its distinctive status by, on the one hand, not imitating the offensive behaviors of the non-Israelites while, on the other, imitating God through observance of the laws that set apart pure from impure species of animals. *Leviticus* 20.22–26, like the other legal passages we have examined, does not present Israelite dietary laws in contradistinction to non-Israelite food practices and does not claim that adherence to these laws renders Israelites unlike non-Israelites, much less that such behavior serves to segregate these populations. Rather, it asserts that adherence to the dietary laws renders Israelites like God, who is solely responsible for effecting the distinction between Israel and the nations ("*I the LORD* . . . set you apart"). Proper behavior with respect to foodstuffs, according to *Leviticus* 20.25, serves the purely symbolic function of expressing Israel's holiness through the enactment of divinely ordained classifications among animal species that are analogous to the divine classification of peoples.

Whether one understands the Hebrew Bible's distinctions between permitted and prohibited varieties of meat to convey lessons about the virtues Israelites ought to embody, to inculcate ethical values about the sacredness of life, or simply to reflect a vision of wholeness and of a properly ordered cosmos, the meaning of these distinctions resides in the foodstuffs themselves.[26] Even if there was, historically speaking, a difference between Israelite and non-Israelite consumption patterns, Biblical texts make no reference to such a contrast and thus ascribe no significance to the differentiating and segregating functions inherently latent in any set of food restrictions. This is not the case with respect to cultic and sexual practices: both *Leviticus* and *Deuteronomy* frame their presentations of divine norms regarding such practices in opposition to the imagined practices of non-Israelites. The former, for example, concludes its catalog of sexual offenses by warning Israelites, "Do not defile yourselves [literally: render yourselves impure] in any of those ways, for it is by such that the nations that I am casting out before you defile themselves" (18.24; cf. *Deut.* 7.1–6, on the difference between Israelite and non-Israelite cultic practices). Neither makes any reference to the practices of the nations when presenting its regulations governing animal species or the blood taboo.[27] The texts that comprise the Hebrew Bible simply do not portray dietary restrictions as playing a role in establishing or preserving the proper social order.

The only instances in which Israelite norms regarding the preparation of meat are presented in contradistinction to those observed by non-Israelites serve merely to highlight the fact that God has already set Israel apart from the nations. *Leviticus* requires Israelites to bring their domestic livestock to the Israelite sanctuary for slaughter in a sacrificial context; the *ger* must offer his sacrifices at the Israelite sanctuary as well, but *Leviticus* tacitly grants non-Israelites the right to perform non-sacral slaughter of livestock animals (*Lev.* 17.3–9).[28] Implicit in this distinction is the notion that Israelites partake of a closer relationship with God than non-Israelites and are therefore held to a higher standard. This notion is explicit in *Deuteronomy* 14.21, which cites the fact that Israelites alone are "made holy to the LORD" to explain why Israelites may not consume carrion meat themselves but may give this culturally acceptable foodstuff to a *ger* or sell it to a foreigner (*nokhri*).[29] These laws—and, indeed, all of the Hebrew Bible's dietary laws—highlight Israel's unique relationship with God, not the dissimilarity between Israelites and foreigners.

The foreign food restrictions we will examine in the remainder of this study serve to classify humanity in various ways: the authorities who formulate such restrictions imagine Them to be not-Us, anti-Us, like-Us, or unlike-Us. Through the process of constructing otherness, of course, these authorities simultaneously imagine the identities of their own communities in relation to those ascribed to foreigners: We are not-Them, anti-Them, like-Them, or unlike-Them. Biblical dietary laws do not rest upon this kind of contradistinction, as they claim to establish Israelites not as dissimilar to foreigners but rather as similar to God. Perhaps Biblical texts regard the difference between Our food and Their food as insignificant because, in fact, there were only negligible differences between Israelite and non-Israelite food practices in ancient Canaan. Perhaps other markers of identity, such as geography or ethnicity, were sufficiently determinative that food-based identity markers were seen as trivial.[30] Whatever the reason, these works imagine the domain of food to be, as Robert Frost puts it, a place "where it is we do not need the wall."

We are now in a position to answer our persistent question regarding the Hebrew Bible's lack of foreign food restrictions and nonchalant attitude toward interaction over food with foreigners. Because the texts that comprise the Hebrew Bible do not conceive of Israelite dietary norms in contrast to those of non-Israelites, they have no reason to express concern regarding food associated with foreigners. The Hebrew Bible locates its markers of communal identity and its barriers to interaction with foreigners in other domains, including those related to cultic and sexual practices. Biblical dietary laws, however, serve in their original context neither to segregate nor to differentiate Us from Them. These laws classify foodstuffs, not people, and play no direct role in maintaining the proper social order.

Our exploration of Biblical dietary laws, spurred by a question that stems from familiarity with the presence of foreign food restrictions in post-Biblical normative literature, thus generates another question we must now pose as we turn our attention to those restrictions: why do Jewish, Christian, and Islamic authorities choose to employ food restrictions as a means of classifying people and, in some cases, as a means of segregating Us from Them? The fact that food-related practices are inherently suitable for such a purpose, after all, does not mean that all such practices are intended to serve this purpose; we find in the Hebrew Bible an example to the contrary. Because dietary laws do not necessarily differentiate or segregate their adherents from outsiders, we should not take the identity-establishing or segregative functions of later foreign food restrictions for granted. Rather, we must consider in what way, to what extent, and for what reasons Jewish, Christian, and Islamic authorities use foreign food restrictions to advance their vision of the proper social order. The fact that, during the Hellenistic period of Jewish history, interpreters of the Bible choose to interpret and extend the Torah's food restrictions in unprecedented ways demands particular attention.

TYPES OF IMPURITY, IN THE BIBLE AND BEYOND

Before turning to that subject, however, it is worthwhile to reflect briefly on a term we have encountered several times in passing: *impurity.* Concepts of impurity appear frequently in discussions about food restrictions not only within the Hebrew Bible but also in later Jewish, Christian, and Islamic literature. The term impurity (Hebrew: *ṭ.m.'.*), however, is too broad and multivalent to be of analytical use without qualification. In the texts we have examined, after all, this term refers to the meat of certain animal species (e.g., pork: *Lev.* 11.7, *Deut.* 14.8), to the person who consumes carrion permitted for consumption (*Lev.* 11.40, 17.15), and to the consequences of abhorrent sexual practices (*Lev.* 18.24, *Ezek.* 33.26). These usages reflect three distinct types of impurity which must be distinguished if we hope to understand the specific significance of impurity rhetoric as it manifests itself in Jewish, Christian, and Islamic discourse about foreigners and their food.

The present study employs a typology of impurity that amalgamates those developed by contemporary scholars of the Hebrew Bible and ancient Judaism on the one hand and medieval scholars of Islamic law on the other.[31] Islamic authorities distinguish between two types of impurity: *ḥadath,* a state endured by human beings after the occurrence of various natural events (e.g., urination, menstruation) and alleviated through the performance of ritual ablutions; and *najāsah,* an intrinsically impure substance (e.g., urine, blood).[32] The first of these categories corresponds to what Jonathan Klawans, in his study of Biblical and ancient Jewish literature, labels "ritual impurity": a more or less unavoidable state, typically impermanent, that afflicts human beings as a result of naturally occurring circumstances rather than sinful activity. Klawans employs the term *ritual* to describe this form of impurity because of its implications: the person who endures such a state may not perform certain rituals and, in many cases, must perform a purificatory ritual in order to return to a state of purity. The Bible also uses the term *impure* to refer to the defilement that results from particularly heinous sin, including illicit sexual activity, idolatry, and bloodshed. Klawans refers to this type of impurity, absent from the medieval Islamic purity system, as "moral impurity" because the transgressions that result in such impurity typically violate moral codes of conduct.[33] Klawans, who focuses his attention on types of impurity that afflict human beings, neglects to include impure animals or other nonhuman objects within his classificatory system. The Islamic category of *najāsah* encompasses this type of Biblical impurity reasonably well.[34] By broadening the category of *najāsah* to refer not only to intrinsically impure substances and animals but to human beings as well, we can also encompass what Christine Elizabeth Hayes refers to as "genealogical impurity," a state that afflicts the offspring of mixed Jewish-gentile marriages according to Hayes's interpretation of works such as *Ezra* and *Nehemiah*.[35]

This study employs the following terms to refer to the three different types of impurity described above; in each case, I have selected adjectival labels that relate to the cause of the impurity.

Intrinsic impurity is inherent in a substance (e.g., carrion or pork) due to its very nature. According to some authorities, intrinsic impurity is inherent in a person bearing the status of "religious outsider" as well. Only a change in the intrinsic nature of a person (e.g., through conversion) or substance (e.g., through the ritual slaughter of an animal) can remove this state of impurity. In many cases, such change is impossible: pork, for example, is impure according to Biblical sources no matter how the pig died, and Spanish proponents of "purity of blood" ideology, which developed in the fifteenth century, hold that converts to Christianity and their descendants remain impure.

Circumstantial impurity is caused by some form of contact with an intrinsically impure substance (e.g., touching or eating carrion) or by the occurrence of a polluting event (e.g., menstruation). One who contracts such impurity is temporarily polluted and may, in certain purity systems, communicate this pollution to others. The circumstances that lead to pollution of this nature are part of normal life experience, are unavoidable in many cases, and are in no way sinful. One who has been affected by these circumstances must adhere to specified norms in order to remove the resulting state of impurity and thus become fit once more for engaging in certain ritual practices.[36]

Offensive impurity refers to the defilement generated by particularly sinful behavior (e.g., illicit sexual activity). One who commits such a grave offense is defiled and cannot easily, if at all, be cleansed of this stain; in some purity systems, this defilement can carry over from one generation to the next. Offensive impurity results from human actions and is therefore neither communicable nor inevitable. On the contrary, religious authorities

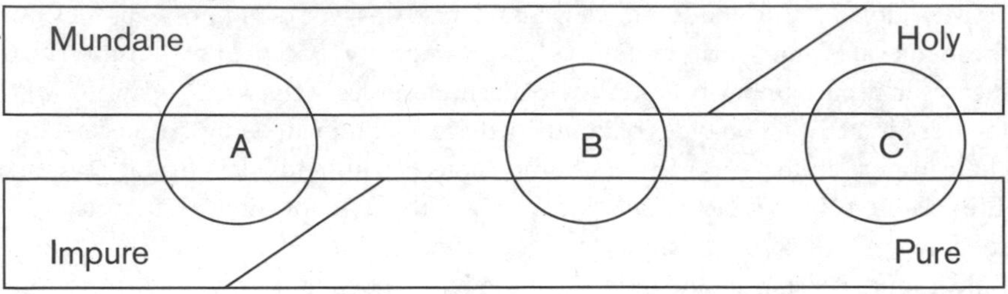

FIGURE 2. HOLINESS AND IMPURITY. An object can be simultaneously mundane and impure (A), mundane and pure (B), or holy and pure (C), but nothing can be holy and impure.

> prohibit their followers from engaging in the offensive behavior that causes such defilement.

In the interest of clarity, references to impurity in the remainder of this study specify its type. I use the term *defiled* solely in association with offensive impurity while the term *polluted* consistently refers to circumstantial impurity. Individuals and substances that fall into the remaining category are simply *impure*. I generally avoid terms such as *clean* and *unclean* because purity and hygiene are independent, albeit overlapping, concepts; such terms, where they appear, should be understood metaphorically.

Given the diversity of meanings associated with the term *impurity*, what unifies these phenomena such that they are described using the same term? The common denominator is that the impure must be kept separate from the holy. The terms *impure* and *holy* are not antonyms: the opposite of "holy" is "mundane," not "impure," and not everything mundane is impure. Rather, the relationship of these terms is one of antithesis: nothing impure can ever be holy (see figure 2).[37] Exposure of the holy to the impure, moreover, can have calamitous consequences. For that reason, the Hebrew Bible instructs that intrinsically impure substances and circumstantially polluted people must be excluded from the precincts of the sanctuary. It warns, moreover, that the offensive defilement produced through heinous sins is so antithetical to God's holiness that it ultimately forces the divine presence to abandon the sanctuary.[38]

We will see as this study progresses that religious authorities often employ impurity rhetoric as a means of denoting the antithetical opposition between Us and Them and of heightening the significance of segregative foreign food restrictions. Whereas Mary Douglas famously suggests that the term impurity refers to "dirt," that is, "matter out of place,"[39] I will demonstrate that this term is consistently used to put select foreigners *in their proper place* within the social order—namely at the negative pole of a spectrum whose positive pole is occupied by the holy, by Us.

PART TWO

Jewish Sources on Foreign Food Restrictions

Marking Otherness

You are unique and Your divine name is unique,
and who is like Your people, Israel, a unique nation on earth?

RABBINIC PRAYERBOOK

3

"They Kept Themselves Apart in the Matter of Food"

The Nature and Significance of Hellenistic Jewish Food Practices

Alexander the Great's conquest of Judea (332 B.C.E.) marks the beginning of a new era in which Judaism, in its various forms, encounters, engages, and reflects in its literature the influence of Hellenistic thought and culture.[1] Shaye J. D. Cohen traces "the beginnings of Jewishness" to this era, as it is in this period that Judaism comes into being as a religious rather than a solely ethnic identity.[2] The redefinition of Jewish identity that occurs during the period of Hellenistic cultural dominance, which extends well into the beginning of the Common Era, necessitates a reimagining by Hellenistic Jews of the distinction between Us and Them and a parallel revision of the systems of classification that give this distinction meaning.[3] Food restrictions play an important role in the way many of these Jews imagine Jewish identity and mark the otherness of non-Jews; these restrictions do not play such a role during earlier periods of Israelite and Jewish history. The nature of these food restrictions and the significance ascribed to them, however, differ considerably between the literary elites of Judea and Alexandria, the two centers that produce the vast majority of Hellenistic Jewish literature.[4]

The Torah, we observed in chapter 2, does not frame its food restrictions in opposition to non-Israelite food practices. Adherence to the dietary laws of *Leviticus* and *Deuteronomy* reflects Israel's holiness—that is, its divinely established distinctiveness—but may not actually distinguish Israelites from foreigners in a manner that would be recognizable to an outside observer. Biblical works written during the era of Persian hegemony (sixth to third centuries B.C.E.), such as *Nehemiah*, reflect the anxieties of a community in competition with foreigners and at risk of losing its sense of distinctiveness. While some works from this era articulate intermarriage prohibitions of unprecedented scope as a means of preserving the ethnic purity of the Jewish community, none employs food restrictions as a means of bolstering Jewish identity. Works from the Hellenistic era, in contrast, regularly use food restrictions for exactly that purpose, albeit in different ways. Alexandrian authors portray adherence to Biblical dietary laws as a primary means by which Jews distinguish themselves from their gentile neighbors who, these authors emphasize, embrace dietary norms quite different from those set forth in the Torah. Various Judean authorities go further by advocating a number of unprecedented foreign food restrictions whose manifest goal is to segregate as well as distinguish Jews from gentiles. Both the new interpretations of Biblical dietary laws and the foreign food restrictions that emerge during this era reflect the internalization by Alexandrian and Judean Jews alike of a particularly Hellenistic mode of thinking. The following comparison of Alexandrian and Judean works, however, reveals sharp differences in the ways authors in these two communities envision the proper place of Jews within the broader social order of the Hellenistic world.

READING BIBLICAL DIETARY LAWS THROUGH A HELLENISTIC LENS IN ALEXANDRIA

Scholars have long recognized the impact of Hellenistic thought on the earliest post-Biblical interpretation of the Torah's dietary laws, the pseudepigraphic *Letter of Aristeas*. This fictional work, written in Greek by an Alexandrian Jew, is generally dated to the second half of the second century B.C.E.[5] A delegation sent to Jerusalem by the Greek king of Egypt inquires into the rationale behind the Jewish dietary laws (*Aristeas* 128–29), and the high priest, Eleazar, responds with a lengthy exposition on the allegorical significance of these regulations. These laws, Eleazar explains, provide Jews a moral compass by promoting the values of cleanliness, righteousness, and memory while discouraging violence, reliance on physical strength, and sexual defilement (vv. 143–58). The last of these vices, Eleazar asserts, is common to the majority of gentiles, who "defile themselves in their relationships, thereby committing a serious offense. . . . We are quite separated from these practices" (v. 152). The great Alexandrian philosopher Philo (d. ca. 40 C.E.) offers a similarly allegorical interpretation of Biblical dietary laws (*Special laws* 4.100–131). Philo depicts those who forsake such laws for the sake of "ministering to the pleasures of the belly and the organs below it" as adopting a life characterized by vice (*Virtues* 182).

The allegorical explanations of Jewish dietary practices found in *Aristeas* and the works of Philo are clearly apologetic in orientation, designed to account for a practice viewed with suspicion by Greeks in terms that Greeks themselves—and, perhaps more importantly, Jews who have adopted a Hellenistic mode of thinking—might find respectable. Indeed, various Greek and Latin authors understand Jewish dietary practices to reflect a kind of misanthropy.[6] Jewish literature from Alexandria reflects awareness of and concern about such calumnies; it is no coincidence that the foremost question the Greek delegation asks in *Aristeas* addresses Jewish dietary laws. Similarly, the *Third Book of Maccabees*, written around the first century B.C.E.,[7] reports that the Jews of Alexandria "kept themselves apart in the matter of food, and for this reason they appeared hateful to some" (*3 Macc.* 3.4). Like *Aristeas, 3 Maccabees* (whose subject matter is unrelated to the other *Books of Maccabees*) directly addresses the fact that the Torah enjoins food practices different from those of the dominant Hellenistic culture. These practices not only set Jews apart from gentiles but also, according to *3 Maccabees*, lead to false allegations of Jewish disloyalty that prompt the king to attempt the mass execution of Alexandria's Jewish population. Philo and the author of *Aristeas* seek instead to demonstrate that these practices cause Jews to live morally exemplary lives and, indeed, instill a commitment to morality superior to that of the typical gentile.

The *Letter of Aristeas* appears to suggest that God imposed restrictions on the food of non-Jews to reduce social interaction between Jews and outsiders. Eleazar, after all, prefaces his interpretation of the Torah's dietary laws by explaining that "in his wisdom the legislator . . . surrounded us with unbroken palisades and iron walls to prevent our mixing with any of the other peoples in any matter, being thus kept pure in body and soul, preserved from false beliefs, and worshipping the only God omnipotent over all creation. . . . So, to prevent our being perverted by contact with others or by mixing with bad influences, he hedged us in on all sides with strict observances connected with meat and drink and touch and hearing and sight" (vv. 139, 142).[8] The "hedges" and "iron walls" of which Eleazar speaks, however, are purely metaphorical and in no way prevent Jews from consuming food associated with foreigners. Thus, for example, Eleazar interprets the Biblical requirement of eating only animals with split hoofs to symbolically represent the fact that Jews are set apart from gentiles and their vices (v. 151). He does not, however, suggest that this requirement necessitates either abstention from meat prepared by gentiles or the segregation of Jews and gentiles during meals. Eleazar's message, simply stated, is: We are superior to Them because We do not eat certain foods which They do. Because Biblical food practices are no longer common to insiders and outsiders alike, the author of *Aristeas* is able to present Jewish norms in contradistinction to the practices of gentiles; the latent potential of Biblical dietary laws as a marker of distinctively Jewish identity thus becomes manifest. It is noteworthy, however, that this author and Philo alike measure the superiority of the Jews on a spectrum heavily influenced by Hellenistic values.

The purely metaphorical nature of the wall that separates Jews from gentiles in *Aristeas* becomes clear as the letter progresses. Eleazar dispatches seventy-two elders to Alexandria so that they may translate the Torah into Greek, whereupon the king invites them to dine with him and share their pearls of wisdom. "Everything of which you partake," he says, "will be served in compliance with your habits; it will be served this way to me as well as to you" (v. 181). The Jewish guests raise no objection to participating fully in these banquets, even though the king's staff prepares and serves the meals to a mixed assemblage of Jews and gentiles (vv. 182–86). Christine Elizabeth Hayes cites this passage to demonstrate that the author of *Aristeas* was not concerned about the circumstantial impurity that might be transmitted if Jews and gentiles sit at the same table. "The Jewish sages are able to dine and share food with the Egyptian king because it is *Jewish food.* It has been prepared according to Jewish dietary rules, and the king's presence and participation does not render the food impure" (emphasis in original).[9] Hayes is right, but for the wrong reason. This text expresses no concern regarding circumstantial impurity, but the food being shared is not "Jewish food," even though it is prepared according to Jewish norms. This is foreign food, prepared by and eaten with gentiles. Nevertheless, neither the king's presence eating with the Jews nor the preparation of the food by his staff renders the food polluted or defiling, and *Aristeas* expresses no concern about the possibility that such a meal might lead to abominable beliefs or behaviors on the part of its Jewish participants either. According to the author of *Aristeas,* Jews need not segregate themselves from gentiles at meals because adherence to Biblical dietary laws, understood allegorically, is itself a sufficient means of maintaining Israel's distinctiveness. Philo also perceives no conflict between adherence to these laws and Jewish commensality with gentiles; indeed, he asserts that Jews and gentiles come together annually to celebrate the translation of the Torah into Greek at an assembly and feast (*Moses* 2.41–42).

Similarly, the dietary restrictions to which *3 Maccabees* refers are unrelated to the identity of the person who prepares or shares the food. After the king rescinds his miraculously thwarted decrees against the Jews, he declares that the Jews should celebrate for seven days and orders a government official (presumably a gentile) to supply the Jews with all the wine and supplies necessary for their feasting (*3 Macc.* 6.30). The king then holds his own banquet celebrating the miraculous turn of events, apparently with Jewish participation (6.34, cf. 6.40). "Keeping apart in the matter of food," it would seem, does not require abstention from food provided by gentiles or from attendance at gentile feasts, at least according to Alexandrian Jewish authorities.

Alexandrian Jews interpret Biblical dietary laws in ways that reflect both their internalization of the mode of thinking dominant within Hellenistic culture and their heightened sensitivity regarding the differences between Jewish and gentile food practices. These Jews understand traditional food restrictions not only as expressions of Israel's holiness but also as markers of the distinction between Us and Them, yet they do not articulate any new restrictions designed to sharpen that distinction or to segregate Jews from gentiles. Jewish literature from Judea, in contrast, does just that.

JUDEAN HEROES AND THEIR ABSTENTION FROM FOREIGN FOOD

The difference between the norms of food consumption valorized in literature from Hellenistic Judea on the one hand and in both pre-Hellenistic and Alexandrian literature on the other is encapsulated in the expanded version of *Esther* found in the Septuagint; this work was translated into Greek by a Jerusalemite in the late-second or early- to mid-first century B.C.E.[10] Among the additions to the original text found in this expanded version is a prayer by Esther, apparently composed in Hebrew, in which the queen asserts: "Your maid servant has not dined at Haman's table, nor have I extolled a royal symposium nor drunk the wine of libations" (*Addition to Esther* C 28).[11] These assertions run counter to the portrayal of Esther found in the original text, in which the heroine raises no objection to the food and drink of outsiders and in which she participates actively in a palace culture structured around symposium-like drinking parties.[12] Esther's newfound disdain for commensality with gentiles and for the royal symposium also differs sharply from the attitude manifest in *Aristeas,* which portrays the elders' banquet with the king as a great honor for the Jewish community. Disdain for food associated with foreigners, however, is commonplace among the heroes depicted in Hellenistic Judean literature, beginning with the Biblical book of *Daniel.*

Daniel, set in the sixth-century Babylonian exile, consists of several distinct sources redacted during the first years of the Ḥasmonean revolt (167–164 B.C.E.); its opening chapter has been dated to the third century.[13] This chapter reports that King Nebuchadnezzar gathered Israelite youths of noble descent to the palace to enter the royal service. "The king provided for them a daily allotment from the king's food and from the wine he would drink" (*Dan.* 1.5). Yet "Daniel resolved not to defile himself with the king's food or the wine he would drink, so he sought permission of the chief officer not to defile himself" (1.8). Ultimately, Daniel arranged for himself and his companions to receive "vegetables to eat and water to drink" instead of the royal rations (1.12).[14] This story about Daniel echoes the account of King Jehoiachin's food rations in 2 *Kings* 25.29–30 (// *Jer.* 52.33–34), where the same reference to "daily allotment" appears. Whereas Jehoiachin accepts the rations, Daniel refuses them. The author of *Daniel* 1, like some later transmitters of *Esther,* presents a hero who adheres to stricter standards regarding the food of foreigners than those reflected in either earlier Biblical texts or roughly contemporaneous Alexandrian sources.

There is no indication either that Daniel's refusal to accept the king's food is motivated by concerns regarding its ingredients or that other Israelite youths, and Jehoiachin before them, ignore Israelite dietary laws. The term used for food, *pat-bag,* is a loan-word whose Persian equivalent refers to any government-supplied ration; it appears in a clearly generic sense elsewhere in the book (11.26). The hyphen inserted into the Hebraized word suggests that *pat-bag* was understood, at least by those who punctuated the text, to relate to the Hebrew word *pat:* morsel or, more specifically, bread.[15] The Septuagint, which translates the term as "the king's table," also understands it to refer generally to all food that the king might serve, including the many foodstuffs unregulated by the Torah. Even if one assumes that meat was a primary component in royal rations, we saw in the previous chapter that the Hebrew Bible contains no prohibition against gentile preparation of meat from permitted animals; it also contains no prohibition against foreign wine.[16] There is no indication in *Daniel* that the food in question is impure (contrast *Hosea* 9.3, *Ezek.* 4.13), and no reason to assume that Daniel is worried about the impurity of its gentile preparers either.[17] Christine Hayes and Jonathan Klawans have demonstrated compellingly that neither Biblical nor Hellenistic Jewish sources express concern regarding the circumstantial impurity of gentiles, and in any case even the water and vegetables which Daniel requests instead of the king's food are susceptible to contracting circumstantial impurity.[18]

Efforts to ascribe impurity-based concerns to Daniel's behavior stem from the misinterpretation of his desire not to "defile himself [*yitga'al*]" in terms of circumstantial impurity. This term is consistently associated in the Hebrew Bible with impurity resulting from offensive behavior—which is to say the performance of a prohibited action—rather than with the occurrence of a natural and unavoidable event.[19] In this case, that action is the consumption of the king's food, and the resulting defilement is unrelated to the purity status of the food or its preparers. Daniel does not believe that eating the king's food is prohibited because the food is polluted; he believes such food is defiling because its consumption is prohibited.[20] As the ingredients of the "king's food" are not themselves problematic, Daniel's concern must relate to the king, which is to say, to the fact that the king—and, more to the point, his cooks—are not Jewish.

Note that the prohibition of foreign food observed by Daniel is evidently linked to the preparation of food by gentiles rather than gentile contact with or possession of the food, as Daniel accepts the king's natural foodstuffs, specifically water and vegetables. This prohibition thus conforms to Claude Lévi-Strauss's distinction between "raw" and "cooked" foods, the latter alone constituting a manifestation of human culture. Similarly, the late second-century B.C.E. *Second Book of Maccabees* reports that Judah Maccabee and his soldiers withdrew to the mountains where "they stayed, eating herbs for food, in order to keep clear of defilement [tou molusmou]" (2 *Macc.* 5.27).[21] Jonathan A. Goldstein rejects as "nonsense" the possibility that Judah and his band ate herbs in order to avoid defilement because, as he correctly notes, "herbs can become unclean and other foods can be ritually [i.e., circumstantially] pure."[22] *Second Maccabees,* however, does not refer to circumstantial impurity in this context but rather to offensive impurity, and it employs the Greek term used to translate the Hebrew terms *to'evah* (LXX *Jer.* 51.4 = 44.4 in the

Hebrew Bible) and *yitgaʾal* (LXX *Dan.* 1.8), both of which relate to offensive impurity. Judah, like Daniel, adheres to a prohibition against food "cooked" by foreigners and regards transgression of this norm as a defiling offense.[23]

The eponymous subject of *Tobit,* composed ca. 250–175 and set in the eighth century B.C.E., boastfully recounts his observance of a similar dietary norm.[24] "After I was carried away captive to Assyria and came as a captive to Nineveh, all of my kindred and my people ate the food of the gentiles [*tōn artōn tōn ethnōn*], but I kept myself from eating the food of the gentiles. Because I was mindful of God with all my heart, the Most High gave me favor and good standing with Shalmaneser, and I used to buy everything he needed" (*Tobit* 1.10–13). [25]

Like Daniel, Tobit abstains from the gentile food consumed by his compatriots in the capital city of the conquering nation, and as a result God shows him favor and elevates his status in the eyes of the foreign king. The food in question—"bread" in Greek, "bread" or *pat-bag* in many medieval Hebrew versions[26]—is characterized as "gentile" (cf. "the king's food" in *Dan.* 1.8) but not as "impure," and there is no reason to assume that it contains Biblically prohibited ingredients. Tobit, like Daniel, adheres to a preparer-based prohibition of foreign food not widely observed among his contemporaries, and the narrator of both works presents the ultimate success of the two heroes as resulting from their scrupulous adherence to these restrictions. The same may be said of two Jewish priests mentioned in passing in Josephus's autobiography: "Even in wretched circumstances"—they had been sent as prisoners to Rome—"they had not abandoned piety toward the deity but were subsisting on figs and nuts."[27] Josephus's emphasis here is not on what the priests ate but rather what they did not eat, namely food prepared by foreigners. None of these Judeans would have consented to partake of the king's food in the manner described in *Aristeas.*

Abstention from the food of foreigners specifically because of its foreignness is also attested in texts discovered at Qumran, many of which reflect the practices of sectarian communities in Hellenistic Judea. Even though these sources routinely condemn nonsectarian Jews and their food as impure, their limited references to the prohibition of gentile food are predicated on a different rationale.[28] *Miqṣat Maʿasei ha-Torah,* according to the reconstruction of Elisha Qimron and John Strugnell, prohibits gentiles from offering sacrifices of grain or meat in the Temple.[29] If these prohibitions were based on the impurity of gentile wheat or animals, however, they would apply equally to the offerings of most Jews, who did not adhere to the standards of purity demanded by the sectarians. The *Temple Scroll* prohibits captured gentile war brides from touching pure items for seven years or eating sacrificial meat during this period.[30] This prohibition, however, cannot stem from the ascription of impurity to foreigners; surely the author of this work does not imagine that someone could marry a woman who for seven years would be impure or in a state of pollution and thus unfit for sexual relations! The status of food associated with a foreigner is evidently unrelated to the foreigner's state of purity.

Qumran documents, *Tobit, Second Maccabees, Daniel,* and the expanded version of *Esther* all presume the existence of an unprecedented prohibition against eating certain types of otherwise permissible food on account of its association with foreigners, a prohibition based on the classification of people rather than of foodstuffs. It is no coincidence that such a prohibition emerges during the Hellenistic era, as the implications of consuming food prepared by foreigners or engaging in commensality with non-Jews were greater in the Hellenistic world than they had been in earlier periods. Whereas Persian culture regarded identity as an inexorable consequence of ethnicity (that is, genealogy),[31] Hellenism is characterized by the notion that identity is malleable, determined by one's education in the Greek language and enculturation into Greek society. Hellenistic civilization, according to Martin Hengel, embraced the formulation of Isocrates: "The designation 'Hellene' seems no longer to be a matter of descent but of disposition, and those who share in our education have more right to be called Hellenes than those who have a common descent with us."[32] As "disposition" is reflected and reinforced through behavioral patterns, the decision to eat the food of Greeks and participate in Greek meals, such as symposium banquets, can bear profound significance for one's identity. It was, in fact, possible for nations to "be willed out of existence by their upper classes' desire to be Greek"; Seth Schwartz suggests that this was precisely the intention of some Judean Jews.[33]

Even Jews who resisted assimilation to Hellenism—including the Hasmonean Maccabees, who staged a successful "anti-Greek" revolt and established an independent Judean kingdom (164–163 B.C.E.)—internalized many aspects of Hellenistic thought and culture.[34] Among the Hellenistic concepts embraced by these Jews are those that relate to identity and the distinction between Us and Them. Just as Hellenistic thinkers employ a binary classification of humanity into Greek-speaking "Hellenes" and non-Greek-speaking "barbarians," ascribing no normative significance to acknowledged differences among foreigners, Jewish thinkers of this era classify all non-Jews as "gentiles."[35] Both Jewish and Hellenistic thinkers, moreover, acknowledge the possibility that They can become Us. Just as barbarians can, in the eyes of the Greeks, "become Greek" by adopting core aspects of Hellenistic culture, gentiles can now become Jews irrespective of their genealogical origins by embracing core Jewish beliefs and practices.[36] More ominously, from the perspective of Judeans opposed to assimilation, Jews can now become Greek and abandon the core elements of Jewishness through a process that includes consumption of food associated with gentiles.

The unprecedented permeability of the border distinguishing Us from Them, I suspect, has much to do with the unprecedented efforts by Judean authorities to employ foreign food restrictions as a means both of marking the otherness of gentiles and of limiting interaction with them. By heightening the contrast between Us and Them with respect specifically to food, a significant component of many cultural activities in the Hellenistic world, foreign food restrictions seek to prevent a member of Our community from becoming one of Them. Such restrictions contribute to the maintenance of a well-ordered society, one in which Jews remain distinct from—and, from their own perspective, superior to—gentiles. Mary Douglas, among others, has observed that dietary practices can establish symbolic separations between intertwined religious populations.[37] The need for such separation was likely acute during the final pre-Christian centuries, when Judean writers grappled with the implications of their increasingly mutable religious identity in the midst of the Hellenistic world. *Daniel* in particular offers a model for achieving success and power under foreign rule while nevertheless avoiding acculturation: despite his education in the Babylonian royal palace, Daniel refuses to internalize Babylonian culture, literally as well as figuratively. Even as he reaches the highest ranks of gentile society, Daniel actively maintains through his dietary practices the distinction that God has established between Israel and the nations.

A similar phenomenon is evident in a popular practice attested in the works of Josephus, namely the refusal by Jews in Judea and neighboring Syria to make use of "foreign" olive oil. Providing this piece of information enables Josephus to demonstrate that the rulers of Syria established and maintained special privileges for Jewish soldiers, authorizing them to be paid in cash so that they could bring their own oil to the gymnasium.[38] In our context, Josephus's offhand remark indicates that a noteworthy number of Jews refrained from utilizing one of the most important and most widely traded foodstuffs in Mediterranean antiquity because of its gentile origins.[39] It also illustrates beautifully the efforts of Jewish soldiers to participate in Hellenistic society while maintaining a sense of Jewish distinctiveness: the Jews in question regularly attend the gymnasium, a quintessential Hellenistic institution, but for symbolic reasons they insist on anointing themselves with "Jewish" oil! Elsewhere, Josephus indicates that Jews continued to refrain from using gentile olive oil during the Great Revolt of 66–73 C.E., when an unscrupulous Jewish general cornered the Jewish oil market and charged exorbitant rates.[40]

No precedent for prohibiting gentile oil can be found in pre-Hellenistic Jewish texts, nor does this restriction appear to be a natural outgrowth of earlier religious law. Martin Goodman argues, quite reasonably, that the relatively late development of restrictions on oil and other gentile foodstuffs "is best explained by social and cultural changes in the lives of Jews in this period rather than the development of novel religious theories" regarding the circumstantial impurity of gentile oil or its putative use in idolatrous practices.[41] As a significant number of Jews in the Hellenistic world feel the need to emphasize their distinctive identity within the broader social order, they choose food—to be more precise, culturally freighted foodstuffs—as a medium through which to express their community's unique holiness.

The Jews' embrace of restrictions limiting their access to the food of foreigners, of course, was far from universal, even in Judea and its environs. Jews aspiring to reach the upper tiers of Hellenistic society were avid participants in its culture of symposium banquets: Josephus tells us that Joseph Tobiad and his son Hyrcanus, paradigmatic "Hellenizers" who parlayed their quick wit and familiarity with Greek language and social mores into lucrative tax-farming contracts, ate regularly at the table of the Ptolemaic king.[42] It is nevertheless striking that Judean literary sources never depict their heroes eating with foreigners, while Alexandrian literary sources regularly do so. To put it differently, Alexandrian sources consistently emphasize Jewish distinctiveness with respect to food in a manner that does not necessitate adherence to any rules absent from the Torah, while Judean sources promote adherence to unprecedented foreign food restrictions. The difference between paradigmatically Alexandrian and Judean notions regarding the nature and significance of Jewish food practices points to the dominance within these two Jewish centers of very different ideas about the dangers and opportunities inherent in food-related social intercourse with gentiles.

THE BENEFITS, AND COSTS, OF JUDEAN FOREIGN FOOD RESTRICTIONS

Both Judean and Alexandrian authors regard one type of food associated with foreigners—food offered in idolatrous sacrifice—to be especially dangerous to Jewish identity. Indeed, the *Books of Maccabees* (excepting the inappropriately-titled *Third Maccabees*) and Philo go so far as to define the consumption of food which gentiles have sacrificed to their deities as an act of apostasy. *First Maccabees,* written around the late second century B.C.E., refers to Jews who offer sacrifices to Greek gods as having "gladly adopted [Hellenistic] religion" (*1 Macc.* 1.43). It contrasts the behavior of these scoundrels with that of the heroic martyrs who "stood firm and were resolved in their hearts not to eat forbidden food. They chose to die rather to be defiled by food or to profane the holy covenant; and they did die" (vv. 62–63).[43] The benefits associated with abstention from food sacrificed to idols evidently exceed the value of life itself. According to *Second Maccabees,* Antiochus IV Epiphanes did not require Jews to offer idolatrous sacrifices but rather, on pain of death, "to partake of the sacrifices," specifically the portions eaten by the inner circle of participants (*2 Macc.* 6.7).[44] Such behavior represents a choice "to change over to the Greek way of life [*ta Hellēnika*]" (v. 9); like the Greeks themselves, *Second Maccabees* regards the consumption of such food as integral to the sacrificial ritual and as a central element of activities that mark one's "Greekness."[45] Similarly, Philo's account of the Biblical Baal-Peor incident indicates that partaking of idolatrous libations and sacrifices proves the sincerity of conversion from Judaism.[46]

It comes as no surprise, therefore, that Jewish authorities in the Hellenistic world treat abstention from food offered to idols as the foremost marker of one's Jewish identity, even though we observed in chapter 2 that the Torah lacks a direct prohibition against eating such food. The authors of *Second Maccabees* and, especially, *Fourth Maccabees* emphasize the importance of such abstention by recounting in glowing detail the martyrdom of those who refused to eat what the latter terms *eidōlothuton*, "[food] offered to idols."[47] This term is found in numerous New Testament and early Christian sources; abstention from food offered to idols, a requirement first articulated in Hellenistic Judean literature, constitutes a crucial marker not only of subsequent Jewish identity but also of early Christian identity (see chapters 6–7). From this point onward, in both the Jewish and Christian traditions as well as in Islamic law, eating food sacrificed to idols is no different from offering such a sacrifice oneself: it unequivocally marks the consumer as one of Them.

Jubilees (ca. 160–150 B.C.E.), a Judean work that retells the Biblical account of events preceding the Revelation at Sinai, goes even further and articulates a blanket prohibition against commensality with gentiles as a means of preventing Jews from succumbing to idolatry. This prohibition is placed in the mouth of Abraham as part of the patriarch's deathbed blessing to his grandson Jacob. "Now you, my son Jacob, remember what I say and keep the commandments of your father Abraham. Separate from the gentiles and do not eat with them. Do not act as they do, and do not become their associates, for their actions are defiled, and all their ways are contaminated, abominable, and detestable" (22.16).[48] Abraham proceeds to explain that gentiles offer sacrifices to the dead, consider trees and stones to be gods, and engage in other abominable practices against which God will guard Jacob (22.17–19). *Jubilees*' Abraham articulates a program of segregation that will benefit Jacob and his descendents by enabling them to remain free from defiling offenses and thus to maintain their distinctive monotheistic identity. Principled abstinence from shared meals with foreigners, possibly echoed in the Septuagint's references to avoiding "the king's table" (LXX *Dan.* 1.8; *Addition to Esther* C 28), is also attested within the New Testament: some Jewish Christ-believers object to such behavior, and stories about Jesus never portray him eating with gentiles (see chapter 6).

Motivated by caricatured images of gentiles and perhaps inspired by *Exodus* 34.15–16 and *Numbers* 25.1–3, which acknowledge the dangers of shared meals with idolaters, some Hellenistic Judeans actively avoid not only idolatry but also, as a preventative measure, commensality itself. Alexandrian works like *Aristeas, Third Maccabees,* and Philo's *Moses,* in contrast, portray commensality with gentiles in positive terms. Their authors would no doubt regard abstaining from common meals as too onerous. One might cite *Joseph and Aseneth,* often ascribed to the Alexandrian Jewish community, as an exception to this rule, but I would suggest otherwise.[49] The narrator of this romance, in which the daughter of an Egyptian official falls in love with Joseph and turns away from her ancestral idolatrous practices in order to marry him, makes a point of stating that servants "set a table before [Joseph] by itself, because Joseph never ate with the Egyptians, for this was an abomination to him" (7.1).[50] In this work, however, Joseph does not consistently abstain from commensality with gentiles. It would seem, therefore, that this verse constitutes nothing more than an inversion of the Biblical statement that Egyptians regarded commensality with Hebrews to be abominable.[51] John M. G. Barclay ascribes the lack of subsequent references to separation at table to "a function of narrative necessity rather than religious laxity: while the earlier disjunction of Joseph at the meal table (7.1) was an important symbol of social alienation, it will not do to insert a jarring note of disharmony into an otherwise happy ending," namely the marriage of Joseph to Aseneth.[52] Barclay's observation points to the fact that separation from gentiles at meals does not constitute a normative Jewish practice in the author's community. It would indeed be a jarring note of disharmony if, at the end of the day, Joseph compromised the values of the author's audience by abandoning a traditional taboo against eating with gentiles! The author of *Joseph and Aseneth* uses rejection of commensality with gentiles as a literary motif but not as an expression of Jewish piety in its own right.

Abstention from food associated with foreigners also functions as a literary motif in *Judith,* composed in Judea circa 104 B.C.E., but in this case there is reason to believe that Judith's behavior reflects norms of piety familiar to the work's intended audience.[53] When the gentile general Holofernes besieges the Jewish town of Bethulia, seeking to kill all of its inhabitants, Judith appears in his encampment with her own food, dishes, and oil (*Jth.* 10.5). Claiming to be the servant of God who will enable Holofernes to punish Israel for its transgression of various dietary laws, Judith offers to provide the general with intelligence that will enable him to conquer the Jews (11.12–16). Upon hearing her offer,

> [12.1] He then ordered them to bring her into where his silver dinnerware was set out and to serve her from his own delicacies [*opsopoiēmatōn*] and wine. [2] But Judith said, "I will eat none of that lest it become a stumbling-block for me. Besides, I have enough with what I brought with me." [3] Holofernes said to her, "But if you run out of what you have, how can we get you more of the same? For there is no one of your nationality [*ek tou genous*] among us." [4] Judith replied, "As sure as you live, my lord, your servant will not exhaust her supplies before the Lord God accomplishes by my hand what He has planned."[54]

Holofernes fails to realize that the plan Judith hopes to accomplish is not his military victory but rather his assassination. When Holofernes later orders Judith to eat and drink with him in the hopes of seducing her (12.10–12), she consumes only the food which her servant had prepared (12.19), thwarting Holofernes' designs and seizing the opportunity to decapitate the drunken general (13.2, 6–8).

Food restrictions function in *Judith* as a plot device: Judith cites the failure of Jews to observe them as the cause of Holofernes' impending victory and her defection to him, so her own highly restrictive attitude toward food serves to convince the general of her sincerity.[55] This observation, however, does not diminish the work's value as an expression of contemporary Jewish attitudes toward the food of foreigners, as Judith's sincerity would be most convincingly demonstrated if she herself adhered to commonly recognized dietary standards. For this reason, Holofernes' statement in *Judith* 12.3 sheds considerable light on the food restrictions familiar to Judeans in the late second century. Holofernes, presumably reflecting a recognizable conception of the classificatory system underpinning Jewish dietary law in the author's community, indicates that Judith's concern does not stem from the ingredients of his food but rather from the "nationality" of those who acquire or prepare it. Indeed, Judith does not specifically refuse foods that might contain prohibited ingredients; she refuses the general's wine and "delicacies," a term that refers to cooked, baked, or otherwise prepared foods consumed with bread (12.1).[56] Judith, like the heroes of other Hellenistic Judean tales, adheres strictly to a preparer-based prohibition of foreign food, specifically foods that have, in Lévi-Strauss's terminology, been "cooked" by a gentile. These restrictions, beyond their symbolic significance as a marker of Jewish distinctiveness, also serve an eminently pragmatic and beneficial function clearly dramatized in *Judith:* they safeguard morally upright Jews from the depravity that stereotypically characterizes gentiles and therefore ultimately save the Jewish community from annihilation. The author of *Aristeas* also imagines gentiles as prone to immoral sexual activity, yet neither he nor any other Alexandrian author advocates the adoption of similar foreign food restrictions.

Alexandrian Jews shared with their Judean counterparts a contempt for the idolatrous and immoral practices they regularly ascribe to gentiles and a concern that Jews might come to adopt these abhorrent behaviors and thus forsake their Jewish identity. Elites in both communities not only believed that Jews ought to remain distinct from gentiles but also shared the conviction that Jewish food practices serve to reinforce this distinction: Barclay identifies idol worship and transgression of Jewish food laws as the two most frequent charges associated with apostasy from Judaism in diasporic literature.[57] Alexandrian Jews were also clearly familiar with the foreign food restrictions emerging within Judea, as the texts of *Daniel, Tobit, Judith, First* and *Second Maccabees,* and the expanded *Esther* all circulated in Greek and entered the Alexandrian scriptural canon of the Septuagint. Nevertheless, the segregative restrictions lauded in these Judean works find no echo in Alexandrian literature. Alexandrian Jewish elites value food restrictions as a strictly symbolic means of expressing their community's holiness and preventing assimilation, apparently believing that Biblical dietary laws are sufficiently robust to maintain Jewish distinctiveness on their own so long as these laws are properly interpreted (see figure 3).

It appears that, from an Alexandrian perspective, the costs inherent in foreign

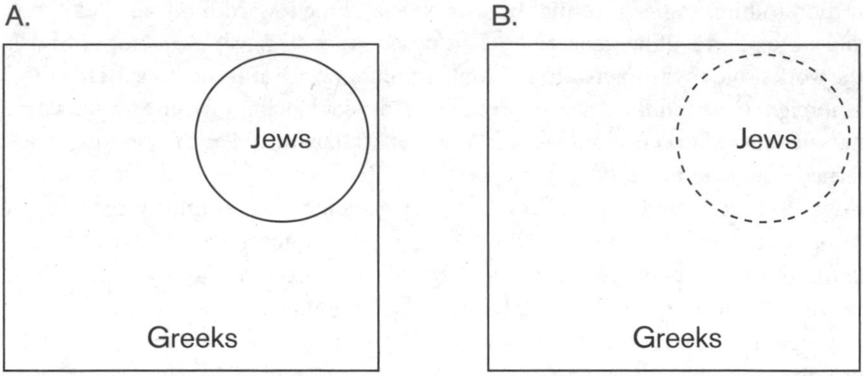

FIGURE 3. JUDEAN AND ALEXANDRIAN CONCEPTIONS OF JEWS AND JEWISH DIETARY PRACTICES. (A) Judeans imagine Jews as a nation separate from and superior to the Greeks. Judean dietary practices, in the form of foreign food restrictions, preserve Jewish distinctiveness through segregation. (B) Alexandrians imagine Jews as a recognizable, respected nation integrated into Hellenistic society. Alexandrian dietary practices preserve Jewish distinctiveness without impeding interaction with Greeks.

food restrictions and their attendant barriers to interaction with gentiles outweigh their benefits. Alexandrian Jews were deeply interested in outreach and in gentile acceptance of their own community as fully Alexandrian. These Jews sought to secure for themselves political rights in their Greek hometown,[58] and their discussions of Jewish food practices reflect a desire to portray Judaism in a manner that those schooled in Hellenistic thought would find respectable. Abstention from food associated with foreigners would stir up undue animosity among non-Jewish neighbors already suspicious about the Jews and their dietary norms. It is possible that Alexandrian Jews would also have been skeptical regarding the benefits of such abstention; Alexandrian literature, after all, expresses less concern about the implications of food-related interaction with gentiles than one finds in contemporaneous Judean texts. To frame this issue more broadly, Alexandrian literature reflects a desire for the social integration of Jews and gentiles even as Jews maintain their religious distinctiveness. Alexandrian elites could only embrace the foreign food restrictions emanating from Judea at the cost of forfeiting that vision of the proper social order.

• • •

John Barclay introduces his study of Diaspora Judaism in the Hellenistic world by citing the blessings of Israel offered by Balaam in Philo's account. "In recounting the story of Balaam, Philo has the seer add an important interpretative gloss to his blessing of this 'people who will dwell alone.' According to Philo's Balaam, their separation will not be territorial ('by the demarcation of land') but will be effected by 'the particularity of their exceptional customs, not mixing with others to alter the ancestral ways.' "[59] This passage is emblematic of the conception of Jewish identity expressed by members of the Alexandrian Jewish elite. What keeps Jews distinct from gentiles is their adherence to traditional practices like Biblical dietary laws, not their geographic or social separation from non-Jews. "Not mixing with others," to these authors, is a state of mind, a set of symbolic behaviors that express Israel's holiness and thus ward off the temptation "to alter the ancestral ways." It is not, however, a program of segregation limiting Jewish access to common meals or to food prepared by gentiles. The "iron walls" erected by Jewish dietary laws are purely metaphorical, as the distinction between Us and Them emphasized in Alexandrian discussions of these laws does not prevent Jews from interacting with gentiles. Quite the contrary: whereas Judean sources regularly portray their heroes as abstaining from foreign food, Alexandrian authors employ shared meals with the gentile king as a literary motif representing Jewish success in their adopted homeland, a sign that gentiles value the presence of the Jews in their midst.

Both Alexandrian and Judean sources depart from earlier Biblical works in their depiction of the norms governing Jewish food practices, but do so in disparate ways. These varied departures reflect the differences in how the Jewish elites of these two centers internalize the paradigms of the Hellenistic culture in which they live. Alexandrians appeal to Hellenistic value systems and concepts of allegory in order to ascribe new virtues to traditional Jewish food practices. Judeans, in contrast, employ Hellenistic ideas about the significance of sacrificial food and the distinction between Us and Them in the process of creating foreign food restrictions that heighten the contrast between Jews and gentiles. The qualitatively different stories about foreigners and their food told by Alexandrians and Judeans—the former valorize Jews who receive food from gentile kings, the latter valorize Jews who refuse to eat such food—externalize the different styles in which Alexandrian and Judean Jews think about the proper relationship between Us and Them. The Alexandrian authors whose works we have examined seek integration into Hellenistic society even as they retain their Jewish distinctiveness, while Judean authors believe that the preservation of Jewishness depends on remaining aloof from Hellenistic society (see figure 4). Benedict Anderson observes that "communities are to be distinguished . . . by the style in which they are imagined." [60] Differences in their styles of thought regarding the proper relationship between Us and Them reflect the different styles in which Alexandrians and Judeans imagine the identity of the Jewish community itself.

The fact that segregative foreign food restrictions are commonplace within works by members of the Judean literary elite reflects a degree of separatist sentiment, even among nonsectarians, unattested in Alexandria.[61] Gentile acceptance and respect are less prominent goals in Judean sources; the desire for autonomy and distinc-

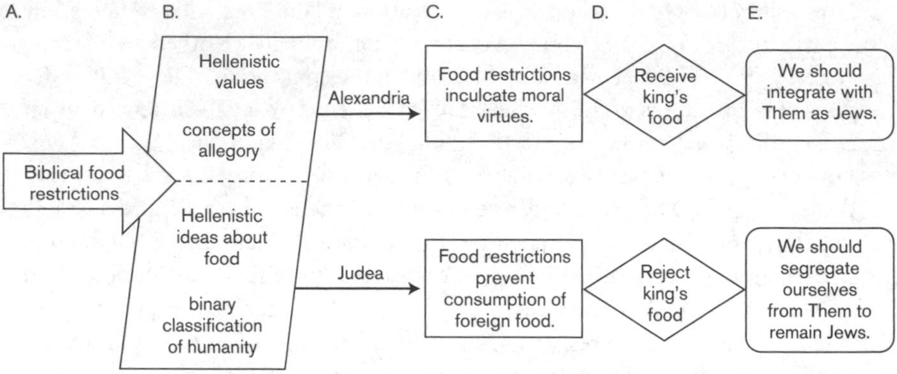

FIGURE 4. THE IMPACT OF HELLENISTIC CULTURE ON JEWISH IDEAS ABOUT FOREIGNERS AND FOOD. (A) Traditional texts and practices (givens), (B) when viewed through internalized cultural paradigms, (C) take on new meanings that, (D) when articulated in normative terms, (E) externalize new ideas about Us and Them.

tiveness, in contrast, is quite apparent. Judeans, unlike their Alexandrian counterparts, evidently believe that Biblical dietary laws alone provide inadequate markers of Jewish holiness and gentile otherness, so they formulate unprecedented foreign food restrictions founded upon classifications of peoples, not foodstuffs. These restrictions inscribe normative barriers to social intercourse across the border between Us and Them while making that border both clear-cut and objectively real. It is indefensible to claim, as some have done, that foreign food restrictions fueled the agenda of the Judean Zealots and sparked the Great Revolt against Rome.[62] Nevertheless, these restrictions do reflect a desire among members of the Judean elite to "dwell alone" in more than merely symbolic terms, despite the costs attendant to this vision of the proper social order. The cultural and symbolic significance associated with the preparation and sharing of food make foreign food restrictions ideally suited for such a separatist agenda.

As this study progresses, we will see that a process similar to the one that shapes the evolution of traditional Jewish food practices in the Hellenistic world plays out in other communities as well. This process involve phases which Peter L. Berger calls the "externalization" of human ideas, the "objectivation" of these ideas as an independent reality, and the "internalization" of these reified ideas by other humans, who repeat the process in each successive generation.[63] We will discover, however, that variegated inputs into this process yield strikingly different outcomes.

4

"These Gentile Items Are Prohibited"

The Foodstuffs of Foreigners in Early Rabbinic Literature

Judean literature from the Hellenistic era reflects the existence of norms absent from earlier Biblical texts: Jews ought not share food with gentiles, and they ought not eat food prepared by such foreigners, especially if that preparation involved the worship of foreign deities. By marking the difference between Us and Them and, moreover, by hindering interaction between insiders and outsiders, these norms serve the social function of preventing undue assimilation. They also construct a sense of Jewish distinctiveness and gentile otherness within a Hellenistic culture that treated identity as mutable and granted little credence to traditional claims regarding Israel's holiness.

The first centuries of the Common Era witness the emergence of Rabbinic Judaism within Hellenistic Judean society, a movement that derives its name from the honorific title "rabbi" (roughly: master teacher) held by its leaders. The rabbis whose opinions appear in the foundational sources of Rabbinic Judaism are known as the Sages, a term analogous to "Church Fathers." The present chapter focuses primarily on the earliest of these foundational sources, which date from approximately the third century and are known as tannaitic literature because they preserve the words of Sages called *tanna'im,* "transmitters." The Sages, who originally constituted an insular group of scholars with little popular support, regarded themselves as the authorized interpreters of God's instruction (*torah*) to Israel as primarily—but not exclusively—contained in the Torah, the first five books of the Hebrew Bible.[1] The Sages devoted considerable energy to elucidating the norms of proper Jewish behavior in legal terms so as to enable punctilious observance of the divine will. Their vision of the law, captured in the literature that came to be known as the "Oral Torah" (complementing the "Written Torah" of the Bible), ultimately achieved dominance in the Jewish world. The Sages did not regard Hellenistic-era literature as authoritative and may well have been unfamiliar with most of the works we examined in the previous chapter.[2] Nevertheless, the Sages were members of Judean society. As such, they inherited, internalized, and interpreted the norms of their community's literary elite governing the food of non-Jews, as well as the distinctively Judean style of thought regarding the proper relationship between Us and Them.[3]

The literature produced by these Sages displays most—arguably, all—of the characteristics which José Ignacio Cabezón associates with "scholasticism": a strong sense of tradition, an interest in language, a tendency toward expansiveness in both breadth and depth of coverage, a conviction that the received canon overlooks nothing and contains nothing unessential, a belief that everything of importance can be known, a commitment to reasoned argument, a high degree of self-reflexivity, and a drive toward the systematic presentation of knowledge.[4] The scholastic mode of thinking, and the last of its aforementioned characteristics in particular, is especially pronounced in the Mishnah (redacted ca. 200 C.E.), the foundation of all subsequent Rabbinic legal discourse. "The Mishnah constructs legal categories, which often appear to be theoretical and abstruse, and then discusses, usually in great detail, the precise definitions and limits of those categories. It creates lists of analogous legal phenomena, and then proceeds to define and analyze every item on the list. It posits legal principles, and devotes much attention to those objects, cases, or times, which seem to be subject to more than one principle at once, or perhaps to none of the principles at all."[5] The process of subjecting vague pre-Rabbinic foreign food restrictions to scholastic analysis that seeks to systematize precise knowledge has a significant impact on the nature and practical ramifications of these laws. This process also reveals the Rabbinic system of classifying humanity.

In the Mishnah and, to a lesser extent, the near-contemporary tannaitic work known as the Tosefta,[6] Rabbinic scholasticism effectively weakens the function of foreign food restrictions as a barrier to interaction with gentiles. Pursuit of order in the realm of ideas, we will see, comes at the expense of norms that seek to preserve order in the realm of social intercourse. Tannaitic Sages, moreover, express greater concern about the foodstuffs of foreigners than about foreigners themselves. By devoting only minimal attention to gentiles within their discussions of foreign food restrictions, the Mishnah and the Tosefta implicitly highlight the fundamental difference between Us and Them: gentiles do not merit scholastic reflection in their own right. The way the authors of these works think (or do not think) about gentiles reflects how they imagine their own community: as uniquely significant.

RABBINIC SCHOLASTICISM AND RESTRICTIONS ON FOOD PREPARATION BY FOREIGNERS

The nature of Rabbinic scholasticism and the impact it has on foreign food restrictions is exemplified in the Tosefta's discussions regarding animal slaughter and other acts of food preparation performed by gentiles. The Toseftan tractate *Sheḥiṭat Ḥullin* ("nonsacrificial animal slaughter") begins by addressing the issue of who may perform a valid act of animal slaughter. As we observed in chapter 2, *Deuteronomy* does not address this issue and *Leviticus* implicitly regards as valid any slaughter performed properly by a non-Israelite member of Israelite society.

[1.1a] All [Jews] are fit to perform animal slaughter, even a Samaritan, even an uncircumcised [Jew], even a Jewish apostate.
[b] An animal slaughtered by a heretic is [regarded as having been slaughtered for the sake of] idolatry.[7]
[c] Animal slaughter performed by a gentile is invalid, and animal slaughter performed by an ape is invalid.
[d] As it says, "You may slaughter . . . and you may eat" [*Deut.* 12.21], [to the exclusion of meat from an animal] that a gentile slaughtered or an ape slaughtered or was slaughtered through its own action.[8]

This passage categorizes butchers according to their status vis-à-vis the Jewish community. Slaughter performed by members of the community is valid, and that of individuals with an ambiguous position relative to its boundaries is similarly permitted (unit a). Slaughter performed by Jews who have attached themselves to another religious community is implicitly valid as well because the butcher, from a rabbinic perspective, remains Jewish. The Sages, however, treat such an act as idolatrous and prohibit consumption of the resulting meat on that basis (b).[9] Slaughter performed by non-Jews, in contrast, is invalid, but the resulting meat is not defined as idolatrous (c).

The prohibition of non-Jewish acts of animal slaughter, according to the Tosefta, derives from *Deuteronomy* 12.21 which, in its original context, allows Israelites to slaughter their domestic animals outside the sanctuary so that the Israelites may eat meat at home. According to the creative exegesis found in unit d, however, this verse also limits the scope of its permission: "you" may only eat the meat of animals which "you" have slaughtered. For that reason, the meat of animals slaughtered by gentiles is legally equivalent to the meat of animals killed by beasts, such as apes, and to carrion meat, whose consumption *Deuteronomy* 14.21 prohibits. Animal slaughter performed by a gentile, even if the act of slaughter conforms to every dictate of Rabbinic law, is invalid simply because the butcher is a non-Jew, someone who is not one of Us. As Jordan D. Rosenblum observes, "Butchery—a cultural practice that separates humans from animals—is now marked by the Tannaim as a distinctly Jewish practice."[10]

It is important to emphasize that the Tosefta's prohibition of slaughter performed by gentiles is unrelated to idolatry. In addition to the distinction between heretics-regarded-as-idolaters and gentiles-regarded-as-apes that opens *Sheḥiṭat Ḥullin*, we learn later in the tractate that

> meat in the possession of a gentile is permitted for benefit; [meat] in the possession of a heretic is forbidden for benefit; [meat] coming out of an idolatrous temple is "the sacrifices of the dead" [*Ps.* 106.28]. This is because they said: slaughter performed by a heretic is [regarded as] idolatry, their bread is [regarded as] the bread of gentiles, their wine is [regarded as] wine offered in libation [to idols], their fruit is [regarded as] prohibited due to failure to tithe, their books are [regarded as] books of divination, and their children are [regarded as] illegitimate. (T. *Ḥul.* 2.20)

According to this tradition, a Jew may derive benefit from meat in the possession of a gentile by, for example, using its fat as a source of fuel. Such benefit, however, is forbidden with respect to meat in the possession of a heretic, in this context apparently a Jewish Christ-believer.[11] Only meat possessed by a heretic is treated as tantamount to the meat of an idolatrous sacrifice. The range and severity of the prohibitions detailed in *Sheḥiṭat Ḥullin* 2.20 reflect an effort on the part of the Sages to establish as firm a barrier as possible between Jews and those seen to pose the gravest danger to them, namely renegade fellow Jews. It is no coincidence that the "uncharacteristic and bitter fury" of this passage, in the words of William Scott Green, is reserved solely for those who "appear to be too close for comfort" and are therefore "especially intolerable."[12] Although some of these restrictions are modeled after those associated with gentiles, the law regarding gentiles is in certain respects less severe because, from the perspective of the Sages, gentiles pose less of a threat to Jewish identity than do heretics.

The fact that the Sages do not imagine gentiles to be especially threatening accounts in part for their readiness to nuance prohibitions related to the food of gentiles by means of borderline cases in which contradictory rules could plausibly apply. Discussion of such scenarios, a common feature in casuistic works of law, serves an academic rather than a practical function, as the utility of a borderline case in clarifying details of the law often comes at the expense of the likelihood that it will actually occur.[13] The Tosefta's discussion of animal slaughter offers a clear example of such scholastic activity on the part of the Sages.

Having distinguished between slaughter performed by Jews and slaughter performed by gentiles, the Tosefta proceeds to sharpen the distinction between these categories by presenting hypothetical cases involving Jews and gentiles engaged cooperatively in the act of slaughter. If a Jew begins to slaughter an animal but a gentile completes the act, the slaughter is invalid unless the Jew has already cut through all or most of the animal's trachea and esophagus. Conversely, if a gentile begins to slaughter an animal and a Jew completes the act, the slaughter is valid and the meat is permitted for consumption (T. *Ḥul.* 1.2).[14] The Tosefta goes on to permit the meat of an animal slaughtered by a Jew and a non-Jew who together wield the knife (1.3a). These cases serve to define with precision the action that constitutes slaughter, namely the severing of most of the trachea and the esophagus: the act of slaughter is valid whenever a Jew has performed this task properly, regardless of circumstances. Applying this principle, the Tosefta proceeds to declare that a Jewish deaf-mute or a minor who severs the trachea and esophagus commits a valid act of slaughter, as does a Jew who performs this action accidentally (1.3b, 1.6a).[15]

Elsewhere, the Tosefta offers a similarly precise definition of the actions that constitute the making of bread and cheese. These foodstuffs, like meat, are products of "cultural transformation," to use Claude Lévi-Strauss's terminology.[16] Just as a Jew must be responsible for the act that turns an animal ("unelaborated") into meat ("culturally elaborated," in contrast to carrion which is "naturally elaborated"), the Tosefta declares that a Jew must perform the crucial transformative acts that turn dough into bread and curds into cheese. It defines these acts as the tasks of baking and setting: "Bread which a Jew bakes, even if a gentile kneaded [the dough], and cheese which a Jew sets, even if a gentile worked [the curds]—this is permitted" (T. *A.Z.* 4.11).[17] By stating that a gentile may prepare the raw ingredients that go into bread and cheese, the Tosefta indicates that this activity is legally inconsequential. Note that the Tosefta is evidently unconcerned by the possibility that gentiles might employ problematic ingredients when making bread or cheese; if it feared this possibility, it surely would not allow gentiles any role in the preparation process. In any case, bread in Mediterranean antiquity was not customarily made with problematic ingredients; we will examine issues related to the ingredients of cheese below.[18]

The orientation of the Tosefta's discussion of bread and cheese toward defining transformative acts of food preparation becomes even more apparent when we consider the statements that immediately precede it: "Their capers, pressed produce, liverwort, and hot water are permitted;[19] their roasted eggs are prohibited; R. Yehudah and his court permitted gentile olive oil by a vote" (T. *A.Z.* 4.11; the last statement implies that olive oil had previously been prohibited).[20] Each of these items is a natural foodstuff that has undergone cultural transformation (capers and liverwort are inedible raw), and ingredients are not at issue as nothing is added to these foodstuffs in the course of their preparation. Tosefta *A.Z.* 4.11 defines an act of food preparation that must be performed by a Jew as one in which a foodstuff is transformed from a fluid or malleable state to a firm state (raw eggs to roasted, dough to bread, curds to cheese; the reverse transformation, olives to oil, had once been prohibited as well, and we will see that the transformation of grapes into wine is especially fraught). The religious identity of the person performing other acts of food preparation is irrelevant; Lévi-Strauss might say that such acts do not impart the preparer's identity onto the foodstuff.

The borderline cases of joint animal slaughter which the Tosefta explores are clearly hypothetical: their function is not to address real-world scenarios but rather to facilitate the development of a more precise definition of a legal concept, "the act of slaughter." In this instance, the Tosefta's definitional activity in no way undermines the practical significance of a prohibition against meat prepared by gentiles, as it is difficult to imagine that Jewish and gentile butchers would regularly engage in the sort of partnership permitted by the Sages. The Tosefta's discussion of the regulations governing bread and cheese, however, demonstrates that definitional exercises of this nature do have the potential to legitimate entirely plausible foreign involvement in food preparation. By specifying the precise acts that constitute the making of bread and cheese, the Sages open the door to gentile involvement in other aspects of the preparation process: a Jewish commercial baker, for example, could readily employ gentile assistants. There is no reason to presume that the Sages intend to create such a practical leniency, which is merely a side-effect of determining the precise legal definition of food preparation, but they nevertheless do just that. As David C. Kraemer observes, "The introduction of definitions—of standards that did not previously exist—makes the law not more onerous but less. By knowing precisely what is forbidden, you also know what is permitted."[21] The Hellenistic Judean idea of a profound distinction between Us and Them that entails avoiding foods which They prepare remains intact in the Tosefta, yet the Sages, by subjecting the methods of food preparation to scholastic analysis, sometimes narrow the scope of traditional foreign food restrictions in significant ways.

THE "INGREDIENTIZATION" OF CONCERNS ABOUT THE FOOD OF FOREIGNERS

Unlike the Judean sources we examined in chapter 3, which express concern about the beliefs and behaviors of gentiles, Mishnaic and Toseftan discourse about foreign food restrictions consistently focuses not on foreigners themselves but rather on their foodstuffs and on the manner in which these foodstuffs are prepared. The Sages express concern regarding whether these foodstuffs have been offered in idolatrous sacrifice and, especially, whether they might contain problematic ingredients. The latter is a topic that no pre-Rabbinic text addresses directly.

Concern about idolatrous sacrifice and problematic ingredients is expressed clearly in Mishnah *'Avodah Zarah* ("Idolatry," literally, "Foreign Worship") 2.3–7, whose structure reflects the Sages' penchant for classification and systematization.[22]

> [2.3] These gentile items are prohibited and their prohibition includes the prohibition of deriving benefit:
>
> wine, gentile vinegar that had once been wine, Hadrianic earthenware,[23]
> and hides [of animals] whose hearts were cut out [in the context of a sacrificial rite]. . . .
>
> [2.6] These gentile items are prohibited but their prohibition does not include the prohibition of deriving benefit:
>
> milk which a gentile drew while no Jew was watching him;
> their bread and [olive] oil;[24]
> boiled foods and pickled foods when their custom is to add wine or vinegar to them;[25]

minced fish,[26] brine containing no small fish,[27] and fish paste;[28]
droplets of asafetida;[29]
and seasoned salt.[30]

These are prohibited, but their prohibition does not include the prohibition of deriving benefit.

[2.7] These are permitted for consumption:
milk which a gentile drew while a Jew was watching him;
honey and honeycombs[31] (even though [honeycombs] drip, they are not considered to be a liquid that renders something susceptible [to contracting pollution]);
pickled foods when their custom is not to add wine or vinegar to them;
unminced fish and brine containing small fish;
leaves of asafetida;
olives caked together in a round.[32]

R. Yose says: Pitted [olives] are prohibited.[33]

The Mishnah presents three lists of gentile foodstuffs, classified on the basis of whether one may consume or derive benefit from them. The Sages treat all gentile wine as having been offered in idolatrous libation, a designation whose implications we will explore at greater length below. According to the Mishnah, gentile wine and foodstuffs that consist entirely of such wine (vinegar and "Hadrianic earthenware," ceramic potsherds soaked in wine), as well as portions of animals sacrificed to idols, are prohibited both for consumption and for the derivation of benefit because of their direct association with idolatry (2.3). Foodstuffs prepared by gentiles that are likely to contain wine or vinegar as an ingredient are prohibited for consumption alone, the same degree of prohibition that applies to all foods liable to contain prohibited ingredients (2.6). Out of concern for the latter, Jews may not consume milk collected by a gentile unless they can verify that the source of the milk is a kosher animal; they may not consume fish products prepared by a gentile unless they can verify that these products contain only kosher fish; and they may not consume foodstuffs suspected of containing nonkosher additives, such as asafetida resin and spiced salt. Gentile foods that do not contain wine products or other prohibited ingredients are unproblematic and not subject to any prohibition (2.7).[34]

Although all of the items addressed on the Mishnah's lists are prepared foods, the classificatory system that underlies these regulations bears no inherent relationship to their foreign preparers: a Jew may not consume food containing idolatrous or nonkosher ingredients regardless of who prepares it. The cause for concern regarding non-Jews expressed in Mishnah *'Avodah Zarah* 2.6–7 (and statements on the same foodstuffs in T. *A.Z.* 4.11–13) is simply that one cannot expect gentiles to utilize only permissible ingredients when preparing food. The Torah, after all, prescribes these laws only upon the Jews, and the Sages draw an even sharper distinction than *Leviticus* by excluding gentiles from the prohibition against consuming blood (*Sifra, Aḥarei* §8).[35] Strictly speaking, then, the Rabbinic prohibitions we have just surveyed are not foreign food restrictions—that is, restrictions stemming from the identity of the preparer or table companion. Gentiles are not significant in and of themselves. Rather, they constitute a category of food preparers that raises instructive questions about the avoidance of prohibited ingredients.[36]

The Mishnah's classification of gentile foodstuffs reflects the systematic application of a simple set of legal principles. Jews may not benefit in any way from foodstuffs directly associated with idolatry and may not consume (but may derive benefit from) foodstuffs that might contain forbidden ingredients; other foodstuffs prepared by foreigners are fully permissible. The redactor of the Mishnah, in fact, seems to go out of his way to present foreign food restrictions and the opinions of fellow Sages as if they conform to these principles even when they do not. He slips the traditional preparer-based prohibitions of gentile bread and olive oil into a list that otherwise consists entirely of foods that contain problematic ingredients (M. *A.Z.* 2.6), despite the fact that there are no grounds for concern about the ingredients of bread or oil in Mediterranean antiquity.[37] We learn in Tosefta *'Avodah Zarah* 4.8 that R. Yose explicitly prohibits not only the consumption of olives pitted by gentiles but also the derivation of benefit from such olives, on the grounds that gentiles sprinkled the olives with vinegar to release their pits. In Mishnah *'Avodah Zarah* 2.7, however, the redactor portrays R. Yose as if he merely prohibits consumption of such olives; the claim that one may not derive benefit from a foodstuff containing a prohibited ingredient contradicts the Mishnah's guiding principles on this subject. The redactor also chooses not to mention rabbinic opinions that conflate the status of foodstuffs which the redactor perceives as belonging to two distinct categories.[38] Redaction, no less than classification and the application of borderline cases, constitutes a powerful tool in the scholastic toolbox as it furthers the goals of systematization and the transmission of tradition.

The redactor of the Mishnah seems to be averse to acknowledging the principle that the very act of food preparation by foreigners might render the resulting foodstuff prohibited for Jewish consumption. For that reason, he employs redactional sleights-of-hand to incorporate norms based on that principle into his legal collection without drawing attention to their underlying rationale. This is true not only with respect to the prohibitions against gentile bread and olive oil but also with respect to gentile meat. We observed above that Tosefta *Sheḥiṭat Ḥullin* explicitly justifies its prohibition against consuming meat from animals slaughtered by gentiles on the grounds that the butcher is not Jewish. Mishnah *Ḥullin* 1.1, in contrast, misleadingly implies that such meat is forbidden for consumption because gentile butchers are prone to perform the act of slaughter incorrectly. The trouble with this notion is that the Mishnah itself states that different rules govern the acts of gentile butchers on the one hand and butchers who often botch the act of slaughter—deaf-mutes, imbeciles, minors, the blind, and those who slaughter at night—on the other. Whereas one may eat meat prepared by error-prone butchers who perform the act of slaughter properly, the Mishnah declares that all animals slaughtered by gentiles are legally equivalent to carrion and thus forbidden for consumption, the same position articulated in the Tosefta.[39]

The effort of the redactor to shoe-horn originally preparer-based restrictions into his own conceptual framework is most evident in the Mishnah's discussions of gentile cheese. This case is worthy of close analysis both because of its relevance in the present context and because we will return to issues relating to cheese, albeit from an Islamic perspective, in chapter 11. In short, the Mishnah asserts that gentile cheese is prohibited because of one of its ingredients—rennet, the enzyme that turns milk into cheese—but cannot find a defensible basis for this claim.

In the ancient world, rennet was derived primarily from the stomachs of suckling animals, in which this enzyme facilitates the digestion of the mother's milk.[40] Cheese makers utilized one of two substances containing rennet: the coagulating milk found inside the stomach of such an animal after its slaughter, referred to in Rabbinic Hebrew as *qeivah* (literally, "stomach"), or the lining of that stomach, *'or shel qeivah* ("the skin of the stomach"). On these forms of rennet, Mishnah *Ḥullin* 8.5 states:

> [a] The *qeivah* of [an animal slaughtered by] a gentile and that of carrion—this is prohibited.
>
> [b] One who sets [cheese] using the *'or shel qeivah* of a valid animal—if it imparts flavor, this is prohibited.
>
> [c] A valid animal that suckled from an invalid animal—its *qeivah* is prohibited; an invalid animal that suckled from a valid animal—its *qeivah* is permitted, because [the *qeivah*] is contained within the animal's digestive tract.

The Mishnah raises three separate issues involving rennet. The stomach contents of an improperly slaughtered animal are prohibited, just like the meat (and, by extension, the stomach lining) of such an animal (a). If the rennet is derived from the stomach lining of an animal whose meat is permitted for consumption, the stomach lining itself must not affect the taste of the cheese, because this circumstance constitutes an impermissible mixture of milk and meat (b). If the rennet is derived from the contents of an animal's stomach, the concern shifts to the origin of those contents, which must be an animal whose milk is permitted for Jewish consumption (c).

Mishnah *Ḥullin* 8.5b–c indicates that the stomach lining is considered to be "meat," that is, part of the animal itself, while the contents of the stomach are not part of the animal. This pair of statements reflects straightforward application of established principles of ingredient-based Jewish dietary law: no mixing milk and meat, and no consuming the milk of a nonkosher animal. The distinction made between an animal and the contents of its stomach reflects the standard Rabbinic conception of physiology. The Sages generally view the body like a doughnut: they regard unabsorbed material in the digestive tract (the hole of the doughnut) as being outside the body itself and therefore not affected by the legal status of that body. Until digested, all substances in an animal's stomach retain the status they possessed prior to consumption.

For this reason, the Mishnah's prohibition of rennet derived from the stomach content of an animal slaughtered by a gentile or of carrion makes no sense. According to 8.5a, the improper manner of an animal's death renders the contents of its digestive tract forbidden for consumption. This statement, however, contradicts the "doughnut physiology" presumed by the continuation of this text. The Tosefta's redactor acknowledges the logical inconsistency of this tradition and attests to its resultant rejection: "The *qeivah* of [an animal slaughtered by] a gentile and that of carrion—this is prohibited. They retracted [this ruling], saying that one may curdle [milk] with the *qeivah* of a gentile or the *qeivah* of carrion without concern" (T. *Ḥul.* 8.12). The redactor of the Mishnah, in contrast, does not address the problematic nature of the prohibition against gentile cheese, even though he was certainly aware of the problem. In its discussion of foreign foods, Mishnah *'Avodah Zarah* recounts a conversation between R. Yehoshu'a and R. Yishma'el, in which the latter refutes the former's arguments that gentile cheese is prohibited on account of its rennet. R. Yehoshu'a, apparently lacking a better justification for the traditional prohibition of gentile cheese, quickly changes the subject (M. *A.Z.* 2.5);[41] the Mishnah's redactor does much the same.

Twice the Mishnah articulates a general prohibition against gentile cheese based on the status of its ingredients and on both occasions fails to provide a plausible rationale for this prohibition. Nevertheless, the Mishnah never questions the existence or continued validity of the requirement to abstain from gentile cheese. We observed above that the Tosefta offers a defensible rationale for such a prohibition based on the transformative nature of the act of setting cheese to harden (T. *A.Z.* 4.11). The Mishnah, apparently because its redactor is uncomfortable with prohibiting foodstuffs on account of their preparer's identity, makes no mention of it. We may note in passing that later Sages cited in the Babylonian Talmud, most likely unaware of the Toseftan statements on this subject,[42] determine that the prohibition of gentile cheese stems from concern that gentiles derive their rennet from the lining of an animal's stomach rather than from the stomach contents (B. *Ḥul.* 116b).[43] Stomach lining, part of the animal itself, is permitted only when the animal has been slaughtered properly, which is to say, by a Jew.

Virtually ignored in all of these Mishnaic discussions about the food of foreigners are the foreigners themselves (see figure 5). The Mishnah, after all, classifies "gentile *items*" (M. *A.Z.* 2.3, 6), not gentiles, and it does so by means of legal principles

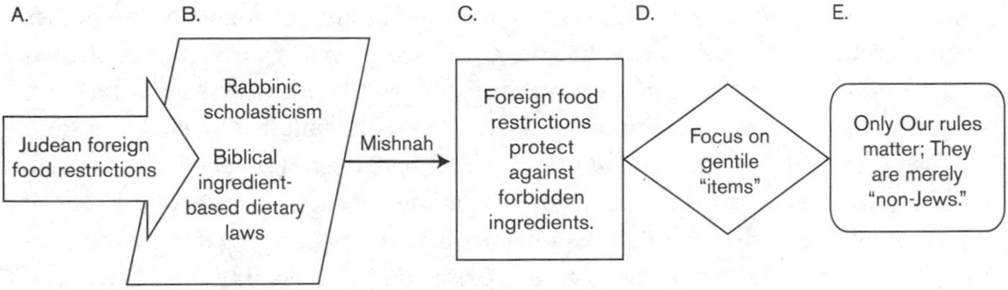

FIGURE 5. THE IMPACT OF SCHOLASTICISM ON THE MISHNAH'S FOREIGN FOOD RESTRICTIONS. (A) Traditional texts and practices (givens), (B) when viewed through internalized cultural paradigms, (C) take on new meanings that, (D) when articulated in normative terms, (E) externalize new ideas about Us and Them.

that have nothing to do with gentiles. Indeed, the scholastically oriented Sages express far greater interest in producing order within the realm of foodstuffs than within the realm of society. This interest reflects the degree to which tannaïtic literature, and especially the Mishnah, treats the food of gentiles as "food for thought," a topic worthy of contemplation within the broader framework of the ingredient-based dietary laws found in the Torah. The Sages, unlike the Torah but in keeping with the practice of their Hellenistic predecessors, emphasize the difference between Our food practices and Theirs. Nevertheless, gentiles themselves warrant little contemplation in their own right within the self-referential, even solipsistic, system of Rabbinic scholasticism. Like the barbarians of Hellenistic discourse, They are significant solely because of the fact that We are not Them: gentiles are, quite literally, "non-Jews."[44]

WINE: AN EXCEPTIONAL CASE THAT PROVES THE RULE

The scholasticism that characterizes normative discourse in the Mishnah and the Tosefta has an especially profound impact on the way these works treat wine that is associated with gentiles. Wine has long been a staple of the Mediterranean diet, and the practice of offering wine libations to the gods was commonplace in the Hellenistic world.[45] Concern about the idolatrous predilections of gentiles alone, however, does not account for the extraordinary lengths to which the Sages go in regulating Jewish association with foreign wine. We have already seen that Mishnah *'Avodah Zarah* 2.3 prohibits deriving benefit from not only from gentile wine but also from wine vinegar. As we observed in Tosefta *Sheḥiṭat Ḥullin* 2.20, the prohibition of benefit which the Sages apply to items associated with idolatry is far more severe than the prohibition of consumption that applies to other forbidden foodstuffs. Mishnah *'Avodah Zarah* 2.4 records a series of disagreements over whether various gentile items associated with wine—beverages stored in vessels that contained it, by-products of its manufacture, and foods prepared with wine or vinegar—are subject to the prohibition against benefit or are merely prohibited for consumption. The last third of Mishnah *'Avodah Zarah,* a section sometimes called "the tractate on libation wine," elaborates a range of regulations extending far beyond issues of consumption, including limitations on Jewish participation in gentile wine production, the precautions necessary for storing and transporting Jewish wine so as to prevent gentiles from accessing it, and the use by Jews of gentile wine presses (M. *A.Z.* 4.8–5.11). The Tosefta contains similar discussions (T. *A.Z.* 4.7–10, 7.1–8.3).

We observed in chapter 3 that the Septuagint's Esther specifically refrains from drinking the wine of libations (*Addition to Esther* C 28); Paul similarly condemns such behavior in idolatrous contexts (*1 Cor.* 10.20–21; see chapter 6). Pre-Rabbinic Judeans and early Christ-believers prohibit food that has been offered to idols because they equate the consumption of such food with idolatry itself. Such restrictions also serve to express the sharp difference between the religious tenets of Jews or Christ-believers and those of the dominant Hellenistic culture. It is unsurprising, therefore, that works from these communities express no concern about many of the wine-related issues that occupy the Sages. Rules that govern the transportation of one's own wine or prevent inadvertent consumption of trace amounts of foreign vinegar, after all, do not further the goal of marking the otherness of gentiles and do not relate to the worship of idols; the Sages themselves acknowledge the latter point by permitting Jews to derive benefit from foods containing gentile wine or vinegar (M. *A.Z.* 2.6, T. *A.Z.* 4.8). Rather, these rules and the discussions about them further a quite different goal, one distinctive to the Sages: to reflect upon every implication, no matter how remote, of the traditional prohibition against Jewish association with gentile wine.

The legal principle expressed through the Mishnah's discussions of foreign wine in all its permutations is that actions associated with idolatry render the objects of those actions, as well as a wide range of related products, permanently forbidden for Jewish use. This principle bears little relevance to the concerns regarding external threats to Jewish identity found in pre-Rabbinic discussions of foreign food restrictions. The Sages imagine that gentiles are inexorably drawn to the worship of false deities, but what really interests them is the determination of how Jews, imagined as unique in their worship of the one true God, should avoid inadvertent association with foreign worship.

The classificatory interests that guide the Mishnah and the Tosefta have led us far afield from the concerns of their Judean predecessors regarding the dangers of gentile culture and interactions with foreigners. Indeed, in their focus on the status of food implicated by idolatry, the Sages gloss over the very foreigners who practice idolatry. Thus, for example:

> If [a gentile] is eating with [a Jew] at a table, and [the Jew] leaves a flagon on the table and a flagon on the side table and leaves [the gentile] and walks out, what is on the table is prohibited [for Jewish consumption] and what is on the side table is permitted. But if [the Jew] said to [the gentile], "Mix for yourself and drink," even what is on the side table is prohibited.[46] [Wine in] open vessels is prohibited; in closed vessels [it is only prohibited if the gentile was left alone long enough] to open it and reseal it and for the seal to dry. (M. *A.Z.* 5.5)

This law apparently presumes that one's gentile companion, if left unsupervised, will immediately offer some of the wine in front of him in libation to the gods, rendering the entire contents of the flagon prohibited, and that he will do the same to the wine being held in reserve if he is given permission to mix it. Gentiles, the Mishnah implies, are so prone to the surreptitious performance of libations that they are wont to open a sealed container of someone else's wine in order to offer a portion to the gods! As Peter Schaefer aptly observes, "One cannot help feeling that the authors of the Mishna . . . exaggerate a bit. One gets the impression that the Gentiles are obsessed with spoiling Jewish wine and making it prohibited for Jews, and that Jews are busy day and night protecting their wine from Gentiles."[47] One also gets the impression that the Sages impute meanings to potentially idolatrous gentile actions without any consideration for how gentiles might understand these acts; the ideas of gentiles themselves, it would seem, merit no attention.[48]

These precautionary measures in the Mishnah and the Tosefta regarding foreign wine, strikingly, do not prevent Jewish interaction with non-Jews. On the contrary, Mishnah *'Avodah Zarah* 5.5 takes for granted that Jews drink together with gentiles and focuses solely on ensuring that the wine consumed by Jews has never been left unattended with a foreigner. Neither the Mishnah nor the Tosefta expresses any concern about the dangers posed by drinking with outsiders nor any desire to separate Jews from gentiles in social settings.[49] In this respect, the Mishnah resembles the works of Alexandrian authorities who also understand food restrictions to distinguish Jews from non-Jews without preventing interaction with gentiles. As Philo puts it, "the particularity of their exceptional customs" naturally restrains Jews from "mixing with others to alter the ancestral ways." As interaction with gentiles poses no danger to Jews, barriers to social intercourse are unnecessary.[50]

This nonchalant attitude toward interaction with gentiles contrasts sharply not only with the attitude found in pre-Rabbinic Judean works such as *Judith* but also with statements found in tannaitic Rabbinic works of Biblical exegesis. Expanding on the incident in *Numbers* 25.1–3 in which foreign women seduce Israelite men into the worship of Baal-peor, *Sifrei* reports that "she would say to him, 'Would you like to drink some wine?' He would drink and the wine would burn within him and he would say, 'Obey me!' She would take out an image of Peor from between her breasts and say to him, 'My master, is it your desire that I obey you? Then bow to this'" (*Sifrei Bemidbar* §131).[51]

Sifrei states that this incident occurred before there was a blanket prohibition of gentile wine, suggesting that the prohibition is designed to limit sexually charged interactions with foreigners. Similarly, *Mekhilta d'Rabbi Shim'on b. Yoḥai,* paraphrasing *Exodus* 34.15–16, warns that eating meat prepared by foreigners will lead to intermarriage and that the gentile wife will then draw the Jew into idolatry. Discussions of foreign food restrictions in the Mishnah and the Tosefta, in contrast, express no hint of concern about intercourse with gentiles, sexual or otherwise. These collections of laws presume that Jews regularly interact with their gentile neighbors in economic and social situations, and neither work makes any effort to prevent such engagement when there is no specific concern regarding the idolatrous practices of non-Jews.[52] When these works address the food of foreigners, the foreigners themselves are often of little concern; what interests the Mishnah and the Tosefta is whether the foodstuff in question falls into a category of items prohibited either for consumption or for benefit. The scholastic mode of thinking that animates these works facilitates the pursuit of a different kind of order than the one that interested pre-Rabbinic Judeans.

THE EIGHTEEN DECREES: A ROAD NOT TAKEN IN THE MISHNAH OR THE TOSEFTA

The Mishnah and the Tosefta depart sharply from pre-Rabbinic Judean literature in their scholastic, foodstuff-oriented approach to the issues associated with food prepared by foreigners, an approach that yields almost as many permissions as prohibitions. This shift in focus away from the stark dangers inherent in the food of foreigners seems to have troubled at least some Sages, who endorsed a broader set of explicitly preparer-based foreign food restrictions. These authorities, however, advance their conception of this traditional Jewish food practice by distinctly Rabbinic means: they ascribe these restrictions to legislation promulgated by a first-century conclave of Sages, thereby justifying the validity of prohibitions absent from the Torah. The authors of such works as *Daniel* and *Jubilees* had no need for such niceties.

Mishnah and Tosefta *Shabbat* both speak of a first-century gathering involving members of the two major schools of Rabbinic thought at which "they voted, and the Shammaites were more numerous than the Hillelites, and eighteen decrees were promulgated on that day" (M. *Sh.* 1.4 // T. *Sh.* 1.16). Although the Mishnah portrays the subject of this conclave as relating to the precautions one ought to take to avoid inadvertently performing prohibited actions on the Sabbath—and even enumerates all eighteen decrees—the Talmuds preserve a variety of lists that provide a very different understanding of the conclave's activity.[53] Several of these lists are related to an account of the so-called Eighteen Decrees ascribed to the mid-second-century R. Shim'on b. Yoḥai, first attested in the Palestinian Talmud (the Yerushalmi, redacted ca. 400). Many historians and scholars of Rabbinic literature have treated this tannaitic account as factually accurate, but there is good reason to be skeptical about the historicity of a fifth-century text describing a first-century event, especially when its account differs radically from the account found in third-century literature.[54] Moreover, the list ascribed to R. Shim'on b. Yoḥai appears to respond to the discussion of prohibited foreign ingredients found in the Mishnah; if so, this list postdates the conclave considerably. Irrespective of its date of origin, comparison of this tradition to Mishnah and Tosefta *'Avodah Zarah* highlights a road not taken in these works, thereby illuminating the way in which the Sages responsible for these collections imagine foreigners and their foodstuffs.

The Yerushalmi attributes to R. Shim'on b. Yoḥai the following statement about the conclave:

> On that day, they promulgated prohibitions against
> [a] their bread, their cheese,[55] their wine, their vinegar,
> [b] their brine, their fish sauce,
> [c] their pickled foods, their boiled foods, their salted foods,
> [d] hulled grain, pounded grain, peeled grain,
> [e] their language, their testimony, their gifts, [marriage to] their sons, [marriage to] their daughters, their first-borns. (Y. *Sh.* 1.4, 3c)[56]

R. Shim'on's list of prohibited foodstuffs consists of four distinct categories: foods that do not exist in nature (unit a), products of fish processing (b), foods that have been "cooked" in some manner (c), and processed grain (d). Although the organization of this list is original, its contents appear to be inspired by our Mishnah, or perhaps a source similar to it. Every item in the first three units appears in the discussions about the food of foreigners found in Mishnah (and Tosefta) *'Avodah Zarah*, although here we find "their salted foods" instead of "seasoned salt." The contents of unit d are unparalleled, but the difference most likely results from a misunderstanding regarding the Mishnah's prohibition of *ḥilaq* (fish sauce, M. *A.Z.* 2.6; this term does not appear in the Tosefta). The author of this account of the Eighteen Decrees apparently understood this term as referring to hulled grain (*ḥelqah*) and proceeded to add two additional types of processed grain in order to reach the desired number of prohibitions.[57]

The logic underlying R. Shim'on b. Yoḥai's version of the Eighteen Decrees is illuminated by a tradition that the Yerushalmi cites in the name of the third-century R. Ḥiyya Rubba: "R. Shim'on b. Yoḥai taught: 'What food you eat you shall obtain from them for money; similarly, the water [you drink] you shall procure . . .' [*Deut.* 2.6]—just as water has not been changed from its natural state, so too [purchase] anything that has not been changed from its natural state" (Y. *Sh.* 1.4, 3c // Y. *A.Z.* 2.8, 41d). In its original context, this verse from *Deuteronomy* conveys instructions by God to purchase food and drink without distinction from the descendants of

Esau. R. Shim'on b. Yoḥai, however, interprets the verse as expressing a limitation of that which Israelites may obtain from outsiders. He draws the line between permitted and prohibited foreign foods at Lévi-Strauss's nature-culture divide. Foods that have been "cooked"—that is, subjected in one manner or another to cultural transformation—by outsiders are prohibited, while those that have merely been handled by gentiles, like the vegetables that Daniel requests, are permissible.

R. Shim'on's concern regarding food prepared by foreigners reflects a desire to separate Jews from the dangerous influences of gentile culture and from assimilation into that culture. His foreign food restrictions seek to advance a vision of the proper social order. Interest in erecting barriers to social intercourse also accounts for the decrees unrelated to food (unit e). Refusal to accept gifts or sacrifices from foreigners, refusal to recognize non-Jews as valid witnesses, and, especially, refusal to learn Greek or condone intermarriage effectively segregate members of the Jewish community from their non-Jewish neighbors.

The attitudes toward foreigners and their food that are attributed to R. Shim'on b. Yoḥai differ considerably from those found in the Mishnah and the Tosefta. These works focus their attention on the ingredients used by foreigners, while the Eighteen Decrees ignore this issue entirely: contrast R. Shim'on's reference to "their pickled foods, their boiled foods" with "the pickled and boiled foods of gentiles when their custom is to add wine or vinegar to them" (T. *A.Z.* 4.8, cf. M. *A.Z.* 2.6). The preparer-based orientation of the Eighteen Decrees is especially evident in its reference to "their salted foods," that is, all foods prepared by salting, rather than to "spiced salt," an ingredient (M. *A.Z.* 2.6; T. *A.Z.* 4.12). R. Shim'on b. Yoḥai's Eighteen Decrees tradition also differs significantly from the Tosefta's preparation-based foreign food restrictions. The Tosefta considers without hesitation joint acts of food preparation, acts that seem to fly in the face of this tradition's separatist orientation and pointed lack of exceptions. As both Talmuds observe, the Eighteen Decrees cannot account for the permission in T. *A.Z.* 4.11 of foods whose cultural transformation does not involve a change of state from fluid to firm.[58] The Eighteen Decrees focus on the foreignness of gentiles; the Mishnah and the Tosefta, in contrast, focus their attention on the ingredients of particular foodstuffs and the processes by which particular foodstuffs are prepared.

Read in light of R. Shim'on b. Yoḥai's Eighteen Decrees, it is even clearer that the permission-strewn Mishnah and Tosefta are not preoccupied by the desire to segregate Jews from gentiles and do not employ legislation for the purpose of social engineering. Rather, these works are motivated by a scholastically oriented desire to plumb the nuances of traditional norms regarding gentile foods within the broader context of Rabbinic law, and gentiles are largely excluded from that self-referential focus. While other works of Rabbinic literature offer vivid caricatures of gentiles that contrast sharply with the portrayal of Jews—gentiles are wicked whereas Jews are righteous, gentiles are animalistic whereas Jews are angelic—the

Tosefta and especially the Mishnah are less engaged in such rhetoric.[59] The analogy of gentiles and apes in Tosefta *Sheḥiṭat Ḥullin* 1.1, for example, does not depict what gentiles are but rather what they are not: Jews. If the message of the Eighteen Decrees is, "We want nothing to do with Them," the Mishnah and the Tosefta convey the implicit message that the only matters worthy of scholastic reflection are those that relate to Us.

• • •

The scholastic mode of thinking that the Sages employ in Mishnaic and Toseftan texts regarding food associated with foreigners results in regulations that allow for considerable Jewish-gentile interaction. We observed that tannaitic Sages reinforce barriers to food-related interaction with heretics but generally do not do the same when addressing foreign food restrictions. Indeed, one might reasonably compare the Sages to the hunters in Robert Frost's "Mending Wall," who remove stones from the border wall in the pursuit of their own agenda. It would be a mistake, however, to conclude that these Sages are interested in effacing the line distinguishing Us from Them, or even in diminishing the significance of food as a marker of that distinction. Quite the contrary: discussions of foodstuffs associated with foreigners in the Mishnah and the Tosefta construct the otherness of gentiles by conveying the sense that gentiles are unworthy of sustained attention in their own right.

Rabbinic discourse about the food of foreigners repeatedly underscores the fact that Jews alone observe the dietary laws and monotheistic worship practices enjoined in the Written and Oral Torahs. As Gary G. Porton puts it, "Gentiles are important primarily because they serve as a means of emphasizing the unique relationship between Israel as an ethnic unit and the central symbols/concepts which serve to define this group in the minds of the authors of our documents."[60] The fact that gentiles have no relationship with these symbols/concepts—or, in the present case, norms—serves to highlight the distinctiveness inherent in Jewish identity: We are holy, They are mundane.[61]

The Mishnah and the Tosefta, like *The Hitchhiker's Guide to the Galaxy* as depicted by Douglas Adams, are compendious works that devote great detail to topics they perceive to be important (the security of Jewish wine, the mechanics of animal slaughter, towels). These works, however, imagine the peoples of the earth to be worthy of little attention: gentiles may safely be dismissed as "mostly harmless."[62] In the binary system of classification which the Sages inherit from their Judean predecessors and, indirectly, from the Greeks, Jews constitute the "1" and gentiles are simply "0," an absence of significance analogous to the blank space on a page that facilitates one's perception of the ink upon it. Gentiles, in the minds of the Sages, are simply non-Jews.

The messages implicit in Mishnaic and Toseftan discussions of these foods—Jews, not gentiles, worship God properly; Jews, not gentiles, are chosen by God; Jewish law is worthy of intense examination while gentile ideas are insignificant—mark the otherness of foreigners and thus reinforce rabbinic notions of self-identity. These discussions suggest that Jews are holy, unique among the peoples of the earth and uniquely significant, because Jews alone distinguish themselves through the fastidious maintenance of divinely ordained (and rabbinically interpreted) classifications of foodstuffs. Foreign food restrictions in the Mishnah and the Tosefta sharpen Jewish conceptions of the social order even while allowing for a range of activities that the heroes of earlier Judean literature proudly avoided. Ironically, scholastic reflection on foreign food restrictions serves the same identity-defining function as separatist-oriented observance of these restrictions. By training rabbinic disciples to think about the nuances of these laws, the Mishnah and the Tosefta also impart a particular style of thinking about the difference between Us and Them and a particular style of imagining Jewish identity itself.

We have seen, however, that the Mishnah and the Tosefta do not tell the whole story. Other tannaitic texts preserve statements that treat foreign food restrictions not as "food for thought" but rather as a means of segregating Jews from gentiles in food-related settings. As we turn our attention to the Talmuds, we will discover that some later Sages also take this approach to foreign food restrictions, and that they employ tools associated with scholasticism as a means of establishing barriers to social interaction with gentiles.

5

"How Nice Is This Bread!"

Intersections of Talmudic Scholasticism and Foreign Food Restrictions

Jewish foreign food restrictions first appear in Judean literature of the centuries following Alexander the Great's conquest. These restrictions reflect, in part, an effort to preserve the distinctiveness of Jewish identity within the Hellenistic world by means of separating Jews from gentiles and gentile practices. The Sages inherit these rules, the underlying notion that food practices distinguish Us from Them, and the even more fundamental concept of a binary classification of humanity into Jews and non-Jews (that is, gentiles).

As we observed in chapter 4, the Mishnah and the Tosefta ascribe to foreign food restrictions a very different set of enactment principles than those implicit in other sources, namely that these restrictions serve primarily as a means of preventing Jews from inadvertently consuming prohibited ingredients. When early Sages acknowledge the preparer-based nature of certain foreign food restrictions, they proceed to define the act of preparation narrowly. Tannaitic discussions of foreign food restrictions reflect the scholastic environment in which Rabbinic law evolved, an environment that fosters the development of abstract categories, nuanced distinctions, and ivory-tower aloofness both from everyday concerns and from the outside world. Because scholastic analysis involves the demarcation of numerous instances in which the food of foreigners is permitted, this analysis entails a significant side effect within the Mishnah and the Tosefta: it dilutes the effectiveness of traditional foreign food restrictions as barriers to social interaction.

Scholastic interest in classification, definition, and analysis characterizes not only the early works of Rabbinic literature but the discourse of the Palestinian and Babylonian Talmuds as well. Many Talmudic Sages, however, also attend to the concerns regarding social interaction between Jews and gentiles that animate pre-Rabbinic (and some tannaitic) texts about Jewish dietary laws. Discussions of foreign food restrictions in the Talmuds reflect a variety of ways in which these and other pragmatic concerns intersect with the scholastic mode of thinking that underpins rabbinic legal interpretation, as well as the ways in which concerns about food overlap concerns about foreigners. The scholasticism that characterizes not only Rabbinic literature but also the work of scholars within other religious traditions, we will see, can itself be used to achieve social objectives.

The Talmuds contain a considerable number of passages regarding foreign food restrictions, each with its own set of intricacies and complications. Zvi Arie Steinfeld has analyzed many of these passages in a series of articles; this chapter draws on his important studies without attempting to replicate their detail.[1] It begins with a brief survey of passages that pursue "ivory tower" goals of classification and legal precision with respect to foodstuffs. The chapter then turns to more sustained analysis of passages that reflect efforts to limit social intercourse with gentiles through commensality-oriented restrictions. This analysis devotes particular attention to the ways in which scholastic methods of interpreting and transmitting sources advance a social agenda. The final third of the chapter is devoted to a close reading of Talmudic texts addressing a single foreign food restriction, the prohibition of bread baked by gentiles. This case study illuminates the interplay of various pedagogical and pragmatic concerns within the scholastic environment of rabbinic academies and the Talmuds they produced. Whether oriented toward theoretical or practical matters, however, all of the authorities whose statements we will examine in this chapter regard non-Jews as indistinct and mostly nondescript. Talmudic Sages construct the otherness of gentiles in order to serve as a contrasting background against which to define Jewish identity.

The Babylonian Talmud (or Bavli, redacted ca. 600) and the Palestinian Talmud (or Yerushalmi, redacted ca. 400) are works of corporate authorship that developed over centuries and that reflect tensions among a variety of opinions.[2] Indeed, the Talmuds reflect to a far greater degree than the Mishnah the characteristic of scholasticism which José Ignacio Cabezón calls "proliferativity": "Scholastics, I maintain, opt for broader (even if inconsistent) canons and for minute and detailed forms of analysis that leave no question unanswered, no philosophical [or legal] avenue unexplored. Rather to include, even if this requires reconciling inconsistent texts or positions, than to exclude, thereby risking the loss of what might be soteriologically [or normatively] essential."[3] This "proliferativity" manifests itself within the Talmuds through dialectical argumentation, a process of question-based dispute about the merits of differing Rabbinic statements.[4] Talmudic dialectic, comprising discussions structured loosely around the text of the Mishnah, is self-consciously diachronic: Sages from different places and times appear in the same passages without engaging in geographically or temporally impossible conversations. In addition to statements and conversations attributed to Sages of the third through fifth centuries, known as *amora'im* ("interpreters"; sing. *amora*), the Talmuds incorporate material attributed to the earlier *tanna'im,* including many statements preserved independently in the Tosefta. Within the Talmuds, tannaitic and amoraic statements alike are embedded within a larger literary framework created by anonymous redactors in a multigenerational process of accretion and reformulation. The Bavli is not only the more extensive and more extensively redacted of the two but also the more authoritative for subsequent Rabbinic law.

FOREIGN FOODSTUFFS IN THE TALMUDIC KITCHEN

Many Talmudic statements regarding the food of foreigners, like their tannaitic predecessors, function within a pedagogical framework of hypothetical argumentation intended to work out nuances of legal categories. These statements were not primarily intended to establish practical guidelines for Jewish behavior.[5] Isaiah Gafni exaggerates only slightly when declaring that the extensive discussions of foreign food restrictions found in the Babylonian Talmud "are nothing more than a continuation of legal discussions drawn directly from the Mishnah and Palestinian legal traditions. Consequently, these passages do not necessarily reflect the contemporaneous circumstances—or even desires—of the authors of these statements themselves."[6]

The Talmuds, following the lead of the Mishnah, devote considerable attention to the problematic ingredients that may be found in food associated with foreigners. For example, we saw in the previous chapter that Babylonian Sages take for granted the existence of an ingredient-based rationale for the prohibition of gentile cheese, as asserted in the Mishnah, and succeed in identifying justifiable grounds for this position (B. *Ḥul.* 116b). The Talmuds similarly identify ingredient-based concerns underlying the prohibitions of such gentile foodstuffs as milk (which might come from a nonkosher animal), asafetida resin (which might be contaminated by nonkosher residue on the knife that extracts it), spiced salt (which might contain nonkosher additives), and most other foodstuffs addressed in tannaitic literature.[7] These prohibitions are unrelated to concerns about the allegedly idolatrous and immoral predilections of gentiles, stemming instead from the simple observation that non-Jews do not observe Biblical and Rabbinic laws regarding foodstuffs prohibited for Jewish consumption. Because such foodstuffs would also be prohibited if prepared similarly by a Jew, the foreign origins of these foods are actually of no legal import. Nevertheless, as we observed in chapter 4, the discussion of specifically foreign foodstuffs serves to mark the otherness of gentiles by emphasizing that Jews alone adhere to Jewish dietary law.

The Talmuds also devote detailed attention to food restrictions based on foreign preparation, in sharp contrast to efforts by the Mishnah's redactor to avoid discussing this form of foreign food restriction.[8] The Yerushalmi preserves traditions ascribed to R. Shim'on b. Yoḥai prohibiting all foods prepared by gentiles, including his account of the Eighteen Decrees. The redactors of the Yerushalmi, however, reject these sweeping prohibitions since, as we have seen, the prohibitions contradict tannaitic statements permitting certain foodstuffs prepared by gentiles.[9] In a parallel passage, the Bavli records and rejects a statement by the third-century Palestinian *amora* R. Yoḥanan similar to one which the Yerushalmi associates with R. Shimʿon b. Yoḥai: "'What food I eat you will supply for money, and what water I drink you will furnish for money' (*Deut.* 2.28)—just as water has not been changed [from its natural state], so too [supply] food that has not been changed [from its natural state]."[10] Acknowledging the existence of preparer-based food restrictions while rejecting their comprehensiveness, the Talmuds proceed to subject these restrictions to scholastic analysis in a manner analogous to the one we encountered in the Tosefta.

Although R. Yoḥanan holds that all food prepared by gentiles is prohibited, he allows a limited degree of gentile involvement in food preparation: "Whether a gentile places [meat on the coals] and a Jew flips it, or a Jew places [the meat] and a gentile flips it, it is permitted. It is not prohibited unless [the grilling is] at the hand of a gentile from start to finish" (B. *A.Z.* 38b).[11] Similarly, R. Yoḥanan reportedly holds that meat roasted by a gentile until it is barely or partially edible may be completely cooked by a Jew for Jewish consumption, and that meat cooked to a barely edible stage by a Jew may be completed by a gentile without becoming prohibited for Jewish consumption.[12] As long as a Jew is substantially involved in the cooking process, the meat is permitted for Jewish consumption because its preparation was not effected solely by a non-Jew; R. Yoḥanan defines prohibited "gentile cooking" as preparation without significant Jewish participation. The Bavli passage in which these statements appear explicitly allows for assistance by one's gentile neighbor in the cooking process and implicitly offers Jewish-gentile interaction as a means of rendering potentially prohibited cooked meat permitted for Jewish consumption. Such leniencies, although in keeping with the letter of preparer-based food restrictions, undermine the latent social function of these laws as a mechanism of segregating insiders and outsiders.

One could argue that R. Yoḥanan and other *amora'im* who articulate leniencies regarding foreign involvement in food preparation are motivated by a desire to make life easier for their followers. It may be, for example, that R. Yoḥanan wished to enable Jews to hire non-Jews to prepare their food, or at least wished to eliminate the problems that would otherwise result from a non-Jewish neighbor's helpful assistance. There is, however, no evidence that R. Yoḥanan had such practical concerns in mind or that he intended to address real interaction between Jews and gentiles. R. Yoḥanan's statements are reminiscent of the Tosefta's borderline cases regarding joint animal slaughter and joint preparation of bread and cheese. In the Tosefta, these cases serve the pedagogical function of defining what constitutes the acts of slaughter, bread baking, and cheese making. R. Yoḥanan's cases are similarly designed to define with greater precision the act of rendering meat fit for consumption in accordance with the principles established by the Torah and earlier Rabbinic authorities. What we find in the Bavli is a series of ivory-tower conversations about the nuances of "meat cooked by gentiles" that have little bearing on the ways insiders ought to interact with outsiders in real life. As we observed in the previous chapter, gaps emerge in the food-restriction-wall setting Jew apart from gentile as a side effect of this interpretive activity. A prohibition of foreign food preparation that originated with an eye toward social segregation has been reworked—one might even say, subverted—in service of the scholastic agenda of Talmudic Sages.

R. Yoḥanan limits the scope of preparer-based foreign food restrictions by the extent to which a gentile is responsible for the preparation. The third-century Babylonian *amora* called Rav, in contrast, applies preparer-based restrictions only to certain categories of food: "All foodstuffs typically eaten on their own are not subject to [the prohibition against] food cooked by gentiles; [only] those eaten with bread are subject to [the prohibition against] food cooked by gentiles."[13] Rav's position is appealing to the redactors of both Talmuds because it is readily reconcilable with traditions found in the Mishnah and the Tosefta.

Rav's exceptions to the prohibitions against food prepared by foreigners, like those offered by R. Yoḥanan, do not seem to stem from practical concerns. There is no reason to presume that the foodstuffs Rav prohibits are more likely to contain prohibited ingredients than others.[14] Classical commentators suggest that Rav's prohibition of food fit for a king (B. *A.Z.* 38a) is intended to prevent the kind of commensality that may result in intermarriage. Unlike *Judith*'s author and some later Sages, however, Rav does not express concern that social intercourse will lead to sexual intercourse.[15] Rather, Rav's distinction is likely based on a nuanced interpretation of Daniel's refusal "to defile himself with the king's food or the wine he would drink" (*Dan.* 1.8).[16] The phrase "the king's food," *pat-bag ha-melekh,* accounts for Rav's distinction between, on the one hand, foods that would be served to a king (*melekh*) and eaten with bread (*pat*) and, on the other hand, foods that do not fit this description. Rav's permission of raw foods reflects Daniel's willingness to eat vegetables and water served by foreigners (*Dan.* 1.12). The precedent established by Daniel both justifies the existence of preparer-based foreign food restrictions absent from the Torah and specifies the scope of these restrictions. The difference of opinion between Rav and R. Yoḥanan stems entirely from their appeal to different Biblical prooftexts.

Rav and R. Yoḥanan each follows his respective understanding of foreign food restrictions to its logical conclusion without evident concern for the potential ramifications of his legal logic. Such lack of consideration for practical implications is commonplace in Talmudic discussions regarding foreign food and clearly manifest in the following passage in the Bavli: "A child who mastered [the laws related to] idolatry at the age of six was asked: What is the law regarding treading [grapes] with an idolater in a wine press? He replied: One may tread [grapes] with an idolater in a wine press. Yet he might offer libations with his hands! They bind his hands" (B. *A.Z.*

56b). A Jew must not benefit from work associated with idolatry, so the question at issue here is whether his gentile co-worker might offer a libation while the two are treading grapes. The suggestion to tie up one's coworker as a means of preventing such behavior is perfectly logical but surely impracticable; it is the kind of suggestion that a six-year-old might make.[17] Nevertheless, the Bavli accepts this proposal as legally convincing and proceeds to address the issue of whether gentiles are capable of offering libations with their feet and whether such action constitutes a valid performance of the ritual. This discussion is not really about effective mechanisms for preventing the offering of libations but rather the potential means by which libations might be offered, as imagined by the Sages on the basis of their own norms for proper worship. What interests the Sages in this context is determining with precision the circumstances that render wine touched by gentiles prohibited, just as in other contexts they seek to determine precisely which circumstances render foodstuffs associated with gentiles prohibited. As we observed in the previous chapter, this scholastic process of interpreting the implications of gentile actions takes place without regard for the ways gentiles themselves understand their own behavior.

The Sages assert that the prohibition against wine touched by gentiles applies even in the absence of evidence that the gentile performed a libational offering. This notion is already expressed in Tosefta *Zavim* 5.8: although the Tosefta ascribes a greater degree of impurity to wine known to have been offered in libation than other gentile wine, it affirms that all gentile wine is prohibited because of concern regarding libations. The Talmuds express similar distinctions in the impurity ascribed to libational wine and "ordinary gentile wine" (*stam yeinam*). They clearly indicate, however, that this distinction has no practical effect on the prohibition against deriving benefit from gentile wine of any sort, much less consuming it or anything made from it.[18] Gentile wine is treated as if it had been offered in libation, irrespective of the likelihood of such activity or the intentions of the gentiles who made it.

The same kind of reasoning underpins the assertion that Jewish wine—that is, wine prepared by Jews alone—becomes prohibited for consumption whenever a gentile touches it, even when it is clear that the gentile did not offer any of that wine in libation. To cite one of several examples addressed in the Bavli, "It once happened in Biram that a gentile climbed a palm tree to take one of its branches. While climbing down, he accidentally touched [Jewish] wine with the tip of the branch. Rav permitted [the Jew] to sell the wine to gentiles. R. Kahana and R. Asi said to Rav, 'But you have taught that even [contact by] a newborn baby renders wine as offered in libation!' He said, 'This statement of mine applies to its consumption—no one said anything about the derivation of benefit!'" (B. *A.Z.* 57a). Rav permits the Jewish owner to sell his wine to a gentile in these cases because it is evident that the gentile infant or tree climber who touched the wine did not intend to do so. Nevertheless, the mere act of gentile contact, even when that contact is indirect and unintentional, renders Jewish wine prohibited for Jewish consumption. Contact with Jewish wine by a gentile who has not completed the process of converting to Judaism also renders the wine prohibited on account of idolatrous libations (*A.Z.* 57a–b): a non-Jew is, by definition, an idolater, and wine touched by an idolater is, by definition, treated as if it has been offered in libation.[19] These conclusions reflect the prevailing interest of Rabbinic literature in defining the permissibility of foodstuffs associated with foreigners on the basis of standardized rules related to the foodstuffs themselves, with only scant attention to the foreigners. If an item associated with a gentile falls into the category of foodstuffs that might contain prohibited ingredients, or if it has been prepared in a manner that qualifies as gentile cooking, or if it has been handled in a manner that triggers concern about idolatrous libations, the item is by definition prohibited for Jewish consumption and, in the latter case, benefit. The gentile's perception of the actions at issue are legally irrelevant to the Sages as they delve into the implications of their own rules and legal principles.

Indeed, Talmudic discussions of gentile wine proceed without regard for the ways in which gentiles actually utilize such wine. The Talmuds never consider the fact that many contemporary gentiles—increasingly Christian and Zoroastrian—do not offer libations in the course of their daily activities.[20] To the extent that wine plays a role in the rituals of these communities, its function is limited to specific ceremonial contexts performed by ritual specialists alone. Despite considerable shifts in the realia of religious life beyond the bounds of their community, however, Talmudic Sages accept without question the presumptions of the already overanxious Mishnah regarding gentile behavior and extend them in accordance with their own internal logic.[21] As Jacob Neusner observes in reference to a different manifestation of this broader phenomenon, "The outsider remained what he had always been, a (mere) pagan, part of a world demanding from Israel no effort whatsoever at differentiation."[22]

The sole exception to the rabbinic notion that gentiles uniformly offer idolatrous wine libations proves the rule. That exception relates to the "resident alien," a term the Sages define as a gentile who accepts for himself the prohibition against idolatry and, according to some Sages, a variety of other Biblical laws. Such a foreigner may be left alone briefly in the presence of Jewish wine without concern that he will offer a portion in libation, although the status of his own wine remains unclear; some, in fact, hold that even the wine of a resident alien is legally equivalent to wine offered in libation.[23] The fact that the resident alien must forswear idolatry before a rabbinic court, coupled with the Talmud's refusal to grant resident alien status to a pair of gentiles known by Sages to refrain from idolatrous worship, indicates quite clearly that the category itself is hypothetical, the product of rabbinic imagination rather than social reality. This category of gentiles is also as close to the line separating Jews from gentiles as one can come while remaining outside the Jewish community: according to some Sages, the resident alien accepts upon himself all Biblical laws except those related to forbidden meats (B. *A.Z.* 64b). Just as the Sages understand Biblical dietary laws to mark their adherents as Jews, members of the holy people set apart from the nations by God, the Rabbinic prohibition of gentile wine as "idolatrous" marks all non-Jews as uniformly mundane, a zero within the Sages' binary system of classifying humanity. Only along the border line itself do the Sages feel any need to entertain more fine-tuned categorical distinctions.

FEAR OF INTERCOURSE, AND INTERDICTIONS AGAINST COMMENSALITY WITH FOREIGNERS

Talmudic authorities, like their tannaitic predecessors, focus primarily on gentile foodstuffs rather than gentile ideas or practices, and they engage in ivory-tower pursuits without regard for concerns regarding Jewish-gentile interaction. In the Talmuds, however, these priorities are far from absolute. The Babylonian Talmud in particular expresses considerable concern regarding an issue that goes unmentioned in the Mishnah, Tosefta, and Yerushalmi, namely the possibility that consuming the food of foreigners might lead to sex with foreigners.[24] Concern about interreligious intercourse plays a role in Babylonian discussions of several foreign food restrictions, including some that have no precedent in earlier Rabbinic literature. These discussions not only mark gentiles as "non-Jews" but also ascribe to gentiles the ability to threaten Jews and their unique state of holiness. Discourse about these foreign food restrictions also demonstrates several ways in which the Sages employ scholastic approaches to the transmission and study of law to further a practical agenda of segregating Us from Them.

Tannaitic sources and the Talmud Yerushalmi only prohibit gentile intoxicants that contain wine or grape products, expressing no concern about other alcoholic beverages. The Tosefta, in fact, explicitly permits consumption of apple wine prepared by non-Jews (T. *A.Z.* 4.12). The Bavli, however, assumes that a generic prohibition of foreign alcoholic beverages exists—perhaps because beer, not wine, was the intoxicant of choice in Babylonia[25]—and merely discusses its underlying rationale. "Why did they prohibit gentile alcohol? Rami b. Ḥama said [in the name of] R. Yiṣḥaq, 'Because of [concern about] marriage.' R. Naḥman said, 'Because of [concern about beverages left] uncovered.' . . . R. Pappa would drink [gentile alcohol] when they brought it to him in the doorway of the tavern; R. Aḥai would drink it when they brought it to his home. Both [understood the prohibition of gentile alcohol as being] because of marriage, but R. Aḥai distanced himself exceedingly [from this possibility]" (B. *A.Z.* 31b). We are told elsewhere that the late third-century Palestinian *amora* R. Yiṣḥaq also states that gentile wine is prohibited "because of their daughters" (B. *A.Z.* 36b).[26] The nature of this rationale, however, allows Sages like R. Pappa and R. Aḥai to redefine the prohibition in terms of commensality. If the underlying concern is that drinking beer in a gentile tavern might lead to fraternization with the gentile regulars and ultimately to sex with their daughters or with women who might be present, then the antisocial act of ordering "takeout" or home delivery of one's alcohol renders the beverage itself permitted for consumption. R. Pappa and R. Aḥai utilize the same form of scholastic reasoning that Sages like R. Yoḥanan use when defining what exactly constitutes forbidden acts of gentile cooking; in this case, however, the effort to achieve greater definitional precision is clearly not hypothetical. These Sages employ scholastic reasoning to navigate conflicting practical concerns: fear of intercourse on the one hand and the desire for beer on the other.

Scholasticism plays a different role in the Bavli's discussion of R. Naḥman's concern about uncovered beverages. Mishnah *Terumot* 8.4 prohibits the consumption of water, wine, and milk left in uncovered containers out of concern that a thirsty snake might have surreptitiously secreted its venom into the liquid. The Sages appear to be quite worried about this threat and cite several cases in which wily snakes succeed in poisoning wine or attempt to do so. Only in the Talmuds, however, is this concern specifically associated with the beverages of gentiles. The Bavli reports that some Sages do not drink gentile water or alcohol because gentiles are not sufficiently scrupulous about covering their beverages; the Yerushalmi raises concern about gentile milk for the same reason.[27] R. Naḥman's prohibition of gentile alcohol because it was left uncovered is, in a sense, ingredient-based, but the accusation that gentiles are lax in their adherence to basic food safety precautions is qualitatively different from the assertion that gentiles fail to follow distinctively Jewish dietary laws. It indicates that gentile food poses a physical danger to Jews and, perhaps more ominously, insinuates that gentiles have developed an immunity to snake venom such that they can afford to be cavalier in leaving their beverages susceptible to contamination.

David C. Kraemer suggests that the Bavli's discussion of snake venom in gentile beverages is an integral component of a broader presentation of outsiders as "snakelike," a portrayal designed to make Jews wary of their gentile neighbors and thus reluctant to associate with them socially, let alone sexually.[28] The second chapter of the Bavli's tractate *'Avodah Zarah*, in which the subject of gentile beverages appears, begins with a discussion of the Mishnaic prohibition against leaving one's animal in the care of a gentile lest the gentile engage in bestiality. The Bavli reports that gentile men are more sexually attracted to the animals of Jews than to their wives, as R. Yoḥanan said, "When the [primordial] snake had intercourse with Eve, he left filth in her." The Talmud proceeds to explain that this filth, transmitted from one generation to the next, was removed from Israel at Mount Sinai but remains in gentiles and, reportedly, results in their inclination toward bestiality.[29] Straying from Rabbinic norms even with respect to evidently permissible interaction with gentiles, the Bavli warns, can result in death: "He who breaches a wall will be bitten by a snake" (B. *A.Z.* 27b, citing *Eccles.* 10.8). The portrayal of gentiles as morally repulsive, mortally dangerous to Jews, and, in a sense, intrinsically subhuman is not new. The Talmuds, however, extend this rhetoric about the otherness of gentiles in such a way as to raise serious questions about the safety of socializing with foreigners and consuming their food; indeed, R. Naḥman ascribes normative significance to this rhetoric.

As Kraemer interprets these Talmudic passages, the Bavli moves beyond merely marking gentile otherness to concretely defining gentile identity as snakelike.[30] This rhetorical technique yields powerful incentives for Us to avoid commensality and other forms of interaction with Them. We should note that this effort to effect a separation between insiders and outsiders depends on the very nature of the transmission of Talmudic materials within Rabbinic academies: it presumes that the audience of the Bavli's discussion of venom in gentile beverages has recently encountered its discussion of snake-derived filth in gentiles. In this instance, the order established within the realm of legal categories and literary units also serves to establish order in the social realm. The redactors of the Bavli take advantage of structural aspects of the scholastic medium through which they transmit their traditions to advance a segregationist agenda.

Manipulation of this medium also enables the Bavli's redactors to create an unprecedented prohibition against commensality with gentiles in the context of gentile wedding banquets.

> [a] It is taught: R. Shim'on b. El'azar says, "All Jews outside the Land [of Israel] worship idols in a state of purity. How so? A gentile throws a [wedding] banquet for his son and invites all the Jews living in his town—even if they eat and drink from their own [food] and their own servant serves them, scripture regards them as if they had eaten the sacrifices of the dead, as it says, 'And he will invite you and you will eat of his sacrifice' [*Exod.* 34.15]."
>
> [b] I might say [that one only worships idols] through the act of eating, but Rava said, "If so, scripture would simply state 'and you will eat of his sacrifice.' What is the significance of 'and he will invite you'? From the moment of the invitation [it is as if the Jew worships idols]!"
>
> [c] Therefore, for the full thirty days [after the wedding], whether he tells you [that a meal is] celebratory or not, it is prohibited [to attend that meal]. From that time onward, if he tells you [that a meal is] celebratory it is prohibited, but if not, it is permitted. And if he says that it is celebratory, until when [is it prohibited]? R. Pappa said: For a full year. And before [the wedding], from when is it prohibited [to attend a meal]? R. Pappa said in the name of Rava: From the time when they place barley in the tub [to make beer].
>
> [d] And is it truly permitted after a full year? Was it not the case that when R. Yiṣḥaq b. R. Mesharsheya came to the house of a certain gentile after a full year and heard the gentile giving thanks [to the gods], he left without eating?! R. Yiṣḥaq b. R. Mesharsheya is different, because he is an important man. (B. *A.Z.* 8a–b)[31]

To understand what is happening in this passage, we will need to examine the statements associated with named Sages independently of the literary context in which the anonymous redactors embed them.

R. Shim'on b. El'azar, a *tanna* active in the early third century, presents the Torah as equating attendance at a gentile wedding banquet with the consumption of food offered to idols. Even if Jews eat kosher food prepared and served by Jews, it is as if they eat "sacrifices of the dead" (a).[32] This rhetoric, however, is not directed against intermarriage or even commensality with gentiles but rather against emigration from the Land of Israel: "All Jews outside the Land worship idols," not merely those who eat with foreigners. As the fourth-century Babylonian *amora* Rava observes, moreover, the infraction described in this text occurs at the moment of invitation rather than the time of the banquet itself (b). It is only because the gentile invites "all the Jews living in his town" that all are implicated in the sin of idolatry irrespective of their behavior. The Tosefta indicates that R. Shim'on b. El'azar's statement originates as the climax to a series of hyperbolic statements condemning emigration: others can demonstrate that leaving the Land of Israel results in death or even abandonment by God, but R. Shim'on b. El'azar can "prove" that any Jew who lives outside the land has essentially abandoned Judaism itself (T. *A.Z.* 4.4–6). There is no indication, however, that R. Shim'on b. El'azar intends his rhetoric about the evils of living in the Diaspora to have legal force, or that he would extend the implications of his statement in the way that the redactors of the Bavli do.

The anonymous voice of the Babylonian Talmud nevertheless portrays R. Shim'on b. El'azar's statement as demonstrating that one should not eat with a gentile for up to a year after his son's wedding (c). This is a non sequitur created by the redactors, who transplanted the structure of unit c from an entirely different discussion about the circumstances under which one ought to insert references to the happiness of Jewish newlyweds into the grace after meals.[33] Not only R. Shim'on b. El'azar but also R. Yiṣḥaq b. Mesharsheya would be surprised by the norms articulated by these redactors: the latter, after all, regards the permissibility of a shared meal as dependent on whether foreign deities were thanked for the food, not whether it occurs in the putative context of a wedding celebration (d). The redactional activity within this passage reflects a concerted effort to craft a new commensality-based foreign food restriction on the basis of sources that neither share this agenda nor support its logic.

What we find in this passage is a novel prohibition against commensality that appears solely at the redactional level of the text and that is based on material borrowed from a different Talmudic passage; this borrowed material is crucial to the literary coherence of our passage even as it disrupts its logical coherence. Ethan M. Tucker has identified all of these factors as characteristic of efforts by the Bavli's redactors to craft material that can be readily transmitted from generation to generation.[34] Tucker observes that the "literary agendas" of the redactors frequently reveal a disinterest in practical legal conclusions. In this case, however, the redactors use the tools of literary craftsmanship to address a practical concern about interaction with foreigners, namely the possibility that social intercourse might lead to more intimate relations. The method by which the Sages compile and revise their legal teachings for transmission becomes in and of itself the vehicle for expressing and justifying an unprecedented law.

We observed in the previous chapter that techniques of redaction, no less than those of classification and distinction, function as tools in the scholastic toolbox of the Rabbinic Sages. Whereas the Sages responsible for tannaitic works employ these tools irrespective of their impact on normative barriers to interaction with gentiles, the redactors of the Bavli wield them to strengthen these barriers and threaten any who would breach the walls. Perhaps the renewed interest of Babylonian Sages in limiting food-related interaction with gentiles reflects their elevated concern about the danger of assimilation, their desire to remain aloof from the broader society, their particular interest in preserving the purity of their genealogical lineage, or some combination of these or other factors.[35] Hypotheses such as these require testing in light of evidence regarding Jewish social history in Sasanid Babylonia, an effort that would unnecessarily distract us from the study of intellectual history.

In the present context, two points regarding the Bavli's discussions of snakelike gentiles and their wedding banquets merit emphasis. First, scholastic modes of thought can themselves be employed in pursuit of a social agenda, albeit only to a limited extent. The redactors of the Bavli are able to create a novel prohibition against commensality, but only one that applies to the specific case of gentile wedding celebrations addressed by R. Shim'on b. El'azar. Any broader prohibition would run counter to the received Rabbinic tradition, and the Talmuds themselves implicitly condone commensality with gentiles in other contexts.[36] Second, the Sages think about gentiles in caricature. The Talmuds depict all gentiles as snakelike and cavalier about basic food-safety precautions, just as they portray all gentiles as idolaters wont to offer libations at a moment's notice. Even when oriented toward practical issues of Jewish behavior when interacting with gentiles, the Sages consider the actual practices or intentions of gentiles to be irrelevant.

TALMUDIC DISCUSSIONS OF GENTILE BREAD

We have seen how Talmudic Sages employ tools associated with scholasticism in a variety of ways. These tools not only further purely academic endeavors, like the clarification of legal categories and the precise definition of prohibited acts, but also, especially in the Bavli, advance practical efforts aimed at preventing social intercourse with gentiles. Talmudic discussions about the prohibition against bread baked by non-Jews illustrate the intersecting factors that influence Rabbinic attitudes toward the food of foreigners and the various approaches Sages take to navigating these confluences. In this case, the factors that shape Rabbinic discourse relate not only to issues of social and conceptual order but also to the needs—and pleasures—of everyday life. Once again, however, the intentions and practices of gentile bakers themselves are not significant factors.

Mishnah *'Avodah Zarah* 2.6 offers no explanation for its blanket prohibition of gentile bread, while Tosefta *'Avodah Zarah* 4.11 indicates that the prohibition only applies when a gentile places the dough in the oven: "Bread which a Jew bakes, even if a gentile kneaded [the dough] . . . this is permitted." The fifth-century Babylonian sage Ravina offers an even broader definition of what constitutes "Jewish" bread: "Bread which a Jew bakes in an oven which a gentile kindled, or which a gentile bakes in an oven which a Jew kindled, or which a gentile bakes in an oven which a gentile kindled but a Jew came and added a woodchip [to the fire], is permitted" (B. *A.Z.* 38b). Ravina's statement is in keeping with R. Yoḥanan's permission of joint Jewish-gentile preparation of meat, which appears in the same passage of the Bavli, and the Tosefta's permission of various other forms of joint food preparation. In a sense, Ravina's statement is even more permissive than those of his predecessors: both the Tosefta and R. Yoḥanan require that a Jew participate directly in the act of baking or cooking, but Ravina considers the act of adding a source of heat to be sufficient to constitute "Jewish baking," even if the Jew never comes into contact with the bread itself.[37] Note that for Ravina, the gentile baker is important only by virtue of the fact that he performs those tasks which a Jew does not perform.

Ravina's ruling opens the door to near total gentile involvement in the baking of bread for Jewish consumption, and many observant Jews over the succeeding millennium and a half have taken advantage of his permissiveness. Nevertheless, there is no reason to presume that Ravina seeks to create a practical loophole in the traditional prohibition of gentile bread. Rather, Ravina appears to be engaged in the academic exercise of exploring borderline cases so as to define with greater precision the nature and scope of this prohibition. He teaches through these cases that any act which subjects dough to increased heat constitutes legally significant participation in the baking process. Ravina's statement exemplifies the tendency in Rabbinic literature to explicate the law and sharpen its categorical distinctions irrespective of the practical ramifications of such explications. We have seen that many Sages ascribe symbolic, boundary-marking significance to foreign food restrictions (Jews observe laws that non-Jews do not) without perceiving these laws as serving the social, boundary-enforcing function of preventing Jews from interacting with non-Jews. Perhaps it was to be expected that symbolic prohibitions against foreign preparation of food would be met with largely symbolic acts of Jewish food preparation.

Not all Sages, however, treat the status of bread baked by gentiles as a matter of purely symbolic interest. Bread, after all, is a significant foodstuff in the Near East, both with respect to its caloric function as a dietary staple and with respect to its cultural function as the basis of any true meal. Some Sages, therefore, seek to permit the consumption of bread baked entirely by gentiles, especially in locations where Jewish bread is scarce, while others react strongly against such efforts. Although the statements of these Sages can readily be explained by reference to practical motivations of various sorts, they too reflect the influence of scholastic thought.

The Yerushalmi reports that the law governing bread baked by gentiles is "among the laws based on obfuscation [*'im'um*]," that is, intentionally ambiguous language. Laws labeled as such permit the performance of otherwise forbidden activities so long as one does not state explicitly that one's action contravenes the law. Thus, for example, it is forbidden to tell a worker during the sabbatical year, "Pick me some vegetables today in exchange for [this coin]," as one may not buy or sell sabbatical produce. One may, however, tell a worker, "Here is a coin; pick me some vegetables today," because in the latter statement the payment is not explicitly linked to the produce. The intellectual gymnastics associated with this sort of intentional ambiguity are paradigmatically scholastic in nature, but in this case the permission of gentile bread is clearly intended to have practical ramifications. Palestinian *amora'im* disagree as to whether engaging in obfuscation so as to consume bread baked by gentiles is legitimate in all circumstances or only when Jewish bread is unavailable. R. Ya'aqov b. Aḥa, who objects to any permission of gentile bread, insists that those who engage in obfuscation must acquire gentile bread not directly from the baker but rather from a *palṭer,* someone who sells the bread of multiple bakers.[38]

The Yerushalmi offers no explanation of how the intentional use of ambiguous language relates to the permissibility of gentile bread. No other Rabbinic text provides additional information on this matter either, but in this case we can compensate for the silence of Rabbinic sources by examining texts from outside the Rabbinic tradition that ascribe normative significance to the words associated with the acquisition of food prepared by foreigners. As we will see in the next chapter, Paul declares that even though Christ-believers may not eat food that has been offered to idols, they may "eat whatever is sold in the market without raising any question on the ground of consciousness" (*1 Cor.* 10.25). Christ-believers may also eat food served in the home of an idolater, "but if someone says to you, 'this has been offered to the gods,' then do not eat it" (10.28). The prohibition against idol food, Paul teaches, applies only when one is aware of the food's sacrificial origins. Paul effectively permits the consumption of food that may well have been offered to idols so long as its idolatrous history remains unspecified, and he encourages his followers to preserve the ambiguity of the food's origins by not asking questions. We will see in chapter 11 that some Muslim jurists also advocate willful ignorance when obtaining potentially problematic foodstuffs. A Shi'i tradition reports that someone asked the Fifth Imam, Muḥammad al-Bāqir (d. 735), about the permissibility of cheese which non-Muslims make using rennet from improperly slaughtered animals. He said: "If this fact is known you may not eat of it, but if the cheese is anonymous such that one cannot know who made it, and the cheese is sold in a Muslim market, then eat it."[39] In related traditions, Muḥammad al-Bāqir specifically instructs Muslims not to ask questions when buying potentially problematic cheese in the marketplace, on the principle that what you don't know can't hurt you. One report adds that he exclaimed, "I like cheese!"[40]

Both Paul and Muḥammad al-Bāqir advocate a "Don't ask, don't tell" policy when it comes to potentially problematic food: if we are unaware that a problem exists and can contrive to remain ignorant of its existence, then we are entitled to the benefit of the doubt. It is reasonable to suggest that this is also what the term *obfuscation* means in the Yerushalmi's discussion of gentile bread: an intentional effort to maintain the ambiguity of the bread's provenance by not asking any questions and thus to evade the prohibition against consuming bread baked by foreigners. This interpretation, inspired by familiarity with Christian and Islamic sources, not only fits the semantic range of the term *'im'um* as used in Rabbinic literature but also accounts for R. Ya'aqov b. Aḥa's stipulation that the permission of gentile bread only applies to bread purchased from a *palṭer.* The act of purchasing bread from someone who sells the wares of multiple bakers is like the act of shopping in the marketplace: because one must make inquiries to determine the origins of any given foodstuff, one can maintain a reasonable modicum of ambiguity by not asking certain questions. In effect, the Sages encourage their followers not to think too much about the merchandise of the gentiles with whom they interact and, by extension, not to think too much about the gentiles themselves either.

R. Yehudah ha-Nasi (fl. ca. 200), known simply as "Rabbi" and traditionally regarded as the redactor of the Mishnah, seems to embrace the logic of obfuscation with respect to bread baked by gentiles. The Bavli's primary discussion of gentile bread (B. *A.Z.* 35b) revolves around multiple interpretations of two different versions of Rabbi's statement on this subject; many of these opinions parallel those voiced in the Yerushalmi. The Bavli's redactors, however, take the liberty of arranging and commenting upon this material in such a way as to address an issue about which their predecessors were apparently not concerned. In the following translation, words and sentences added by these redactors are italicized.[41]

> [a] R. Kahana said in the name of R. Yoḥanan: No court permitted [foreign] bread.
>
> [b] *Does this imply that someone did permit it? Yes,* for when R. Dimi came [from Palestine], he said: Once Rabbi went out in the fields and a gentile brought him professionally baked bread prepared from a *se'ah* of flour.[42] Rabbi said, "How nice is this bread—why did Sages see fit to prohibit it?"
>
> [c] *Why did Sages see fit to prohibit it!? Because of [concern about] marriage! Rather, why did Sages see fit to prohibit it in the field?*
>
> [d] *The people thought that Rabbi had permitted the bread, but this is not the case; Rabbi did not permit the bread.*

[e] R. Yosef (some say R. Shemu'el b. Yehudah) said: That was not what happened. Rather, once Rabbi went to a certain place and saw that bread was scarce for the disciples. He said, "Is there no *palṭer* here?"

[f] The people thought he meant a gentile *palṭer,* but he only meant a Jewish *palṭer.*

[g] R. Ḥelbo said: Even for those who think [he referred to] a gentile *palṭer,* this [permission] applies in places where there is no Jewish *palṭer,* but not in places where there is a Jewish *palṭer.*

[h] *R. Yoḥanan said:* Even for those who think that Rabbi permitted [foreign] bread, this applies in the fields but not in town.

[i] *Why is this? Because of marriage.*[43]

Our analysis of this passage will proceed in roughly chronological order, rather than in the sequence crafted by the redactors.

We begin with R. Dimi's account of Rabbi's encounter with an appealing loaf of bread baked by a gentile (b); R. Dimi, active in the early fourth century, regularly traveled between Palestine and Babylonia and was an important conduit of Palestinian traditions to Babylonian Sages. Expressing his astonishment that foreign bread should be prohibited, Rabbi apparently permits its consumption without reservation. To paraphrase Rabbi's exclamation in light of the Yerushalmi's discussion of obfuscation, "This bread looks delicious! I see nothing wrong with it, and I don't want to hear about anything wrong with it either!"

The notion that Rabbi abrogated the prohibition of foreign bread, however, was evidently unpalatable to many later Sages. R. Yoḥanan, a third-century Palestinian authority apparently reacting to the tradition later transmitted by R. Dimi, flatly declares that no court permitted eating bread baked by gentiles (a), and he suggests that Rabbi himself did not do so either. "Even for those who think that Rabbi permitted [foreign] bread," R. Yoḥanan insists, "this applies in the fields but not in town" (h). R. Yoḥanan uses the unusual vocabulary of "town" and "fields" to refer respectively to locations where Jews are present or absent;[44] he thus limits Rabbi's putative permission of gentile bread to places where there are no Jews from whom to acquire bread. By referring specifically to "the fields," R. Yoḥanan is able to suggest that Rabbi himself had this qualification in mind when he accepted a loaf of foreign bread "in the fields," even though R. Dimi's account, when read on its own, gives no indication that Rabbi suffered from a lack of bread baked by Jews.

The fourth-century Babylonian R. Yosef (or his contemporary, R. Shemu'el b. Yehudah) also objects to the notion that Rabbi permitted the consumption of foreign bread, insisting that R. Dimi's account must be inaccurate. According to his alternative account, Rabbi was shocked to discover that Rabbinic disciples had no bread and therefore exclaimed, incredulously, "Is there no *palṭer* here?" (e). In R. Yosef's account, like the one offered by R. Yoḥanan, Rabbi specifically addresses a case of scarcity. The patriarch's question does not itself indicate his position regarding the permissibility of consuming bread acquired from a gentile *palṭer,* and R. Yosef claims that it is a mistake to conclude that Rabbi permitted eating bread sold by such a merchant, even in cases of necessity (f). R. Yosef's colleague R. Ḥelbo, in contrast, understands "Is there no *palṭer* here?" to indicate that Rabbi did in fact permit the consumption of bread sold by gentile merchants in the absence of Jewish merchants from whom one can obtain bread (g). R. Ḥelbo, like R. Yaʿaqov b. Aḥa in the Yerushalmi, stipulates that gentile bread must be acquired in a setting in which one can plausibly maintain the ambiguity of its origins. Note that R. Ḥelbo and R. Yosef utilize the language ascribed to Rabbi to limit the scope of Rabbi's permissiveness, just as R. Yoḥanan utilizes the language of R. Dimi's account for this purpose. By doing so, these Sages are able to claim that they are merely interpreting the opinion of Rabbi himself. In a scholastic environment that highly values the received tradition, this technique of retrojection through exegesis enables later authorities to mask their own innovations.

The named authorities in this passage all focus their attention on gentile bread itself, to the exclusion of the gentile baker. The anonymous redactors, in contrast, worry about the people—more specifically, the women—associated with gentile bread. No named Sage in either the Yerushalmi or the Bavli links gentile bread to concern about marriage with foreigners, but we have seen that some *amora'im* justify the prohibition of gentile alcohol by reference to intermarriage fears and that the redactors of the Bavli seem particularly interested in discouraging if not prohibiting food-related interaction with foreigners. For that reason, they interject a sharp retort to the rhetorical question R. Dimi ascribes to Rabbi: "Why did Sages see fit to prohibit it!? Because of [concern about] marriage!" The redactors, fearful as they are of the prospect that commensal intercourse will lead to sexual intercourse, can only imagine Rabbi offering a lenient ruling about gentile bread "in the fields" (c). The redactors here appropriate R. Yoḥanan's term for a place without Jews from whom to acquire bread and use it to refer to a place where there are no gentiles to marry. (The redactors fail to explain how Jews are supposed to acquire gentile bread in a place where there are no gentiles.) Drawing from R. Yosef's playbook and perhaps protesting too much, the redactors also insist that Rabbi did not in fact permit the consumption of gentile bread, even "in the fields," and that claims to the contrary reflect a popular misunderstanding (d). By inserting a lengthy digression in the middle of R. Yoḥanan's statement (a + h), the redactors structure their discussion of gentile bread so that it begins with an emphatic statement that the prohibition of such food remains in full force. This structure, moreover, implies that R. Yoḥanan himself shares the redactors' concern about intermarriage (i).[45]

In sum, the redactors portray the prohibition of gentile bread as an essential bulwark against intermarriage despite the fact that none of the Sages whose words they preserve understands this prohibition in such a manner. The redactors employ elements of existing traditions—R. Yoḥanan's town/fields distinction and R. Yosef's claim that there was a misunderstanding—to reach conclusions that make sense in light of their own marriage-oriented understanding of foreign food restrictions while masking the novelty of their interpretation. In the process, the redactors radically alter the nature of R. Yoḥanan's distinction and obscure the concern about bread scarcity and the preference for bread purchased from a *palṭer* expressed in the statements they compile. As we saw when considering the Bavli's prohibition against attending gentile wedding-related meals, redactional activity creates an unprecedented commensality-based foreign food restriction in response to concern about sex with foreigners.

A variety of practical concerns underlies the attitudes toward gentile bread that we have encountered in Talmudic texts. One is concern about intermarriage: the prohibition against gentile bread, according to those who fear marriage with non-Jews, ought to function as a barrier to social interaction and ought to remain intact even in places where bread baked by Jews is scarce. Another is concern about the scarcity of a staple foodstuff: some Sages seek to relax the prohibition against gentile bread to one degree or another when bread baked by Jews is difficult to obtain. R. Dimi's account of Rabbi's statement reflects the implicit presence of a third concern: in marveling over the appetizing loaf of bread he has been given, Rabbi seems not to be motivated by concern for sufficient food but rather by a desire for tasty food. The same concern may motivate a suggestion in the Yerushalmi that one may contrive to permit foreign bread even without a compelling need to do so, and it may also underlie the interest of R. Pappa and R. Aḥai in purchasing alcohol from a gentile tavern. As we observed in passing, the motivating force of good food also plays a role in some Islamic discussions about cheese. In our Talmudic texts, the attitudes influenced by these social, nutritional, and gastronomic concerns play themselves out in the context of scholastic discourse among the *amora'im* and shape the ultimate redaction of this discourse as well. At the same time, the Talmuds also preserve amoraic discourse about bread and other foodstuffs that seems to address no practical concern but rather is motivated by the pursuit of ever more precise understandings of the law.

Permissive or not, practically oriented or not, Rabbinic statements regarding foreign bread—and all food associated with gentiles—reflect a scholastic milieu that prizes concepts and categories. Indeed, the fact that the Talmuds give voice to these diverse approaches to the significance of foreigners and their food, even as these approaches work at cross-purposes, reflects the "proliferativity," to return to Cabezón's term, of Rabbinic scholasticism. As we will see in many of the chapters to follow, the scholasticism characteristic of Rabbinic literature manifests itself in various works by Christian and Islamic authorities as well. We will also see, however, that these authorities pay far more attention to foreigners than one finds in the food-oriented discourse of the Sages. Christian and Islamic authorities define the identity of their own communities through comparison with specific identities which these authorities themselves ascribe to adherents of other religions. Rabbinic literature, in contrast, simply depicts gentiles as lacking the identity ascribed to Jews, an identity expressed and reinforced through adherence to and reflection upon a wide variety of food restrictions.

"A UNIQUE NATION"

The Rabbinic liturgical epigraph with which part II began emphasizes the incomparability—and thus, the holiness—of God and of God's people: "You are unique and Your divine name is unique, and who is like Your people Israel, a unique nation [*goy*] on earth?" Jewish sources offer a variety of glimpses into what it is that sets this singularly holy community apart from the indistinct mass of mundane "nations" (*goyim*) and how Jewish authorities perceive the archetypical gentile (*goy*). As William Scott Green observes, the opposition between Jews and gentiles "forms a necessary outer limit for, and thus is a constitutive element of, any culture or religion we choose to mark as Jewish. Had there been no nations, Israel would have had to invent them."[46] The existence of actual nations beyond the bounds of Israel, however, should not distract us from the degree to which the gentiles we encounter in Jewish literature are Jewish inventions all the same. Whether portrayed as seductively attractive or morally repulsive, dangerously negligent or benignly helpful, avid idolaters or equivalent to apes, the images of gentiles found in our sources reflect the imaginations of their authors. The most common motif in Jewish discussions of foreign food restrictions is that gentiles are all alike by virtue of the fact that they are, by definition, non-Jews. Foreign food restrictions serve to mark the otherness of gentiles, those who lack the characteristics constitutive of Jewish identity; only rarely do these restrictions ascribe characteristics to gentiles themselves.

The binary division of Us and Them into Jew and non-Jew, holy and mundane, is not a foregone conclusion; we will see in the following chapters that Christian and Islamic authorities employ more complex systems for classifying humanity. Nor, for that matter, is this division found in quite so stark a manner within the Hebrew Bible. The rhetoric of Israel's uniqueness is most certainly present in Biblical texts: the phrase "a unique nation on earth" comes from *2 Samuel* 7.23 (= *1 Chron.* 17.21) and the theme of Israel's distinctiveness, as we saw in chapter 1, is prominent in the Torah. Many of these texts, however, regard distinctions among non-Israelites to be of considerable significance. *Deuteronomy,* for instance, applies different laws to Israelite relations with the peoples resident in the Promised Land (7.1–2), with Ammonites and Moabites (23.4–7), with Edomites and Egyptians (23.8–9), with *gerim,* and with foreigners (both 14.21, to cite one example). Jewish authors of the post-Biblical period, in contrast, regard distinctions among non-Jews to be of no real consequence, much as Hellenistic thinkers were content in most contexts to dismiss all non-Greeks as barbarians.

The development of foreign food restrictions in Hellenistic Judea and its environs reflects an effort to define more clearly the boundary between Us and Them at a time when existing boundaries are perceived to be insufficient. The fact that scholastic interpretation by early Sages effectively weakens the function of these restrictions as barriers to social interaction reflects a lack of concern about gentiles in the Mishnah and the Tosefta: as non-Jews, gentiles are to a large extent nonentities in these works. We have seen, however, that scholasticism is not antithetical to practical concerns about social interaction with foreigners. The Bavli demonstrates a variety of ways in which scholastic modes of interpretation and transmission can themselves be used to erect barriers between insiders and outsiders. The fact that foreign food restrictions can constitute barriers separating Jews from gentiles is perhaps less surprising than the fact that they can demarcate the boundary between insiders and outsiders without seriously impinging on interaction across that boundary. Indeed, the latter function is fundamental to the former even as it exists independently both in sources about foreign food restrictions and in many discussions of other kinds of dietary law. Separation presupposes distinction, but distinctiveness can be maintained without separation. What underlies both functions is an interest in classification and differentiation, and discourse about foreign food restrictions provides opportunities to sharpen these classificatory endeavors in various ways.

As we shift our attention from the Rabbinic descendants of Hellenistic Judaism to its Christian offspring, we will see even greater emphasis placed on the purely symbolic significance of dietary laws in general and foreign food restrictions in particular. We will also, however, discover that Christian authorities ultimately embrace the barrier-establishing social function of foreign food restriction to a far greater degree than their Rabbinic counterparts. The differences between Christian and Jewish discussions of foreign food restrictions reflect not only different attitudes toward ingredient-based dietary laws but also, and more importantly, a fundamental difference in how authorities from each tradition imagine the ideal social order and classify its constituent parts.

PART THREE

Christian Sources on Foreign Food Restrictions

Defining Otherness

Jesus left that place and went away to the district of Tyre and Sidon. Just then a Canaanite woman from that region came out and started shouting, "Have mercy on me, Lord, Son of David: my daughter is tormented by a demon!" But he did not answer her at all. His disciples came and urged him, saying, "Send her away, for she keeps shouting after us." He answered, "I was sent only to the lost sheep of the house of Israel." But she came and knelt before him, saying, "Lord, help me." He answered, "It is not fair to take the children's food and throw it to the dogs." She said, "Yes, Lord, yet even the dogs eat the crumbs that fall from their masters' table." Then Jesus answered her, "Woman, great is your faith! Let it be done for you as you wish." And her daughter was healed instantly.

MATTHEW 15.21–28

Although those Jews had been called to sonship, they degenerated to the level of dogs, while we who were dogs received the strength, through God's grace, to cast off our former irrationality and to rise to the honor of sons. How do I prove this? "It is not fair to take the children's food and throw it to the dogs." Christ was speaking to the Canaanite woman when he called the Jews "children" and the gentiles "dogs." But see how thereafter the order was changed about: they became dogs, and we became the children. Paul said of the Jews: "Beware of the dogs, beware of the evil workers, beware of those who mutilate the flesh! For it is we who are the circumcision" [Phil. 3.2–3]. *Don't you see how those who at first were children became dogs?*

JOHN CHRYSOSTOM, *DISCOURSES AGAINST THE JEWS* 1.2.1–2

6

"No Distinction between Jew and Greek"

The Roles of Food in Defining the Christ-believing Community

The first adherents of what we now call Christianity were, of course, Hellenistic Jews from Judea and the surrounding provinces. Like the early Sages, they inherited not only the Jewish scripture but also Jewish ideas and practices of their time and place. Among the latter are the notion of a binary distinction between holy Jews and mundane gentiles, a distinction marked in no small measure by differences in dietary practice, and Judean restrictions that limit access to otherwise permissible food associated with foreigners. Belief that Jesus was the messiah (Greek: *christos*), however, radically affected the manner in which these Jews understood their ancestral texts and traditions. Some Christ-believing Jews embraced a new style of thinking about the relationship between Jews and gentiles, maintaining that one need not be Jewish at all in order to gain full membership in the community of those who believe in Jesus as Christ. The success of proselytizing efforts among gentiles—the "gentile mission"—determined the fate of the Church, as gentiles quickly came to outnumber Jews within the Christ-believing community. These gentile Christians developed a conception of Christianity as a religion not only separate from Judaism but also in direct opposition to it.[1] The evolution of norms regarding food in general and food associated with foreigners in particular reflects the evolution of Christian identity itself. As Hal Taussig perceptively frames the formation of this identity, "In the beginning was the meal."[2]

The New Testament offers glimpses into the beginnings of the gentile mission and the styles in which the earliest Christ-believers imagined their community's identity; because they did not conceive of this identity as being wholly separate from or necessarily opposed to Judaism, it is anachronistic to refer to these figures as "Christians." Of particular relevance for the present study are several of the Pauline letters, written in the fifth decade of the first century, and *Acts of the Apostles*, written in that century's eighth decade as the continuation of the *Gospel of Luke*. These works emphasize the importance within the Christ-believing community of the common table. Indeed, *Acts* lists "the breaking of bread" among the core activities of those who embrace the gospel and accept baptism (*Acts* 2.42).

In Paul's words about membership in the Christ-believing community, "there is no distinction between Jew and Greek . . . for 'everyone who calls on the name of the Lord shall be saved'" (*Rom.* 10.12–13, citing *Joel* 2.32). The Hellenistic Jews whose works we considered in chapter 3, in contrast, believe quite strongly in the distinction between Jew and Greek, and many of the earliest Christ-believers shared that conviction. Paul and fellow advocates of the gentile mission, therefore, face the challenge of reconfiguring the traditional Jewish conception of the proper social order, made manifest in Judean foreign food restrictions. The magnitude of this challenge becomes apparent when we reflect upon the portrayal of Jesus at table in the Gospels. Although the Gospels famously recount that Jesus ate with "tax collectors and sinners" (*Matt.* 9.11 // *Mark* 2.16 // *Luke* 5.30), people on the margins of Jewish society, it is surely significant that we never hear of Jesus eating with gentiles.[3] Quite the contrary, Jesus compares gentiles to "dogs" who are unfit to share the food of the Jewish "children"; "the dogs under the table" may "eat the children's crumbs," but gentiles may not sit at Jesus' table as equals and have no right to expect Jesus' attention (*Mark* 7.27–28; cf. *Matt.* 15.26–27, part of the first epigraph introducing part III).[4] Jesus himself had no interest in ministering to gentiles: "I was sent only to the lost sheep of the house of Israel," he declares (*Matt.* 15.24).

If Jesus shared meals with gentiles—or, more precisely, if the authors of the Gospels imagined that Jesus had done so—there would surely be reference to this in their works.[5] Those who subsequently argued for the legitimacy of eating with gentiles could have made their point quite simply and effectively: "What would Jesus do?" Rather, our sources indicate that Jesus, a Jew conveying his message to the Jewish community of Judea, observed the foreign food restrictions discussed in chapter 3. This practice implies that Jesus' conception of the social order was more similar to that of his Judean predecessors than that of his Christ-believing successors.[6] As Stephen G. Wilson observes, "The reluctance of early Christians to embark on a Gentile mission"—and, I would add, to relax traditional foreign food restrictions—"is to be explained not simply by reference to their disobedience or their Jewish scruples, but by acknowledging a far more fundamental factor, namely that in all probability they shared the same view as Jesus."[7]

Many Jewish members of the Christ-believing community, like their ancestors, regarded food restrictions in general and foreign food restrictions in particular as an important means both of marking the otherness of gentiles and of effecting a separation from them. For that reason, New Testament passages addressing these restrictions provide important insights into the ultimately successful efforts of those who sought to redefine this community and its boundaries. These passages address two separate issues, which we will examine in turn: the dietary laws incumbent upon gentile as well as Jewish Christ-believers, and the norms governing commensality with fellow Christ-believers.

THE DIETARY LAWS INCUMBENT UPON GENTILE CHRIST-BELIEVERS

Paul, an educated and observant Jew who experienced a vision of the risen Christ, understood himself to be Christ's apostle (that is, messenger) to the gentiles to proclaim the salvation that comes through association with Jesus Christ. In that role, Paul wrote several letters that address directly the applicability of Jewish food restrictions within the Christ-believing community, primarily as they apply to gentile Christ-believers; the Pauline letters are the earliest texts in the New Testament canon.[8]

Best-known among Paul's statements about food is his teaching to the Christ-believing community in Rome.

> I know and am persuaded in the Lord Jesus that no [food] is forbidden in itself; but it is forbidden for anyone who thinks it forbidden.[9] If your brother or sister is being injured by what you eat, you are no longer walking in love. Do not let what you eat cause the ruin of one for whom Christ died. . . . Do not, for the sake of food, destroy the work of God. Everything is indeed pure, but it is wrong for you to make others fall by what you eat; it is good not to eat meat or drink wine or do anything that makes your brother or sister stumble. (*Rom.* 14.14–15, 20–21)

Paul writes these words to the gentile Christ-believers in Rome and agrees with them that they may eat "anything" (14.2).[10] Paul tells them, however, that there are values more important than eating whatever one wishes. One such value is to "welcome those who are weak in faith" (v. 1), who, out of concern for Jewish dietary laws, "eat only vegetables" (v. 2). "Those who eat must not despise those who abstain, and those who abstain must not pass judgment on those who eat, for God has welcomed them" (v. 3). God has permitted members of the Christ-believing community to eat all foods, yet Paul demands that those who take advantage of this permission act "in love" toward those who observe the ingredient-based food restrictions of the Hebrew Bible and subsequent Jewish tradition. When necessary, the "strong" should voluntarily abstain from food that the "weak" regard as impure.[11]

In his words to the Romans, Paul conveys a central message of his gospel to the gentiles, namely that gentile Christ-believers, because they are not Jews, are not bound by Jewish law. There is nothing wrong with abstaining from certain foods, or with treating certain days on the Jewish calendar differently from others, but there is also nothing wrong with treating all days and all food alike (vv. 2–6; cf. *Col.* 2.16, whose authorship is disputed). Paul does not seem to mind that some Christ-believers observe these laws while others do not, and he certainly does not encourage Jewish Christ-believers to consume foods prohibited in the Torah in order to eliminate the difference between Jews and gentiles. Paul affirms the right of gentiles to full membership in the community of Christ-believers while continuing to live free from Jewish law; he does not address the continued applicability of that law to Jews. Whereas earlier Jewish writers like the author of *Aristeas* seized upon Biblical dietary practices as a marker of one's Jewishness, Paul insists that the dietary practices of Christ-believers do not constitute an essential expression of their identity.

The rhetoric in *Romans* notwithstanding, Paul does not in fact allow gentile Christ-believers to eat "anything." On the contrary, Paul instructs the Christ-believers of Corinth to abstain from food offered to idols (*eidōlothuton*).[12] The *First Letter to the Corinthians* was not actually the first that Paul wrote to the community he founded among the gentiles of that city; after leaving Corinth to found additional churches in Syria and Asia Minor, he sent an earlier letter that has not survived. The leadership of the Corinthian church wrote back to Paul challenging some of his teachings. *First Corinthians,* Paul's response, addresses the challenge of preserving a distinct community of monotheistic Christ-believers in the midst of a nonmonotheistic culture. Paul portrays abstention from *eidōlothuton* as crucial to this task.

The challenge that faced Corinth's community of Christ-believers is epitomized in *1 Corinthians* 5.9–11: "I wrote to you in my letter not to associate with sexually immoral persons, not at all meaning the immoral of this world, or the greedy and robbers, or idolaters, since you would then need to go out of the world. Now, however, I am writing to you not to associate with anyone who bears the name of brother or sister who is sexually immoral or greedy, or is an idolater, reviler, drunkard, or robber. Do not even eat with such a person." Paul taught Corinthian Christ-believers to shun idol worship and sexually immoral activities—fundamental messages of the Hebrew Bible and the Jewish tradition—and also to shun people who engage in these and other offensive behaviors. The majority Corinthian population, however, worshipped Greek gods and embraced Hellenistic culture, whose norms of sexual propriety differ in some respects from those of the Bible. Did Paul wish for his followers to "go out of the world," to cut off all contact with society at large as did Judean sectarians and, to a lesser extent, nonsectarian elements of the Judean elite? No, he clarifies, Christ-believers should not pass judgment on outsiders and need only shun members of their own community who engage in offensive behavior (vv. 12–13). Such sinners should be cut off even from table fellowship, which Paul regards as a defining marker of membership in the Christ-believing community.

Implicit in the commensality prohibition of *1 Corinthians* 5.11 is the permission of sharing meals with an idolater or a sexually immoral person who is not a "brother or sister." Such commensality was a core element of participation in Greco-Roman society: meals were central to social life, and attendance at them signified and enhanced one's social status along with one's attendant economic and political power.[13] Meals in the Hellenistic world, however, were not "secular" affairs. They frequently involved the offering of sacrifices to the gods, the consumption of food that had previously been sacrificed, or the invitation of a god to partake of the meal. The symposium that concluded a formal dinner consisted of drinking significant quantities of wine, a portion of which had been offered in libation, and frequently devolved into sex acts which the authors of the Hebrew Bible regarded as offensive and defiling.[14] Participation in the meals of outsiders thus raised serious questions regarding the boundary separating Christ-believers from their neighbors. Paul, in a manner reminiscent of the Alexandrian Jewish authors whose works we encountered in chapter 3, values participation in the broader society even as he rejects certain behaviors associated with it: Christ-believers may attend gentile meals but nevertheless must adhere to their community's distinctive religious norms. To that end, Paul condemns acts of sexual immorality (*porneia*, 6.12–20) and, after addressing issues related to marriage and chastity, proceeds to discuss at length and with careful nuance the issue of *eidōlothuton* (8.1–11.1).[15]

A faction of the Corinthian Christ-believing community considered the consumption of food offered to idols as permissible in all circumstances; Paul cites from their arguments in the course of responding to them. In their words, "we know that all of us possess knowledge" (8.1) that "no idol in the world really exists" as "there is no God but one" (v. 4); if neither idols nor multiple gods exist, no food can truly be offered to them or defiled by them! Moreover, "food will not bring us close to God" (v. 8) in any case, so the act of eating or abstaining is ultimately irrelevant.[16] The freedom claimed by these "knowers" to eat *eidōlothuton* contrasts sharply with the opinion of many Hellenistic Judean writers, most notably the authors of the *Books of Maccabees*, who consider all food offered to idols to be prohibited.[17] Paul adopts an intermediate position.

Paul begins his response by chiding the "knowers" for boasting of their knowledge, both because they may know less than they think and because love of God and of one's fellow is more important than knowledge (8.1–3). He reminds them that not everyone possesses their knowledge about the nonexistence of idols: "Since some have become so accustomed to idols until now, they still eat [their food] as food offered to an idol, and their consciousness, being weak, is defiled" (v. 7).[18] The sense of Paul's statement is that some Christ-believers mistakenly believe that the food they eat has been offered to a real deity. This misunderstanding of the reality of multiple deities results in real defilement because the act of eating food that one regards as having been offered to idols is a paradigmatic form of idolatry itself. For that reason, Paul says, even someone who rejects idolatry and understands that idolatrous sacrifice has no effect on the status of the foodstuff itself must take care lest his decision to consume *eidōlothuton* "not somehow become a stumbling block to the weak" (v. 9). A member of the Christ-believing community must not cause harm to a fellow member, and that alone is sufficient grounds for one to forego the "right" to eat *eidōlothuton.* Paul proceeds to recount the ways in which he foregoes his own rights for the sake of others as an example for how the "knowers" ought to behave (9.1–23); at the conclusion of his discussion about food offered to idols, he reiterates the importance of foregoing one's liberty to further the glory of God and the salvation of humanity (10.29b–11.1).

Paul's rhetoric about concern for the "weak" serves to make his resistant audience of "knowers" more receptive to his critique of their position. Who can argue with the importance of love and concern for one's fellows?[19] In *1 Corinthians* 10, Paul's critique grows sharper as he turns the knowers' attention to the limitations of their knowledge and ultimately rejects entirely their "right" to eat *eidōlothuton.* The Israelites surely knew God during their desert journey, yet some of them nevertheless became idolaters, engaged in sexual immorality, and put Christ to the test; their punishments, Paul warns, ought to serve as an example to us all. It is noteworthy that Paul emphasizes eating and drinking as the core components of idolatry in his references to the Golden Calf and Baal-peor incidents (10.7–8). Because knowledge alone does not prevent idolatry, Paul instructs his followers to "flee from the worship of idols" (v. 14) by avoiding food sacrificed to them. In particular, Paul highlights the incompatibility of eating such food on the one hand and participating in the communion at the ritual core of the Christ-believing community on the other, as the former expresses a relationship with demons antithetical to relationship with the Lord (vv. 20–21).[20] Because the distinction between monotheism and idolatry is absolute, Paul no less than other Hellenistic Jewish authorities forcefully prohibits the consumption of *eidōlothuton* and regards abstention from such food as a crucial marker of one's membership in a minority religious community. Paul holds that We are those who do not eat food offered to idols, and anyone who would knowingly and willfully do so is by definition one of Them.

Significantly, however, Paul permits the consumption of food whose association with idolatry is unknown.

> Eat whatever is sold in the market without raising any question on the ground of consciousness, for "the earth and its fullness are the Lord's" [*Ps.* 24.1]. If an unbeliever invites you to a meal and you are disposed to go, eat whatever is set before you without raising any question on the ground of consciousness. But if someone says to you, "this has been offered to the gods," then do not eat it, out of consideration for the one who informed you, and for the sake of consciousness—I mean the other's consciousness, not your own. (*1 Cor.* 10.25–29a)

In the Greco-Roman world generally and in Corinth specifically, much of the meat—as well as various other foodstuffs—available in the public marketplace came from sacrifices in local temples.[21] Furthermore, "unbelievers" regularly served sacrificial food at home, particularly on festive occasions of various sorts.[22] Even without being informed explicitly of its sacrificial origins, there was always a reasonable chance that the food one would receive in the market or at a gentile's home had been offered in sacrifice. Paul was aware of these facts and shared the Jewish community's abhorrence of *eidōlothuton,* but nevertheless permitted all food of unspecified origins obtained in the marketplace or a gentile's home. Later, Islamic authorities articulate similar leniencies with respect to potentially problematic meat found in the public marketplace, but whereas they stress the "the outward appearance of Islam" borne by such food,[23] Paul makes no demand that the food appear "Christian" so long as it lacks any outward appearance of idolatry. If one can reasonably imagine that the food has no association with idolatry, it poses no problem.

Paul's leniency regarding potentially idolatrous food rests on a form of contrived ignorance similar to that of some Talmudic Sages regarding foreign bread. If we do not know for certain that the foodstuff is prohibited and we manage to avoid acquiring such knowledge, we may benefit from the doubt. Paul's willingness to advocate such ignorance with respect to a foodstuff so freighted with cultural significance likely relates to his understanding of idolatry itself: Paul agrees with the Corinthian "knowers" that the act of sacrifice has no real impact on the food that has been sacrificed (10.19). Whereas most rabbinic discussions of foreign food restrictions are preoccupied by the status of the food itself, Paul consistently maintains that it is not food but the act of eating it with a certain mindset that is potentially defiling.[24] Paul informs his audience in Rome that no food is intrinsically impure or prohibited (*Rom.* 14.20), but at the same time he warns that a person sins by eating food he or she regards as prohibited (v. 23). Similarly, Paul prohibits eating food with the awareness that it is *eidōlothuton* (*1 Cor.* 8.7) and regards as a grave offense the act of consuming such food in contexts where one's mindset is expressed through ritual, such as in a temple or at a meal associated with a sacrifice (10.10, 21). When one is not conscious of a foodstuff's idolatrous associations, however, there is nothing problematic in the act of eating it.

Because one's ideas about the food are all that matters, Paul instructs the Corinthians not to make inquiries regarding food that is only potentially associated with idolatry and to regard it as "the Lord's" food rather than an idol's food unless explicitly informed otherwise. Paul's *eidōlothuton* prohibition marks gentile Christ-believers as distinct from their unbelieving neighbors while allowing them wide latitude for neighborly interaction. Paul imagines gentiles to be separable from their idolatry, as he allows for association with the former but not the latter. Church Fathers seeking rapprochement with Greco-Roman society, we will see in chapter 7, make the most of this distinction.

Paul teaches that gentile Christ-believers need not adhere to Jewish law, including Biblical dietary restrictions, but that they must abstain from food offered to idols and from sexual acts which the Jewish tradition deems offensive. Abstention from

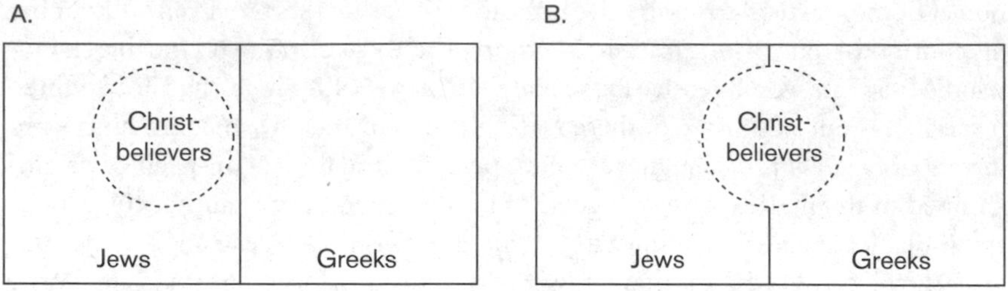

FIGURE 6. EARLY CONCEPTIONS OF THE IDENTITY OF THE CHRIST-BELIEVING COMMUNITY. (A) Some early Christ-believers regard their community as Jewish and thus demand that Greeks accept Judaism in order to become members. Biblical dietary law and foreign food restictions mark the boundary between Jews and Greeks. (B) Paul and the author of *Acts* hold that Jews and Greeks alike may be members of the Christ-believing community, irrespective of adherence to Biblical dietary law. Adherence to the Apostolic Decree marks gentile Christ-believers as distinct from other Greeks but does not prevent interaction with them.

forbidden animal species is not a marker of Christ-believing identity, but abstention from *eidōlothuton* is. *Acts of the Apostles* reports that the apostles and elders gathered in Jerusalem, Paul among them, convey roughly the same message in a statement known as the "Apostolic Decree."[25]

> It has seemed good to the Holy Spirit and to us not to impose on you any burden except these necessities:
> the abstention from what has been offered to idols [*eidōlothuton*],
> from blood,
> from that which was strangled,
> and from fornication [*porneia*].
> If you keep yourselves from these, you will do well. (15.28–29; cf. 15.19–20, 21.25)

Some Jewish Christ-believers believe that only Jews are eligible for full membership in the Christ-believing community and therefore demand that gentiles wishing to join the community must first become Jews by assuming the obligations of Jewish law. This demand is expressed metonymically in *Acts* through the requirement of male circumcision (15.1), but applies equally to the requirement of adherence to Biblical dietary restrictions. The leaders gathered in Jerusalem reject this definition of Christ-believing identity. Holding that Jewishness is not essential to Christ-believing identity, the apostles and elders declare that gentiles and Jews alike can be full members of the Christ-believing community (see figure 6). The Apostolic Decree indicates that Christ-believers are not uniformly obliged to adhere to the entirety of Jewish law but are obliged to follow four norms of behavior foreign to Hellenistic culture but fundamental within Jewish thought.

Condemnation of *porneia* and *eidōlothuton,* frequently juxtaposed in the Hebrew Bible and Hellenistic Jewish literature, appears in the Apostolic Decree, *1 Corinthians,* and *Revelation* (2.14, 20). The Apostolic Decree, however, also enjoins adherence to two related aspects of Biblical dietary law: gentile Christ-believers may not consume blood or the meat of animals slaughtered in a manner that does not cause their blood to drain out. We observed in chapter 2 that the Hebrew Bible applies these prohibitions to non-Israelites and regards consumption of blood or meat with blood in it as an offense on par with the cardinal sins of idolatry and illicit sexual behavior. It is not surprising, therefore, that Jewish leaders of the Christ-believing community would require gentiles to maintain these fundamental and divinely established norms regarding food in addition to mandating abstention from *eidōlothuton.*

Many scholars, however, maintain that the Decree does not relate to food but rather is intended to provide baseline moral instructions to gentile Christ-believers. Some support this interpretation by appeal to a variant of the Decree found in a single Western manuscript and attested in various Christian works into the fifth century. According to the Western text, the Apostolic Decree instructs gentiles to abstain "from what has been offered to idols and from blood and from fornication." In the absence of the prohibition of "that which is strangled," found in all other New Testament manuscripts, one can argue that the reference to "blood" in this passage indicates a prohibition against shedding blood, not consuming it.[26] The appeal of this version to modern scholars is that it looks like a list of the three primary cardinal sins of Biblical Israel, as well as Rabbinic Judaism and early Christianity: idolatry, murder, and illicit sexual behavior.[27] The first of these general categories, however, must be inferred from what is actually a specific dietary prohibition regarding food offered to idols, and the term *blood* in the Western text may still refer to a foodstuff rather than serve as a shorthand reference to bloodshed. Indeed, early Western Church Fathers, no less than their Eastern counterparts, understood the Apostolic Decree as prohibiting the consumption of blood; this position was first rejected by Augustine at the turn of the fifth century.[28]

The interpretation of the Apostolic Decree as a statement of basic morality not only runs counter to the evidence of ancient manuscripts and the earliest interpretations of *Acts,* it also fails to account for the function that *Acts* ascribes to the Apostolic Decree. As Marcel Simon puts it, "The question which the Apostles are facing and to which the Decree provides an answer is not to tell the gentile Christians what rule of life they have to obey in order to be saved . . . it is, more simply, to decide under what conditions they will be admitted to full religious fellowship with their brethren of Jewish birth. And it is *a priori* likely that these conditions should be of a ceremonial character."[29] To phrase this point differently, the apostles and elders gathered in Jerusalem seek to establish markers that identify gentile Christ-believers both as similar to their Jewish counterparts and as distinct from other gentiles in the Hellenistic world. In doing so, they wish to supplant the markers of the

Jew-gentile distinction most commonly recognized by Jews and Greeks alike, namely circumcision and abstention from such Biblically forbidden foodstuffs as pork.[30] Basic moral norms, however, do not function as effective markers of identity: both We and They, after all, condemn murder. *Acts*, moreover, refrains from caricaturing gentiles as immoral, reserving its limited use of negative images for Jews who reject the teachings of Christ-believing missionaries. The food restrictions contained in the Apostolic Decree serve as an effective mechanism for marking Christ-believing gentiles as distinct from unbelieving gentiles.[31] Paul's statements about food offered to idols also further this goal.

Paul and the authors of the Apostolic Decree reject the notion that adherence to Biblical dietary law constitutes a significant marker of identity, but we should bear in mind that this notion itself is of relatively recent vintage. The Torah, after all, does not treat abstention from forbidden foods as an identity marker either. The substance of these Christ-believing teachings, moreover, does not contravene Jewish norms of the period. Neither Paul nor the apostles encourage Jewish Christ-believers to violate Biblical dietary laws, and early Sages would agree that gentiles are not obligated to observe these laws. The Sages would also affirm Paul's message to the Corinthians that one need not treat meat whose sacrificial origins are unknown as idolatrous.[32] In these respects, the teachings of these early Christ-believers are "Jewish."

The point at which Paul and his fellow apostles and elders depart from Biblical and Jewish precedent is their vision of the proper social order: these Christ-believers reject the significance of the distinction between Israel and the nations found in the Bible and emphasized in other works of Hellenistic Jewish literature. As Paul explains, "There is no longer Jew or Greek, there is no longer slave or free, there is no longer male and female; for all of you are one in Christ Jesus" (*Gal.* 3.28). Paul is, of course, well aware of the differences between the members of these opposed pairs, but he insists that each has an equal place in the Christ-believing community, despite their differences. By defining gentiles ("Greeks") not as Them but rather as part of Us, Paul indicates that We are not necessarily Jews: what defines Us is the fact that We are Christ-believers.

COMMENSALITY AND THE CREATION OF A CHRIST-BELIEVING COMMUNITY

Paul and his fellow apostles reject the notion that adherence to Biblical dietary law in its entirety constitutes a significant marker of Christ-believing identity. Instead, they employ adherence to taboos against *eidōlothuton* and, according to the Apostolic Decree, blood as a primary marker of one's identity as not-Them. By doing so, these apostles express their conception of the Christ-believing community as fully accessible to Greeks yet distinct from mainstream Hellenistic culture. Referring back to figure 6 above, discourse about the dietary laws incumbent upon gentile Christ believers serves to shift the circle of Christ-believers from existing entirely within the Jewish community to straddling the boundary that separates Jews from Greeks. In order to efface that divisive boundary within the Christ-believing community, Paul and *Acts* emphasize the importance of commensality between Jewish and gentile believers. Commensality of this nature creates the unified community of Christ-believers in which "there is no longer Jew or Greek."[33]

Paul addresses the issue of commensality in his *Letter to the Galatians,* in which the apostle defends the truth of his "gospel for the uncircumcised" (*Gal.* 2.7). Central to Paul's message is that faith in Jesus Christ, rather than observance of the law, is the sole prerequisite for salvation (v. 16). Paul therefore insists that gentile Christ-believers are full and equal members of the Christ-believing community who must be treated as such even if they do not adhere to all Jewish norms. For this reason, Paul sharply rebukes Cephas (elsewhere called Peter) for his behavior in Antioch.[34] Cephas, Paul reports, commonly ate with gentile Christ-believers, but when "certain people came from James," one of the leading apostles in Jerusalem, Cephas "drew back and kept himself separate for fear of the circumcision faction. And the other Jews joined him in this hypocrisy, so that even Barnabas was led astray by their hypocrisy" (vv. 12–13). The refusal of commensality, as Paul makes clear in *1 Corinthians* 5.11, constitutes a sign of exclusion from the Christ-believing community.

Paul's condemnation of Cephas's behavior in the incident at Antioch is absolute (*Gal.* 2.11, 14), in contrast to his nuanced statements in *1 Corinthians* and *Romans.* It is clear, therefore, that the shared meals in question did not involve *eidōlothuton* or ingredients prohibited to Jews. Rather, the issue at stake in Antioch is that Cephas has transgressed the Hellenistic Judean prohibition against commensality with gentiles, attested in *Jubilees* and in the Septuagint's references to heroes who abstain from "the king's table."[35] Alternatively, the "circumcision faction" may insist on abstinence from food prepared by foreigners. In either case, this faction holds that Jewish Christ-believers ought to adhere to Judean foreign food restrictions even with respect to gentiles who share their belief in Christ. Cephas and those who follow his example seem to feel that they ought to observe these traditional restrictions as well, at least in the presence of those who came from James.

Commensality establishes its participants as part of a common Us, while foreign food restrictions mark their targets unequivocally as Them. The apostle who emphasizes unity and mutual respect among Christ-believers, therefore, cannot compromise on this matter. There must be "no distinction between Jew and Greek" among those who call upon the name of the Lord (*Rom.* 10.12), so traditional Jewish foreign food restrictions must be abandoned within the Christ-believing community. Although Paul recognizes that Jews and gentiles differ in their practices and even fosters these differences, he refuses to allow such differences to divide the community. While there can be diversity in *what* Christ-believers eat, he implies, there must be uniform agreement that all community members may eat *with* one another as equals at the common table, because We are all, first and foremost, Christ-believers.[36]

Acts of the Apostles conveys a similar message by linking commensality between Jewish and gentile Christ-believers with the gentile mission itself: the former becomes permissible with the validation of the latter. In *Acts,* however, Peter (Paul's Cephas) stands up to the "circumcised" Christ-believers of Jerusalem when they challenge his decision to preach the gospel to the household of the centurion Cornelius, the act that effectively inaugurates the gentile mission.[37] "Why did you go to those who are uncircumcised and *eat with them?*" they ask, focusing on the act of commensality rather than that of proselytization (11.3, emphasis added). Peter himself acknowledges the traditional prohibition against eating with gentiles, but contends that it no longer applies. As he tells Cornelius and the gentiles with him, "You yourselves know that it is unlawful for a Jew to associate with or to visit a gentile; but God has shown me that I should not call any person mundane or impure" (10.28, cf. 11.12; *Acts,* here and elsewhere, equates hospitality with the sharing of food). Peter—who, like his interlocutors in Jerusalem, initially desires to observe traditional Jewish norms about food consumption (10.14)—asserts that God has eliminated the distinction that once existed between Jews and gentiles, a distinction made manifest through foreign food restrictions.[38] The legitimacy of Peter's decision to preach to gentiles and accept their hospitality is validated by the Holy Spirit itself, which descends upon the gentiles who embrace Peter's gospel just as it descended upon Jewish Christ-believers earlier (10.44–47; cf. 2.4, 11.15–17).

While circumcision and its absence function as metonyms for Jews and gentiles, commensality functions in both the incident at Antioch and the Cornelius episode as a symbol for the equality of all Christ-believers and the unity of the Christ-believing community. It seems, moreover, that the author of *Acts* goes out of his way to integrate the issue of commensality into the Cornelius episode. After all, Peter draws the conclusion that "I should not call any person forbidden or impure" from a vision in which he is called upon to consume forbidden and impure animals (10.13–16). While the voice in Peter's vision refers to the *food* that Peter regards as forbidden and impure (using the grammatical neuter, vv. 14–15), we are told that Peter understands the voice to refer not to foodstuffs but rather to *human beings* (grammatical masculine, v. 28), and thus concludes that he may accept the hospitality of gentiles and engage in commensality with them.[39] *Acts,* like Paul in *Galatians,* apparently seeks to confront directly a common practice among Jewish Christ-believers associated with the circle of James in Jerusalem, namely the refusal to share meals with gentile Christ-believers. Such behavior, both *Acts* and Paul insist, is antithetical to the gentile mission, a mission directly authorized by God. *Acts* further undermines the legitimacy of discrimination against gentile Christ-believers by reporting that James himself interprets the Cornelius episode as evidence that gentiles turning to God no longer need to embrace the entirety of Jewish law (15.13–21). Gentile Christ-believers, all of the apostles and elders agree, are bound solely by the terms of the Apostolic Decree.

As *Acts* presents it, the promulgation of the Apostolic Decree constitutes a crucial turning point in the history of the early Christ-believing community because it provides an accessible means for gentiles to become full members of that community. The remainder of the work focuses on the gentile mission and makes frequent reference to the hospitality and shared meals associated with Paul's efforts to spread the gospel to the nations.[40] Upon her baptism in Philippi, a God-fearing gentile named Lydia urges Paul and his companions to accept her hospitality: "'If you have judged me to be faithful to the Lord, come and stay at my home.' And she prevailed upon us" (16.15). Lydia recognizes that the true test of one's acceptance within a community is if its members will accept one's hospitality and, with it, one's food. Some members of the Jewish communities that attracted "God-fearers" like Lydia would not have accepted Lydia's offer; the Christ-believers do. Similarly, when Paul's jailor in Philippi was baptized, "He brought them up into the house and set food before them" (16.34). When Paul was rejected by the Jews of Corinth, "he said to them, 'Your blood be on your own heads! I am innocent. From now on I will go to the gentiles.' Then, leaving [the synagogue], he went into the house of a man named Titius Justus, a [gentile] God-fearer; his house was next door to the synagogue" (18.6–7). Since the Jews of Corinth spurn Paul's teaching, he turns to the gentiles, who prove to be much more receptive of his message. The unmistakable implications of Paul's decision to leave the inhospitable synagogue and accept the hospitality of a neighboring gentile are reinforced by other rhetorical aspects of *Acts* that foreshadow the future of Christian–gentile and Christian–Jewish relations. Unlike pre-Christian works of Hellenistic Jewish literature, which portray gentiles without distinction as idolatrous and immoral non-Jews who ought to be avoided, *Acts* offers vivid and generally positive portrayals of individual gentiles while reserving its negative stereotypes for Jews and their institutions.

The final act of commensality in *Acts* is especially revealing.[41] On a ship lost at sea, Paul takes bread from the ship's provisions, gives thanks, breaks the bread, and begins to eat, as do the other 276 passengers (27.33–37). Paul's actions allude to those of Jesus, who fed the multitudes and those in distress in the same manner (*Luke* 9.16, 24.30; cf. 22.19). Jesus, however, is only said to break bread with Jews;[42] Paul breaks bread with gentiles who, for the first time in *Acts,* are not already Christ-believers. This act culminates the shift that occurs in *Luke–Acts:* whereas Jesus himself offers the kingdom of God to social outcasts but solely within the Jewish community, his disciples, correctly discerning the divine will following the rejection of Christ by the Jews, bring the gospel to the gentiles and offer them as well both physical and spiritual sustenance.

Through its accounts of shared meals, *Acts* demonstrates the expansion of the Christ-believing community to incorporate gentiles as equals. The abandonment of Jewish foreign food restrictions reflects and furthers the creation of a new communal identity whose definition is unrelated to the distinction between Jews and gentiles. Hellenistic Judean authors from before the time of Jesus endeavor to erect a barrier to interaction with gentiles by telling stories about exemplary figures who abstain from foreign food and by expressing unprecedented food-related norms in quasi-legal terms. The author of *Acts* draws on the same techniques—telling stories about the food practices of exemplars and recounting their normative statements—to dismantle this barrier and foster a new model of interaction between Jews and gentiles within a community that would no longer regard their differences as significant.

. . .

Even before the gentile mission had produced a demographic transformation of the Christ-believing community, proponents of that mission effected a transformation of their community's sense of identity and conception of the proper social order. Norms regarding food, we have seen, played a significant role in the process of creating a unified community that straddled the line setting Jews apart from gentiles. Proponents of the gentile mission take for granted the existence of a difference between Jews and gentiles and explicitly acknowledge its continued relevance in certain spheres: the exemption of gentiles from Jewish dietary laws and other distinctive practices demonstrates that one can be a "gentile Christ-believer" just as one can be a "Jewish Christ-believer." What Paul and *Acts* reject is the notion that the distinction between Jew and gentile should affect the definition of "Christ-believer": differences between the dietary practices of Jews and gentiles, they declare, should no longer be regarded as significant markers of identity. The elimination of restrictions preventing Jews from eating with gentiles conveys the message that members of both groups belong to a single community, a community set apart from the surrounding Hellenistic culture in part through the abstention from blood and food offered to idols. By embracing gentiles as part of Us rather than constitutive of Them, the Christ-believing community ceased to define itself as a "Jewish" community even though many of its members remained observant Jews.

7

"Be on Your Guard against Food Offered to Idols"

Eidōlothuton and Early Christian Identity

The earliest advocates of the gentile mission could not have imagined the impact that their outreach would have on the composition of the Christ-believing community, its self-definition, and its attitudes toward the Jews and gentiles who remained outside its bounds. Because this mission proved far more successful than efforts to persuade Jews to accept Jesus as the messiah, the Christ-believing community and its leaders increasingly hailed from gentile backgrounds. These individuals rejected the religious traditions of their ancestors, but they did not regard their new religious identity as Jewish either. On the contrary, they understood themselves to be "neither Jew nor Greek" (*Gal.* 3.28), interpreting Paul's words about faith in God through Christ from a very different perspective than Paul himself had done. They were "Christians," and over the second and third centuries they created the notion of "Christianity" as a distinct religion. This definitional process was multifaceted and has been the subject of numerous scholarly studies. The present work focuses narrowly on the role played in this process by Christian attitudes toward the permissibility of various foodstuffs, especially foodstuffs associated with foreigners. These attitudes reflect the styles in which Christian authorities imagined Jews and idolatrous gentiles (in Christian parlance, the term *gentile* often refers to non-Christian non-Jews) and thus the style in which they defined Christianity as neither the former nor the latter.

The Church Fathers, as the early leaders of what ultimately became orthodox Christianity are called, faced challenges in their efforts to define the Christian community that Jewish authorities in the Hellenistic world did not. The Jews constituted an ethnic-religious community whose existence was recognized by insiders and outsiders alike. While Jewish authorities redefined the nature and boundaries of their community, they were able to build upon a firmly established foundation. In contrast, the Roman government refused to recognize the legitimacy of Christianity and, as we have seen, early Sages regarded Jewish Christ-believers not as non-Jews but rather as heretics. Church Fathers, therefore, needed not only to mark the otherness of Them but also to establish a commonly recognized definition of Us. This task was all the more challenging because unlike Jews, who were able to define the identity of their community in contradistinction to a single foil, Church Fathers needed to define Christianity in relation to two different non-Christian foils (see figure 7). Discourse about Christian food practices provided Church Fathers a powerful vehicle for charting a path between the Scylla of Judaism and the Charybdis of Hellenistic idolatry.

Church Fathers employed the rejection of the Hebrew Bible's dietary laws as a means of highlighting the distinction between Christians and Jews. Although Paul in *Romans* 14 preached respect for those who observe traditional ingredient-based restrictions, later letters ascribed to Paul take more stridently dismissive stances toward these practices. "For the pure all things are pure, but for the defiled and unbelieving nothing is pure," declares the author of *Titus*, insinuating that those who regard certain foods as unfit for consumption do so because "their minds and consciousness are defiled" (*Tit.* 1.15). The author of *1 Timothy* teaches that God created all food as good and that none should be rejected; those who hold otherwise, he asserts, have been ensnared by demonic teachings (*1 Tim.* 4.1–4).

Second- and third-century Church Fathers regularly disparage continued observance of "the tiresome legislation about meats,"[1] focusing particular attention on Jewish abstention from pork. The pseudepigraphal *Letter of Barnabas* derides this and other aspects of Jewish practice as based on a flawed understanding of the Hebrew Bible: Moses conveyed "spiritual" messages through Biblical food restrictions, "but because of their fleshly desires the people accepted them as though they referred to actual food."[2] The message of the Church Fathers is thus the inverse of Hellenistic Jewish rhetoric about the dietary laws reflected in such works as *Aristeas:* We are superior to Them because They do not eat certain foods while We do. Rejection of Jewish food restrictions and the accompanying slurs against "carnally minded" Jews serve both to distinguish Christianity from Judaism and to define the former as the antithesis of the latter in crucial respects.[3] Indeed, such rhetoric denies Jewish claims to the possession of a special relationship with the divine in order to advance Christian claims to the mantle of Israel's holiness.

At the same time, Church Fathers distinguished their community from the majority population of the Greco-Roman world by steadfastly affirming the Apostolic Decree's prohibitions against eating blood, strangled meat, and food offered to idols. Abstention from *eidōlothuton* in particular constituted one of the most important markers of Christian identity in the centuries immediately following Jesus' death. Early Christian authorities glorify as martyrs those who refuse to offer sacrifices

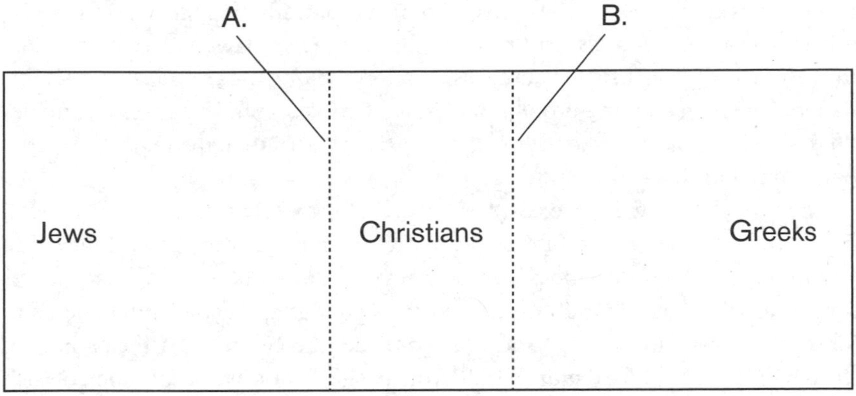

FIGURE 7. THE EARLY CHURCH: "NEITHER JEWISH NOR GREEK." (A) We (Christians) eat all foods; They (Jews) do not. (B) They (Greeks) eat food offered to idols; We (Christians) do not.

or consume sacrificial food, they look askance at Christians who engage in such behavior under duress, and they impugn so-called heretics with the charge of eating *eidōlothuton* willingly. Christian discourse regarding sacrifice and its by-products reflects a rhetorical embrace of Christianity's status as an "illicit" religion persecuted by an empire that defined the loyalty of its subjects in terms of sacrifices on behalf of the emperor. The Apostolic Decree thus comes to function not only as a golden mean between the excesses of Jewish law and the abhorrent dietary practices associated with idolatry but also as a means of defining its adherents as "neither Jew nor Greek."

With the Christianization of the empire, the prohibition of sacrifice became state policy. As a direct result, condemnation of *eidōlothuton* ceased to play a significant role in Christian self-definition within the Roman world. That shift left Jews as the most significant external foil against which to define Christianity, a development whose implications we will explore in chapter 8. This chapter focuses on Christian restrictions against food offered to idols and their role in defining the distinct identities of Christianity on the one hand and what came to be known as "paganism" on the other.

THE SYMBOLIC SIGNIFICANCE OF REFUSING SACRIFICIAL FOOD

Early Christian authorities are uniform in their condemnation of food offered to idols; indeed, they frequently describe abstention from *eidōlothuton* as constituting a decisive difference between "Christians" and "Greeks."[4] Many of these authorities, in keeping with the Apostolic Decree, also prohibit the consumption of blood.[5] They do not regard these prohibitions as contradicting in any way the permission of eating "all foods" irrespective of Jewish dietary laws—a permission that the vast majority of Christian authorities endorse. Quite the contrary: this combination of permissions and prohibitions, equally rooted in the New Testament, defines what it means to approach food as a Christian because it distinguishes Christians from both Jews and Greeks.

The *Didache,* a late first- or early second-century work, is unusual in advocating continued adherence to Biblical dietary restrictions: "If you can bear the entire yoke of the Lord, you will be perfect, but if you cannot, do what you can. As for food, bear what you can, but be very much on your guard against food offered to idols, for it is worship of dead gods."[6] Even those who cannot bear the entirety of the Bible's laws about food must refrain from *eidōlothuton,* as consumption of such food is tantamount to the practice of idolatry itself. Paul, the Apostolic Decree, and the Didachist articulate three different positions regarding the extent to which gentiles ought to observe Biblical dietary law, but all agree with Jewish authorities who identify the refusal to eat food offered to idols as a crucial aspect of monotheistic identity within the Hellenistic world.

Unyielding opposition to consuming *eidōlothuton* remains a feature of early Christian literature even after Christian authorities collectively reject all dietary regulations absent from the New Testament. Aristides, the earliest Christian apologist whose work survives, faults Jewish adherence to various ritual practices, including their concern for "the purity of foods" (*Apology* 14.4). At the same time, he proudly declares that Christians "do not eat from food that has been offered in sacrifice to idols, because [Christians] are pure" (15.4).[7] Like Paul, Aristides links Christian abstention from *eidōlothuton* with abstention from idolatry and sexual immorality, behaviors associated with Greeks and barbarians but anathema to the "pure" Christian community. This purity—Aristides employs the language of *Tit.* 1.15, but "holiness" better captures his intent—stems from the avoidance of defiling behaviors rather than the avoidance of foods falsely labeled impure or polluting.

Justin Martyr, a key figure in second-century efforts to define Christian orthodoxy and distinguish Christianity from Judaism, proudly declares that "those from the gentiles who have come to know God, Creator of the world, through the crucified Jesus would submit to every torture and punishment, even to the extremity of death, in order not to worship idols or eat food offered to idols" (*Dialogue with Trypho* 34.8).[8] Justin's assertion that Christian heretics eat *eidōlothuton* (35.2), reminiscent of charges found in *Revelation* 2.14, 20, is echoed by Irenaeus of Lyons (*Against Heresies* 1.6.3). Praises of Christians who prefer torture to sacrificial food and rebukes of heretics for allegedly eating such food without concern reflect the importance of the *eidōlothuton* prohibition in the self-definition of nascent Christian "orthodoxy," as well as the community's embrace of persecution as a badge of authenticity.

During the first Christian centuries, the offering of sacrifices on behalf of the emperor was a key element of political culture within the Roman Empire.[9] Refusal to participate fully in this culture not only set Christians apart from the larger Greco-Roman population, it also drew the wrath of Roman officials and at times resulted in Christian martyrdom.[10] One of the earliest accounts of such martyrdom is provided by Pliny the Younger, who would test suspected Christians by demanding that the accused utter an invocation to the gods, offer wine libations and incense before a statue of the emperor, and revile the name of Christ; those who refused were executed. Reporting to the emperor (ca. 110) on the success of his efforts, perhaps with some exaggeration, Pliny indirectly highlights Christian refusal not only to offer sacrifices but also to purchase meat that had been sacrificed by others. "There is no doubt that people have begun to throng the temples, which had been almost entirely deserted for a long time; the sacred rites which had been allowed to lapse are being performed again, and flesh of sacrificial victims is on sale everywhere, though up till recently *scarcely anyone could be found to buy it.*"[11] The significance of consuming *eidōlothuton* is also attested in a document associated with the emperor Decius's edict of 250 requiring that all Romans offer sacrifices to the gods. In a certificate of compliance, the offerant declares, "I have always sacrificed to the gods, and now in your presence, in accordance with the terms of the edict, I have done sacrifice and poured libations and *tasted the sacrifices,* and I request you to certify to this effect."[12] Martyrdom accounts similarly emphasize refusal to consume food offered in sacrifice by others.[13]

Because of the symbolic significance of eating food offered to the gods and inspired by the model set by Christian martyrs, Christian authorities followed in the footsteps of their Jewish predecessors in forcefully prohibiting not only the offering of sacrifice but also the consumption of sacrificial food. Cyprian, bishop of Carthage (d. 258), took a firm stance against readmitting into the Church those who ate such food, depicting in vivid language the unfitness of these Christians to partake of Eucharistic communion:

> People coming back from the altars of Satan approach the Lord's sacred body, their hands still foul and reeking; while still belching, one may say, from the poisonous food of the idols—their breath even yet charged with the foulness of their crime and with the stench of their repulsive death-feast—they desecrate the body of the Lord, whereas Sacred Scripture cries aloud against them: "He that is clean shall eat of the flesh, and if any man shall eat of the flesh of the saving sacrifice which is the Lord's, and his own defilement be upon him, that man shall perish from among his people."[14]

Concern directed specifically toward the consumption of *eidōlothuton* is also expressed in ecclesiastical laws promulgated at the Council of Ancyra (in Asia Minor, 314). Two of the canons from this council impose supplementary penalties upon those who, having been forced to offer sacrifices, proceed to share in "the meals made for the idols" (cc. 4–5), while a third imposes punishment even on "those who participate in shared meals on gentile festivals in a place set aside for gentiles, bringing and eating their own food" (c. 7).[15] These canons reflect the continued significance of the *eidōlothuton* prohibition as a marker of Christian identity into the fourth century. The last in particular highlights the fact that Christian authorities, following in Paul's footsteps, are concerned about the nature of one's behavior—participation in a festival meal—not the nature of the food one consumes.[16]

At the same time as Church Fathers stood firm against the consumption of *eidōlothuton*, they also sought to portray Christians as full-fledged participants in Greco-Roman society. Consider, for example, the words of Tertullian (fl. ca. 200), who elsewhere declares that Christians are distinguished from their Greek counterparts in their abstention from blood and food offered to idols.[17]

> Are we not human beings living among you, with the same manner of nourishment, dress, and equipment, the same necessities of life? For we are not Brahmans or naked Indian sages living in the woods, exiled from life. We bear in mind that we owe thanks to the Lord our God, the Creator; we reject no fruit of His work. (Obviously, we do exercise moderation, lest we make excessive or improper use of them.) So, it is not without the forum, not without the meat market, not without the baths, shops, factories, inns, your market days and other opportunities for commerce that we live with you in this world. . . . Even if I do not attend your rituals, nevertheless, even on that day, I am a human being! . . . At the feast of Bacchus I do not recline at the public table, as is the custom of gladiators eating their last meal; nevertheless, wherever I may be I dine from your supplies.[18]

Tertullian makes the case that the unusual religious norms of Christianity in no way prevent its adherents from participating actively in Greco-Roman society and ought not prevent the acceptance of Christians within that society. Tertullian, like his rabbinic contemporaries, offers a carefully—and, perhaps, artificially—circumscribed notion of idolatry and embraces interaction with idolaters outside that prohibited sphere.[19] Earlier Jewish apologists in Alexandria advanced similar arguments in their own efforts to gain acceptance as equal citizens. By emphasizing Christian willingness to consume the food of non-Christians, however, Tertullian implicitly highlights the difference between members of his own community and the Jews, whose dietary restrictions and refusal to share food with gentiles were disparaged by Christians and non-Christians alike. Tertullian's insistence on the willingness of Christians to share food with idolatrous gentiles reflects the degree to which Christians, too, defined themselves as gentiles.

By the third Christian century, both the permission of eating all types of meat and the prohibition of consuming food offered to idols had become firmly established within what was becoming the orthodox Church; these tenets of Christian dietary practice are, in fact, often juxtaposed.[20] Significantly, Church Fathers understood these dietary norms as symbolic boundary markers distinguishing Christians from non-Christians, not as barriers to social interaction with non-Christians.

Tertullian, even more forcefully than Paul before him, emphasizes that nothing prevents Christians from sharing meals with foreigners or eating food that foreigners prepare in nonsacral contexts. Similarly, the expectation that Christians ought to eat all kinds of meat without distinction does not prevent them from occasionally eating vegetarian fare or kosher meat at table with Jews or with Christ-believers who adhere to Jewish law; Justin reports that some Christians refuse to eat with the latter, but indicates that such abstention from commensality is unnecessary (*Dialogue with Trypho* 47). The food restrictions of the early Church function in the same manner as those articulated within Alexandrian Jewish literature and early Rabbinic literature: they affirm the identity of insiders through contradistinction with the food practices of outsiders without impinging on interactions that involve permitted foodstuffs. With the Christianization of the Roman Empire, however, the distinction that had once been marked through the *eidōlothuton* taboo disappeared.

THE IMPLICATIONS OF EMPIRE AND "PAGANISM" FOR DEFINING CHRISTIAN IDENTITY

The canons of Church councils often reflect the concerns of their participants: clerics gathered in Ancyra, for example, were quite clearly concerned about the implications of the compulsory idolatry mandated by imperial authorities in the first years of the fourth century. It is striking, therefore, that by the end of the fourth century prohibitions against *eidōlothuton* drop out of Greek-language canons, even those that paraphrase the Apostolic Decree.[21] This is not to say that the authors of such canons approved the consumption of food offered to idols. They surely did not, but they no longer felt any need to express their condemnation.

Idolatry constitutes the primary foil against which Church Fathers define the Christian community in its first centuries. With the Christianization of the Roman Empire, a process that nominally began with Constantine's conversion in 313 and accelerated under the reign of Theodosius I (379–95), this contrast and the associated prohibitions of *eidōlothuton* rapidly receded to irrelevance.[22] As sacrifice constituted the epitome of traditional Roman religion, in the eyes of Christian authorities and in those of the pre-Christian Roman emperors, it is unsurprising that Roman emperors invested in the success of Christianity actively sought to abolish its practice. The *Theodosian Code,* a collection of legislation issued by Constantine and his successors to 437, contains no fewer than fifteen laws proscribing sacrifice.[23] Roman law, unlike earlier Christian sources, does not address Christian consumption of food offered to idols, as it attempts instead to eliminate the existence of such food entirely. From the rhetoric of fifth-century laws on the subject, it seems as though the emperors believed that their efforts were largely successful. Theodosius II, for example, refers in 423 to "the pagans who survive"; the very term *pagani,* originally referring to country peasants but now a derogatory reference to adherents of traditional nonmonotheistic religions, reflects the changed religious climate in the urban centers of the Roman Empire.[24] No new imperial legislation regarding idolatrous sacrifice was promulgated after the middle of that century. Ecclesiastical authorities active in the imperial heartland similarly neglected the subject.[25]

Early Christian authorities, following in Paul's footsteps, carefully distinguish the practice of idolatry from the Greco-Roman population that engaged in this practice. They insist that Christianity's implacable opposition to idolatry, reflected in its strong *eidōlothuton* taboo, in no way contradicts its eagerness to engage idolaters, represented in its openness to commensality and foods prepared by foreigners. Once idolatry ceased to pose a serious challenge—weakened to the point that Christians can dismiss it as "paganism," a superstitious holdover surviving only among country bumpkins and the uncivilized—the already porous boundary separating Christians from other gentiles lost much of its significance. The distinction between Christians and Jews, however, retained its symbolic potency.

The difference between Christian attitudes toward Jews on the one hand and toward gentiles on the other is apparent in the canons of the earliest surviving ecclesiastical council, a synod of early fourth-century Spanish clerics meeting in Elvira (present-day Granada) prior to the conversion of Constantine. Among these canons we find the following series:

> 15. No matter the large number of girls, Christian maidens are by no means to be given in matrimony to gentiles lest youth, bursting forth in bloom, end in adultery of the soul.
> 16. Catholic girls ought not be given in marriage to heretics if they are unwilling to change over to the Catholic Church. They shall be given to neither Jews nor heretics for there can be no fellowship for the faithful with the unfaithful [nulla possit esse societas fideli cum infidele]. If parents act against this prohibition, they shall be excluded [from communion] for five years.[26]
> 17. If any should perchance join their daughters in marriage to the priests of the idols, they shall not be given communion even at the end.[27]

These canons prohibit marriage to non-Christian husbands in all cases. Parents are only punished, however, if they give their daughters in marriage to Jews, heretics (which is to say, non-Catholic Christians), or, worst of all, idolatrous priests. Intermarriage with other gentiles, although discouraged, goes unpunished. The Elviran distinction between gentiles and priests reflects Paul's distinction in *1 Corinthians* 10.27–28 between the food of "unbelievers" on the one hand and food offered to idols on the other: gentiles themselves are not perceived as posing a significant threat to Christian identity so long as they are not directly involved in idolatry.[28] The fact that marriage to a Jew is subject to a severe penalty while marriage to a gentile goes unpunished reveals that Christian clerics deem the former action far more dangerous than the latter.

Some Christ-believers of Paul's day questioned whether gentiles who merely abandoned idolatry could be equal members in a community consisting primarily of Jews. The clerics of Elvira, in sharp contrast, prefer such gentiles over Jews, who are now regarded as posing a threat to Christian faith as dangerous as heresy. Strikingly, these clerics justify their concern about Jews and heretics by reapplying Paul's statement condemning interaction between Christ-believers and idolaters: "For what partnership is there between righteousness and lawlessness? Or what fellowship [societas] is there between light and darkness? What agreement does Christ have with Beliar? Or what does the believer share with the unbeliever [fideli cum infidele]? What agreement has the temple of God with idols?" (2 *Cor.* 6.14–16).[29]

With the decline of idolatry and, thus, *eidōlothuton,* Christian discourse regarding the food of foreigners comes to focus exclusively on Jews, the new "unbelievers." Church Fathers, like their Rabbinic counterparts, view gentiles as "mostly harmless," but the perceived danger of the Jew, along with his potential value as a foil for defining Christianity, remained undiminished. Whereas the Sages and the Church Fathers alike imagine gentiles as "non-Jews" or "non-Christians" (in mathematical terms, 0 rather than 1), Christians come to imagine Jews as "anti-Christians" and to define Christianity itself as "anti-Jewish" (1 and -1). This conception of Judaism as antithetical to Christianity, bolstered through rhetoric of impurity and the association of Jews with heretics and idolaters, provides fertile grounds for the development of unprecedented restrictions against Jewish food beginning in the fourth century. That process, as we will see in the following chapter, begins at Elvira.

8

"How Could Their Food Not Be Impure?"

Jewish Food and the Definition of Christianity

Anti-Jewish rhetoric is entwined in the very formation of Christianity. In the words of Miriam S. Taylor, this rhetoric reflects "an internal logic in which the invalidation of Judaism emerges as a theoretical necessity in the appropriation of the Jewish God and the Jewish Bible for the church. . . . The church's portrayal of Judaism is expressed in terms of a dualism opposing Christians and Jews which is built into the very logic and into the very structure of Christian teaching."[1] The Church Fathers perceive holiness in zero-sum terms: only one religious community can stand in a unique relationship with the divine and can possess the authoritative understanding of divine revelation. Judaism must be wrong if Christianity is right, and it is essential to prove that Judaism is wrong because of the fact that Jews lay claim to the same God and the same Biblical texts as do Christians. Discourse about the meaning and continued applicability of Biblical law in general and Biblical food restrictions in particular figures prominently in Christian anti-Jewish rhetoric.

As we observed in the previous chapter, Church Fathers declare that Jewish adherence to Biblical dietary law reflects the falsehood of Judaism's "carnality" and the failure of Jews to appreciate the true allegorical meaning of the Old Testament. These traits stand in opposition to Christianity's embrace of the spirit and of Truth itself. Consumption of all foods defines Christians as "not-Jews" and affirms the authority of New Testament statements about food, such as, "For the pure all things are pure" (*Tit.* 1.15; cf. *Mark* 7.19, *1 Tim.* 4.4). Figure 8 displays another dualistic representation of Christian and Jewish food practices, found in an early thirteenth-century *Bible moralisée.*[2] The offering of the Eucharistic Host, which becomes the body of Christ, the "lamb of God," is contrasted with the carnal Jewish offering of a physical lamb, which Jews raise up toward heaven in a futile gesture and then slaughter in accordance with

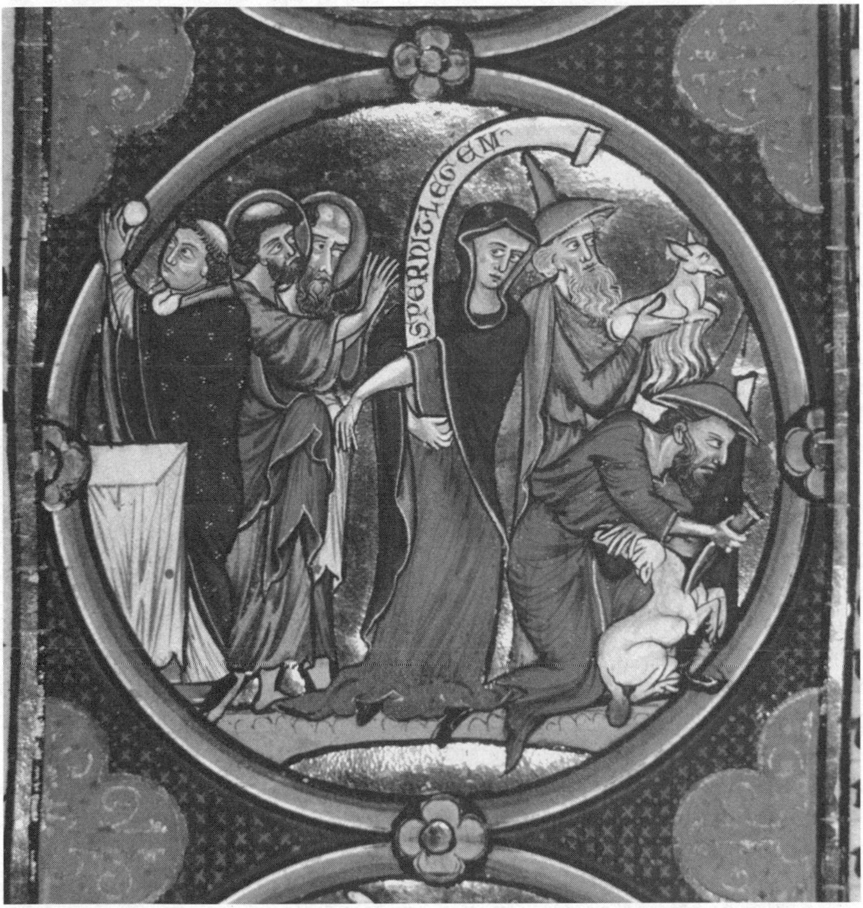

FIGURE 8. A CHRISTIAN IMAGE OF JEWISH ANIMAL SLAUGHTER. "This [i.e., *Esther* 1.9–12] signifies that Synagoga, invited to the faith, treated the praching of the faith with contempt on account of her legalistic sacraments." *Bible moralisée*, Vienna, Österreichische Nationalbibliothek, codex 1179, folio 186a. Courtesy of the Österreichische Nationalbibliothek.

Jewish law. As Sara Lipton observes, "The Christian sacrament appears elevated, open, and clean, whereas the Jewish ritual appears hunched, closed, and bloody." The scroll carried by the woman in the center of the image, a personification of the Jewish community, completes the contrast: it states that Synagoga, through her very adherence to Jewish food practices, "spurns the law" that she thinks she obeys. Precisely because the Jews understand Biblical law literally, they fail to observe it properly. Indeed, adherence to Jewish food practices constitutes the reason for Jewish rejection of everything that the Eucharist symbolizes: the image's caption states that Synagoga "treated the preaching of the faith with contempt on account of her legalistic sacraments." Only members of the Holy Church truly understand God's nature and correctly adhere to God's law. God, we shall see, demands abstention solely from *eidōlothuton*—and food associated with Jews.[3]

Most of the foreign food restrictions we have encountered thus far mark the otherness of foreigners without defining those foreigners in any detail. Daniel's refusal to eat the Babylonian king's food, for example, indicates that We are not Them but conveys no information either about the king or about the substance of the difference between Jews and gentiles. Similarly, many Rabbinic foreign food restrictions highlight the truism that gentiles are non-Jews but, in the process of doing so, portray gentiles as nondescript nonentities. Prohibitions against food offered to idols define the difference between Us and Them to a degree—They worship idols, while We worship God alone—but the fact that both Jewish and Christian authorities are able to distinguish gentiles from their idolatry indicates that even these regulations do not ascribe specific significance to gentile identity. Christian prohibitions of food associated with Jews, in contrast, serve to define Judaism as the very antithesis of Christianity, arguably to a greater degree than other Christian laws relating to Jews.[4] These restrictions highlight the opposition between Us and Them, an opposition which contributes to the construction of Christian identity: not only are We not Them, We are Their mirror image and Our rituals (e.g., the Eucharist) are the mirror image of Theirs (e.g., kosher animal slaughter). Discourse about food associated with Jews reveals the styles in which Christian authorities imagined Jews and the ways these authorities employed that image as a foil against which to define Christianity itself.

The foreign food restrictions we will examine in this chapter are among the thousands of "canons" (from the Greek *kanon,* rule) promulgated in late antiquity and the Middle Ages by individual bishops or, more frequently, by councils of clerics. The high Middle Ages witnessed both increasing papal influence over canon law in the Latin West and the development of canon law as a science in the nascent European universities. Medieval scholars rightly perceived a qualitative difference between the "old law" promulgated before the twelfth century and the "new law" that succeeded it. The present chapter focuses on "old law," especially that of the fourth through ninth centuries; we will explore subsequent Christian discussions about foreign food restrictions in chapters 12 and 13. The geographic scope of this chapter extends from Spain to Sasanid Babylonia. I have chosen not to organize this material along geographical lines because the same themes and rhetorical techniques appear across the breadth of Christendom.

Christian foreign food restrictions define Jews in two different and, indeed, contradictory ways: as equivalent to or worse than heretics, which is to say insiders gone horribly bad, and as equivalent to or worse than idolaters, which is to say the ultimate outsiders. As we examine each set of these portrayals in turn, however, we will discover that they frequently share a common feature: the ascription of impurity to Jews and their food. This similarity reflects the fact that both conceptions serve to define Judaism as the antithesis of orthodox Christianity, which constitutes the true successor to the mantle of Biblical Israel's holiness. In the third section of this chapter, we will explore both the ways in which impurity rhetoric contributes to Christian portrayals of Jews and the ways in which the internal logic of this rhetoric itself shapes the nature of Christian foreign food restrictions. Examination of the impurity rhetoric used by Christian authorities of the early Middle Ages also affords us an opportunity to consider the way such rhetoric functions in Jewish sources.

JEWS IMAGINED AS HERETICS (ONLY WORSE): PROHIBITIONS AGAINST COMMENSALITY

The clerics gathered in Elvira, whose heightened concern about Jews we encountered in chapter 7, promulgate the earliest attested Christian foreign food restrictions relating to Jews. These clerics regard Jews and heretics as equivalent in canons about sexual intercourse (cc. 16, 78), but they single out Jews in a pair of food-related canons:[5]

> 49. Those who possess [agricultural produce], which they received from God with an act of thanksgiving, are warned not to let Jews bless their produce, lest their blessing render ours ineffectual and weak. If anyone dares to do so despite this prohibition, he shall be cast out from the church completely.
> 50. Indeed, if any of the clergy or the faithful takes food with Jews, it is decided that he shall be kept from communion in order that he be corrected as he should.[6]

The first of these canons expresses the incompatability—indeed, the oppositional relationship—between Christianity and Judaism. Jewish blessings, the clerics at Elvira warn, counteract the effect of Christian blessings, and anyone who would allow Jews to offer their blessings over Christian food has no place within the Christian community. Because Christianity and Judaism stand in mutual opposition, Christians must also shun commensality with Jews. Those who eat with such outsiders are, fittingly, forbidden from eating with insiders, as "communion" in Elviran canons refers to social as well as sacramental participation in the Christian community.[7] These clerics embrace Paul's message that communion defines community, and they wield the prohibition of commensality not only as a means of disciplining wayward Christians but also as a means of segregating Jews from Christian society.

Both of these canons, like the canon on marriage to Jews discussed in chapter 7, employ Pauline language that was not originally directed toward Jews. The language of canon 50 is reminiscent of Paul's instruction not to share food with Christ-believing sinners (*1 Cor.* 5.11),[8] yet Paul permits eating with those who do not belong to the Christ-believing community. The application of Paul's commensality prohibition to Jews reflects the equation of Jews and heretical Christians expressed in Elviran canons about sexual activity and also suggests that Elviran clerics regard Jews as sinners who have an especially pernicious influence upon the Christians with whom they interact. Canon 49 expresses this fear through its allusion to *1 Timothy*, which speaks of a time to come in which some will renounce the faith by paying attention to those who demand abstinence from food "which God created to be received by the faithful with an act of thanksgiving" (*1 Tim.* 4.3). The clerics gathered at Elvira understand this prophecy to refer to Christians who accommodate Jewish food-related practices, and they thus imagine Jews as "those who hypocritically speak falsehood" and convey "the teachings of demons" (4.1–2).[9] The consistent use of Pauline language in Elviran canons about Jews demonstrates that their authors are concerned with what Jeremy Cohen aptly terms "the hermeneutical Jew," a construct derived not from social interaction but rather from scholarly engagement with sacred texts. The hermeneutical Jew is a figure imagined for the purpose of serving as a foil for the construction of Christian identity.[10]

Christian clerics, like their Rabbinic counterparts, prize the establishment and preservation of proper categories. In contrast to the Rabbinic focus on classifying foodstuffs, however, Elviran authorities are interested solely in the classification of foreigners. Their classificatory system reveals a spectrum of foreigners ranging in danger from mostly harmless gentiles to utterly abhorrent idolatrous priests; Jews are positioned closer to the latter than the former, defined as similar to yet more dangerous than Christian heretics. As ecclesiastical concern about idolatry waned, Jews came to occupy the negative extreme of this spectrum.

Authorities from across the Christian world of late antiquity express in their own ways the conception of Jews as especially threatening analogues to heretics and, through the extension of Paul's teachings, promulgate their own prohibitions against commensality with Jews. A Syriac canon composed in the 530s by the anonymous Syrian Orthodox (Jacobite) author of the "Canons from the East" (i.e., Babylonia) bars all Christians who eat with Jews from partaking of the Eucharist. The preceding canon, in contrast, merely reprimands clerics who eat with heretics and says nothing about laity engaging in such behavior.[11] A similar juxtaposition of prohibitions against commensality with heretics and with Jews appears in the canons of the Council of Epaone, convened in 517 in Burgundy:

> 15. If a cleric of elevated rank should participate in the meal of any heretical cleric, he shall not have the peace of the Church for the duration of a year; if junior clerics do so, they shall be flogged. As for the meals of Jews, our law has prohibited even a layperson [from participating]. Whosoever has become defiled by the meals of Jews shall not break bread with any of our clerics.[12]

Here again, interaction with Jews is clearly more objectionable than interaction with heretics. There is no reason to presume that the authors of these canons were familiar with the canons from Elvira.[13] Rather, the similarities in their images of the Jew reflect the fact that these images derive from a common set of sacred texts and serve the common agenda of oppositional Christian self-definition.

The Council of Epaone was one of six councils convened in the regions of Gaul between the late fifth and mid-seventh century to prohibit commensality with Jews. The Council of Mâcon (convened in 581 or 583), like that of Epaone, prohibits participation in Jewish meals on penalty of expulsion from all association with Christians, and declares that the offender has been "defiled by [Jewish] impieties." The prohibitions of commensality with Jews promulgated at the Third Council of Orléans (538) and the Council of Clichy (626 or 627) are accompanied not by the rhetoric of offensive defilement but rather by concern about Christian inferiority to Jews. Specifically, these councils prohibit Jews from owning Christian slaves and forbid the marriage of Christian women to Jewish men.[14] References to both inferiority and impurity appear in the earliest Gallic canons regarding commensality, promulgated at the Council of Vannes (in Brittany, ca. 461–91) and, in slightly altered form, at the Council of Agde (in Narbonne, 506). The latter version of this canon ultimately became a centerpiece of medieval Latin canon law regarding commensality with non-Christians.

> All clerics [added at Agde: and laity] should henceforth avoid the meals of Jews, nor should anyone receive them at a meal. Since they do not accept the common food served by Christians, it would be unbecoming and sacrilegious for Christians to consume their food. This is because they would judge what we eat with the permission of the Apostle to be impure and because clerics [Agde replaces "clerics" with "Catholics"] would begin to feel as though they were inferior to the Jews if we were to consume what they serve while they disdained what we offer.[15]

The prohibition of commensality with Jews, including inviting Jews to Christian meals, is here justified by means of two distinct rationales, both based on the fact that Jews adhere to food restrictions absent from Christianity. It is sacrilegious for Christians to participate in any meal that accommodates Jewish conceptions of food impurity, and it is unbecoming for Christians to participate in an exchange of food that, because of the asymmetry involved in accommodating the demands of Jewish norms, might generate feelings of inferiority on the part of Christians.

Gallic councils address Jewish food more often than any other issue associated with Jews. This frequency is especially striking because some of the councils that prohibit commensality took place in regions where there were no Jews with whom to share meals.[16] The use of impurity-related rhetoric in many of these canons also calls for an explanation, as such rhetoric is absent not only from otherwise comparable Eastern and Elviran commensality canons but also from the Pauline text that inspired these prohibitions. It makes sense that bishops would object to the accommodation of Jewish dietary norms on the grounds that Christians ought not be subservient to demands made by Jews, but why should the very fact that Jews judge certain food to be impure matter to Christians, and for what reason might the consumption of Jewish food result in the defilement of the Christian? Examination of Augustine's teachings regarding Manichean dietary practices sheds light both on the use of impurity-related rhetoric in many of the commensality prohibitions articulated in Gaul and on the frequent condemnation of shared meals with Jews.

Manicheism, a religion with affinities to Christianity and Zoroastrianism that Catholics regarded as a heresy and a serious threat, promotes an especially stringent set of food restrictions. The proponents of this tradition whom Augustine of Hippo (d. 430) engages in disputation cite Biblical passages, including the Apostolic Decree, as prooftexts supporting Manichean practices (*Answer to Faustus* 31.2, 32.3). Augustine, seeking to reclaim the Bible for Catholic orthodoxy alone, denies legitimacy to all ingredient-based food restrictions, even the prohibitions against blood and bloody meat which earlier Church Fathers endorse (32.13; we will examine this passage more closely in chapter 11). The Apostolic Decree's food restrictions originally functioned as a means of distinguishing the Christ-believing community within its gentile surroundings: We abstain from Biblically taboo foods which They (i.e., Greeks) eat. Augustine, seeking to distinguish the orthodox from the heretical, dismantles these prohibitions in order to define Christianity in terms of its absolute and principled rejection of ingredient-based dietary restrictions: We interpret the Bible properly and therefore eat all foods, whereas They (i.e., Manicheans) do not.

Augustine accompanies his rejection of Manichean dietary practices with a sharp jab at Manicheans themselves for adhering to such norms. Employing the Pauline dictum, "For the pure all things are pure, but for the defiled and unbelieving nothing is pure" (*Tit.* 1.15), Augustine asserts that only true Christians, those who regard all food as pure, are themselves intrinsically pure. The preoccupation of Manicheans with the impurity of food, in contrast, reflects the "defiled" state of the Manichean mind—a state, Augustine explains, that stems from Manicheism's heretical beliefs about the body of Christ (*Answer to Faustus* 6.6).[17] More broadly, Augustine asserts that the very act of distinguishing "pure" and "impure" foods in the Christian era manifests one's failure to understand the true significance of Christ; the judgment of food constitutes an act of blasphemy and thus a defiling offense in its own right (19.10, 31.4).[18]

The logic of Augustine's teachings about the meaning of Biblical food restrictions and the implications of regarding certain foods as impure applies not only to Manicheans but also to Jews.[19] This logic accounts for the rhetoric employed by Catholic clerics in Gaul. Jewish judgment of food, the clerics at Vannes and Agde maintain, embodies the Jews' rejection of Christ, reason enough for Christians to abstain from meals in which consideration of Jewish dietary norms plays a role.[20] The clerics gathered in Epaone and Mâcon draw on the language of offensive defilement which *Tit.* 1.15 applies to those who deem certain foods to be impure. Just as Augustine regards Manicheans who adhere to norms of dietary purity as defiled, these clerics treat Christians who partake of a meal prepared in accordance with such norms to be defiled.

The clerics at Epaone, strikingly, do not assert that those who share meals with heretics are similarly defiled, perhaps because Arians, the local "heretics," did not adhere to distinctive dietary regulations. No Christian authority, moreover, expresses concern about commensality with gentiles. Indeed, Augustine actively encourages such behavior: "People living in this world, after all, cannot help living with others of that sort; nor can they win them for Christ, if they altogether shun their company and conversation."[21] Foreign food restrictions highlight the degree to which, especially in the absence of idolatrous gentiles and impurity-obsessed heretics like the Manicheans, Jews constitute a class unto themselves.

Gallic anticommensality canons, even those that do not explicitly associate Jews with heretics, follow Augustine in defining everyone who contests the meaning of the Christian Bible as a heretic, subject to Paul's prohibition against shared meals with Christian sinners. Augustine's definition of Catholic Christianity as a religion intolerant of dietary regulations also accounts for the striking frequency of Gallic prohibitions against commensality with Jews. Over the course of the fifth and sixth centuries, Catholics and Arians competed for control of Christianity in Gaul; as Catholics gained ascendancy in any given region, they convened a synod to establish laws for it and mark their dominance. Prohibitions of commensality appear disproportionately in the canons of these initial councils.[22] This pattern suggests that bishops regarded the rejection of Biblical dietary laws, and thus of shared meals with the paradigmatic contemporary adherents of these laws, the Jews, as a significant component of what it means to be Catholic: We are those who anathematize Jewish food practices.[23] Jews, these clerics feel, constitute a heretical foil crucial to the construction of orthodox identity even when they are not present in the local Christian community. While there is no evidence that the term *Jew* functions as a code word for *Arian* in the canons of Gallic councils, condemnation of Jews nevertheless advances the cause of Catholic orthodoxy because proponents of that orthodoxy were able to brand their opponents as "judaizers" and thus, by definition, not truly Christian.[24]

The commensality prohibitions we have examined thus far define Christian orthodoxy in contradistinction to Judaism, imagined to be an especially dangerous Christian heresy. To be a full member of Christian society, a participant in its ritual and nonritual meals, is to abstain from sharing meals with Jews and, especially for Catholics, to reject Jewish food restrictions. An oath imposed on Jewish converts by Catholic authorities in seventh-century Visigothic Spain encapsulates these diametrically opposed conceptions of Christianity and Judaism.[25] After an extensive declaration of Catholic faith, the converts declare that they

> reject, abominate, and execrate the Jewish rite and its festivals, Sabbath, and circumcision of the flesh, with all its superstitions and other observances and ceremonies. We promise that we shall live under Catholic law, eating common food with Christians, with the exception of food which our nature and not superstition rejects, for "all creatures of God are good" [*1 Tim.* 4.4]. We promise that neither we nor all those on whose behalf we make this covenant shall have any association with Hebrews who have not yet been baptized, and we vow not to participate or intermingle with them in any commerce, conversation, or any sort of fellowship until they too, by God's mercy, shall attain the grace of baptism.[26]

Life "under Catholic law," according to this oath, is exemplified through the consumption of all foods, in accordance with Pauline teachings as understood by Augustine, and through avoidance of interaction with Jews. Just as Rabbinic Sages define adherence to Biblical dietary laws as emblematic of Jewish identity and employ foreign food restrictions as a means of emphasizing the centrality of these laws, Christian authorities view the anathematization of such laws as emblematic of Christian identity and express this rejection through restrictions on Jewish food. These restrictions remind new and old Christians alike that their identity depends upon the rejection not only of Jewish dietary practices but also of social intercourse with Jews and participation in Jewish festivals.

JEWS IMAGINED AS IDOLATERS (ONLY WORSE): PROHIBITIONS AGAINST UNLEAVENED BREAD AND OTHER FOODS

Prohibitions of commensality that associate Jews with Christian heretics effectively subsume Jews under the canopy of Christianity in order to more forcefully exclude them from Christian communion, perhaps because their authors regarded Judaism as uncomfortably close to Christianity to begin with. Prohibitions against foods associated with Jewish holidays, in contrast, define Jews as the ultimate outsiders, equivalent to if not worse than idolaters on account of their rejection of Christ. Both sets of prohibitions establish Judaism as an intrinsically impure antithesis of Christianity, but each constructs its hermeneutical Jew from a different set of prooftexts. As a result, each highlights a different aspect of Jewish—and thus Christian—identity. Although logically incompatible, Christian authorities nevertheless had no qualms about associating Jews with heretics and idolaters alike. The clerics of Elvira, we have seen, depict Jews through allusions to Pauline statements about both sinful Christians (c. 50) and unbelieving idolaters (c. 16). As Averil Cameron observes, "What may seem now to be distinct and separate sets of issues—Christianity versus Judaism, Christianity in relation to polytheism, the true as opposed to 'false' beliefs within Christianity—were close together in the minds of early Christians and approached in very similar ways. Naturally the edges became blurred."[27] More than merely blurring the edges, however, Christian foreign food restrictions reflect the equation of Jews with heretics and idolaters, even as they bear witness to a narrowing focus of Christian concern toward Jews alone. Perhaps because of Latin Catholic antipathy toward food-specific dietary restrictions, prohibitions targeting Jewish holiday foods appear predominantly in canons from Greek- and Syriac-speaking communities in the Near East.

The earliest attested prohibition of foods related to Jewish holidays appears in a mid to late fourth-century collection associated with the Council of Laodicea, a collection that contains a variety of food-related canons.[28]

> 37. It is not permitted to accept festival-related things sent from Jews or heretics or to celebrate their festivals with them.
> 38. It is not permitted to receive unleavened bread from Jews or to take part in their impieties.
> 39. It is not permitted to celebrate Greek festivals with Greeks or to take part in their godlessness.[29]

The authors of these canons, who equate Jews, heretics, and adherents of Hellenistic religions, express concern about Christian participation in the holidays of these outsiders. They single out as particularly problematic the acceptance of holiday-related gifts (of food? the text is ambiguous) and matzah, the unleavened bread Jews bake for Passover. The so-called "Canons of the Apostles," a late fourth-century collection reliant in part on Laodicean material, similarly prohibits Christians from fasting with Jews, celebrating their holidays, or accepting "gifts associated with their festivals, such as unleavened bread or anything similar to this" (c. 70).[30]

The Apostolic Decree's prohibition of food offered to idols seems to be the model that underlies Christian prohibitions of Jewish holiday-related foodstuffs. This connection is made explicit in a canon from the Council of Isho'yahb I, Patriarch of the (Nestorian) Church of the East (585), which declares that food associated with the festivals of Jews, heretics, and pagans "is a portion of that which has been set aside for their sacrificial offerings" (c. 25).[31] Just as the conflation of Judaism and heresy renders Jews subject to Paul's prohibition against commensality with sinful Christians, the conflation of Judaism and paganism results in the notion that Jewish holiday foods are equivalent to food offered in idolatrous sacrifice.

Concern about "pagan" festivals and about heretics remains strong in Isho'yahb's sixth-century Church of the East, which was situated in the Zoroastrian-dominated Sasanid Empire and enmeshed in an intense rivalry with (Jacobite) Syrian Orthodox Christianity. Prohibitions against the sacrificial meat of pagans also appear after the Arab conquest in a set of Syriac canons from Antioch, formerly a part of the Roman Empire.[32] After the Christianization of the Roman Empire, however, ecclesiastical authorities within its bounds rapidly dismiss paganism and its rituals as irrelevant, and they tend not to address heretics by means of food restrictions either. Judaism and its holidays, however, remain a persistent concern throughout Christendom—even, as we have seen, in places without Jews.

Prohibitions against food offered to idols disappear entirely from Greek-language canons by the end of the fourth century, only to be replaced by prohibitions against food associated with Jewish holidays.[33] The Canons of the Apostles, for example, prohibits consumption of meat from carrion and other animals whose blood was not drained but neglects to mention meat offered to idols (c. 63). Likewise, bishops convened in Constantinople by Justinian II at the Council in Trullo of 692 state, "Divine scripture has commanded us to abstain from blood and from what is strangled and from fornication," editing *eidōlothuton* out of the Apostolic Decree (c. 67).[34] In their canon addressing Christian association with Jews (c. 11), however, these bishops make a point of prohibiting consumption of the Passover matzah.[35] Unleavened bread takes the place of *eidōlothuton* as the foodstuff whose rejection defines Christian identity because Christian authorities come to imagine Judaism, not idolatry, as the primary antithesis of Christianity.

It is probably no coincidence that the shift in Christian self-definition from "We believe in one God (unlike the Greeks)" to "We believe in Christ (unlike the Jews)" occurs during the period in which disputes over Christology divided rival factions claiming the title of Christian orthodoxy. As we observed above, condemnation of the Jews indirectly furthers the agenda of clerics able to brand their Christian opponents as "judaizers." Condemnation of Jewish matzah may indirectly serve to highlight the danger inherent in accepting the unleavened bread of the Eucharist from the wrong cleric.

Ephrem the Syrian (d. 373) expresses eloquently the horrors associated with matzah and the Jews who prepare it.[36] The refrain of Ephrem's nineteenth "Hymn on Unleavened Bread" declares that Christ's body, which unleavened bread itself symbolizes, has rendered the Jews and their matzah obsolete. Nevertheless, the text of the hymn makes clear that both Jews and matzah pose grave dangers to Christians.

> Do not take, my brothers, that unleavened bread from the People whose hands are filthy with blood,
> Lest the filth that fills their hands cling to that unleavened bread.
> Although meat is pure, no one eats from that which was sacrificed to idols because it is defiled—
> How impure therefore is that unleavened bread which the hands that killed the Son kneaded!
> It is abhorrent to take food from a hand that is defiled with the blood of animals—
> Who, then, would take from that hand which is completely defiled by the blood of prophets?
> Let us not, my brothers, eat along with the drug of life the unleavened bread of the People which is, as it were, a drug of death.

> For the blood of Christ is served in the unleavened bread of the People and dwells in our Eucharist.
> The one who received it in our Eucharist received the drug of life. The one who ate it with the People received the drug of death,
> Because that blood, which they cried out might be upon them, is served on their festivals and their Sabbaths,
> And whoever associates himself with their festivals, upon him as well is the spattering of the blood.[37]

Jews, according to Ephrem, are impure on account of the defilement generated by the murder of prophets and, especially, of Christ himself. That defilement besmirches all who participate in Jewish festivals and clings to the unleavened bread which Jews prepare, presented here as equivalent to an idolatrous sacrifice. Indeed, matzah embodies the blood of Christ itself, the blood which Jews called as a curse upon themselves and their descendants (*Matt.* 27.25). Ephrem also alludes in this passage both to the Apostolic Decree and to Paul's warning to the Corinthians that one cannot partake of both the body of Christ and the sacrificial food of idolaters (*1 Cor.* 10.16–21).

Two sermons pseudonimously ascribed to Ephrem warn that those who eat with Jews and idolaters will also join them in hell.[38] Christ alone possesses the keys to eternal life; by definition, pseudo-Ephrem teaches, all other religions are satanic and traffic in that which is impure and abominable. The clerics at Elvira and the author of the "Canons from the East" prohibit commensality with Jews by analogy to Paul's prohibition against eating with sinful Christians. These sermons, drawing on Paul's teaching, "You cannot partake of the table of the Lord and the table of demons" (*1 Cor.* 10.21), instead define Jews as idolaters.

Paul, Church Fathers, and the Elviran clerics are careful to distinguish gentiles from their idolatry. Nothing, these authorities emphasize, is wrong with gentiles themselves, and Christians must abstain only from association with a specific act which only some gentiles perform. Rhetoric equating Jewish food with *eidōlothuton,* in contrast, applies to all Jews uniformly. Ephrem justifies the prohibition against matzah by reference to the act of crucifixion, for which every Jew bears personal responsibility. A sermon attributed to Caesarius, Catholic bishop of Arles (d. 542), does the same but extends that prohibition to all foodstuffs associated with Jews: "The food and drink of the Jews is sacrificial, cursed just as they cursed the Lord, since they crucified their God and Lord; therefore it is cursed, it has borne their faithlessness."[39] Similarly, Jacob of Edessa (d. 708) prohibits consumption of all "bread, wine, or similar items" prepared by Jews on the grounds that they have been touched by "the impure hands of the Jews"; Jacob warns that even a Christian who borrows a Jew's wine press or the like may "become defiled by those who are sinners." Excepting cases of necessity, those who eat Jewish food "shall be cast out from the Church of God and from association with the faithful as one who is impure and despised and abominable, and they shall be numbered among the Jews until they purify themselves through repentance."[40] Unleavened bread may be the paradigmatic foodstuff expressing the Jews' rejection and crucifixion of Christ, but all Jewish food is forbidden as if sacrificed to idols because it all bears the curse and the stigma of impurity under which Jews are imagined to live.

The first of John Chrysostom's *Discourses against the Jews,* preached in Antioch in 386, offers valuable insights into the logic underlying rhetoric that brands Jews, their holidays, and their food as idolatrous and impure.[41] Chrysostom (d. 407), whose sobriquet attests to the power of his "golden tongue," attacks the popular belief that Jews are holy and worthy of emulation by citing scripture to prove that Jews are dogs and stiff-necked beasts who refused the yoke of God. Because they are ignorant of the Father and crucified the Son, they plainly do not worship God; their synagogues must therefore be places of idolatry and dwellings of demons (1.3). Because they abuse and do violence to the scriptures, moreover, the Jews are "exceedingly impure and accursed."

> So it is that I exhort you to flee and shun their gatherings. The harm to our weaker brothers is not slight; providing an excuse for the Jews' madness is no small matter. For when [your brothers] see you, who worship the Christ whom [the Jews] crucified, reverently following Jewish ritual, how can they fail to think that everything the Jews do is the best? How can they not think that our ways are worthless when you, who accept Christianity and follow its practices, run to those who degrade them? Paul said: "If others see you who have knowledge eating in the temple of an idol, might they not, since their consciousness is weak, be emboldened to eat food sacrificed to idols?" [*1 Cor.* 8.10] And I say: If others see you who have knowledge come into the synagogue and watch them blow trumpets, might they not, since their consciousness is weak, be emboldened to admire Jewish practices? (1.5.7)

Chrysostom, deftly appropriating Paul's anti-*eidōlothuton* rhetoric, charges that Christian "knowers" who choose to attend Jewish rituals place their weaker brothers at risk just as they would by entering an idolatrous temple. Demons, he continues, dwell in the synagogues and, more ominously, in the souls of the Jews themselves. Jews possess "impure souls" and have become so accustomed to bloodshed that they sacrifice their own children to the demons (1.6). Moreover:

> They killed the Son of your Master, yet you have the audacity to come together with them? The one whom they killed has honored you by making you as His brother and co-heir, yet you dishonor Him by honoring those who murdered and crucified Him and by attending their festival gatherings? You enter into their profane place and pass through their impure doors and share in the table of demons—for that is what I am persuaded to call the fast of the Jews after the God-slaying. How can those who have set themselves in opposition to God be anything but worshippers of demons? (1.7.5)

In this sermon, John Chrysostom offers a banner example of the hermeneutical Jew. He weaves together stock rhetorical accusations and a range of Biblical prooftexts to construct a monstrous antithesis of Christianity and thereby persuade his flock to avoid participation in Jewish festivals.[42] Chrysostom structures his argument along the lines of *1 Corinthians* 8–10, first encouraging his audience to avoid synagogues for the benefit of those with a "weak consciousness" and later demonstrating that participation in Jewish festivals—tantamount to sharing in "the table of demons"—is anathema for one who believes in Christ.[43] In his second discourse, Chrysostom presses this point further: "After you have gone off and shared with those who shed the blood of Christ, how is it that you do not shudder to come back and share in his sacred banquet, to partake of his precious blood?" (2.3.5). Paul, of course, intended his instructions to the Corinthians to apply specifically to practices associated with traditional Hellenistic religion. According to Chrysostom, however, "the impiety of the Jews is equal to that of the Greeks, while their guile is much more dangerous" (1.6.4). Jews, not Greeks, constitute the true threat to Christianity, so Christian identity is now defined by avoidance of Jewish rituals even more than by abstention from idolatrous rites.

THE LOGIC AND IMPLICATIONS OF JEWISH IMPURITY

Whether they portray Jews as the ultimate outsiders on account of their rejection of Christ or the most threatening of insiders on account of their willful misinterpretation of the Bible, Christian prohibitions of food associated with Jews define Judaism as antithetical to Christianity: if Christians are "1," Jews are "-1" even as gentiles are merely "0." The rhetoric of impurity plays a significant role in rendering Jews in a more negative light than gentiles and, indeed, serves to place Jews at the negative pole of the Christian spectrum of humanity. This function reflects the fact that the impure is that which can never be holy and, indeed, must be kept far removed from that which bears the mantle of holiness; the mundane, in contrast, poses no threat to the holy. The ascription of impurity to an entire class of people finds no precedent in the New Testament. Paul, after all, does not brand Christian sinners as impure when prohibiting commensality with them, and *Acts* refers only to "the defilement that comes from idols" (*Acts* 15.20), not to the defilement of idolaters themselves.

The forcefulness of Christian impurity rhetoric with respect to the Jews stems in no small measure from the way in which Christian authorities collectively conflate the three types of impurity described at the end of chapter 2. Jews are defiled because they shed blood—most notably the blood of Christ—and because they embrace false beliefs about God and the dietary laws. These timeless offenses result in a permanent state of intrinsic impurity, vividly expressed by Chrysostom through the image of Jewish synagogues and souls infested by demons. As Ephrem the Syrian and Jacob of Edessa make clear, Jewish impurity is especially dangerous because, like certain forms of circumstantial pollution, it is contagious: Jewish food, especially but not exclusively symbolically significant foodstuffs, takes on the impurity of its preparers, and those who eat such food become "Jews" by association. By marshaling attributes of all three types of impurity found in Biblical literature and coupling them with attributes that the Christian Bible associates with other objectionable groups, Christians construct a Jew who is more negative than the sum of his attributes. This hermeneutical Jew functions as a magnet that attracts negative depictions precisely because the Jew is imagined to be the polar opposite of true Christianity and thus the embodiment of everything which Christians do not want to be themselves.[44]

Because ecclesiastical authorities intertwine their self-definition as Christians with their hermeneutically derived definition of Jews, however, the nature of the imagined Jewish foil carries with it profound implications for the identity and proper behavior of Christians. By asserting that Jewish blessings have the power to counteract those of Christians (c. 49), for example, the clerics gathered at Elvira imagine Jews as powerful and Christians, consequently, as vulnerable. The ironic implications of Christian imagination regarding Jews are especially evident in prohibitions of Jewish foods premised on rhetoric regarding Jewish impurity. We have seen that Christian authorities like Jacob of Edessa and the clerics gathered at Epaone insist that Christians, to maintain their own identity as the holy people, must avoid the impure food of Jews whenever possible. Of course, *Titus* 1.15 also teaches, "For the pure all things are pure," and no less an authority than Augustine defines Christianity by its rejection of the notion that food can be impure. The inexorable logic of rhetoric about Jewish impurity, however, nevertheless demands, even from heirs to the Augustinian tradition, an embrace of the notions that Jewish food is impure and its consumption by Christians forbidden.[45] As Paul himself observes regarding the "weak" Christ-believers of both Rome and Corinth, food truly is forbidden to those who imagine it as impure or idolatrous.

The logic and implications of Jewish impurity are expressed clearly in the work of Agobard, archbishop of Lyons from 816 to 840. Agobard draws together the various strands of thought about Jews and their food we have been following in this chapter, along with many of the texts we have examined, in his treatise *On Jewish Superstitions.*[46] He cites the prohibitions against commensality promulgated at Agde, Epaone, and Mâcon (§§4–6), as well as the example set by Hilary of Poitiers, who not only refused to share meals with Jews and heretics but even refrained from greeting them in the street (§2).[47] On the basis of these and other sources from late antiquity, Agobard continues, "one ought to direct greater denunciation toward fellowship with Jews—behavior which must be cursed and avoided—than toward fellowship with other heretics because, although all properly deserve to be denounced for being hostile toward the truth, those who express greater hostility are especially deserving." After all, he observes, heretics only dissent from some of the Church's tenets and thus are only partial blasphemers, but the Jews proclaim falsehoods about everything, blaspheming against Christ and his Church in their entirety and cursing Christ at every available opportunity (§9).[48] Agobard, who is unfamiliar with Greek and Syriac sources, does not interpret restrictions against Jewish food as extensions of the New Testament's prohibition of food offered to idols. Like Chrysostom and Ephrem, however, Agobard portrays Jews as infested by "the impure spirit of idolatry" and asserts that Jews are more abhorrent than either Biblical unbelievers like the Amalekites or contemporary pagans like Muslims; indeed, Jews are nothing less than the Antichrist (§§19–22).[49]

The theme of Jewish impurity is a consistent refrain in *On Jewish Superstitions.* Agobard, introducing his discussion of canons about the Jews, summarizes their contents as follows: "Every Christian must avoid completely all association with Jews, who are intrinsically most impure" (§3). He devotes the bulk of this treatise to a presentation of scriptural evidence demonstrating the need for such avoidance, with particular attention to the avoidance of Jewish food. The charge of Jewish impurity introduces this presentation:

> Because they are so greatly and in so many ways polluted by the defilement of mind and deed, through them are fulfilled directly the words of the prophet Haggai. On God's order, he asked the priests: "If someone polluted by a corpse touches any of these"—clearly referring to "bread or meat or wine or oil or any other food" [*Haggai* 2.12]—"is it not impure?" The priests replied and said, "It is impure." Thereupon Haggai said, "That is how this people and that is how this nation appears before me, says God, and likewise all of the works of their hands" [*Haggai* 2.13–14]. (§11)[50]

Haggai, prophesying metaphorically, blurs the line between the noncontagious offensive defilement resulting from Israelite sinfulness and the contagious circumstantial pollution caused by contact with corpses. Agobard takes Haggai's words literally and deduces from them the charge that both Jews and their food are contagiously impure on account of Jewish sinfulness. The theme of impurity returns once more at the climax of Agobard's discourse on Biblical prooftexts. Even though scripture permits sharing meals with unbelievers, Agobard declares, this permission cannot be applied to the Jews because their food is impure. "We know the food of those who are impure is impure because of their sinfulness in mind and conscience. For how could their food not be impure, how could their granary and storehouses not be cursed?" (§24).[51] This definition of Judaism and Jewish food underlies Agobard's insistence that Christians may not consume meat or wine prepared by Jews, despite the fact that none of the canonical sources that Agobard adduces contain such prohibitions. Amulo (d. 852), Agobard's successor to the see of Lyons, states explicitly that Jewish wine is prohibited because it "has become polluted by their activity."[52]

Jeremy Cohen makes a compelling case that Agobard's anti-Jewish rhetoric is an element of the archbishop's broader concern for establishing a properly ordered Christian empire, a concern that dominated Agobard's career. Jews, Agobard asserts, occupy an inappropriate position in Carolingian society and are the beneficiaries of imperial privileges which they do not deserve. In Cohen's words, Agobard believes that "imperial Jewish policy has resulted in nothing less than the disgrace of Christianity, which numerous Christians aggravate when they persist in eating with the Jews and spending time in their company."[53] Agobard expresses no desire to eliminate Jews from the realm, but he is vociferous in demanding that Jews be put in their proper place as despised witnesses to the truth of Christianity. The very definition of Christianity as the positive polar opposite of Judaism (1 and -1) necessitates legal and rhetorical measures, foreign food restrictions prominent among them, that accomplish this task. The degree to which impurity rhetoric advances Agobard's agenda—and, indeed, that of so many other Christian authorities of late antiquity and the early Middle Ages—belies Mary Douglas's famous definition of impurity as "matter out of place."[54] Quite the contrary, Christian assertions that Jews are impure, and the foreign food restrictions that derive from such assertions, function as a means of placing Jews where they belong within the proper social order: at the negative pole of the Christian worldview and in an inferior position within Christian society.

The absence of comparable impurity rhetoric in Jewish discourse about foreign food restrictions offers further indication that Jewish authorities do not perceive the difference between Us and Them in antithetical terms and do not treat gentiles as a foil against which to construct Jewish identity. Within the worldview exemplified in such discourse, gentiles are not impure (-1 on our spectrum), but rather merely mundane (0); consequently, gentiles merit little attention in their own right.[55] Both Qumranic and Rabbinic authorities, like their Christian counterparts, ascribe impurity to the food of Jewish heretics in the process of defining orthodoxy in contradistinction to a heretical foil.[56] Ultimately, however, the Sages come to view Christianity not as a heretical offshoot of Judaism but rather as an archetypical gentile religion. For that reason, at the same time Christians begin to treat Jews as the primary foil against which to define Christian identity, Talmudic Sages dismiss Christianity as having no particular significance for the construction of Jewish identity.[57] Both sets of authorities engage in the process of imagining not only their own community but also those outside its bounds, yet they do so in fundamentally different styles. The role which impurity rhetoric does or does not play in these acts of imagination reveals significant information about Jewish and Christian styles of thought about foreigners and, we will see in part IV, Islamic styles of thought on this subject as well.

THE DOGS AND THE CHILDREN, THE IMPURE AND THE HOLY

Discourse about foreign food restrictions serves to express both Jewish and Christian ideas about the proper place of Jews and gentiles within an ideal society. Hellenistic Jews of Alexandria imagine themselves as members of a distinctly holy community nevertheless integrated into the broader society; they interpret Biblical dietary laws as a means of marking their distinctiveness but refrain from endorsing foreign food restrictions. Judeans, in contrast, employ foreign food restrictions as a means of emphasizing through symbols and social practice not only Jewish distinctiveness but also the divide that separates Jews from gentiles, the holy from the mundane. This divide remains fundamental in Rabbinic literature about foreign food restrictions, in which the most significant characteristic of non-Jews is the very fact of their non-Jewishness.

The food-related discourse we have examined in the last three chapters reflects the ways in which Christian authorities transformed the Jew-gentile dichotomy in the process of defining a new religious community that, although positioned outside of both categories, nevertheless lays claim to the mantle of Israel's holiness. This transformation is apparent in the two epigraphs that introduce part III. Jesus' own unwillingness to eat with gentiles and his reluctance to "take the children's food and throw it to the dogs" by ministering to a gentile woman (*Matt.* 15.26) dissolves within a generation or two of his death into an embrace of commensality among Jewish and gentile Christ-believers. Such behavior symbolizes the unified nature of a Christ-believing community in which the differences between Jews and gentiles have become inconsequential; as Paul teaches, "In Christ Jesus you are all children of God through faith" (*Gal.* 3.26). Foreign food restrictions nevertheless continue to mark the distinctions between Christians and idolaters on the one hand and Christians and Jews on the other. As notions of the proper social order shift, foreign food restrictions are dismantled and constructed accordingly.

With the Christianization of the Roman Empire, the distinction between Christians and idolaters receded in the minds of many Christian authorities, but such was not the fate of the distinction between Christians and Jews. As Chrysostom and, later, Agobard assert on the basis of Jesus' words to the gentile woman, "Although those Jews had been called to sonship, they degenerated to the level of dogs, while we who were dogs received the strength, through God's grace, to cast off our former irrationality and to rise to the honor of sons" (Chrysostom, *Discourses* 1.2.1; cf. Agobard, *On Jewish superstitions* §11). Jesus, like the later Sages (T. *Ḥul.* 1.1), understands his community to be a Jewish one and employs animal imagery as symbolic of the mundane status of gentiles. Christians, in contrast, define themselves in opposition to Judaism and imagine Jews as analogous to animals in order to reinforce their assertions that Jews are impure and thus cut off from the holiness associated with Biblical Israel.[58]

Imagined foreigners are not unique to Christian discourse. The Sages, we have seen, imagine gentiles in various contexts related to foreign food restrictions to be obsessive performers of libation and sexual perverts, as well as helpful neighbors. The common need to imagine foreigners, however, in no way predetermines the nature of the resulting image. The choice by Jewish authorities to imagine gentiles as generally insignificant and the choice by Christian authorities to imagine Jews as gravely dangerous are both just that: choices. These choices reflect the ways in which religious authorities imagine the identity of their own community and, more specifically, the ways in which they stake their claim to holiness. Islamic authorities make yet different choices about the way they portray foreigners, reflecting a different set of ideas about identity and holiness.

The ways in which Jews and Christians imagine foreigners relate to a Biblical notion that both communities embrace: "Israel" possesses a monopoly on holiness and an exclusive relationship with the divine. Each community lays claim to the title of Israel in its own fashion and imagines its outsiders accordingly. The Qur'an, in contrast, rejects the very premise that underlies Jewish and Christian claims. It makes no difference who constitutes *verus Israel* if, as the Qur'an asserts, Israel is not the bearer of intrinsic holiness and God has not established an exclusive relationship with a single people.[59] The Qur'an thus sets the stage for a third style of imagining the identities of Us and Them, one in which the possession of an authentic relationship with the divine, and thus the claim to a measure of holiness, is not necessarily limited to a single community.

PART FOUR

Islamic Sources on Foreign Food Restrictions

Relativizing Otherness

The Messenger of God, may the prayer and peace of God be upon him, said, "Whoever recites our prayers and worships in the direction of our qiblah *and eats the meat of our slaughtered animals, that person is a Muslim who has the protection of God and the protection of His messsenger, so do not betray God through your treatment of those under His protection."*

ṢAḤĪḤ AL-BUKHĀRĪ §393

9

"Eat the Permitted and Good Foods God Has Given You"

Relativizing Communities in the Qur'an

Qur'anic dietary laws, like those of the Hebrew Bible and the early Christian community, express their adherents' relationship to God without in the process segregating the Qur'an's community of "believers" from outsiders.[1] Like early Christian counterparts, Qur'anic discourse functions as a means of defining these believers in contrast to idolaters on the one hand and Jews on the other—communities associated with distinct dietary practices.[2] Indeed, both the limited set of meat-related regulations endorsed by the Qur'an and its rhetoric regarding the Jews and their more extensive dietary norms closely resemble those articulated by Christian authorities.[3]

Given our recent encounter with the ways Christians came to employ such anti-Jewish rhetoric, we might anticipate that the Qur'an sharply condemns the consumption of Jewish food. In fact, however, the Qur'an declares that "the food of those who were given the Book"—that is, meat prepared by Jews and Christians—"is permitted to you, and your food is permitted to them" (Q. 5.5). This statement, atypical within the present study because it explicitly permits the consumption of food associated with foreigners, expresses the notion that We and They share crucial attributes in common. Consumption of meat from the same butchers, as the epigraph to part IV makes clear, constitutes a significant marker of identity. The notion that God has established an ongoing relationship with more than one religious community through the revelation of a scripture, moreover, reflects a core attribute of the Qur'an's worldview: holiness is not exclusive to Us.[4] Consequently, the Qur'an and later Islamic authorities do not define adherents of other religions simply as "not Us" or "anti-Us," the paradigms we have encountered in Jewish and Christian discourse regarding profane and impure foreigners. Rather, Islamic sources imagine outsiders to be "like Us" or "unlike Us" to various degrees. To return to our numerical spectrum in which insiders are assigned the value "1," Jewish and Christian authorities define gentiles as "0," Christian authorities define Jews as "-1," and the Qur'an assigns Jews and Christians alike a value less than 1 but greater than 0. By relativizing the otherness of religious foreigners, the classificatory system developed by Islamic authorities serves to define Islam itself in relation to other religions, foremost among them Judaism and Christianity.

The foundations of this distinctly Islamic approach to the classification of foreigners may be seen in passages of the Qur'an that address the intertwined themes of meat-related food restrictions, foreign dietary practices, and the food of foreigners. Qur'anic discourse about meat-related food restrictions regularly juxtaposes the dietary norms which believers ought to follow with the beliefs and practices of foreigners, demonstrating that adherence to these norms marks believers as distinct from idolaters and Jews. Passages that address these restrictions, however, express three different, albeit overlapping, ideas about the relationship between the Qur'an's audience of believers and members of other religious communities. Surahs ascribed to the Meccan period of Muḥammad's prophethood (ca. 610–22) portray these dietary laws as a golden mean between two undesirable sets of food practices: those of idolaters on the one hand and those of Jews on the other. Believers, unlike idolaters, possess accurate knowledge of the divine will with respect to food but, as non-Jews, are not bound by the punitively rigorous laws which God imposed upon the Children of Israel. Most passages about dietary laws in surahs associated with the Medinan period (622–32), in contrast, emphasize the distinction between believers and Jews while rhetorically associating the latter with idolaters.[5] Whereas Meccan surahs treat Jews separately from idolaters, Medinan surahs conflate these communities. We have already seen, however, that one Medinan verse, Qur'an 5.5, does not use dietary law as a means of distinguishing Us from Them. This verse instead employs the permission of Jewish and Christian meat as a means by which to articulate a fundamental similarity between those who accept the divine revelation that is the Qur'an and those who received earlier revelations. This chapter will examine Meccan and Medinan texts in turn.

MEAT RESTRICTIONS AND THE QUR'AN'S GOLDEN MEAN IN MECCAN SURAHS

On four occasions and with only minimal variation, the Qur'an expresses the dietary norms that believers—and, indeed, humanity in general—ought to observe.[6] The least elaborate of these expressions reads as follows: "God has only prohibited for you carrion [*maytah*], blood, the meat of swine, and meat over which [a being] other than God has been invoked. As for one who is compelled, neither desiring [to eat such food] nor intending to transgress, surely God is Forgiving, Merciful"

(16.115; cf. 6.145, 2.173, 5.3).[7] *Sūrat al-anʿām* ("Cattle") elaborates upon the last of these four food restrictions. This surah enjoins believers to "eat from that over which God's name was mentioned, if you truly believe in His revelations" (6.118) and cajoles believers for refraining from consumption of such food when it is not otherwise prohibited, lest they appear to observe unfounded food restrictions (v. 119). Believers must, however, avoid transgression. "And do not eat from that over which the name of God has not been mentioned; it is indeed a sinful act. The devils inspire their friends to dispute with you; but if you obey them, then you will surely be idolaters" (v. 121). The act of eating meat from an animal slaughtered without the invocation of God marks the consumer as an idolater, perhaps because the Qur'an assumes another being was invoked instead; we encountered similar rhetoric in the *Books of Maccabees* and the New Testament.

The Qur'an's catalog of food restrictions, which appears in Meccan and Medinan surahs alike, resembles the prohibitions expressed in the New Testament's Apostolic Decree.[8] The apostles and elders in Jerusalem instruct gentile Christ-believers to abstain from food offered to idols, blood, and strangled meat (*Acts* 15.29), injunctions that retained their force among Eastern Christians well into the Islamic period.[9] Qur'anic and New Testament prohibitions of food offered to beings other than God are functionally equivalent, and their prohibitions of blood are identical. The Greek term *pnikton* (strangled meat), which refers to the meat of an animal which has not been slaughtered in the manner necessary for its blood to drain out, corresponds to the Arabic *maytah*.[10] Only the Qur'an's prohibition of pork would be foreign to many Eastern Christians, whose authorities seized upon consumption of the pig as a symbol of the distinction between Christian and Jewish dietary practices; the Qur'an here affirms a taboo found not only in the Torah but also in pre-Islamic Arabian society.[11]

That the contents of Qur'anic dietary laws closely resemble those found in Jewish and Christian texts should come as no surprise. The Qur'an, after all, presents itself as the divinely authored Book previously revealed to the Jews as the Torah and to the Christians as the Gospels. Adherence by the believers to norms shared by Jews and Christians merely reflects the common origins which the Qur'an itself ascribes to these three communities and, indeed, serves to bolster the Qur'an's own authority as successor to the Torah and Gospels. Of greater significance for the purpose of understanding Qur'anic ideas about the identity of its believers is the fact that Meccan surahs consistently express norms about meat within a rhetorical context similar to the one employed in *Acts of the Apostles*. We observed in chapter 6 that *Acts* uses food-related practices both to represent the establishment of a new community united by its belief in Christ and to set gentile Christ-believers apart from their idolatrous counterparts without requiring them to become Jews. The Qur'an, I suggest, employs the rhetoric of the golden mean in its presentation of the dietary laws for the same purpose: discourse about food restrictions furthers the goal of establishing a new, emphatically monotheistic, community distinct from and preferable to Judaism.

The most extensive discussion of food practices in the Qur'an appears in *Sūrat al-an'ām* (6.135–47). This passage begins by reporting that "wrongdoers" dedicate some of their food not to its true Creator but rather to the demigod-like partners whom they have ascribed to God.[12] These idolatrous wrongdoers—who go so far as to kill their own children for the sake of these partners—allege that God has decreed a series of bizarre meat-related food restrictions, allegations that the Qur'an repeatedly dismisses as "fabrications" (vv. 135–41). In truth, God created all crops and animals for the use of humankind and only prohibited consumption of carrion, blood, pork, and that over which a being other than God was invoked. Qur'anic idolaters, like the gentiles depicted in Hellenistic-era Jewish literature, lack accurate knowledge about God and the divine will; as a result, they engage in abhorrent practices. Believers, in contrast, possess true knowledge, which is made manifest in their awareness of God's revelation regarding permitted and prohibited meat and in their ability to demonstrate the falsehood of the idolaters' claims (vv. 142–45).

Sūrat al-an'ām contrasts the limited meat-related regulations that believers ought to observe not only with the bizarre practices ascribed to idolaters but also with the more extensive restrictions incumbent upon Jews. "As for the Jews, We prohibited every animal with undivided toes and We prohibited the fat of cattle and sheep, except what their backs or entrails carry or what is mixed with bones. This is Our recompense to them for their transgression. We are surely Truthful. If they accuse you of speaking falsely, say: 'All-encompassing is the mercy of Your Lord, but His wrath cannot be turned back from the sinful people'" (6.146–47). The Qur'an presents the burdensome dietary restrictions observed by Jews as a form of punishment for Israelite transgressions.[13] These regulations, unlike those fabricated by idolaters, are authentically divine in their origin, yet there is no reason for any non-Jew to observe them. The Qur'an, like the Church Fathers, teaches that believers in God's final revelation are not Jews and ought not adhere to all the dietary prohibitions found in the Torah.

In establishing the dietary practices of the believing community as preferable to two undesirable alternatives, *Sūrat al-an'ām* is careful to maintain the distinction between its foils. It does so both by discussing each foil separately and by employing different terminology with reference to each. Idolaters are "wrongdoers" (*al-ẓālimūn*) whose claims about the divine will are based on "fabrication" (*mā yaftarūn*). The "sinful" Jews (*al-qawm al-mujrimīn*), in contrast, adhere to an authentic revelation, albeit one that stems from their "transgression" (*baghyihim*) and therefore does not warrant emulation. The Jews may without warrant accuse believers of speaking falsely (*kadhdhabūka*), but they neither fabricate false claims about God nor transgress the divinely ordained dietary laws endorsed by the Qur'an.

Golden-mean rhetoric also plays a role in the portrayal of meat-related food restrictions within *Sūrat al-naḥl* ("Bees"). Those who do not believe God's revelations, apparently a reference to idolaters (see 16.98–100), are the ones who fabricate falsehood (*yaftarī al-kadhb*) and who will ultimately suffer great punishment (16.104–5). Believers who turn to unbelief (*kufr*) will suffer grievously as well, excepting those who were compelled to abandon the community against their will; the latter can look forward to God's merciful forgiveness (vv. 106–13). "Eat, then, the permitted and good foods God has provided you and give thanks for God's kindness, if you truly worship Him" (v. 114). True adherence to God's will, the Qur'an declares, is manifest through the consumption of permissible foods—which is to say, everything but carrion, blood, pork, and that over which a being other than God has been invoked (v. 115)—and the act of giving thanks to God. The act of giving thanks sets believers apart from the unbelievers who deny God's grace (v. 112), while the act of eating "permitted and good foods" sets them apart from those who "fabricate falsehoods" about God and who will suffer great punishment (vv. 116–17), namely idolaters.

Sūrat al-naḥl then adds, "We prohibited for the Jews that which We related to you previously. We did not wrong them; rather, they wronged themselves" (v. 118). This reminder, followed by an exhortation to repentance, serves to demonstrate God's ability to punish as well as to be merciful. Believers who behave as they should are rewarded with mercifully lenient laws and the promise of greater kindness in store, but those who transgress may find themselves in the situation of the Jews or, worse, that of idolaters or unbelievers. Like its counterpart in *Al-anʿām,* this passage carefully maintains the distinction between idolaters and Jews through its structure and its terminology, although in this case the Jews are "wrongdoers" while "falsehood" and "fabrication" alike are imputed to idolaters. The terms that apply to each of these foreign communities are interchangeable in these two passages, but the dietary practices of these communities and the relationship of each to the norms that apply to believers are kept distinct. Discourse about food restrictions functions in both of these passages to define the identity of the believing community: We are non-Jewish monotheists.

By positioning its own dietary regulations in contrast to those associated with idolaters and Jews, the Qur'an establishes proper food practices as a divinely ordained golden mean between two undesirable extremes, the former being false and the latter excessively rigorous. Observance of Qur'anic dietary restrictions serves to affirm the monotheism of the believers and to distinguish them from idolaters, while consumption of foods prohibited under Jewish law distinguishes believers in the Prophet's revelation from their Jewish counterparts. Indeed, the Qur'an's insistence that believers ought to consume all "permissible and good" foodstuffs implies that behavior to the contrary constitutes either a denial of God's authentic revelation or a rejection of the leniency God has mercifully extended to the believers.

Not only Qur'anic dietary laws themselves but also their accompanying rhetoric of pagan ignorance and Jewish transgression find parallels in Christian literature. There is much within the Qur'an, of course, that is quite different from Christian beliefs and practices. The similarity in this case, I would suggest, stems from the fact that the Qur'an's Meccan surahs and early Christian authorities alike seek to carve out an intermediate space for their followers between the same two established communities. Meat-related food restrictions and their accompanying rhetoric, wielded successfully by Christians, are deployed in the Qur'an for the same purpose.

SHARING "THE TABLE": BELIEVERS AND PEOPLE OF THE BOOK IN MEDINAN SURAHS

We observed in part III that Christian authorities, after initially portraying their community's food practices in contrast to the idolatry of the gentiles on the one hand and the excessive restrictiveness of the Jews on the other, come to equate Jews and idolaters in the process of defining Judaism as antithetical to Christianity. A similar rhetorical progression can be found within the Qur'an. Medinan surahs, which make no reference to dietary practices associated with idolatry, emphasize the difference between the freedom of believers to eat all permitted foods and the punitive restrictions incumbent upon Jews. These surahs, unlike their Meccan counterparts and like Christian sources, also conflate Judaism with idolatry in the process of portraying Jews (and, to a lesser extent, Christians) as especially hostile to the community of believers and particularly misguided in their understanding of the divine will. The Qur'an, however, departs from the path taken by Christian authorities: it affirms the affinity between believers in its revelation and the recipients of previous scriptures. Jews and Christians, far from being "anti-Us," are actually "like Us" to a significant degree, and We, in turn, are like Them. Food-related passages in the aptly named *Sūrat al-māʾidah* ("The Table," surah 5) express this distinctive conception of foreigners through their depictions of the complex relationship between the Qur'an's believers and those who had been given the Book before them.

Before turning to *Al-māʾidah,* however, we should briefly consider food-related passages found in three other Medinan surahs. Through their reapplication of motifs found in Meccan texts, these surahs cast "People of the Book," especially Jews, as tantamount to idolaters. *Sūrat al-baqarah* ("The Cow"), much like *Al-naḥl,* enjoins the consumption of "permitted and good" foodstuffs—which is to say, everything other than carrion, blood, pork, and food over which an entity other than God was invoked—as a sign of obedience to God (2.168–73). Reading this passage out of context, one could readily conclude that its message is identical to that of its Meccan counterparts: adherence to the Qur'an's limited food restrictions distinguishes believers from idolaters. Polemic in *Al-baqarah,* however, is consistently directed not against idolaters but rather against the People of the Book. The repetition of familiar anti-idolatry rhetoric in this context suggests that Jews and Christians too follow in Satan's footsteps (v. 168), impute statements to God without knowledge (v. 169), and are unbelievers who prefer the teachings of their ancestors to those of God (vv. 170–71). The unbelief of Jews past and present is further detailed in *Sūrat al-nisā'* ("Women"), which reiterates, "It was because of the wrongdoing of the Jews that We forbade them good foods which had been permitted to them" (4.160). Consumption of good food distinguishes those who walk on the divinely ordained path from those who oppose them. In the midst of extended polemic against the People of the Book, *Sūrat Āl Imrān* ("The Family of Imran") declares that "All food was permitted to the Children of Israel before the Torah was revealed, excepting what Israel [i.e., Jacob] prohibited for himself.[14] Say: Bring the Torah and recite it if you are truthful! Whoever fabricates falsehood about God afterward, those are truly the wrongdoers" (3.93–94). According to this surah, the Jews falsely deny that the distinctive food restrictions found in the Torah constitute punishment for their sinfulness. Jews are now depicted not only as wrongdoers but also as fabricators of falsehood with respect to God. Idolaters are absent from these Medinan passages, but the attributes associated with those idolaters in Meccan surahs now apply to the Jews. We observed in chapter 8 that rhetoric of this nature serves to define the Jews as inimical to the monotheistic community that employs it, irrespective of the fact that Jews also lay claim to monotheism.

Whereas the "unbelievers" we encountered in the Meccan *Sūrat al-naḥl* are evidently turncoats from the community of believers which the Qur'an itself addresses, in *Al-mā'idah* and other Medinan surahs the term *unbelief* (*kufr*) frequently refers to Jews and Christians who profess false theology or dismiss the authenticity of the Qur'an. For example, the table that gives *Sūrat al-mā'idah* its name descends from heaven upon Jesus' request as edible evidence of Jesus' prophethood and God's providence. God warns that those who unbelieve after receiving such a clear sign—for instance, by ascribing divinity to Jesus himself—will be subject to unparalleled punishment, while those who acknowledge the truth will be rewarded (5.109–20).[15] *Sūrat al-mā'idah* places the recipient of the Qur'an in the lineage of Moses and Jesus, prior messengers who received substantially the same revelation found in the Qur'an and who conveyed the same truth to their communities. The Qur'an thus confirms and supersedes prior scriptures while revealing the falsehood espoused by some Jews and Christians (vv. 15–19, 44–48).[16] The food-laden table, one might say, represents the truth that God has provided to all three scriptural communities. The presence of Jews and Christians around this metaphorical table, however, does not legitimate the deceitful truth-claims of these outsiders, nor does it negate their hostility toward God's ultimate revelation.

Much of *Al-mā'idah,* like the preceding surahs, is devoted to polemic against Jews and Christians, both as separate communities and collectively as "those who were given the Book" or "People of the Book."[17] "Believers," God warns, "do not take the

Jews and the Christians as allies; they are only allies with one another. Whoever of you who takes them as allies is surely one of them; indeed, God does not guide the wrongdoing people" (v. 51). Jews are wont to mislead believers, accept false statements, devour unlawful gain, and tamper with God's revelations (vv. 41–44); Christians falsely assert that Christ is God or that God is a Trinity (vv. 72–73). Jews and Christians alike mock the religion of the believers, falsely claim to accept its beliefs, hasten toward sin, and ally themselves with unbelievers (vv. 57–66, 80–81), although Jews and idolaters are more hostile toward the believers than Christians are (v. 82). By linking Jews and Christians, Jews and idolaters, People of the Book and those who unbelieve, *Al-mā'idah* highlights the threats posed to the believing community and its convictions by those who received earlier revelations despite their commonalities. This surah acknowledges that all who espouse correct beliefs and behave properly, including those who are Jewish or Christian, will be rewarded on the Last Day (v. 69); it warns, however, that all who engage in unbelief and denounce God's revelations are destined for hell (v. 86). Although this warning certainly applies to members of the believing community as well (cf. v. 10), in the present context it falls most heavily on foreigners and thus sharpens the thrust of the earlier caution that believers who associate with Jews and Christians will become foreigners themselves.

Strikingly, *Sūrat al-mā'idah*'s scathing critique of foreigners and its frightening portrayal of their behavior is followed immediately by a call for believers to eat all foods God has permitted them: "Believers, do not prohibit the good things which God has permitted you, and do not transgress, for God does not love the transgressors. Eat of the permitted and good things which God has provided you. Fear God in whom you believe" (5.87–88). The consumption of divinely permitted foods, implicitly contrasted with those that the Jews and idolaters of verse 82 refuse to eat, distinguishes believers equally from all foreigners—We alone enjoy all of God's bounty—even as it functions metonymically as an expression of reverence for God. Rather than repeating the familiar meat-related prohibitions in this context, however, *Al-mā'idah* instead addresses a variety of other food-related laws: the expiation of unfulfilled oaths by means of feeding the needy or fasting, the prohibition of wine, and regulations about hunting while on pilgrimage (vv. 89–96). This departure from the pattern we encountered in other surahs likely stems from the fact that *Al-mā'idah* addresses the prohibitions of meat in its opening verses (1–5), an atypical passage in its own right.[18]

Unlike the passages we examined earlier, in which the meat-related food restrictions incumbent upon the community of believers are juxtaposed with those of idolaters and Jews, the opening verses of *Sūrat al-mā'idah* address these laws in the context of rules about hunting and the pilgrimage, the theme to which this surah returns later. The dietary regulations, as it were, now stand on their own two feet within the broader framework of Qur'anic law: no contrast with foreign practices is necessary. This version is also unique in that it contains a running gloss of the terms to which we have grown accustomed.

> Prohibited to you are carrion, blood, the meat of swine, meat over which [a being] other than God has been invoked, that which has been strangled or beaten to death, that which falls to its death, that which is gored or mangled by wild beasts—unless you perform a proper act of slaughter—and that which was sacrificed before a [pagan] stele or which you divided using divining arrows, for each of these is a sinful act. Today, those who unbelieve despair of your religion; do not fear them, but fear Me. Today, I have perfected your religion for you, fulfilled My grace upon you and approved Islam as your religion. [As for] one who is compelled [to eat prohibited food] by reason of hunger without intention to sin, surely God is Forgiving, Merciful. (5.3)

This verse glosses *carrion* as animals whose death was caused by strangulation, beating, a fall, or another animal's horns or teeth—in short, by any means other than "a proper act of slaughter" (*dhakāt*), a human-initiated act which causes the animal's blood to drain out.[19] The requirement of proper slaughter does not prohibit hunting, as the surrounding verses explicitly permit such activity so long as the hunter is not in the sacred state associated with the pilgrimage and invokes God (vv. 1–2, 4). Sacrifice before a pagan stele and the use of divining arrows in association with meat, both defined as sinful acts, are tantamount to the invocation of a being other than God. "Compulsion" as a mitigating factor for transgression of these norms is here defined as referring specifically to hunger.

Although foreign dietary practices are absent from this passage, foreigners themselves are not. In the midst of *Sūrat al-mā'idah*'s account of the dietary regulations we find a pair of statements, each beginning with the word *today*, expressing the despair of the unbelievers and the perfection of Islam. The location of these remarks seems to express the oft-attested notion that observance of Qur'anic food restrictions—no more and no less—constitutes a defining characteristic of the nascent Islamic community in contrast to those who fall outside its bounds. The dietary laws, moreover, reflect the uniquely perfect nature of the divinely ordained religion that is Islam, much as *Leviticus* portrays Israelite dietary practices as reflecting that community's distinctive status in God's eyes (*Lev.* 20.24–26). As Marion Holmes Katz observes, the reference to fulfillment of God's grace (*ni'mah*) links these laws to the broader theme of God's covenant with the community of believers, a theme that is prominent in Medinan surahs and central to *Al-mā'idah*. The term *today* (*al-yawm*), in addition to its possible reference to a specific moment of revelation, also links this passage to the Last Day, when those who adhere to the Qur'an's injunctions will be rewarded and those who fail to do so will receive the punishment they have earned. Adherence to Qur'anic dietary laws in the present world symbolically reflects the ultimate distinction between these two groups.[20]

Even though Jews and Christians are among those who "despair of your religion" and are destined for eternal punishment, and despite the polemics against these communities that appear later in the surah, *Al-mā'idah* does not advocate abstention from Jewish or Christian food. Quite the contrary: "Today the good things are permitted to you, and the food of those who were given the Book is permitted to you, and your food is permitted to them. So are the chaste women among the believers and the chaste women among those who were given the Book before you, provided you give them their dowries and take them in chastity, not in wantonness or as mistresses. If anyone denies the faith, his work shall be in vain, and in the world to come he will be among the losers" (5.5). The term *food* (*ṭaʿām*) in this verse is best understood as referring to all foodstuffs that God has not prohibited and especially to permissible meat, the subject of the passage as a whole. Indeed, the permission of "good things" (*al-ṭayyibāt*) appears in many of the meat-related Qur'anic passages we have been examining (16.114; 2.168, 172; 5.4, 87).[21] Qur'an 5.5 indicates that believers may eat otherwise acceptable food prepared by Jews and Christians; the prohibition of food over which God's name has not been mentioned (6.121), in contrast, implies that believers may not eat the meat of animals slaughtered by non-monotheistic foreigners. Believers may also marry Jewish and Christian women yet may not marry male or female idolaters, to whom the Qur'an ascribes a status inferior to that of Muslim slaves (2.221). Qur'an 5.5 does not, however, permit the marriage of a believing woman to a Jewish or Christian man. As Yohanan Friedmann observes, "A marriage of a Muslim woman to a non-Muslim man would result in an unacceptable incongruity between the superiority which the woman should enjoy by virtue of being Muslim, and her unavoidable wifely subservience to her infidel husband."[22] Muslims ought to be superior to non-Muslims, just as their religion is superior to all others. Although Qur'an 5.5 condones a partially porous boundary between believers and People of the Book by allowing food exchange across this border, it still maintains the distinction between these groups and is quite conscious of the hierarchical nature of the relationship which it addresses.

It is precisely the concern regarding intermarriage that prompts warnings about commensality in the Torah and foreign food restrictions in such diverse sources as the Babylonian Talmud and the canons of the Third Council of Orléans. Qur'an 5.5, implicitly acknowledging the connection between the food of foreigners and intermarriage, permits both so long as the believing male audience adheres to established standards regarding acceptable foodstuffs and acceptable wives. According to the Qur'an, there is nothing inherently problematic with the food of People of the Book or with the relationships that may result from interaction at the dinner table.

What accounts for the Qur'an's unparalleled permissiveness regarding food prepared by and, presumably, eaten with Jews and Christians? Gordon Newby has argued that Qur'an 5.5 expresses the desire to integrate Jews into the nascent Islamic community: "Dietary practices have bound Jews together and separated them from the rest of the world, and it is reasonable to expect that Muḥammad's motives are to use the same device to weld together his new community. From the perspective of this legislation, Jews could be included in the *ummah* if they were to accept Muḥammad's definition of *kashrut*."[23] This verse, however, is not directed toward Jews (or Christians, for that matter) but rather toward the believers themselves, who are permitted to share food and engage in a certain form of marriage specifically with those who are outside of their community. Friedmann interprets Qur'an 5.5 from the opposite perspective. Drawing on the traditional ascription of this passage to Muḥammad's Farewell Address, he conjectures that "once the great victory of Islam over its adversaries had been assured, the time was ripe to symbolize this victory by permitting the Muslims to take women of the vanquished in matrimony."[24] Friedmann recognizes, however, that his explanation of the verse in light of Islamic superiority fails to account for the permission of Jewish and Christian food as equivalent to that of believers, a permission that expresses a measure of equality between these traditions rather than the subservience of Jews and Christians to the newly dominant Muslims.

Neither Newby nor Friedmann is entirely wrong, however. Qur'an 5.5 indicates that those who were given the Book are part of the holy community of believers in a certain respect, and are inferior to the Qur'an's believers in other respects: They are simultaneously like Us and unlike Us. Jews and Christians are inferior to believers on the conceptual level, in that their scriptures have been superseded by the Qur'an, and also on the social level; the latter is manifest in the well-known tax that People of the Book must pay to their Muslim overlords (9.29). At the same time, those who were given the Book share with their Muslim counterparts a belief in the one true God and a commitment to obeying the divine will as conveyed in authentic revelations. The affinity of all who received a scripture is expressed through the permission of Jewish and Christian food. Qur'anic marriage regulations spell out the relative otherness of different types of non-Muslims in greater detail. People of the Book, as non-Muslims, are inferior to Muslim women but not so inferior as to preclude marriage to Muslim men. Idolaters, in contrast, are inferior even to Muslim slaves and therefore are utterly unsuitable for marriage to a Muslim.[25]

The statement permitting (male) Muslims to take the food and daughters of those who were given the Book is predicated on the presumption that these "goods" meet Qur'anic standards of permissibility. Qur'an 5.5 stipulates that women among the believers and the People of the Book alike must be chaste and must be taken in marriage appropriately, but regards the beliefs of monotheistic nonbelievers, in contrast to those of idolaters, as posing no obstacle to marriage. Similarly, this verse presumes that the food of those who were given the Book, no less than the food of believers, is "good," which is to say that it conforms to the standards of permissibility articulated in previous verses. Although the Qur'an speaks disparagingly of the overly burdensome dietary laws observed by Jews, it never entertains the possibility that either Jews or Christians violate the basic meat-related norms God has established for the believing community. The early Islamic community understood abstention from carrion, blood, and meat offered to idols to be the common heritage of Abraham's spiritual descendants.[26] Both Jewish and Eastern Christian sources, moreover, indicate that members of these communities practiced forms of slaughter in which the butcher invoked God's name and drained the animal's blood.[27] As the Qur'an regularly emphasizes that believers can and should eat all food that is not explicitly prohibited by God, the permission of Jewish and Christian food follows naturally from that food's presumed conformity to Qur'anic norms.

The presumption that Jews and Christians adhere to the dietary norms enjoined upon believers reflects the Qur'an's acceptance of Judaism and Christianity as legitimate religions whose adherents, despite all their faults, observe fundamental divine ordinances. This stance is crucial to the Qur'an's rhetoric about its own authority as the latest and most perfect revelation of God's will. The identity of the Qur'an's community of believers rests not only on establishing the difference between this community and its predecessors but also on establishing the relationship among these communities. The Qur'anic category of Us derives its meaning not from a dichotomy between Us and Them but rather from the existence of a continuum along which the distinction between Us and Them is, at one point, blurred. The permission of food exchange across the border between believers and People of the Book symbolically reflects this blurriness and the affinity that binds all those who have shared the metaphorical table that is God's revelation.

Sūrat al-mā'idah, and verse 5.5 in particular, encapsulate the Qur'an's image of the People of the Book as they stand in relationship to adherents of Islam. The Book which Jews and Christians revere is no less divine than the Qur'an itself and the laws they observe no less authentic than those incumbent upon believers, but some Jews and Christians ignore, distort, or falsify God's teachings. The Qur'an is the culmination of the history of revelation that included the Jewish and Christian Bibles, but Jews and Christians fail to recognize that fact and act with malice toward those who do believe. People of the Book, on account of their sinfulness, will ultimately receive the punishment they deserve, just as the Children of Israel received punitive food restrictions in recompense for their transgressions; in this respect, Jews and Christians are no different from idolaters and unbelievers. Yet while the ultimate superiority of adherents to Islam should be manifest in society, Jews and Christians are less inferior than other nonbelievers by virtue of the Book which God gave them. Qur'anic foreign food restrictions make manifest this difference between the status of People of the Book and other nonbelievers.

Qur'anic discourse about food restrictions and the food of foreigners defines the community of believers as distinct from idolaters and from Jews while highlighting the danger Jews and, to a lesser extent, Christians pose to that community. Nevertheless, finally—indeed, according to traditional authorities, in the Prophet's

Farewell Address—the Qur'an declares that We, members of the nascent Islamic community, are like Them, Jews and Christians. People of the Book are, in certain respects, holy. Jews, Christians, and Muslims partake in the same manner of the food, literal and metaphorical, that God has graciously provided, and permission to consume "the food of those who were given the Book" ascribes normative significance to the relationship that exists among these communities. The fact that some Jews and Christians reject or abuse some of that food neither nullifies this relationship nor prevents Muslims from sharing food with People of the Book. Because Qur'anic passages about food restrictions express a number of overlapping distinctions among foreigners, however, Islamic authorities with fundamentally different conceptions of the relationship between Us and Them have been able to find scriptural support for their contradictory ideas.

10

"'Their Food' Means Their Meat"

Sunni Discourse on Non-Muslim Acts of Animal Slaughter

The importance of food practices as a marker of Islamic identity, implicit in the Qur'anic passages we examined in the previous chapter, is made explicit in a ḥadith (an orally transmitted account of a statement) ascribed to the Prophet Muḥammad: "Whoever recites our prayers and worships in the direction of our *qiblah* and eats the meat of our slaughtered animals, that person is a Muslim who has the protection of God and the protection of His messenger."[1] This ḥadith, which appears as the epigraph to the present unit, encapsulates the definitional issues inherent in Islamic discussions regarding animal slaughter. Jews and Christians do not recite "our prayers" nor, following the so-called *qiblah* controversy of Muḥammad's Medinan years, do they worship facing in the same direction as Muslims.[2] These differences illustrate the fact that Jews and Christians do not belong to the Islamic category of Us. To the extent that these non-Muslims share Islamic standards with respect to animal slaughter, however, Jews and Christians are not simply Them either. We have seen, moreover, that the Qur'an explicitly treats meat prepared by Jews and Christians as equivalent to the meat of animals slaughtered by Muslims. What, then, is the nature of the relationship between People of the Book and Muslims, or between People of the Book and other non-Muslims? The style in which Islamic authorities think about Jews and Christians as "Them," we will see, reflects the style in which these authorities define the meaning of "Us."

The relative otherness of different groups of outsiders rests at the heart of Islamic discourse regarding the permissibility of food associated with foreigners. Sunni authorities uniformly permit the consumption of meat from animals slaughtered by Jews and Christians, commonly referred to in Islamic legal literature as Scripturists (sing. *kitābī*).[3] With only the rarest exception, however, Sunnis do not extend this permission to meat prepared by other non-Muslims, often referred to generically as Magians (*majūs*) even though this term properly refers to Zoroastrians alone.[4] The Sunni distinction between animal slaughter performed by Scripturists and animal slaughter performed by Magians reflects an embrace of the distinction between People of the Book and idolaters, expressed in such verses as Qur'an 5.5: Scripturists, according to Sunni authorities, are more similar to Muslims than are Magians.

Most Shiʿi authorities, in contrast, forbid the consumption of all meat prepared by non-Muslims and even go so far as to treat nearly all food associated with foreigners as impure. These authorities equate Scripturists and Magians, emphasizing and elaborating upon Qur'anic rhetoric that highlights Jewish enmity toward the believers and associates People of the Book with idolaters. This divergence in Sunni and Shiʿi attitudes toward the food of Jews and Christians reflects not only a difference of opinion regarding the relationship that exists between Islam and earlier monotheistic traditions but also, and more fundamentally, a difference in the ways Sunnis and Shiʿis conceptualize Islam itself. As such, discourse about the food of foreigners constitutes one of the numerous fronts in the Sunni–Shiʿi war of ideas regarding authority within the Islamic world.

Islamic law is based not only on the Qur'an but also and especially on the Sunnah, the practice of Muḥammad and those closest to him as reported through thousands of ḥadiths. Sunnis and Shiʿis, however, ascribe legitimacy to different collections of ḥadiths, stemming from different early Islamic figures. Shiʿis—properly speaking, the *Shīʿat ʿAlī*, partisans of ʿAlī—believe that authority to guide the Islamic community after the Prophet's death rests in the hands of his descendants through his cousin and son-in-law ʿAlī b. Abī Ṭālib (d. 660), descendants known as the Imams. Shiʿi ḥadith collections and works of law consequently preserve the statements and practices of Muḥammad and the Imams. The majority Sunnis, in whose collections the ḥadith cited above appears, turn instead to ḥadiths associated with Muḥammad and Muslims who lived during the Prophet's lifetime (Companions of the Prophet) or shortly thereafter (Successors). In doing so, Sunnis assert that authority rests in the practice of the Prophet's community, as understood by its members; for that reason, Sunnis are known formally as *ahl al-sunnah wa-'l-jamāʿah*, those who follow the Sunnah and communal consensus.

Although the primary division within Islamic law is between Sunnis and Shiʿis, each group consists of multiple factions. Sunni authorities eventually coalesced into four schools of legal thought—Mālikī, Ḥanafī, Shāfiʿī, and Ḥanbalī—each oriented toward the teachings of an eponymous eighth- or ninth-century "founder." The three major groups of Shiʿis—the Zaydīs, the Ismāʿīlīs, and the Imāmīs—differ regarding the true chain of Imams; legal scholars within each group orient themselves toward the teachings transmitted within their own particular community. By the tenth century, when these various divisions had crystallized, the contours of Sunni positions regarding foreign food were already fully formed; Shiʿi attitudes on the subject continued to develop into the eleventh century.

The present chapter focuses primarily on Sunni discourse about the food of foreigners.[5] It begins by examining the general status within Sunni law of meat prepared by non-Muslims and then explores two subjects to which Sunni jurists devote particular attention: the definition of slaughter-related acts forbidden to Magians and the status of problematic Scripturists. The issues that preoccupy Sunni jurists who address these subjects, we will see, relate not to the borders of the Islamic community but rather to the boundaries surrounding the larger group of those who received divine revelations. The very differently oriented discourse about foreign food restrictions found in Shiʿi sources is the subject of chapter 11.

SCRIPTURISTS AND MAGIANS ALONG THE SUNNI SPECTRUM OF FOREIGNERS

Sunni authorities downplay the significance of several Qur'anic distinctions between People of the Book and non-Scripturists. Most choose, for example, to interpret the Qur'an's injunction to kill idolaters who do not accept Islam (Q. 9.5) as applying solely to Arabs, thus justifying the practice of offering all non-Arab foreigners the alternative of paying the punitive *jizyah* tax, which Qur'an 9.29 applies solely to People of the Book. These authorities incorporate everyone who pays this tax into the umbrella category of *ahl al-dhimmah,* "protected peoples," imposing upon all *dhimmīs* without distinction a variety of laws intended to reinforce their inferior status within Islamic society. Thus, for example, Scripturists and Magians alike may not serve in positions of authority over Muslims; they may not ride horses, bear arms, build especially tall buildings, adopt honorific titles, or otherwise put on airs of elevated social status; they must, moreover, rise when Muslims wish to sit and provide hospitality to traveling Muslims upon request.[6] Foreign food restrictions, however, differ from most *dhimmī* laws in that they are reflexive rather than imposed: they apply not to foreigners but rather to Muslims themselves, regulating what food a Muslim may or may not eat.[7] Although Sunni authorities apply imposed *dhimmī* laws equally to all foreigners, they do not regard all *dhimmīs* as equal when it comes to the reflexive laws governing Muslim consumption of food associated with foreigners and Muslim marriage to non-Muslim women. Rather, Sunni authorities carefully distinguish between Scripturists and Magians with respect to these laws, and they use foreign food restrictions in particular as a means of relativizing the otherness of different types of non-Muslims. If Muslims are "1" and idolaters are "0," Scripturists fall somewhere around the midpoint of the Sunni spectrum of humanity while Magians fall near its bottom.[8]

Sunni authorities unanimously permit Muslims to eat the food of Jews and Christians, including the meat of the animals these Scripturists slaughter, while forbidding meat prepared by other non-Muslims. This position, unsurprisingly, is commonly grounded in Qur'an 5.5, which the exegete Muḥammad b. Jarīr al-Ṭabarī (d. 923) glosses as follows:

> "And the food of those who were given the Book is permitted to you": And the meat of slaughtered animals prepared by the People of the Book, the Jews and Christians—they are those to whom the Torah and the Gospels were given and revealed and whose religion is based on one or both of them—is permitted to you. God says: It is permissible for you to eat this, in contrast to meat prepared by all polytheists who do not have a scripture, for example Arab polytheists and worshipers of images and statues.[9] As for individuals who are not members of communities that confess the unity of God (whose name is great) and that observe a religion of the People of the Book, the meat of their slaughtered animals is forbidden to you.

Al-Ṭabarī asserts that "food," *ṭaʿām,* means "meat from a properly slaughtered animal," *dhabāʾiḥ.* Qur'an 5.5, he explains, allows Muslims to eat the meat prepared by a Jewish or Christian butcher, to the exclusion of meat prepared by polytheists who lack an authentic scripture. Al-Ṭabarī supports this interpretation with no fewer than twenty statements ascribed to a variety of Companions and Successors and provides no contradictory opinions.[10] In the words of the eminent Companion of the Prophet, ʿAbd Allāh b. al-ʿAbbās (Ibn ʿAbbās, d. 687/8): "'their food' means their meat."[11] Several later authorities offer more elaborate justifications for this interpretation of Qur'an 5.5: *food* is a generic term and therefore must encompass the specific subcategory *meat;* meat is the explicit subject of the previous Qur'anic verses; meat is the only kind of food—in contrast to such foods as bread and olive oil—whose preparation involves a religious ritual such that the identity of the preparer might be relevant.[12]

Sunni authorities also justify the permission of meat from animals slaughtered by Jews (and, by extension, Christians) through appeals to the practice of the Prophet. Upon conquering the Jews of Khaybar, Muḥammad accepts a gift of roasted lamb prepared by one of his new subjects.[13] The Prophet, Sunni authorities observe, considers the meat of an animal slaughtered by a Jew to be a perfectly acceptable foodstuff; the fact that this particular lamb was laced with poison in a failed assassination attempt is legally beside the point. The permissibility of meat from animals slaughtered by Scripturists is further supported by another event associated with the Battle of Khaybar, recounted in most of the major Sunni ḥadith collections.[14] The most expansive account of this incident appears in the *Sīrah,* the hagiography of the Prophet by Muḥammad Ibn Isḥāq (d. ca. 767), known primarily in the recension of ʿAbd al-Malik Ibn Hishām (d. 833 or 828). According to that version, ʿAbd Allāh b. Mughaffal al-Muzanī (d. 676/7) reported the following:

> I took a bag of fat from the booty of Khaybar and carried it off on my shoulder to my companions, when the man who had been put in charge of the spoils met me and took

> hold of the end of it, saying, "Give it to me! We must divide this among the Muslims." I said, "No, by God! I will not let you take this!" He began to try and pull the sack away from me. The Messenger of God saw that we were doing this and smiled, laughing. Then he said to the person in charge of the spoils, "Don't insist—let him have it." So he let go of it and I hurried off to my companions and we ate it.[15]

In most versions of this account, the Prophet says nothing but merely smiles. This smile, however, is regarded by most Sunni interpreters as evidence that Muḥammad objects neither to taking such spoils from the battle before the official distribution of booty nor to the consumption of fat presumed to derive from an animal which a Jewish butcher slaughtered.

The Prophet's nonchalant attitude toward Jewish meat epitomizes and reinforces the Sunni position on the subject of animal slaughter performed by Scripturist butchers who, Sunnis presume, generally adhere to Qur'anic norms on this subject.[16] Neither Muḥammad nor his Sunni successors, however, are similarly sanguine with respect to meat associated with other types of foreigners. Sunni authorities are quick to contend that the Prophet, even as a youth, never ate meat from animals which had been sacrificed to idols, a taboo observed even before the revelation of the Qur'an by the "Abrahamic" Zayd b. ʿAmr b. Nufayl.[17] Many also cite a ḥadith in which Muḥammad instructs his followers to treat Zoroastrians as People of the Book in all respects except for the permission of eating their meat and marrying their women. Among the earliest to cite this tradition is Yaʿqūb Abū Yūsuf (d. 798), one of the founding figures of what came to be the Ḥanafī school of law. Abū Yūsuf teaches: "Although *jizyah* is taken from the Magians, it is not permitted to marry their women nor to eat their meat, as is permitted with the People of the Book. There is no difference of opinion about this."[18] As Qur'an 5.5 refers explicitly to those who were given the Book, its permission cannot apply to other non-Muslims. The only early Sunni authority said to disagree with this distinction between slaughter performed by Scripturists and slaughter performed by Magians is Ibrāhīm b. Khālid Abū Thawr (d. 854), who is sharply condemned for his unorthodox opinion that animal slaughter performed by Magians is no more problematic than that undertaken by Jews and Christians.[19]

The Sunni distinction between meat from animals slaughtered by Jews and Christians on the one hand and Magian meat on the other reflects an embrace of the hierarchical spectrum of humanity implicit in Qur'an 5.5. The most important distinction is between Muslims and non-Muslims, but Sunnis further divide the latter between Scripturists and non-Scripturists and grant this secondary distinction lasting normative significance. Jews and Christians, whose inferiority to Muslims is expressed through imposed *dhimmī* laws and the prohibition against intermarriage with Muslim women, are nevertheless granted limited parity with Muslims in recognition of their adherence to religions that were in fact revealed by God. One might say that if Muslims are holy, Jews and Christians are somewhat holy. Because of this likeness, Scripturist women are suitable partners in marriage and Scripturist acts of ritual slaughter are valid. The exclusion from these permissions of Zoroastrians and other thoroughly mundane foreigners expresses the notion that Magians are more unlike Muslims.

The spectrum of foreigners expressed through discourse about non-Muslim acts of animal slaughter advances conceptions of Islamic identity in various ways, many particular to Sunni authorities. The legitimacy Sunnis grant to Judaism and Christianity as "like Us"—monotheistic traditions founded upon authentic sacred scriptures—serves ultimately to bolster the truth claims of Islam as the successor to these traditions. By including Scripturists within a very broad definition of Us, one might say, Sunnis also enlarge the community of consensus with respect to certain core principles of Islam; recall that the notion of consensus rests at the core of Sunni self-definition. Ascription of correct beliefs to Jews and Christians, moreover, bolsters Sunni claims with respect to the authority vested in the community of Muslims: if even Jews and Christians possess true knowledge, how much more so must Muslims possess such knowledge, especially those who lived during the time of the Prophet. The permission of meat from animals slaughtered by Jews and Christians also makes manifest the permissive nature of Islamic law itself, a theme that Sunni authorities are fond of emphasizing and of contrasting with the exceedingly rigorous norms associated with Jewish law.[20] Additionally, the permission of eating Jewish and Christian meat granted by members of the comfortably ensconced superior community within Islamic society fulfills a social function: it highlights the hierarchical relationship between the dominant Muslims and the subordinate Scripturists which it symbolically and only marginally relaxes.

• • •

The status of foreign meat within Sunni law constitutes a symbolic marker of conceptual categories rather than an incentive for Muslim–Scripturist relations on the one hand or a barrier to interaction with Magians on the other. The permissibility of meat prepared by Jews or Christians does not facilitate interaction over meals to any significant degree. A Magian, moreover, may serve his or her Muslim neighbor quite a range of other foods, and a Sunni may share with Magians meat from an animal which a Muslim slaughtered. Indeed, Muḥammad b. al-Ḥasan al-Shaybānī (d. 804/5), among the founders of the Ḥanafī school, regards as authoritative various traditions permitting the bread, soft cheese, vinegar sauce, and other nonmeat foodstuffs prepared by Magians, and he specifically permits eating with Magians when they mumble in observance of the Zoroastrian practice of not speaking during meals.[21] Other ḥadiths highlight the fact that Muslims are permitted to employ Magians as domestic servants; to eat the fruit Magians pick, the butter they prepare, and the fish they catch; and generally to consume all Magian food with the exception of that which requires ritual slaughter.[22] Just as Biblical dietary law reflects the distinctive status of Israelites without actually separating them from non-Israelities, Sunni law regarding animal slaughter expresses the notion that Scripturists are categorically distinct from Magians without preventing interaction between Muslims and non-Scripturists.

The permission of food-related interaction between Muslims and Magians, however, masks the fact such interaction became increasingly unlikely in the regions of the Islamic world that produced most works of Islamic law. Even if we take estimates of medieval conversion to Islam with the grain of salt they deserve, there is little reason to presume that Muslims living in North Africa, the Near East, or even Iran had many opportunities to eat foods prepared by Zoroastrians or other non-Scripturists, or to abstain from eating the meat of animals slaughtered by such Magians.[23] Nevertheless, Islamic authorities continue to address the status of food associated with Magians throughout the Middle Ages, just as Church councils promulgated laws about Jews even when none are present. A significant reason for doing so, I would suggest, is that discourse about the food of Magians furthers scholastic efforts to clarify important legal categories, both with respect to the act of food preparation and with respect to the distinction between Scripturists and non-Scripturists.[24] Borderline cases related to the act of food preparation, we will see, occupy the attention of Sunni and Shiʿi jurists alike; we observed in chapters 4 and 5 that Rabbinic Sages also devote considerable attention to such cases. Only Sunnis, however, regularly address borderline cases that serve to clarify the identity of non-Muslim food preparers because only for Sunnis does discourse about food serve as a means of defining foreigners with any degree of precision. We will consider each set of cases in turn.

WHAT MAKES MEAT FOREIGN? DISCUSSIONS ABOUT JOINT MUSLIM-MAGIAN HUNTING

Sunni and Shiʿi authorities from across the Islamic world devote considerable attention to scenarios involving a Muslim and a Magian who go hunting together, attention made all the more extraordinary by the fact that most Muslims would have been hard-pressed to find Magian hunting partners. Joint hunting—like joint animal slaughter, joint cooking, and joint baking in Rabbinic literature—constitutes a borderline case useful for identifying which specific actions must be performed by insiders and which may be performed by foreigners. The pedagogical function of these cases accounts for discussions that are in other respects overly extensive, impractical, and, for most Muslims, hypothetical.

In Islamic law, hunting is ritual slaughter by other means, to be employed when the animal one wishes to kill cannot be constrained so that a butcher can slit its throat.[25] The Ḥanafī Abū Bakr b. Masʿūd al-Kāsānī (d. 1189) expresses the implications of this understanding of hunting for discussions regarding the identity of the hunter: "As for one whose slaughtered meat you may eat, in accordance with what we have already stated, eat the game which he hunts with the arrow or the hunting animal. As for one [whose act of animal slaughter] is not [permitted], do not [eat from his game], because the fitness of the butcher is a precondition for all forms of slaughter, the preferable and the unavoidable alike."[26] Because Magians are legally unfit to perform the act of animal slaughter, Muslims may not consume meat from the game they kill either. But what exactly makes the meat of a game animal "Magian"?

Members of the Shāfiʿī school express particular interest in the case of joint Muslim–Magian hunting and develop numerous permutations of this case in order to flesh out the details of various general principles of law. A representative discussion appears in the *Wajīz* of Muḥammad b. Muḥammad al-Ghazālī (d. 1111), an intentionally concise work whose author nevertheless devotes more than half of his discussion about the religious requirements for a butcher to the issue of joint participation in the act of animal slaughter. After stating that the butcher must be a Muslim or Scripturist rather than an idolater or Magian, and after briefly reviewing Shāfiʿī opinions regarding children of mixed marriages (which we will examine below), al-Ghazālī writes:

> If a Magian and a Muslim are partners in the act of slaughter, it is prohibited. The same applies if each sends an arrow or a hunting dog at a game animal. But if one of them strikes the animal first, beginning the act of slaughter, its legal status follows that hunter. If the Magian's dog chases the quarry toward the Muslim's dog, who kills it, its meat is permitted. If the Muslim's dog exhausts the quarry but the Magian's dog then catches it and kills it, the animal is carrion and the Magian must offer compensation to the Muslim.[27]

Joint slaughter—for example, if a Muslim and a Magian each cut only part of the jugular vein—is prohibited because of the principle that prohibition always trumps permission in circumstances when rules leading to both alternatives apply simultaneously. This logic also accounts for the prohibition of game animals killed by the animate or inanimate agents of both a Muslim and a Magian hunter. Al-Ghazālī clarifies, however, that the act of slaughter occurs at the moment the fatal blow is delivered: if a Muslim's dog strikes first and a Magian's dog joins the fray subsequently, the quarry is still permitted for Muslim consumption. Establishing the precise sequence of events, then, is crucial to determining the legal status of game animals, a point emphasized by many jurists; if the sequence is unknown, the meat is prohibited for consumption. Indirect assistance by the Magian hunter—in this case the work of the Magian's dog in chasing the quarry toward the Muslim's dog—is legally insignificant. Al-Ghazālī's final point is that a Muslim acquires ownership of a game animal by exhausting it. If the Magian's dog subsequently kills that animal, rendering it unfit for Muslim consumption, the Magian hunter is required to remunerate the Muslim for property damage.

Various authorities from other schools of legal thought also engage in discussion of joint hunting, sometimes adding further permutations to the mix. Of note is the interest in this subject among Zaydī and, especially, Imāmī authorities, whose discussions frequently echo both the content and language of earlier Shāfiʿī works.[28] If a Muslim hunter uses a dog trained by a Magian, the game this dog catches is permitted for Muslim consumption no less than if a Muslim butcher had used a Magian's knife: what matters is the agent, not the implement.[29] If a Muslim sends his dog and a Magian goads the dog on, thus increasing its speed and helping it to reach its quarry, the animal it kills is permitted: only the direct agent is legally relevant.[30] If a Muslim and a Magian jointly send the same dog, whatever it kills is prohibited: when both permission and prohibition apply, the prohibition trumps.[31] If a non-Muslim sends his dog and converts to Islam before the dog reaches its quarry, the game is nevertheless prohibited for consumption because the person who sent the dog was not Muslim at the time of sending it. (Conversely, if a Muslim apostasizes between the time he sends the dog and the time the dog kills the quarry, the game remains permitted.)[32]

It is hard to imagine that any Muslim could keep all of these regulations straight while pursuing game in the company of a Magian hunting partner, an action that itself is never prohibited or even discouraged. Nor does it seem likely that jurists were actually interested in regulating the behavior of Muslim hunters. Rather, the question of joint hunting seems to have taken on a life of its own in scholastic contexts as a framework within which to consider the implications of laws prohibiting animal slaughter by foreigners and, specifically, to articulate the precise definition of slaughter in the context of hunting. There is no reason to assume that Islamic authorities were familiar with the similar discussions found in Rabbinic literature or to attribute the scholastic mode of thinking found in both Jewish and Islamic sources to common origins. Borderline cases are an obvious mechanism for clarifying legal categories, and the need to define "food prepared by foreigners" is intrinsic to the very notion of preparer-based foreign food restrictions. Discussions of borderline cases like joint hunting, however improbable they may be, thus play an important pedagogical and classificatory role in Islamic as well as Jewish and Christian legal discourse.

WHO IS A SCRIPTURIST? BORDERLINE CASES ONLY SUNNIS CARE ABOUT

Sunnis, as we have seen, hold that "animal slaughter performed by all Muslims and Scripturists is permitted, but the meat of [animals slaughtered by] Magians and idolaters is not permitted."[33] Borderline cases involving joint Muslim–Magian hunting expeditions serve to clarify the second half of this rule by defining "the meat of Magians." Sunnis employ other cases to clarify the first half of this rule through elucidation of the term *Scripturists.*[34] One such case relates to the children of mixed Scripturist-Magian parentage.[35] Mālik b. Anas (d. 795) and members of the Mālikī school hold that the child's religion always follows that of the father; these jurists apply to the children of non-Muslim parents the same legal principle that applies to children of Muslim fathers and Scripturist mothers.[36] Some Shāfi'ī jurists affirm Mālik's opinion, while others follow the opinion of the school's eponymous founder, Muḥammad b. Idrīs al-Shāfi'ī (d. 820), who prohibits meat slaughtered by all butchers of mixed Scripturist-Magian parentage on the basis of a principle we have already encountered, namely that conflicts between permission and prohibition are resolved by following the restrictive alternative.[37] Ḥanafī authorities advance a more permissive stance than their Shāfi'ī counterparts: a child born to a Scripturist and a non-Scripturist is a Scripturist because, as al-Kāsānī explains, the law presumes that the child would adopt the superior religion.[38] Discourse about children of mixed parentage provides a forum for debating which generic legal principles ought to apply in borderline cases, as well as a means of determining the precise contours of the border between Scripturists and non-Scripturists.

The preeminent Imāmī jurist Muḥammad b. al-Ḥasan al-Ṭūsī (d. 1066/7) addresses both the Ḥanafī and Shāfi'ī opinions but dismisses this dispute as irrelevant because, according to Shi'is, all non-Muslims are unfit to perform the act of animal slaughter.[39] Thus, while Shi'i jurists participate actively in discussions regarding joint Muslim–Magian hunting, they take no part in Sunni discussions that clarify the border between Scripturists and non-Scripturists. Rabbinic Sages, who treat all gentiles as equally "not Us," also see no need to address borderline cases of this nature. Sunni discourse about problematic Scripturists illuminates a distinctive element of Sunni thought regarding foreigners, namely their treatment of Jews and Christians as "like Us." Opinions regarding the food of borderline Scripturists reveal both the reasons that underlie this style of thought and the limits of Sunni tolerance with respect to Jews and Christians.

Some cases involving problematic Scripturists, like those involving joint Muslim–Magian hunting, are clearly devoid of practical relevance, serving only to clarify the boundaries of legal categories. Numerous authorities, for example, address the permissibility of meat from animals slaughtered by Sabians (*ṣābi'ūn*). Modern academics have been unable to identify the Sabians, listed in the Qur'an alongside Jews and Christians among those communities whose faithful will receive God's reward (Q. 2.62, 5.69; cf. 22.17); many scholars, in fact, hold that Sabians never actually existed.[40] During the Middle Ages, Sabians survive solely within the imagination of Islamic jurists and exegetes, but this fact does not prevent Islamic authorities from addressing the laws that apply to meat prepared by such imagined individuals.[41] Aḥmad b. Muḥammad al-Ṭaḥāwī (d. 933) reports that although Abū

Ḥanīfah al-Nuʿmān b. Thābit (d. 767) permitted Sabian meat on the grounds that Sabians, like Christians, believe in a scripture, the other "founders" of the Ḥanafī school, Abū Yūsuf and al-Shaybānī, disagreed because Muslims do not recognize the legitimacy of the Sabian scripture.[42] Maḥmūd b. ʿUmar al-Zamakhsharī (d. 1144) offers a different account of the opinion held by Abū Yūsuf and al-Shaybānī. Sabians, he reports in their names, actually constitute two distinct groups: "One group recites the Psalms and worships angels; the other group does not have a scripture to recite and worships stars, and these are not of the People of the Book." Meat associated with the former group is permitted, but not that of the latter.[43] Other authorities permit Sabian acts of animal slaughter on the grounds that the Sabians are quasi-Jews who keep the Sabbath or that Sabians constitute a subset of Christianity.[44] Still others condemn the consumption of Sabian meat on the grounds that Sabians fall upon the spectrum between Christianity and Magianism because of their belief in the influence of the stars, or perhaps they fall somewhere between Judaism and Magianism and have no religion.[45] These opinions—and similar statements regarding the Samaritans, who do at least exist[46]—indicate that the elevated status among non-Muslims which Sunnis accord to Scripturists derives from and depends specifically upon the fact that Scripturists revere at least some portion of the Bible.

The most hotly contested case of problematic Scripturists within Sunni discourse involves the Banū Taghlib, a large and powerful Monophysite tribe in Iraq often portrayed in legal literature as emblematic of Arab Christians in general.[47] Numerous tradents report that ʿAlī, the Prophet's cousin and son-in-law (d. 660), declared, "You may not eat the meat of animals slaughtered by the Christians of the Banū Taghlib"—or, in some versions, "by Arab Christians"—"because they do not adhere to any tenet of Christianity except the drinking of wine!"[48] Al-Shāfiʿī, in the *Kitāb al-umm,* cites this tradition approvingly, along with a caustic statement attributed to the second caliph, ʿUmar b. al-Khaṭṭāb (d. 644), that Arab Christians are not People of the Book in any respect.[49] Other early authorities, including Ibn ʿAbbās (d. 687/8), the eminent Syrian traditionist Ibn Shihāb al-Zuhrī (d. 742), and the Kufan jurists Ibrāhīm al-Nakhāʿī (d. 714) and al-Shaʿbī (d. 720s) have no qualms about the Banū Taghlib and their slaughter. Ḥadiths associated with these figures often cite prooftexts indicating that conversion to Judaism or Christianity remains possible (Q. 5.51) and that some members of these communities do not really know the contents of books they revere (2.78). Arab Christians may be recent Christians or ignorant Christians, but they are Scripturists nonetheless and entitled to treatment as such.[50]

At stake in the early debate over the status of animal slaughter performed by members of the Banū Taghlib is the legitimacy of Arabs who embrace a religion other than Islam. The Qur'an, after all, is God's revelation to the Arabs, so toleration of Arab Christians is fraught with greater implications than toleration of other Christian communities.[51] The notion that all Arabs ought to be Muslims accounts for 'Umar's particular anger toward Arab Christians and 'Alī's assertion that the Banū Taghlib merely wish to remain free of Islam's prohibition against alcohol. Refusal to tolerate outsiders who are "too close for comfort" and therefore especially threatening is a phenomenon which we have encountered in other traditions as well. Recall that Rabbinic authorities prohibit the meat of animals slaughtered by heretics to a greater degree than meat prepared by gentiles, and that early medieval bishops permit commensality with pagans but prohibit members of their flock from eating with Jews. Some Christian authorities expressly articulate their fear that toleration of Jewish dietary practices might undermine belief in the authority of the New Testament. A similar concern regarding the threat posed by a group of unduly similar outsiders seems to underlie restrictive Sunni traditions regarding Arab Christians. Permissive authorities, in contrast, seem to feel that Arab Christians pose no particular threat to the Qur'an and therefore refuse to limit the scope of the Qur'anic permission of Scripturist animal slaughter.

Although al-Shāfi'ī cites the ethnically oriented statements of 'Alī and 'Umar approvingly, he himself shifts the terms of debate regarding Arab Christians from ethnicity to chronology. Al-Shāfi'ī distinguishes between those who converted to Judaism or Christianity before the revelation of the Qur'an and those who converted afterward: he permits meat prepared by the descendents of early converts but prohibits meat prepared by more recent converts and their descendents.[52] What concerns al-Shāfi'ī is the principle that Islam constitutes the perfect religion, a principle threatened by toleration of converts who choose Judaism or Christianity over Islam. Islam, he asserts, tolerates those who were grandfathered into Scripturist religions, whatever their ethnicity or original faith tradition; pre-Islamic converts, after all, associated themselves with the best form of religion then in existence. Those who convert to Judaism or Christianity after the time of Muḥammad, however, effectively reject their obligation to believe not only in God but also his final Prophet. Muslims, al-Shāfi'ī maintains, cannot condone the rejection of this basic Islamic truth claim. Al-Ṭabarī, in contrast, rejects al-Shāfi'ī's opinion as having no basis in either Qur'an or ḥadith. He insists that Muslims interpret the Qur'anic permission of "the food of those who were given the Book" as referring to all Scripturists, including all converts to Judaism and Christianity.[53]

While Ḥanafī, Ḥanbalī, and Mālikī authorities consistently hold that conversion is not an impediment to full Scripturist status, adherents of the Shāfi'ī school frequently cite with approval their founder's distinction between early and late converts.[54] Yaḥyā b. Sharaf al-Nawawī (d. 1277) offers an even more elaborate version of this distinction in his discussion of animal slaughter performed by Jewish and Christian butchers. In one category, he places both butchers directly descended from the original Children of Israel and those whose ancestors converted to Judaism or Christianity before these traditions were corrupted: it is to these people that the Qur'an refers when permitting the food and women of those who were given the

Book. The Qur'an's permissions, he states, do not apply to the descendants of those who converted after the revelation of the Qur'an. Al-Nawawī assigns Scripturists who do not know precisely when their ancestors converted to this second category; this position may be the basis for restrictions imposed upon Jewish butchers by Shāfiʿī courts in fourteenth-century Jerusalem.[55] As for butchers whose ancestors converted to Judaism or Christianity between the time their religion became corrupted and the time of its abrogation by the Qur'an, al-Nawawī places them into his first category only if they adhere to the true elements of their religion (as defined by Islamic authorities, of course) while avoiding the corrupt aspects. Al-Nawawī also considers the status of Jews whose ancestors converted before the time of Muḥammad but after that of Jesus.[56]

Al-Nawawī's distinctions are utterly impracticable: not only is it unrealistic to expect that Scripturist butchers could document in detail a millennium or more of ancestry, Islamic authorities themselves are uncertain about when Judaism and Christianity became corrupted and whether Jesus abrogated Judaism in whole or just in part. Practicality, however, is not the motivating factor behind al-Nawawī's reasoning. What interests him are the classificatory implications of Islamic conceptions regarding Judaism and Christianity as made manifest through the permissibility of acts of animal slaughter. The same may also be said regarding earlier and simpler statements on the subject of ethnically or chronologically problematic Scripturists. At stake is not the permissibility of meat prepared by specific non-Muslim butchers but rather the definition of "Scripturists" as a category of religious foreigners.

Sunni discussions of problematic Scripturists reflect the scholastic mode of thinking which Islamic authorities employ when considering relationships among religious communities within the ideal social order. These discussions occur within ivory-tower seclusion: information about non-Muslims derives from the Qur'an and from legal reasoning, not from encounters with foreigners, let alone the manner in which non-Muslims define themselves. The most important characteristic of Scripturists, from the perspective of Sunni authorities, is evidently their reverence for part or all of the Bible, whose authority underpins the greater authority of the Qur'an itself. Many of these discussions, moreover, reinforce the conclusion reached in the first section of this chapter, namely that the legitimacy Islam accords to Judaism and Christianity through the permission of Scripturist acts of animal slaughter ultimately serves to bolster the legitimacy of Sunni truth claims. It is because of this notion that various Sunni authorities, Shāfiʿīs in particular, are unwilling to extend legitimacy to Scripturists who, by their very affiliation with a religion other than Islam, challenge core principles of Islam. Shiʿis, we will see, eliminate the distinction between Scripturists and non-Scripturists in the course of defending a somewhat different set of Islamic principles.

11

"Only Monotheists May Be Entrusted with Slaughter"

The Targets of Shiʿi Foreign Food Restrictions

In sharp contrast to their Sunni counterparts, who carefully distinguish Scripturists from Magians when discussing acts of animal slaughter, classical Shiʿi authorities make a point of treating all non-Muslims alike with respect to their foodstuffs. Muḥammad b. al-Ḥasan al-Ṭūsī (d. 1066/7), regarded as the last and greatest of the early Imāmī authorities, authored the definitive expression of Imāmī opinions regarding the food of foreigners, one that aptly summarizes classical Zaydī attitudes as well.[1]

> Ritual slaughter may not be performed by non-Muslims. Whenever an unbeliever of any sort of unbelief—whether a Jew, Christian, Magian, or idolater—performs the act of ritual slaughter, whether he mentions God's name during this act or does not mention it, one may not eat the resulting meat. . . . All food which unbelievers handle or touch with their bodies is not permitted for consumption; because they are impure, food becomes polluted through their contact with it. God has been lenient in the permission of using grain and similar foods that do not contract impurity even when [non-Muslims] touch them with their hands.[2]

Not only does al-Ṭūsī reject the fitness of Scripturists and Magians alike to perform the act of animal slaughter, he declares that all non-Muslims suffer from a communicable form of impurity that renders most foods they touch polluted. Only dry and unprocessed foodstuffs like grain, which are not susceptible to contracting circumstantial pollution, are excluded from this general prohibition of food associated with foreigners. Sunnis, in contrast, express no concern that the touch of a non-Muslim renders foodstuffs impure, although some worry that non-Muslim dishes might contain trace remnants of wine or forbidden meat.[3]

Just as the limited legitimacy which Sunnis grant to Scripturists through the permission of Scripturist meat serves to bolster the legitimacy of Sunni conceptions regarding the community of Muslims, Shiʿi refusal to distinguish between Scripturist and non-Scripturist butchers supports distinctly Shiʿi conceptions of Islam. Indeed, Shiʿi rejection of Sunni norms regarding the foodstuffs of non-Muslims functions as a form of anti-Sunni polemic. Whereas Jewish and Christian foreign food restrictions distinguish insiders from the outsider targets of these restrictions, Shiʿi foreign food restrictions serve primarily as a means of distinguishing Shiʿis from Sunnis: We are those who refuse to eat the food of non-Muslims. The true target of Shiʿi foreign food restrictions, therefore, is the Sunni community; Jews and Christians, one might say, get caught in the intra-Islamic crossfire.[4]

Shiʿis face an uphill battle in their efforts to justify prohibitions against nearly all foodstuffs associated with all non-Muslims. The Qur'an, after all, distinguishes People of the Book from idolaters, declaring that "the food of those who were given the Book is permitted to you" (5.5). The second section of this chapter examines the manner in which Shiʿi authorities reconcile their positions with those expressed in the Qur'an. This examination provides the opportunity to reflect on the use of scripture within Jewish and Christian discourse about foreign food restrictions as well. Neither the Hebrew Bible nor the New Testament, after all, provides evident support for many of the statements articulated by later interpreters of these works either. The chapter's final section analyzes Sunni and Shiʿi discourse regarding cheese, a borderline case that reveals the affinities between Islamic authorities at loggerheads with one another.

SHIʿI DISCOURSE REGARDING THE MEAT AND OTHER FOODSTUFFS OF NON-MUSLIMS

The opinions expressed by al-Ṭūsī regarding non-Muslim impurity and acts of animal slaughter are first articulated in the eleventh century. The earliest sources regarded as authoritative by Shiʿi authorities, in contrast, do not differ from their Sunni counterparts with respect to these subjects.[5] Consider, for example, the statement on this subject found in the late eighth-century *Majmūʿ al-fiqh:*

> Zayd b. ʿAlī (d. 740) reported to me from his father from his grandfather from ʿAlī [b. Abī Ṭālib (d. 660)], peace be upon him, who said, "The meat of animals slaughtered by Muslims is permitted to you if they mentioned the name of God over it, and the meat of animals slaughtered by Jews and Christians is permitted to you if they mentioned the name of God over it, but you may not eat the meat of animals slaughtered by Magians or Arab Christians, for they are not of the People of the Book.[6]

Zayd, regarded as an Imam by his followers, the Zaydīs, reports that ʿAlī both acknowledges and ascribes normative significance to the distinction between Scripturists and Magians; as we saw in Sunni sources, ʿAlī pointedly excludes Arab Christians from the former category. ʿAlī emphasizes that the invocation of God is an essential and absolutely required component of the act of animal slaughter, but he takes for granted that People of the Book are competent to utter such an invocation. There are indications that the *Majmuʿ al-fiqh* and other early works of Zaydī law also distinguish between Scripturists and other non-Muslims with respect to issues associated with impurity.[7]

Later Zaydī authorities hold that all acts of animal slaughter performed by non-Muslims are invalid "even though it is well known that Zayd b. ʿAlī would permit meat prepared by Jews and Christians."[8] The Zaydī al-Qāsim b. Ibrāhīm al-Rassī (d. 860), for example, discourages purchasing meat from Jews and Christians "because they are not among those who can be entrusted with [the invocation of God], as they include impermissible [words] in it."[9] The "Four Books," the authoritative collections of Imāmī ḥadith, contain several traditions according to which Jaʿfar al-Ṣādiq, revered by Imāmīs as the Sixth Imam (d. 765), prohibits meat produced through Jewish and Christian acts of animal slaughter for this very reason. In other ḥadiths, Jaʿfar declares that such acts are invalid "whether they invoke [God] or not": "[the essence of] ritual slaughter is the name [of God], and none but monotheists [*ahl al-tawḥīd*] may be entrusted with it." By "monotheists," Jaʿfar clearly means "Muslims," the term found in an otherwise identical statement preserved in a separate ḥadith.[10] Jaʿfar's statements call into question the monotheistic credentials of Jews and Christians.

Other statements ascribed to Jaʿfar in the Four Books, in contrast, allow Muslims to consume meat prepared by any butcher who invokes God properly, regardless of the butcher's religious tradition. In one such ḥadith, Jaʿfar explicitly permits ritual slaughter performed by Jews, Christians, Magians, and "all others who dispute the religion [of Islam]," even as he acknowledges that ʿAlī forbade Muslims to eat meat prepared by Magians and Arab Christians.[11] In these traditions, the validity of slaughter performed by Jews and Christians has nothing to do with possession of an authentic scripture but rather stems the fact that Qur'an 6.118 enjoins Muslims to "eat that over which the name of God was mentioned" without further specification.[12] This permissive stance is endorsed by al-Nuʿmān b. Muḥammad (d. 974), chief jurist of the Fātimid Empire and the foremost legal authority within the Ismāʿīlī branch of Shiʿism, and by Muḥammad b. ʿAlī Ibn Bābawayh (or Ibn Bābūyah, d. 991/2), a prominent Imāmī jurist.[13]

Ninth- and tenth-century Shiʿi authorities, along with the ḥadiths they cite, offer different bottom lines regarding the permissibility of non-Muslim meat but agree that there is no meaningful distinction between Scripturists and other non-Muslims, the opinions of Sunni authorities and even of ʿAlī himself notwithstanding. These sources attest to a new and distinctly Shiʿi conception of the People of the Book, one in which possession of an authentic scripture is legally insignificant. Sunnis, in deference to Jewish and Christian reverence for the Bible, regard Scripturists as "like Us" and therefore place Scripturists in the middle of a spectrum whose poles are marked by Muslims and idolaters. Shiʿi discourse about foreign food restrictions emphasizes that Jews and Christians are "unlike Us" while endorsing an effectively binary conception of humanity that sets Muslims on one side and all non-Muslims on the other.[14]

I suggested in chapter 10 that the elevated status of Scripturists within Sunni discourse serves in part to enlarge the community of consensus regarding core principles of Islam and to bolster Sunni claims regarding the authority possessed by the community of Muslims as a whole. The permission of meat from animals slaughtered by Jews and Christians symbolically reinforces the "big tent" conceptions regarding communal identity and the diffusion of knowledge endorsed by Sunnis. Shiʿi assertions that People of the Book are equivalent to other non-Muslims, in contrast, undermine these conceptions in favor of an elitist model. Indeed, these assertions advance a distinctly Shiʿi understanding of Islam: true knowledge of God and the divine will is accessible only through the teachings of the Imams. Thus, for example, one ḥadith reports that a Christian marveled at the knowledge displayed by Jaʿfar al-Ṣādiq—"By God! He is the most knowledgeable among humans, the most knowledgeable among all that God has created!"—when the Imam informed his followers that Christians invoke Christ rather than God during their acts of animal slaughter.[15] Traditions like this imply that Sunnis, who do not acknowledge the esoteric knowledge possessed by the Imams, lack crucial information and are consequently prone to transgression.

The *Īḍāḥ*, a work of anti-Sunni polemic pseudonimously ascribed to Abū Muḥammad al-Faḍl Ibn Shādhān (d. 873/4),[16] subjects Sunnis to ridicule and condemnation on account of their willingness to eat meat prepared by Jews and Christians. Such behavior, the author argues, puts Muslims at risk of violating the injunction of Qurʾan 6.121: "Do not eat [meat] from that over which the name of God has not been mentioned; it is indeed a sinful act. The devils inspire their friends to dispute with you; but if you obey them, then you will surely become idolaters." Sunnis, however, blindly trust their Jewish enemies to mention God's name properly when performing the act of ritual slaughter and even twist the meaning of Qurʾan 5.5 to permit meat from animals that Christians slaughter in the name of Christ![17] The *Īḍāḥ* cites a ḥadith in which Muḥammad's confidant Abū Bakr (d. 634), a Sunni hero, expresses remorse for never having asked the Prophet about the permissibility of Jewish and Christian slaughter practices. If Abū Bakr was unsure about whether Muslims may eat Jewish and Christian meat, pseudo–Ibn Shādhān exclaims, on what basis can Sunnis be certain of their claims? "So which of the two factions is right in safeguarding itself from that which ought to be feared," he asks in conclusion, "the one that stays clear of [non-Muslim meat] or the one that audaciously approaches it?" The willingness of Sunnis to consume meat prepared by Jews and Christians demonstrates their ignorance and unconscionable laxness, in contrast to the piety that characterizes Shiʿis.

Ninth- and tenth-century Shiʿi statements regarding non-Muslim meat consistently focus on the actions of non-Muslims. Restrictive authorities express concern that Jewish and, especially, Christian butchers might fail to invoke God or might invoke a being other than God during their act of ritual slaughter, while permissive authorities allow meat prepared by non-Muslim butchers because and on condition that they perform the act of slaughter in accordance with Islamic norms. Eleventh-century Zaydī and Imāmī authorities, in contrast, emphasize the beliefs of non-Muslims, not their behaviors. Whereas the ninth-century al-Qāsim forbids the purchase of Jewish and Christian meat on the grounds that Jews and Christians include inappropriate language in their divine invocation, Mu'ayyad bi-'llah Aḥmad b. al-Ḥusayn (d. 1020), a fellow Zaydī, declares such meat prohibited on the grounds that Jews and Christians, like Magians and Muslim apostates, are unbelievers (*kuffār*).[18] The Imāmī jurist and theologian Muḥammad b. Muḥammad al-Mufīd (d. 1032) also treats Jews and Christians as unbelievers no different from idolaters because they do not truly understand God or the divine will. After all, al-Mufīd observes, if Jews and Christians possessed accurate knowledge they too would reject Trinitarian theology, abstain from wine, and acknowledge the authenticity of Muḥammad's prophecy. Because non-Muslim butchers are ignorant about God, they are unfit to invoke God and therefore incapable of performing a valid act of ritual slaughter.[19] In the words of al-Mufīd's disciple, ʿAlī b. al-Ḥusayn al-Sharīf al-Murtaḍā (d. 1044), "Even when they do invoke God's name, they actually invoke other than God, exalted be He, because they do not know God on account of their unbelief (*kufr*)."[20] Once non-Muslims are defined as categorically unfit to invoke God, there can be no grounds for permitting their acts of animal slaughter; al-Ṭūsī, in his ḥadith collections, makes a point of explaining away traditions to the contrary as referring solely to cases of necessity.[21]

The delegitimation of Jewish and Christian acts of animal slaughter on the grounds that non-Muslims lack true knowledge of God furthers Shiʿi efforts to delegitimize the knowledge possessed by Sunnis. Only through the Imams, Shiʿis teach, can one acquire true understanding of the divine will. The equation of People of the Book and idolaters, moreover, lays the groundwork for the more incendiary assertion that Sunnis hostile to the Imams are also equivalent to idolaters: those who reject the authority of the Imams, whom God has selected as the proper leaders of the Muslim community, by definition spurn God's will and thus cannot be true Muslims.[22] Shiʿi authorities further highlight the contrast between their own norms regarding non-Muslim meat and those of their Sunni persecutors by authorizing Shiʿis to practice dissimulation in the presence of hostile Sunnis who might harm Shiʿis refusing to eat such meat.[23] These statements portray Sunnis as functionally equivalent to the Greek and Roman authorities who demanded that Jews and early Christians consume food offered to idols. Shiʿis equate Jewish and Christian acts of animal slaughter with idolatry, but their primary animus is not directed toward Jews or Christians; rather the subjects of condemnation are Sunnis who insist that Muslims ought to consume the meat prepared by Scripturists.

At the same time that Shiʿi authorities develop a blanket prohibition against meat prepared by non-Muslims, they also formulate a conception of non-Muslim impurity that effectively places most other foodstuffs prepared by non-Muslims off-limits for Shiʿi consumption. Early Shiʿi sources ascribe impurity solely to Magians and idolaters, but the notion that all non-Muslims are equally impure becomes dominant concurrently with the notion that all non-Muslims are equivalent with respect to their acts of animal slaughter. Imāmī ḥadith collections attest to the presence of differing ideas regarding the implications of non-Muslim impurity: some traditions indicate that such impurity is communicable to Muslims via prepared foodstuffs, while others express concern solely about foodstuffs that might contain impure ingredients such as pork or wine. The latter position persists into the early eleventh century, when it is endorsed by al-Mufīd, but from the middle of that century onward Imāmīs and Zaydīs alike consistently hold that the impurity intrinsic in non-Muslims is itself communicable to foodstuffs, which are therefore prohibited for Muslim consumption.[24] The Shiʿi move toward ascribing a contagious form of intrinsic impurity to non-Muslims occurs in the wake of the decisive Sunni shift away from ascribing such impurity to any human being and may constitute an intentional rejection of that development.[25] It should come as no surprise that Shiʿis also deem as impure Sunnis hostile to the Imams.[26]

Al-Murtaḍā formulates the argument that proves decisive in establishing the notion that foods touched by non-Muslims are impure; it is probably not coincidental that this argument appears in a polemical work defending Imāmī norms distinct from those of the Sunnis. Regarding the Imāmī contention that "all food touched by an unbeliever—a Jew, a Christian, or anyone else whose unbelief has been established with clear evidence—is prohibited," al-Murtaḍā cites the Qur'anic prooftext, "truly, the idolaters are impure (*najas*)" (9.28). Non-Muslims, al-Murtaḍā explains, are intrinsically impure (*najis*) in a literal and not merely a figurative sense, and for that reason food touched by non-Muslims becomes impure. Of those foods associated with foreigners, Shiʿis may only consume "grains and the like," the phrase al-Murtaḍā uses to refer to dry, unprocessed foods not susceptible to contracting impurity. The distinction between unprocessed "natural" and processed "cultural" foodstuffs, central to Lévi-Strauss's interpretation of food symbolism, is manifest in Rabbinic and Eastern Christian discourse as well. The reason non-Muslims are impure—and, we have seen, the reason their acts of animal slaughter are invalid—is that they embrace false beliefs (*kufr*).[27] Al-Ṭūsī, in the citation with which this chapter begins, reiterates the position of al-Murtaḍā regarding both the invalid nature of non-Muslim acts of animal slaughter and the impurity of other non-Muslim foodstuffs; subsequent Imāmī and Zaydī authorities follow suit.[28]

The definition of all non-Muslims as idolaters, manifest in Shiʿi discourse regarding both animal slaughter and impurity, collapses the gradated spectrum of humanity articulated by Sunnis into an effectively binary system that resembles the Rabbinic Jew-gentile dichotomy.[29] Indeed, both systems reflect the notion that We alone possess true knowledge of God's will. Shiʿi ascription of impurity to non-Muslims also calls to mind Christian assertions regarding Jewish impurity, a state which both Shiʿis and Christians associate with the false theology of the Jews. In both cases, impurity rhetoric serves to forcibly distance outsiders deemed too close for comfort. The similarities between Shiʿi discourse about the food of foreigners on the one hand and that of Jewish and Christian authorities on the other, however, are largely superficial. Unlike the similarity we observed in chapter 9 between Qur'anic and early Christian discourse about Jews, these similarities do not stem from parallel applications of the same concepts regarding foreigners.

Shiʿi and Jewish authorities alike define all foreigners as idolaters and place them all at the "0" mark on their respective spectrums of humanity. Shiʿis, however, make a point of equating Scripturists and idolaters through their discourse about the food of foreigners whereas Jewish authorities simply fail to distinguish among types of gentiles when discussing foreign food restrictions. Shiʿi food restrictions do not merely mark foreigners as "non-Muslims," they highlight the degree to which foreigners are "unlike Muslims" so as to contrast Shiʿi norms with those of Sunnis. The ascription of impurity to Scripturists furthers this goal: the impure cannot possibly be like Us, holy by virtue of Our adherence to the divine will. Although Shiʿis and Christians alike employ impurity rhetoric, they use it for different purposes. Christians brand Jews as impure "anti-Christians" ("-1") in order to define Jews as heretics, but Shiʿis brand Jews and Christians as impure in order to define *Sunnis* as heretics, in part because of false Sunni beliefs with respect to the status of Scripturists.[30] The real target of Shiʿi discourse about the food of Jews and Christians are not Scripturists themselves but rather Sunnis. Indeed, if there is a "-1" on the Shiʿi spectrum of humanity, the bearers of this dubious distinction are "anti-Shiʿi" Sunnis.

"GRAINS" AND AGAINST-THE-GRAIN SCRIPTURAL INTERPRETATION

Shiʿi authorities are well aware that their prohibitions of nearly all foodstuffs associated with non-Muslims seem to contradict the evident meaning of the Qur'an's declaration that "the food of those who were given the Book is permitted to you" (Q. 5.5). These authorities, moreover, recognize the importance of this verse in Sunni discourse about acts of animal slaughter and its potency in polemic against the more restrictive Shiʿi norms. For these reasons, Shiʿis make a point of reconciling Qur'an 5.5 with their conceptions of religious foreigners and proper dietary practices. The ability of Shiʿis to effectively redefine the meaning of this verse reflects the fact that Shiʿi ideas, shaped by the Qur'an, also shape the meaning of the Qur'an itself within the Shiʿi community. The dialectical nature of the relationship between the Qur'an and Shiʿi thought exemplifies Wilfred Cantwell Smith's definition of "scripture" as "a relation between a people and a text." More broadly, Smith observes, "at issue is the relation between a people and the universe, in light of their perception of a given text."[31] Shiʿi perceptions of Qur'anic discourse about the food of foreigners, reinforced through the use of Qur'anic prooftexts in anti-Sunni polemics, reflect and reinforce the manner in which Shiʿis imagine the place of their own community within the broader social universe.

Shiʿi authorities may disregard the evident meaning of Qur'an 5.5, but their ideas regarding non-Muslim acts of animal slaughter are most certainly in keeping with other Qur'anic statements. Recall that the Qur'an itself equates Scripturists and idolaters in certain contexts. Shiʿi discourse regarding animal slaughter, moreover, orients itself toward a pair of verses in *Sūrat al-anʿām:* "Eat from that over which God's name was mentioned . . . and do not eat from that over which the name of God has not been mentioned" (6.118, 121). Even the earliest Shiʿi authorities, who distinguish Scripturists from Magians, emphasize the importance of these norms: the *Majmūʿ al-fiqh,* for example, cites ʿAlī as specifying that meat prepared by Jewish, Christian, or Muslim butchers is only permitted for consumption if the butcher invoked God. The authorities we encountered above who permit the meat of properly slaughtered animals irrespective of the butcher's religious identity support their stance by appeal to 6.118, while those who regard all meat prepared by non-Muslims as unfit for consumption often cite verse 121. Whether permissive or restrictive, norms based on these verses need not distinguish among types of foreigners. Indeed, we will see in chapter 13 that Sunni authorities struggle to preserve such a distinction while reconciling the permissive 5.5 with restrictive verses like 6.121.

For those who believe that the requirement of a proper invocation is paramount and that Jewish and Christian butchers either cannot be trusted to perform this vital task or are incapable of doing so effectively, the Qur'an's permission of "the food of those who were given the Book" cannot possibly refer to meat. Thus the Imāmī exegete ʿAlī b. Ibrāhīm al-Qummī (fl. ca. 900) explains that "by 'their food,' God refers to grain and fruit, to the exclusion of the meat which they have slaughtered, for they do not mention the name of God over their slaughter."[32] Similarly, restrictive ḥadiths associated with Muḥammad al-Bāqir (the fifth Imāmī Imam, d. ca. 735) and Jaʿfar al-Ṣādiq explain that this verse refers to grains, lentils, chickpeas, legumes in general, and similar foodstuffs.[33] The *Īḍāḥ,* in the course of its anti-Sunni polemic, contends that Qur'an 5.5 refers exclusively to "food that does not have the breath of life."[34] Al-Mufīd, who cites 6.121 as proof that the term *food* in Qur'an 5.5

cannot refer to Jewish or Christian meat as Sunnis claim, explains that "the word 'food' in its generic sense refers specifically to breads and nourishing grains, to the exclusion of meat." Elsewhere, al-Mufīd explains the verse as referring to "their grains or dairy products" or, perhaps, to meat prepared by Jews and Christians who have converted to Islam.[35]

Al-Mufīd and his predecessors employ the Qur'an's prohibition against animal slaughter performed without a proper invocation of God in 6.121 to limit the scope of the Qur'an's own permission of "the food of those who were given the Book" to nonmeat foodstuffs. Al-Murtaḍā, al-Mufīd's disciple, instead interprets Qur'an 5.5 in light of a different prooftext: "Truly, the idolaters are impure" (9.28). As we observed above, al-Murtaḍā ascribes a communicable form of intrinsic impurity to non-Muslims on account of their false beliefs. For that reason, al-Murtaḍā insists that one must understand Qur'an 5.5 as referring solely to pure foodstuffs, like grains. Just as the Qur'an surely does not permit eating pork prepared by Jews or Christians, it must not permit eating other impure foods either.[36]

Al-Murtaḍā's argument elegantly justifies the restrictive statements found in earlier Shi'i sources regarding not only non-Muslim acts of animal slaughter but also the impurity of non-Muslim foodstuffs. What makes this argument so brilliant as an act of scriptural exegesis is the way it reframes earlier statements in a wholly original manner. To the best of my knowledge, no earlier Shi'i authority interprets Qur'an 9.28 as evidence for the impurity of all non-Muslims and their foodstuffs.[37] When earlier authorities interpret Qur'an 5.5 as referring to "grains and the like," moreover, they use grain as an example of a non-meat foodstuff. Al-Murtaḍā redeploys this traditional interpretation as a reference to foods that are not susceptible to contracting impurity, namely natural foodstuffs that remain dry and unprocessed. He chooses to overlook earlier statements, including those of al-Mufīd, that allow Muslim consumption of Jewish and Christian foods susceptible to contracting impurity, such as fruit, fish, bread, and dairy products.

Al-Murtaḍā, having internalized the teachings of his Imāmī predecessors, takes for granted that all religions other than Islam are tantamount to idolatry, that all idolaters are intrinsically impure, and that foodstuffs prepared by non-Muslims consequently become polluted. Through the unprecedented act of grounding these convictions in Qur'an 9.28, al-Murtaḍā is able to draw upon the authority of the Qur'an itself to support distinctly Shi'i conceptions regarding religious foreigners and to neutralize the Qur'an's own permission of Jewish and Christian foodstuffs. Western scholars commonly assume that Shi'i notions regarding the impurity of non-Muslims stem from this interpretation of Qur'an 9.28, but, historically, the reverse is true: the classic Shi'i interpretation of Qur'an 9.28 retroactively justifies preexisting Shi'i notions regarding the impurity of non-Muslims.[38] Shi'i authorities shape the meaning of the text at the core of their own educational curriculum through a dialectical process that ensures an ongoing fit between the community and its scripture.

Shiʿi authorities who believe that there is no significant difference between Jews and Christians on the one hand and Magians and idolaters on the other cannot imagine that the Qur'an might suggest otherwise. These authorities, therefore, interpret Qur'an 5.5 against its natural grain—in this case by limiting its impact to grains. The most persuasive among these authorities do so by marshaling not only supporting statements of the Imams but also prooftexts from elsewhere in the Qur'an to bolster their interpretations. The limits and focus of the interpreter's imagination not only constrain the potential meanings of the Qur'an but also expose exegetical possibilities latent in the Qur'anic text. Al-Murtaḍā's application to all non-Muslims of the Qur'anic dictum, "Truly, the idolaters are impure," is an elegant case in point. To those who already regard all non-Muslims as tantamount to idolaters and ascribe impurity to their food, this prooftext offers both compelling logic for their claim and an unimpeachable source for its accuracy. Indeed, al-Murtaḍā's reading of this verse justifies in admirable fashion the Imāmī practice of reading Qur'an 5.5 as referring to grains, and his interpretation is so compelling that subsequent Imāmī and Zaydī authorities employ it consistently. Only an outside observer might notice that this interpretation of Qur'an 9.28 runs against the grain not only of the Qur'anic text itself but also the manner in which Sunnis and even early Shiʿis understand both this verse and the Islamic system of impurity more broadly.

Al-Murtaḍā and his colleagues are not the only religious authorities we have encountered who seek to reconcile their own norms regarding foreigners and food practices with scriptural texts whose evident meaning contradicts those norms. Various Jewish and Christian authorities also engage in what an outside observer might call the innovative misinterpretation of scripture. (We have not encountered such activity among Sunni authorities in this study because Sunni norms regarding foreigners and their food conform to those evident within the Qur'an itself.) The presence of against-the-grain interpretations within the Jewish, Christian, and Islamic traditions alike provides further support for Wilfred Cantwell Smith's contention that the common denominator uniting all members of the literary genre we call scripture is the dialectical nature of the relationship between the text and its community of interpretation.

Recall that R. Shimʿon b. Yoḥai and R. Yoḥanan interpret Biblical verses that authorize the Israelites to obtain food and water from foreigners as referring exclusively to foodstuffs which, like water (and, al-Murtaḍā would add, grain), remain in their natural state. This entirely nonevident explanation of *Deuteronomy* 2.6 and 2.28, like Shiʿi interpretations of Qur'an 5.5, reconciles traditional prohibitions against foods prepared by foreigners with a scriptural verse that appears to contradict them. The redactors of the Bavli, we observed, interpret the statements of earlier Sages in radically original ways as well. Because the redactors regard these statements as no less "scriptural" than those found in the Hebrew Bible, they must reconcile these statements with their own norms. Al-Ṭūsī does the same with ḥadiths that permit the consumption of meat prepared by Jewish and Christian butchers deemed by later authorities as unfit to perform the act of animal slaughter.

Augustine's willful elimination of the Apostolic Decree's prohibitions against blood and the meat of animals whose blood has not been drained offers an especially clear example of the redefinition of a scriptural passage along the lines later used by Shiʿi authorities like al-Murtaḍā. The Apostolic Decree, like its Qurʾanic counterparts, enjoins Christ-believers to abstain from blood, the meat of animals that have been strangled to death, and food offered to idols (*Acts* 15.28–29). Augustine's interpretation of the Decree in *Answer to Faustus* 32.13 vividly illustrates Paula Fredriksen's observation that this work constitutes "a book of scriptural reclamation": Augustine seeks to reconcile the New Testament with the practices of his own Christian community while combating claims that scripture supports Manichean practices such as the abstention from certain foods.[39] To that end, Augustine asserts that the Decree's prohibition against blood, if not in fact an allegorical reference to bloodshed, was merely a temporary measure intended to bridge the gap between Jewish and gentile Christ-believers. The prohibitions against blood and the meat of strangled animals, he declares, no longer bind Christians. "If perhaps there are still a few who are afraid to touch these things [i.e., improperly slaughtered birds and rabbits], they are laughed at by all the others. Thus in this matter that statement of the Truth has hold on the minds of all: 'It is not what enters your mouth that defiles you but what comes out of it' [*Matt.* 15.11]."[40] Augustine explains the Old Testament's prohibition against carrion as nothing more than a sensible medical precaution, although one has to wonder why earlier Christian authorities (e.g., Canons of the Apostles, c. 63) would have required something so obvious. He cites Paul to demonstrate that although Christians must abstain from food known to have been offered to idols, there is nothing intrinsically wrong with such food itself.[41]

Both Augustine and al-Murtaḍā engage in similar efforts to reinterpret scriptural passages that contradict accepted conceptions of proper dietary practice (see figure 9). They begin from a culturally conditioned premise that scripture cannot mean what it appears to mean: the Apostolic Decree could not possibly establish a permanent prohibition against consuming certain foodstuffs because We eat foods it prohibits, the Qurʾan could not possibly permit all Jewish and Christian foodstuffs because We know that They are impure. Each of these authorities is also motivated by a polemical impulse that gives urgency to the task of scriptural reinterpretation. Both appeal to commonly-held knowledge within their own community—no (Latin) Christian cares about eating meat whose blood has not been drained, the food of non-Muslims is impure (according to Shiʿi authorities)—and both clinch their arguments by means of a prooftext from elsewhere in scripture. The end result is the reconciliation of scripture with the community's evolving presumptions, values, and worldviews, as well as the "reclamation" of a contested text from heretics who offer a contrary interpretation.

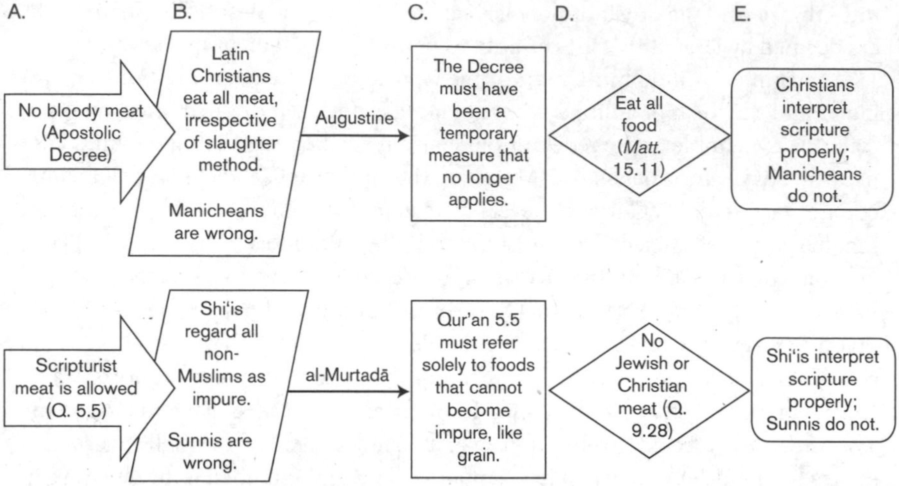

FIGURE 9. THE IMPACT OF SCRIPTURAL INTERPRETATION: AUGUSTINE AND AL-MURTAḌĀ. (A) Traditional texts and practices (givens), (B) when viewed through internalized cultural paradigms, (C) take on new meanings that, (D) when articulated in normative terms, (E) externalize new ideas about Us and Them.

The Bible, the Qur'an, and other works that achieve the status of scripture within Jewish, Christian, and Islamic communities exercise profound influence on subsequent discourse regarding foreigners and their food, but these works do not predetermine the outcomes of such discourse. The divergence of Sunni and Shi'i positions regarding the relative otherness of Scripturists and the status of their foodstuffs clearly illustrates the fundamental yet limited role of the Qur'an in shaping Islamic thought. Sunnis and Shi'is ground their very different conceptions and norms in the same Qur'anic texts, but the meaning of these texts within each community derives from the particular interpretive dialectic that occurs within the community's elite circle of scholars. Jewish and Christian authorities also shape the meaning of the very texts that shape their own ideas; the evolution of the "hermeneutical Jew" within Christian thought to encompass characteristics originally associated with heretics and idolaters offers a case in point. Religious authorities imagine members of other religions within a framework shaped by sacred texts and traditions, but their own imaginations also play a significant role in shaping that framework. Norms that seek to preserve the proper relationship between Us and Them develop within this multifaceted and continuously evolving matrix of ideas about identity and the proper social order. Indeed, the evolutionary dynamic encapsulated in figure 9 (as well as figures 4 and 5) applies to most, if not all, instances of development within religious thought about foreigners and their food.

SUNNIS, SHIʿIS, AND PROBLEMATIC CHEESE

The present chapter, like the authorities whose ideas it examines, focuses primarily on the differences between Sunnis and Shiʿis with respect to norms regarding the food of non-Muslims and the meaning of associated Qurʾanic verses. Indeed, thus far we have observed more similarities between Shiʿis and Jews or Christians than we have between Shiʿis and Sunnis. Lest we end on such a misleading note, the final section of this chapter examines a borderline case—cheese prepared by non-Muslims—that demonstrates the close affinities between Sunni and Shiʿi discussions of foreigners and their food. Michael Cook, in a detailed and carefully argued article tracing the evolution of Islamic discourse on this subject, finds no substantive difference between Sunnis and Shiʿis: although some authorities affiliated with each of these groups prohibit cheese prepared with rennet derived from an animal that is not slaughtered properly, most find ways to prove that such cheese is unproblematic.[42] There is, in fact, a significant difference between Sunni and Shiʿi treatment of this subject which Cook overlooks, but his overall impression is correct: Sunnis and Shiʿis address the same borderline case, apply the same scholastic mode of thought, and reach the same conclusions using many of the same arguments. It is proper, therefore, to speak of pan-Islamic and not merely Sunni and Shiʿi discourse with respect to foreign food restrictions. Islamic discourse on this subject, moreover, is quite distinct from its Jewish and Christian counterparts, similarities notwithstanding. Examination of the case of foreign cheese can help us clarify the nature of the relationship between the conversations about food and foreigners occurring in each of our religious traditions.

Hard cheese (Arabic, *jubn*) offers an ideal borderline case in legal systems that regulate animal slaughter: it is commonly made with an ingredient derived from dead animals, namely rennet, yet cheese is not commonly perceived as a meat product and does not serve comparable caloric, social, or religious functions in the Near East. We observed in chapter 4 that Rabbinic Sages debate the status of cheese associated with gentiles and devote particular attention to issues related to rennet. Dozens of Islamic authorities also address the permissibility of cheese produced with rennet derived from a prohibited animal. The classic test case for Sunnis involves cheese made by Magians.

Sunni traditions present cheese as a quintessentially Iranian, and thus Zoroastrian, food; indeed, Muḥammad and his Arab companions seem to be unfamiliar with this exotic foodstuff. Aḥmad b. al-Ḥusayn al-Bayhaqī (d. 1066) reports that when Muḥammad conquered Mecca and encountered a piece of cheese, he exclaimed, "What is this?" His companions replied, "This is food made in the land of Iran."[43] A ḥadith cited by Aḥmad b. Ḥanbal (d. 855), eponymous founder of the Ḥanbalī school, also associates cheese with Iran and identifies the relevance of this origin: "We think it was made with carrion."[44] Because Magian slaughter is by definition improper and hence equivalent to carrion, one can readily argue that cheese made from a product of Magian slaughter is forbidden for Muslim consumption. A handful of early authorities reportedly adhere to this logic; these authorities prohibit cheese known to contain rennet from carrion, specifically include Magian cheese under the rubric of prohibited Magian slaughter, or permit only cheese made by Muslims, Jews, and Christians.[45] The most prominent Sunni proponent of the prohibition of Magian cheese is Mālik b. Anas, many of whose followers also object to the use of carrion-derived rennet.[46] The prohibition of foreign cheese also appears in Zaydī literature: according to al-Hādī ilā al-Ḥaqq Yaḥyā b. al-Ḥusayn (d. 911), "it is reprehensible [to eat] the cheese made by Scripturists and Magians because they make them with the rennet of carrion."[47] As Mu'ayyad bi-'llah explains, animals slaughtered by foreigners are legally equivalent to carrion, so the rennet they use in making cheese, by definition, comes from carrion.[48]

Most Sunni and Shi'i authorities, however, find ways to render the problematic origins of rennet legally irrelevant. One apparent motivation for these efforts is expressed in several traditions cited by the Imāmī collector Aḥmad b. Muḥammad al-Barqī (d. ca. 893/4). "Someone asked Abū 'Abd Allāh [Ja'far al-Ṣādiq], peace be upon him, regarding cheese, and he said, 'Truly, eating it is pleasing to me!' He then called for it and ate it." Ja'far's father, Muḥammad al-Bāqir, also expressed his fondness for cheese.[49] The Sunni traditionist 'Abd Allāh b. Muḥammad Ibn Abī Shaybah (d. 849) reports that Ibn 'Abbās and 'Abd Allāh b. 'Umar especially enjoyed Iraqi cheese.[50] Love of cheese does not constitute the legal basis for its permission, but these traditions may point to an underlying motivation for finding ways to permit problematic cheese. Food restrictions have costs, both economic and gastronomic, that Islamic authorities may have wished to minimize in certain circumstances. R. Yehudah ha-Nasi's encounter with an attractive loaf of gentile bread may similarly have prompted his permission of that foodstuff (B. *A.Z.* 35b).

Islamic authorities employ four basic approaches to permitting the consumption of Magian cheese. The first approach is to deny the existence of any problem. Cheese, according to proponents of this argument, is not meat at all and therefore cannot be forbidden on the grounds of improper animal slaughter. As the caliph 'Umar b. al-Khaṭṭāb reportedly said when asked about rennet, "Truly, milk cannot die [*yamūt*]!" that is, it cannot become carrion (*maytah*).[51] Numerous Shi'i traditions report that Ja'far permits not only rennet derived from carrion but also such items as horns, hoofs, bones, teeth, fangs, hair, wool, feathers, eggs, and milk.[52] According to what Cook calls the "exception theory," the improper death of an animal affects only its meat; the rest of the carcass and its contents are excepted from the prohibition of carrion and regarded no differently than if proper slaughter had occurred.

A variant of the exception theory involves reference to the Qur'an. A tradition found in multiple Sunni collections reports that the Prophet, asked about the permissibility of clarified butter, cheese, and animal pelts, replied, "The permissible is that which God permitted in His Book, and the prohibited is that which God prohibited in His Book, and that which He passed over in silence is that which He absolves from guilt."[53] According to this argument, the very logic that extends the prohibition of Magian meat to cover cheese made from Magian rennet is flawed because the Qur'an implicitly exempts cheese from its food restrictions.

The second approach Islamic authorities employ when permitting problematic cheese relies on what Cook labels the "ignorance theory": if you don't know that the cheese is problematic, you don't have to worry about it. When ʿUmar b. al-Khaṭṭāb's son, ʿAbd Allāh (d. 693), was asked about Magian cheese, he declared, "I buy what I find in the Muslim markets, and I don't ask questions about it." (The person reporting this statement, Ibn ʿUmar's client Nāfiʿ [d. 730s], commented dryly upon his return from Iran, "If Ibn ʿUmar had seen the Magians do what I've seen them do, I think he would have declared this reprehensible!")[54] In the words of Muḥammad al-Bāqir, "If you know that [cheese] contains carrion then you may not eat it, but if you do not know, then buy and sell and eat. By God, when I go to the market, I buy meat and butter and cheese there and—by God—I don't think that all of those Berbers and blacks mention the name [of God]!"[55] Sunni and Shiʿi traditions alike encourage the practice of not asking too many questions in the marketplace.[56] In one Shiʿi ḥadith, Jaʿfar declares that cheese should be presumed to be made of permitted ingredients and insists that two witnesses to the use of rennet derived from carrion are required to overrule that presumption.[57]

A third and related argument for the permission of all cheese, attested solely in Shiʿi sources, involves what Cook refers to as the "mixture theory." Several traditions report that Muḥammad al-Bāqir, asked to explain the permission of all cheese, states: "Everything that contains permitted and prohibited ingredients is permitted to you unless you yourself recognize the prohibited ingredient and can name it."[58] In this variant of the what-you-don't-know-can't-hurt-you argument, what matters is not that most food sold in the Muslim marketplace is permissible but that most of the content of the specific foodstuff in question—and all of its evident content—is permissible. By this logic, all cheese, even that which definitely contains carrion-derived rennet, would be permitted in principle because the prohibited substance is not evident once it is mixed with milk.[59]

Sunni sources attest to a fourth method—a "ritual theory"—of permitting all cheese: even if Magian cheese contains rennet from a prohibited source, a Muslim can render the cheese fit for consumption through performance of a ritual act. A particularly colorful account preserved in several forms by Ibn Ḥanbal illustrates this case. The Prophet was brought a piece of cheese, and his companions—apparently because they suspected that it contained rennet from carrion—began to beat it with a stick. Muḥammad, however, instructed them to "take a knife to it, mention God's name over it, and eat it."[60] This tradition seems to regard the standard Islamic invocation of God prior to eating as sufficient to render Magian cheese fit for consumption, as if such cheese was no different from any other foodstuff. Similar instructions, sometimes without reference to the knife, can be found in several other traditions, including one found in an Imāmī collection.[61]

Cook suggests that the early Islamic prohibition of foreign cheese and the "exception theory" used to overcome this prohibition derive from Rabbinic sources. (Recall that the Sages grant an "exception" from the general prohibition against eating the meat of improperly slaughtered animals to rennet derived from the stomach contents of such animals.) Cook recognizes that similarities between Jewish and Islamic law do not necessarily indicate a genetic link connecting the two traditions, primarily because both draw on a common Near Eastern heritage. He contends, however, that because the similarities in this case are so close and unusual, they can best be explained in terms of such influence.[62] In fact, concern about rennet is not as unusual as Cook assumes it to be, and on close examination the exception theories articulated in Islamic sources bear little relation to their Rabbinic counterparts.

Among those who regulate meat preparation or consumption and are aware of how cheese is made, concern about rennet is natural. Indeed, Jews and Muslims are not unique in regarding cheese as a meat product. Bishops gathered in Constantinople at the seventh-century Council in Trullo, for example, declare that during Lent Christians "should abstain from all manner of meat, as well as from eggs and cheese, these being the fruit and products of the things from which we abstain."[63] The Rabbinic exception theory, moreover, is quite different from the version attested in Imāmī sources. The Sages treat stuff in an animal's digestive tract as if it is in the hole of a doughnut—not part of the animal's body—whereas Imāmīs exclude all nonmeat animal parts from the prohibition of carrion. The grouping together of rennet and bones would make no sense in a Rabbinic context.[64] While the Sages too are relatively lenient regarding certain foods found in the marketplace and have standard formulas for disregarding small quantities of prohibited foodstuffs when mixed with permitted ingredients, they do not apply these arguments in the case of cheese made from gentile rennet. Indeed, the Sages go out of their way to maintain the prohibition of gentile cheese despite grounds for its permission, whereas most Islamic authorities attempt to do the opposite.

The similarities between Rabbinic and Islamic discussions of problematic cheese are conceptual rather than necessarily genetic: there is no reason to posit the influence of one discussion upon the other because the ideas common to both most likely developed independently. Both communities of legal interpreters dwell on the topic of cheese because the distinctive characteristics of this foodstuff make it an ideal borderline case through which to work out nuances of the law in a scholastic setting. Just as discussions of joint slaughter and joint hunting serve the pedagogical function of defining with precision who has killed an animal, discussions of cheese define the extent to which improper slaughter affects the status of that animal's constituent parts. There is no reason to think that Islamic discussions of joint slaughter were inspired by their Rabbinic counterparts (found only in the relatively obscure Tosefta), and, similarly, no reason to presume that Muslims were familiar with or inspired by the details of Rabbinic cheese regulations. The similarities we observed in Jewish, Christian, and Islamic approaches to the reconciliation of scripture and communal norms are similarly conceptual rather than genetic in nature. It is possible that similarities between early Christian and Qur'anic portrayals of Jews reflect the influence of the former upon the latter, but these similarities could just as easily derive from the application of common concepts that developed independently.

Because borderline cases serve to flesh out the precise boundaries of legal categories, differences in their outcomes from one interpretive community to the next highlight the presence of different underlying systems of classification. The Imāmī permission of both rennet and bones from carrion, for example, stems from a style of thought that classifies animal products as meat or nonmeat, whereas the Sages distinguish between what is inside the body and what is outside. The subtle difference between Imāmī and Sunni statements permitting cheese made with such rennet, unnoticed by Cook, reflects the different styles in which these authorities think about non-Muslims. Whereas Sunni sources uniformly address Magian cheese, Imāmī authorities refer specifically to rennet derived from carrion, not cheese prepared by Magians or other non-Muslims. To the best of my knowledge, the sole Imāmī tradition that specifically addresses Magian cheese is restrictive: "There is no harm in eating any cheese, whether made by a Muslim or another, but it is reprehensible to eat something like rennet that has been in the vessels of the Magians and the People of the Book because they are not cautious about carrion and wine."[65] Foreign rennet, according to this tradition, becomes polluted by direct or indirect contact with the intrinsically impure foodstuffs used by foreigners; as a result, it is reprehensible to eat foreign cheese. Although al-Murtaḍā and later Imāmī authorities do not address the topic of cheese in their synthetic works, they would most probably regard all cheese made by foreigners as polluted and thus forbidden for consumption on the grounds that the intrinsic impurity of non-Muslims is communicable to moist and processed foodstuffs. The difference in the borderline cases discussed by Sunnis and Shiʿis—Magian cheese on the one hand, cheese made with rennet derived from carrion on the other—reflects the different ways these Islamic authorities think about non-Muslims.

Sunnis and Shiʿis define non-Muslims differently, but they employ many of the same sources, questions, interpretive strategies, and modes of thinking when discussing foreigners and their food. These authorities speak the same language, literally and metaphorically, and Shiʿis like al-Murtaḍā and al-Ṭūsī clearly understand themselves to be in dialogue with their Sunni counterparts. Indeed, it is precisely because Sunnis and Shiʿis engage in a common discourse about foreigners and their food that the latter are able to use this discourse as a means of setting Shiʿis apart from the larger Sunni community. Shiʿi efforts to define Sunnis as anti-Shiʿi—and, one might add, Christian efforts to define Jews as anti-Christian—highlight the degree to which We and They are in fact similar in many respects.

HERMENEUTICAL FOREIGNERS AND THE COMMON TABLE

In chapter 8, we encountered Jeremy Cohen's concept of "the hermeneutical Jew," an offspring of scripturally infused Christian imagination that bears scant resemblance to the actual Jews whom Christians might encounter in their daily lives. The image of the hermeneutical Jew, however, is not designed to be accurate but rather to be useful: the hermeneutical Jew, as an embodiment of all that orthodox Christianity rejects, serves a crucial function in the creation of Christian identity. Islamic authorities also draw upon their own scripturally infused imagination to construct hermeneutical Jews, as well as hermeneutical Christians, Magians, and idolaters. These imagined foreigners likewise function as foils for the construction of Islamic identity, albeit in a more nuanced fashion than their Christian counterpart. Despite their reverence for the same Qur'anic text, however, Sunnis and Shiʿis formulate radically different hermeneutical foreigners. These differences reflect both the inherent malleability of the meaning ascribed to texts revered as scripture and the differences between Sunni and Shiʿi conceptions of Islamic identity itself. We can understand the relationship between Sunni and Shiʿi versions of the hermeneutical foreigner by returning to the metaphor of the common table developed in our earlier discussion of *Sūrat al-māʾidah.*

The Qur'an, we observed, portrays Jews, Christians, and Muslims alike as recipients of the same holy sustenance and as adherents of the same basic set of dietary regulations even as it rebukes Jews and Christians for their rejection of the Prophet and for their hostility toward his community of believers. Jews and Christians are thus simultaneously "like Us" and "unlike Us." Sunnis employ discourse about the food of foreigners to highlight the similarity between Muslims and Scripturists while contrasting this relationship with that of Muslims and Magians. These authorities go so far as to debate the status of children from Scripturist-Magian intermarriages and of imagined foreigners like Sabians in order to establish with greater clarity the distinction between Scripturists and other non-Muslims. Shiʿis, in contrast, downplay this distinction and, indeed, the very relationship between Muslims and People of the Book. They instead highlight the degree to which Jews and Christians are unlike Muslims in their practices and beliefs: whereas Sunnis insist that Muslims and Scripturists alike eat of the same meat, Shiʿis assert emphatically that this cannot be the case.

The difference between Sunni and Shiʿi portrayals of Jews and Christians, however, stems not only from different conceptions of Them but also from the application of different definitions of Us. Sunnis choose to draw expansive borders around the broadly defined community of believers while Shiʿis opt instead for highly constrained borders that exclude many of those whom Sunnis include. The Shiʿi common table, one might say, is considerably smaller than its Sunni counterpart, and it has no room for those who are insufficiently "like Us." Sunni and Shiʿi images of the hermeneutical foreigner result both from the attributes ascribed to that figure and from the positioning of that figure relative to the boundaries of Our community.

The hermeneutical foreigner at the center of classical Shiʿi discourse about foreign food restrictions differs considerably from that of the Qur'an itself. We have seen, however, not only that Shiʿis are able to reconcile these different images of Jews and Christians but also that such differences are commonplace. Among the communities examined in this study, it is the Sunnis who are atypical in their close conformity to the portrayal of foreigners found in scripture.

Sunnis are also atypical in their use of discourse about foreign food restrictions to convey precise and nuanced conceptions of identity, both Ours and Theirs. The Christian hermeneutical Jew is a blunt instrument, roughly hewn and useful for clobbering one's opponents. Its Sunni counterpart, in contrast, is finely tuned: Sunni norms governing Jews and Christians are carefully calibrated to express the ways in which They are like Us even while highlighting through *dhimmī* regulations the inferiority that befits those who are not Us. Indeed, we have seen that Sunni discourse about foreign food restrictions is distinctive in its orientation toward marking the boundary not between insiders and outsiders but between different degrees of outsiders. Shiʿis calibrate their hermeneutical foreigner carefully as well, but not for the purpose of providing a nuanced depiction of non-Muslims: Shiʿis position their Jewish and Christian foils in such a way as to reflect well on Shiʿis and poorly on Sunnis. In contrast to their Christian, Sunni, and Shiʿi counterparts, the Jewish authorities we have encountered thus far do not employ foreign food restrictions as a means of constructing hermeneutical foreigners at all. If anything, the Jewish discourse we examined earlier conveys the message that gentiles are not worth thinking about in any detail.The different nature of these hermeneutical foreigners reflects, not only the different styles in which Islamic, Christian, and Jewish authorities think about the relationship between Us and Them, but also, and more fundamentally, the different styles in which these authorities imagine the identity of their own community.

PART V

Comparative Case Studies

Engaging Otherness

To man the world is twofold, in accordance with his twofold attitude.

The attitude of man is twofold, in accordance with the twofold nature of the primary words which he speaks.

The primary words are not isolated words, but combined words.

The one primary word is the combination I–Thou.

The other primary word is the combination I–It; *wherein, without a change in the primary word, one of the words* He *and* She *can replace* It. . . .

If It *is said, the* I *of the combination* I–It *is said along with it*. . . .

There is no I *taken in itself, but only the* I *of the primary word* I–Thou *and the* I *of the primary word* I–It.

MARTIN BUBER, *I AND THOU*

12

"Jewish Food"

The Implications of Medieval Islamic and Christian Debates about the Definition of Judaism

The final part of this work builds upon the conclusions regarding the emergence of Jewish, Christian, and Islamic foreign food restrictions developed in earlier chapters. Explicitly comparative in nature, the case studies in the following chapters depart from the single-tradition focus that characterizes each of the preceding parts. For these reasons, it is appropriate to preface the present chapter with a synopsis of the conclusions of parts I–IV and an introduction to all three of the remaining chapters.

LOOKING BACK, AND LOOKING FORWARD

Foreign food restrictions, like all aspects of culture, are both products and shapers of the human imagination. As Peter L. Berger has observed, humans "externalize" themselves, using both physical and mental activity to collectively produce the ordered and meaningful world which they inhabit. Through what Berger terms "objectivation," this cultural world and its constituent elements become givens, both as things distinct from the human beings who created them and as forces powerful enough to shape human thought and behavior. Thus, to cite some of Berger's examples, humans invent a plow and then cannot help but structure their agricultural activity in accordance with the plow's capabilities and limitations; they invent a language and then cannot help but think in terms of its grammar; they invent norms and then cannot help but feel obligated to obey them. Through "internalization," Berger's term for enculturation, the individual human being absorbs into his or her own subjective consciousness the externalized and objectivated products of a community's collective consciousness, embracing to a greater or lesser degree the way in which that community orders and interprets its world.[1]

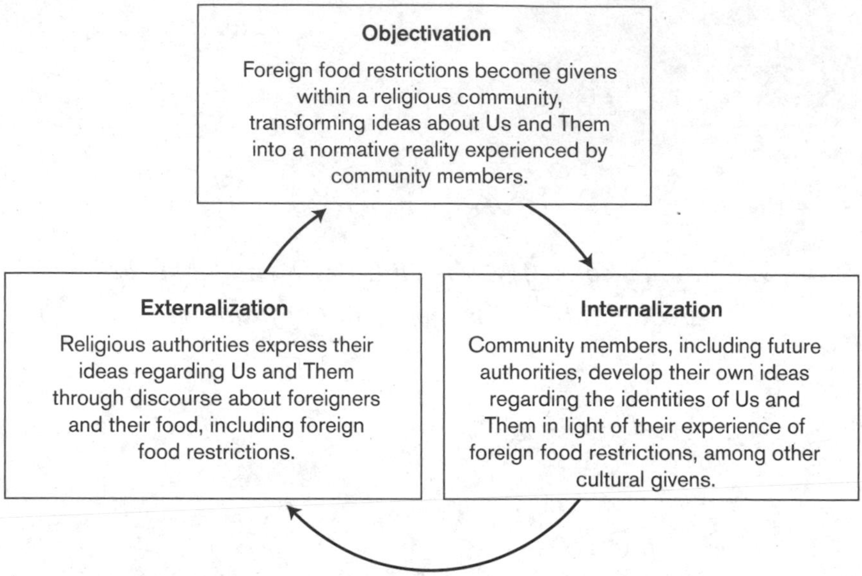
Objectivation
Foreign food restrictions become givens within a religious community, transforming ideas about Us and Them into a normative reality experienced by community members.
Externalization
Religious authorities express their ideas regarding Us and Them through discourse about foreigners and their food, including foreign food restrictions.
Internalization
Community members, including future authorities, develop their own ideas regarding the identities of Us and Them in light of their experience of foreign food restrictions, among other cultural givens.

FIGURE 10. FOREIGN FOOD RESTRICTIONS AND THE TRANSMISSION OF IDEAS ABOUT US AND THEM. An application of Peter L. Berger's dialectical theory of society.

Applying Berger's terminology to religious discourse regarding foreign food restrictions (see figure 10), we may say that such discourse externalizes the worldviews of those who participate in its production, interpretation, and dissemination. We have seen that the ideas and values expressed through discourse about foreigners and their food relate to issues of communal identity and the proper ordering of human society: how and why We differ from Them, how and where the lines between Us and Them are drawn, how members of Our group ought to interact with and, indeed, imagine Them. The worldviews expressed through this discourse, interesting in their own right, become important as intellectual forces through the processes of objectivation and internalization, by means of which they outlive their creators and shape the ideas and practices of future generations. Foreign food restrictions—laws that confront Jews, Christians, and Muslims as real and authoritative givens—transform traditional worldviews into givens by establishing normative barriers to social intercourse along imagined lines separating Us and Them, and, perhaps more importantly, by portraying these lines to be self-evidently significant. Food restrictions, although not always intended to do so, constitute an ideal medium through which to translate ideas about Us and Them into reality because of the significant biological and social roles which food and meals play in human culture: We may only ingest food prepared by or shared with those who are sufficiently similar to Us to pose no danger to Our identity. Those who observe these restrictions at meals internalize not only nutrients but also the worldviews the restrictions transmit. Enculturation into a community's food-related practices, especially when accompanied by the study of scholarly discourse about these practices, fosters the intergenerational continuity both of communal identity and of associated ideas regarding foreigners and the proper social order. We have seen that these ideas evolve when other cultural givens (e.g., Hellenistic ideas or Rabbinic scholasticism) shape the internalization of traditional notions or when especially creative religious authorities (e.g., Augustine and al-Murtaḍā) introduce new interpretive twists.[2]

The ideas externalized through discourse about foreign food restrictions, objectivated in the norms themselves, and internalized through adherence and study relate to the classification of foodstuffs and, more importantly, of foreigners. Underlying these classificatory systems is a desire on the part of religious authorities to articulate and enact the imagined identity of their own communities by means of distinguishing Us from Them, a distinction which different religious communities imagine in qualitatively different styles. We have seen, however, that Jewish, Christian, and Islamic authorities alike employ common techniques to further their distinct classificatory agendas. Representatives of all three traditions employ scholastic modes of thinking, including reflection on pedagogically oriented borderline cases. These authorities all make use of impurity rhetoric to highlight the distinction between insiders and certain groups of particularly significant outsiders. They also all engage scriptural texts in innovative ways, especially for the purpose of constructing ideologically useful hermeneutical foreigners.

Two implications of a Bergerian depiction of the dialectical relationship between religious communities and their foreign food restrictions deserve emphasis in the present context. First, these restrictions, like all cultural products, are not created once and for all: the longevity of these norms depends on the degree to which members of religious communities continue to ascribe value to them. Medieval authorities, we will see, go out of their way to reaffirm traditional foreign food restrictions and their underlying conceptions of foreigners. This phenomenon attests not only to the power of traditional norms in shaping the ideas and practices of those who study them but also to the importance that medieval authorities, having internalized traditional foreign food restrictions, ascribe to these norms. We will also see that medieval authorities introduce subtle but significant changes in these norms and their underlying ideas. They do so by means of the same processes of externalization through which the norms were originally created, including the application of scholastic forms of analysis and the innovative interpretation of canonical texts.

Second, the ideas about foreigners that become cultural givens through foreign food restrictions—and, thus, that become internalized by members of future generations and externalized once more through their own words and deeds—reflect the imaginations of those who produce, interpret, and disseminate these norms. As Berger reminds us, cultural phenomena like foreign food restrictions are products of human minds: in this case, specifically Jewish, Christian, or Islamic minds. We have had repeated occasion to observe that the style in which insiders imagine outsiders varies from one religious tradition to another and bears scant resemblance to the manner in which adherents of other religious traditions imagine themselves. These different styles of thought, and the correspondingly different manners in which Jewish, Christian, and Islamic authorities classify Us and Them, reflect the distinctive styles in which these authorities imagine their respective communal identities.

Setting aside for the moment an important exception that we will encounter in chapter 14, Jewish authorities classify humanity in binary terms: Jewish and gentile ("1" and "0"). Jewish foreign food restrictions generally mark the otherness of gentiles as not-Us without assigning any further significance to Them, although Talmudic prohibitions regarding foreign wine take for granted that They are idolaters. The discussions of foreigners and their food we explored in part II devote no serious attention to the distinctions that exist among gentiles, evidently because the Sages and their Hellenistic predecessors perceived such details to be of no consequence: gentiles are imagined as indistinct and nondescript. Jewish identity, as expressed through the medium of foreign food restrictions, is unrelated to the particular identities of non-Jews; all that matters is that They are not Us.

The self-definition that emerges from Christian foreign food restrictions, in contrast, relates directly to the identity Christians ascribe to certain foreigners, namely Jews. Whereas Jewish authorities divide the world into Us and not-Us, Christian authorities employ a more complex classification of humanity. The prohibition against food offered to idols expresses the opposition of Christianity and "paganism" ("1" and "0"), although it does so in such a way as to leave the door open to social intercourse between Christians and non-Christian gentiles. The oft-repeated and multifaceted prohibitions against food associated with Jews, in contrast, go further by defining Judaism in contradistinction to Christianity ("1" and "-1"). This definition is advanced through a process that involves both the construction of firm barriers to social intercourse and the ascription of negative characteristics to Jews, including the attribute of impurity. Imagined as the mirror image of authentic, holy Christians, Jews fail to understand God's revelation, spurn God's teachings, reject God Himself, and demonstrate unending hostility toward God's true believers. Christians ought to have nothing in common with Them because They are the antithesis of Us.

Islamic sources regarding foreign food restrictions employ a third paradigm for the classification of humanity and the imagination of religious foreigners. Jews and Christians, albeit in different ways, construct the identities of Us and Them in oppositional terms: They are not-Us or anti-Us ("0" or "-1"). Islamic authorities focus instead on the relationships that exist between Us and various groups of Them. Jews and Christians, as adherents of pre-Islamic revelations, are simultaneously like

Us and unlike Us (greater than 0 but less than 1), and both aspects of Their identity are important to Islamic self-identity. Sunnis and Shiʿis, as we have seen, differ in their conceptions of the relationship that exists between Muslims and Scripturists: the former, emphasizing likeness, locate Jews and Christians somewhere in the middle of a spectrum whose poles are marked by Muslims and idolaters, while the latter emphasize unlikeness so as to place Scripturists very close to the idolatrous end of the spectrum. These differences result directly in different portrayals of Jews and Christians. Sunnis imagine Scripturists as faithful adherents of God's dietary laws, while Shiʿis imagine these non-Muslims not only as unfaithful to divine laws but also as incapable of preparing food properly on account of their flawed faith and the resulting impurity. Islamic conceptions of the relative otherness of Jews and Christians reflect the different manner in which Sunnis and Shiʿis conceive of their own identities. Sunnis, who emphasize the value of communal consensus, make a point of including Scripturists in the broad community of those who revere (some of) God's holy revelations. Shiʿis, who emphasize the importance of fealty to the teachings of the Imams, intentionally downplay the relationship between true Muslims and those who dismiss the significance of the Imams.

Medieval discourse about foreigners and their food elaborates upon these various systems for the classification of humanity. Participants in this discourse, which occurs primarily within scholastically oriented circles of thought, explore in ever greater depth the implications of traditional conceptions regarding imagined foreigners. Medieval Jewish, Christian, and Islamic authorities also encounter actual foreigners and grapple with the realization that They do not, in fact, consistently behave in accordance with Our conceptions of Them. The combination of new data and increasingly intensive analysis yields fascinating results that shed valuable light on Jewish, Christian, and Islamic conceptions of religious foreigners and of their own self-identity. Juxtaposition of Jewish, Christian, and Islamic treatment of parallel subjects facilitates the identification and analysis of key similarities and differences among the styles of thought which authorities within these traditions employ and among the styles by which these authorities imagine the identities of their own communities.

The final part of this book presents a series of case studies that explore medieval Jewish, Christian, and Islamic discourse regarding food associated with adherents of other Abrahamic traditions. These case studies reveal the practical implications of the differences between Jewish, Christian, and Islamic spectrums of humanity. They also demonstrate the significance which religious authorities ascribe to traditional conceptions of the proper relationship between Us and Them and to the foreign food restrictions that transform these ideas into cultural givens. The stakes are so high when discussing these subjects that religious authorities brand peers with whom they disagree as facilitators of sinfulness and even as heretics or apostates. The conceptions made real through foreign food restrictions are so important that many authorities endorse restrictions that contradict the economic and social interests of their community, the statements of earlier authorities regarding these norms, and even the core values of their own religious tradition. In the face of evidence that foreigners do not conform to Our ideas about Them, religious authorities nevertheless insist upon preserving their traditional systems for classifying humanity. The reason medieval religious authorities go to such great lengths is that traditional conceptions of Them—and, more importantly, of the relationship between Us and Them—have become deeply enmeshed with fundamental conceptions of Our identity. As Martin Buber observes in the passage that constitutes the epigraph to this part of the book, the identity of the *I* (Us) depends on the *It* (Them) with which it stands in relationship: "If *It* is said, the *I* of the combination *I–It* is said along with it. . . . There is no *I* taken in itself . . . "[3]

MAY MUSLIMS EAT MEAT THAT JEWISH BUTCHERS REJECT?

Christian and Islamic authorities alike decry what they perceive to be the excessive stringency of Jewish dietary law. Indeed, these authorities go so far as define their respective communities in part through the rejection of Jewish food practices: because God favors Us over Them, We are free to eat meat which They refuse to consume. Christian rhetoric regarding the unnecessary rigors of Jewish dietary law and the permissiveness of Christianity is well known, and Ze'ev Maghen has documented a similar dynamic within Sunni sources.[4] This general tendency notwithstanding, many Sunni and Latin Christian authorities also specifically prohibit the consumption of certain cuts of meat permitted under Islamic and canon law but forbidden under Jewish law when that meat is prepared by a Jewish butcher. The very logic of the manner in which these authorities imagine Jews as anti-Christians or unlike Muslims, paradoxically, sometimes necessitates Christian and Muslim adherence to food practices identical to those observed by Jews. Scholastic debates over the status of meat that Jewish butchers reject—an instructive borderline case—reveal significant variations in the ways individual Islamic and Christian authorities imagine the relationship between Judaism and their own traditions, as well as the importance these authorities ascribe to the proper conception of Judaism.

Sunnis, unlike their Shiʿi counterparts, presume that Jewish butchers can and do observe all Qur'anic norms governing the act of animal slaughter; Sunnis therefore permit the consumption of meat that Jewish butchers prepare. This permission, we observed in chapter 10, serves to advance a Sunni conception of Islam's own identity as the successor to a series of authentic religious traditions. Sunni authorities, however, recognize that Jews adhere to a stricter set of norms than those incumbent upon Muslims. Biblical dietary law, after all, prohibits a number of animal species and cuts of meat that Islamic law permits; recall that the Qur'an explains these additional regulations as divine punishment for Israelite stubbornness (e.g., Q. 6.146). Rabbinic law imposes still further restrictions on the suitability of specific members of permitted animal species, among them the requirement that the lungs of a slaughtered animal be intact (see B. *Ḥul.* 46a–49a). An otherwise permitted animal whose condition upon death renders its meat prohibited is called *ṭerefah* in Hebrew, rendered as *al-ṭarīf* or the like in the Islamic texts we will examine. Given the difference between Jewish and Islamic dietary norms, may a Muslim eat meat prepared by a Jewish butcher that is prohibited to Jews yet perfectly permissible for Muslims? The answer hinges on the style in which Islamic authorities imagine Jews and their food practices.

Mālikī jurists tend to prohibit, or condemn as reprehensible, Muslim consumption of meat prepared by a Jew that the Jew himself may not eat: Muslims, in effect, must adhere to Jewish dietary law when acquiring meat from a Jewish butcher. Mālikī discourse on this subject focuses primarily on Qur'anic hermeneutics: does meat rejected as nonkosher by a Jewish butcher qualify as "the food of those who were given the Book" which Qur'an 5.5 authorizes Muslims to eat?[5] 'Abd al-Mālik Ibn Ḥabīb (d. 852/3) offers a succinct and representative statement of Mālikī opinions on the subject:

> God forbade to the Jews everything with undivided toes [*ẓufr,* Q. 6.146], including camels, onagers, ostriches, geese, and everything that does not have split hoofs or divided toes, to the exclusion of chickens and other small birds with divided toes, which the Jews eat—all of this is the statement of Mujāhid [b. Jabr, a Successor, d. ca. 720]. If a Jew slaughters anything which is prohibited to them, it is not permissible for a Muslim to eat it. [Ibn Ḥabīb proceeds to identify all of the fatty portions of meat which God forbade to the Jews in Qur'an 6.146.] We may neither consume nor derive benefit from any of these fatty portions of their slaughtered meat which are prohibited to them. As for that which is not forbidden to them in the text [of scripture] but rather some of them prohibited it—for example, *al-ṭarīf* and the like—it is reprehensible for us to consume or derive benefit from it because this is not of their food; this [ruling] is lenient relative to some of Mālik's disciples.[6]

According to Ibn Ḥabīb, the Qur'anic permission of Jewish food does not include foodstuffs which God prohibited to the Jews in the Qur'an and should not include foodstuffs which Jews have chosen to treat as prohibited, such as *al-ṭarīf,* either.[7]

Mālikī authorities are uniform in prohibiting the meat of an animal categorically forbidden to Jews which a Jewish butcher nevertheless slaughters, such as camel meat, but debate the status of nonkosher cuts of meat from an otherwise permitted animal. Some allow Muslims to eat the fatty portions of animals slaughtered by Jews on the grounds that "proper slaughter renders the entire animal, fat and all, permitted; slaughter does not apply to some parts [of the animal] but not others."[8] This position treats the Qur'an's permission of "the food of those who were given the Book" as a reference to the meat of animals which Scripturists may validly slaughter rather than solely to the portions of meat which Scripturists may actually consume. Other Mālikīs prohibit or condemn Muslim consumption of the fatty portions of animals slaughtered by Jews because, in the words of ʿAbd al-Wahhāb b. ʿAlī al-Baghdādī (d. 1031/2), "the permissibility of meat from a slaughtered animal depends on whether its butcher regards it as permitted or prohibited in accordance with his beliefs."[9] When the Qur'an permits "the food of those who were given the Book," it refers precisely to food which Jews and Christians consider to be permitted. This latter position understands Qur'an 5.5 as granting independent authority to Scripturist norms about animal slaughter.[10]

Mālikī jurists, especially those who fall into the camp exemplified by ʿAbd al-Wahhāb, imagine contemporary Scripturists to be "living letters of scripture," to use the phrase coined by Bernard of Clairvaux in reference to the Jews of Christendom.[11] Jewish butchers observe traditional dietary laws to which the Qur'an itself ascribes authority, and Muslims who wish to consume the meat such butchers prepare must therefore adhere to food restrictions from which Muslims are normally and rightfully exempt. It bears emphasizing, however, that the "Jewish dietary laws" to which Mālikī jurists refer are Qur'anic rather than Jewish: these jurists imagine Jews to be living letters of *Islam's* scripture. For example, Ibn Ḥabīb's assertion that Jews may not eat geese is based not on Jewish practice—Jews consider geese to be kosher—but rather on an Islamic interpretation of the Qur'an's reference to animals with "undivided toes."[12] Familiarity with the actual practices of Jews, such as the refusal of Rabbinic Jews to consume the meat of animals with lung defects, merely adds additional grist to the hermeneutical mills of Islamic scholars. Differences among Islamic attitudes toward the permissibility of Jewish meat, in turn, reflect the different ways in which Islamic jurists choose to interpret the Qur'an as it applies to contemporary Jews.

Mālikīs imagine Scripturists as the bearers of authentic divine teachings that consequently have a real impact on the permissibility of the meat their butchers prepare. For these jurists, discourse about Jewish and Christian slaughter practices offers a means of demonstrating the degree to which Scripturists are like Muslims: We grant weight to Their beliefs about prohibited meat because the Qur'an accords the People of the Book a relatively elevated status among non-Muslims. The logic inherent in this discourse, of course, indirectly attests to the ultimate authority of the Qur'an and thus to the superlative status of Muslims themselves. The ex-Mālikī ʿAlī b. Aḥmad Ibn Ḥazm (d. 1064), in contrast, employs discourse about Jewish meat as a means of emphasizing the irrelevance of Jewish norms in the face of the Qur'an's ultimate authority.

Ibn Ḥazm became a principal spokesman for Ẓāhirism, a numerically insignificant but intellectually important school of jurisprudence which taught that Islamic law should be based on the Qur'an and Prophetic ḥadiths, to the exclusion of other jurisprudential sources employed by Mālikīs and other Sunni jurists. Ibn Ḥazm singles out for particular opprobrium those Mālikīs who defer to the Jewish prohibition of meat from animals with lung defects, "one of the things on which neither the Qur'an nor the Sunnah provides a text which says that it is prohibited to the Jews." Indeed, Ibn Ḥazm observes, concern about lung defects is unique to followers of Rabbinic Judaism, one among several competing streams of Judaism in the medieval Islamic world. "These [Mālikīs]—may God assist both us and them—see to it that they do not eat any animals slaughtered by the Jews about which there is disagreement between the elders of the Jews—may God curse them—and they are wary of contradicting Hillel and Shammai, the two elders of the Rabbanites!"[13] The fact that Jews themselves disagree regarding the legal relevance of lung defects furthers Ibn Ḥazm's sarcastic rhetoric, but Jewish understandings about the laws of animal slaughter are actually irrelevant to Ibn Ḥazm's argument. Ibn Ḥazm uses this case as a banner example of jurisprudence based on sources other than the Qur'an and reliably transmitted Prophetic ḥadiths. His argument, therefore, applies not only to Rabbinic dietary regulations but also to laws of Biblical origin.

In his code of Ẓāhirī law, *Al-muḥallā,* Ibn Ḥazm holds that Muslims may eat any meat permitted by the Qur'an which a Jew slaughters in accordance with Islamic norms, irrespective of the butcher's personal beliefs regarding the meat's permissibility.

> Even if a Jew slaughters a camel or a hare it is permitted for us to eat its meat, as we need not concern ourselves with what the Torah does or does not prohibit to them. . . . The Qur'an states, and consensus affirms, that the religion of Islam has abrogated all prior religions and that whoever adheres to what is found in the Torah or Gospels instead of following the Qur'an is an unbelieving idolater whose religion will not be accepted (cf. Q. 3.85). Because this is the case, God, exalted be He, has nullified all laws in the Torah, Gospels, and other religions, and has made the law of Islam obligatory for all divine and human beings: nothing is prohibited except that which it prohibits; nothing is permitted except that which it permits; nothing is required except that which it requires.[14]

Ibn Ḥazm denies any legitimacy to normative Jewish practice in order to drive home his point that the Qur'an is the only authoritative revelation and that Islam supersedes religions based on earlier scriptures. For that reason, the dietary laws revealed to the Scripturists prior to the time of Muḥammad are obsolete and legally irrelevant.[15] After all, Ibn Ḥazm observes, the Qur'an declares that "the food of those who were given the Book is permitted to you *and your food is permitted to them*" (Q. 5.5, emphasis added). Jews and Christians—indeed, all peoples—are bound exclusively by the dietary regulations that govern Muslims. As further evidence for the permission of all meat which Jews prepare in accordance with Islamic norms, Ibn Ḥazm cites the traditions about Muḥammad's encounters with Jewish meat we encountered in chapter 10, including the incident in which Muḥammad apparently condones consumption of the fatty portions of animals slaughtered by Jews. Ibn Ḥazm argues that the act of proper slaughter cannot logically apply to one cut of meat but not another cut equally permissible for consumption by Muslims.[16]

Ibn Ḥazm goes so far as to brand Mālikīs as apostates on account of their restrictive opinions regarding Jewish meat. Those who allege that Jewish prohibitions against the consumption of camels or certain fatty portions remain in force and who ascribe significance to the beliefs of Jewish butchers, Ibn Ḥazm contends, effectively deny that the Qur'an is God's final and uniquely authoritative revelation. In truth, all that matters is that the butcher is legally fit to perform animal slaughter and that he or she does so in accordance with Qur'anic norms.[17] Ibn Ḥazm believes that authority rests exclusively in the Qur'an and Prophetic Sunnah and, for that reason, he demands that Muslim consumers pay no attention to Jewish norms regarding meat. Whereas Mālikīs endorse the notion that Muslims ought to acknowledge the continued authority of Jewish food practices on account of the close relationship between the Qur'an and prior revelations, Ibn Ḥazm insists that these practices are utterly devoid of authority because the Qur'an is fundamentally different from its obsolete predecessors. The assertion that those who disagree on this point are apostates reflects the importance Ibn Ḥazm ascribes to his conception of the relationship between the Qur'an and the Torah and, thus, between Islam and Judaism.

Islamic discourse about problematic Jewish meat, including that of Ibn Ḥazm, occurs primarily within Mālikī circles. Most other Sunni authorities neglect the issue entirely, while those who address it in passing tend, like Ibn Ḥazm, to permit all meat slaughtered by Jews that meets Islamic standards of permissibility.[18] The noteworthy exception, both in terms of his sustained attention to the subject and his restrictive opinions, is Muḥammad b. Abī Bakr Ibn Qayyim al-Jawziyyah (d. 1350), a disciple of the great Ḥanbalī jurist Ibn Taymiyyah; Ibn al-Qayyim's *Aḥkām ahl al-dhimmah* contains the most thorough discussion of Scripturist meat in medieval Sunni literature.[19] Unlike Ibn Ḥazm and many Mālikīs, who treat all types of problematic Jewish meat alike, Ibn al-Qayyim makes a point of distinguishing between the permissibility of camel meat or cattle fat and meat from animals with lung defects.

Ibn al-Qayyim breaks with the dominant opinion of his own Ḥanbalī school in favor of the Māliki position prohibiting "camels, ostriches, ducks, and anything without divided toes" that Jewish butchers slaughter. He explains that this position is rooted in three self-evident premises: (1) Certain animals are prohibited to Jews, as the Qur'an declares. (2) These prohibitions remain in force because their enactment principle remains in force: Jews continue to transgress in their refusal to accept Muḥammad and his message. (3) Proper slaughter cannot be performed by a person who considers an act of slaughter to be improper.[20] The Jewish butcher Ibn al-Qayyim has in mind, one should note, is evidently a devout adherent of the Qur'an as explicated by Sunni jurists: Qur'an 6.146 notwithstanding, most actual Jews regard ducks, like geese, as kosher and do not believe that Jewish dietary practices constitute a punishment for past or present transgressions.[21] Because Ibn al-Qayyim's hermeneutical Jew is bound by Qur'anic law, however, he need not concern himself with lung defects. "This prohibition, although known to one of their sects, is not in the text of the Torah. Their statement regarding it is not accepted, in contrast to the prohibition of animals with undivided toes or prohibited fat."[22] On this subject, Ibn al-Qayyim embraces the opinion of Ibn Ḥazm, albeit without acknowledging his source.

Ibn al-Qayyim devotes a lengthy discourse—extending over ten printed pages—to the permissibility of the fatty portions of animals slaughtered by Jews, singling out Ibn Ḥazm's opinion on the subject for detailed analysis and harsh criticism.[23] The difference of opinion between these jurists stems from the different ways in which each imagines the Jews. In response to Mālikīs who defer to Jewish norms on account of the elevated status which the Qur'an ascribes to Scripturists, Ibn Ḥazm imagines Jews as subject to the same dietary regulations incumbent upon Muslims. Because the Qur'an supersedes all prior scriptures, distinctively Jewish beliefs are irrelevant and the fatty portions of animals which Jews slaughter are permissible, just like those of animals slaughtered by Muslim butchers: Jews ought to be like Us. Ibn al-Qayyim shares Ibn Ḥazm's exclusive focus on norms of Qur'anic origin, but he emphasizes that the Qur'an itself imposes unique dietary restrictions upon the Jews, including the prohibition against certain cuts of meat. This emphasis on the degree to which Jews who reject Islam are unlike Us reflects the broader tendency in Sunni literature to imagine Jews as the bearers of an oppressively heavy yoke of legal obligations, the yoke from which God freed believers in the revelation granted to Muḥammad.[24] Indeed, Ibn al-Qayyim insists that adherence to the rigorous dietary laws described in the Qur'an constitutes a defining attribute of Judaism: Jews who reject Islam yet adhere to the norms applicable to Muslims, he declares, are heretics. Ibn al-Qayyim thus establishes a definition of what it means to be an orthodox Jew—adherence to laws spelled out in the Qur'an—and insists that a butcher must conform to this definition if he is to be regarded as a legitimate Jew from the perspective of Islamic law. Ibn al-Qayyim regards his conception of Jews to be so central to Islamic identity that, turning the rhetorical tables, he brands Ibn Ḥazm as an apostate for denying the distinctive set of Qur'anic food restrictions incumbent upon Jews.

Ironically, the only way Ibn al-Qayyim can express his belief that Jews, unlike Muslims, are still bound by distinctive restrictions with respect to meat is to subject Muslim patrons of Jewish butchers to these rules as well. Ibn al-Qayyim must therefore explain away the fact that Muḥammad himself apparently permits consumption of the fat of animals slaughtered by Jews.[25] Ibn al-Qayyim's bottom line, that Muslims must adhere to Jewish dietary laws despite the permissive language found in the Qur'an and Sunnah, is the very outcome that Ibn Ḥazm decries. Jews do not eat certain cuts of meat permitted to Muslims, and for that reason Muslims themselves may not eat these cuts when prepared by Jews, even though God and Muḥammad have permitted Muslims to eat them? Precisely, a critically reflective Ibn al-Qayyim might reply: only through prohibitions against Our consumption of Their food can We grant normative expression to Our ideas about Them. The ascription of a particular identity to a group of religious outsiders must carry consequences for the insiders who embrace the classificatory system that assigns this identity. Mālikīs implicitly acknowledge the same principle, employing the prohibition against consumption of meat which Jewish butchers deem nonkosher as a means of acting upon the Islamic notion that Jews indeed adhere to an authentic divine revelation and are therefore like Us to a significant degree. Ibn Ḥazm, in contrast, rejects this prohibition as a means of demonstrating his conviction that the Qur'an nullifies God's revelation to the Jews. For Ibn Ḥazm, what matters most is that Jews are not Us and that We ought to ascribe no significance whatsoever to Their norms.

Sunni authorities imagine Jews in a variety of different, albeit complementary, ways: Jews observe laws found in an authentically divine revelation and are therefore like Us (Mālikīs); Jews observe laws found in an obsolete revelation and are therefore not like Us (Ibn Ḥazm); Jews, because they are unlike Us in their rejection of God's final revelation, must adhere to a distinctive set of laws (Ibn al-Qayyim). Each in its own way, these conceptions of the Jews and of the relationship between Judaism and Islam bolster the self-identity of Sunnis as the heirs to an ancient history of divine revelations and adherents of God's last and uniquely authoritative revelation. While it is possible to hold all three of these conceptions simultaneously, the debate over the status of nonkosher Jewish meat demonstrates that the practical implications of these conceptions are not always compatible. The authorities we have examined, however, agree that We ought to give expression to Our ideas about Them through Our treatment of Their food, even when doing so runs against the grain of Our typical attitudes toward food restrictions.

The willingness of Islamic jurists to prohibit certain types of Jewish meat—despite their commitment to legal permissiveness regarding food in general and Jewish meat in particular—reflects the fact that only action on the part of Muslims can grant substance to the imagined identities Muslims project upon the Jews. The strong rhetoric of apostasy that these jurists wield against those with whom they disagree, moreover, illustrates the significance that these authorities ascribe to their particular conceptions of Judaism and of the proper relationship between Us and Them. The same may be said regarding Christian responses to the very question we have been exploring, but these responses differ in fundamental ways from their Islamic counterparts.

MAY CHRISTIANS EAT MEAT THAT JEWISH BUTCHERS REJECT?

Whereas Sunnis permit meat they define as "Jewish" and debate whether cuts that Jews regard as nonkosher fit this definition, Latin Christian jurists, like Shi'i authorities, are unequivocal in prohibiting the consumption of "Jewish" meat. As we saw in chapter 8, medieval Christians regarded the act of kosher animal slaughter as the antithesis of the Eucharistic offering, an embodiment of and explanation for the Jews' rejection of Christian doctrine. A pair of dueling opinions about the borderline case of meat that Jewish butchers reject as nonkosher, however, sheds light on differences of opinion that underlie the surface uniformity of medieval Christian statements on the subject of Jewish food.[26] Angelo di Castro, a prominent fifteenth-century professor of law at Padua, and John Capistran, a powerful Franciscan (d. 1456, later beatified), address the status of meat from the hindquarters of animals slaughtered by Jewish butchers. Medieval European Jews, wary of violating the Biblical prohibition against eating the thigh muscle (*Gen.* 32.33), refused to consume such meat themselves.

The thoroughly scholastic tenor of the debate between di Castro and Capistran partially obscures the fact that the permissibility to Christians of hindquarters from animals slaughtered by Jews was of considerable practical significance in late medieval Italy. Meat was a dietary staple in this region and, as Ariel Toaff has observed, kosher beef and lamb would have been prohibitively expensive if Jewish butchers were unable to sell the hindquarters to Christians. Indeed, Jewish communities were so troubled by the prospect of foregoing the consumption of beef and lamb that they regularly threatened to relocate if sales to Christians were forbidden. In order to ensure that the Jews of their municipality would not act on such a threat, civil authorities generally condoned the sale of hindquarters to Christian consumers. Ecclesiastical authorities, however, regularly decried such behavior; members of the Franciscan order were especially vocal on this subject and occasionally managed to persuade local officials to stamp out the practice.[27] (To the best of my knowledge, Islamic debates regarding the status of meat that Jewish butchers prepared but refused to eat themselves had no significant social or economic consequences for Jews in the lands of Islam, perhaps in part because Jews in the Islamic world held that most of the hindquarters are kosher.)

Di Castro took it upon himself to address the issue of hindquarters from animals slaughtered by Jews in a responsum that begins by stating the basic law with respect to this subject matter:

> If a Jew purchases an entire lamb or calf, slaughters it and prepares it in other ways in accordance with his rites, and takes possession of the forequarters of that animal which, according to his law, are permitted for his own consumption, but then sells, gives, or otherwise yields the hindquarters (which, according to his law, are not permitted for his own consumption) to a Christian aware of these circumstances, it is clear that the

> Christian who accepts and consumes this meat has committed a mortal sin. This is because he has violated Christian law, according to which it is prohibited for a Christian to make use of the unleavened bread of the Jews, and the term "unleavened bread" is understood to refer to all of their food, as becomes clear from the following canon.[28] The meat in this case is called "Jewish food" because it was purchased by a Jew and prepared and slaughtered by a Jew in accordance with Jewish rites.[29]

All agree that Christians may not consume the hindquarters of Jewish animals because such meat constitutes "Jewish food." But what if the meat in question never becomes "Jewish"? Di Castro offers the following scenario: a Jewish butcher contracts with a Christian butcher for the Jew to slaughter the Christian's animal and purchase only the forequarters, while the Christian butcher proceeds to sell the hindquarters to a Christian customer. No less an authority than Pope Innocent III condemned this very arrangement, which, Innocent says, local princes condone as a favor to their Jewish subjects.[30] Di Castro, however, makes the case that such an arrangement is perfectly legal. "It is apparent that the butcher [who sells the hindquarters to a Christian] does not make use of Jewish food in this case and that the purchaser does not make use of such food either, because the meat in question is not Jewish as it is not his to sell. As such, it is impossible to call [this meat] 'his food,' because the possessive pronoun 'his' signifies ownership."[31] By ensuring that the Jew never actually owns the animal's hindquarters, Christians may sell and consume that portion of the animal without sinning.

Not content with merely permitting Christian consumption of the hindquarters which Jews refuse to purchase from Christian butchers, di Castro makes the case that such behavior demonstrates commitment to Church doctrine and makes manifest the superiority of Christianity over Judaism.

> When a Christian does not eat food prepared by Jews and, to the contrary, eats the very food which Jews reject and refuse to prepare for themselves, this act does not render the Christian inferior to the Jew but rather superior, because it attests to the truth of the Apostle and the Christian law which does not distinguish among foods. This is obvious to one who properly considers the matter. Were it otherwise, it would follow that consumption of everything which the Jews reject in accordance with their law is a sin, which is ridiculous. To not eat such food is in fact to distinguish among foods, which is to judaize and to sin![32]

Christianity and Judaism, according to di Castro, offer diametrically opposed teachings with respect to food restrictions, so Christians must consistently do the opposite of what Jews do: they must not distinguish among foods in the manner of the Jews, they must not eat Jewish foods, and they must eat the foods which Jews reject. Someone who refuses to eat the hindquarters spurned by Jewish consumers, di Castro insists, effectively embraces Jewish dietary laws and thus "judaizes," which is to say that he engages in the heretical act of blurring the distinction between Christianity and Judaism.[33] By defining "Jewish foods" as foodstuffs owned by Jews, di Castro places the hindquarters of Christian animals slaughtered by Jews into the category of "non-Jewish foods," like pork, that Christians not only may but in fact ought to eat in order to demonstrate their opposition to Judaism and its dietary regulations.[34] The act of purchasing hindquarters from Jewish butchers, di Castro contends, is not merely economically or politically expedient; it makes manifest the mirror-image nature of the relationship between Us and Them and therefore carries positive religious significance. According to di Castro, Christians who refuse on principle to eat the meat that Jews reject are heretics.

Capistran, who embraces the traditional prohibition against Christian consumption of the rejected hindquarters produced through Jewish acts of animal slaughter, declares di Castro to be "thoroughly inclined toward excusing sinfulness."[35] In a sharply worded refutation to di Castro's responsum, Capistran focuses not on the issue of who owns the meat but rather on the fact that Jews have handled it.

> If they judge that which is touched by us to be impure and for that reason refuse to purchase or consume meat slaughtered by Christians like us, how can it be fitting for Christians to eat the meat which the criminal and putrid hands of the unbelieving, faithless Jews treat as refuse? . . . We ought not deign to eat that which [has acquired] the impurity of their hands and feet, especially the wine which their feet have pressed, even if we are their hired servants; failure to avoid such foods slanders our glory.[36]

Capistran grounds the prohibition of Jewish food on the notion that Jews themselves are impure sources of pollution. For that reason, it makes no difference whether or not Jews own the animals they slaughter, as di Castro suggests. Christians must act in opposition to Jewish practice: because Jews reject our food as impure, we must reject all food which they touch as impure. Capistran's use of impurity rhetoric to trump di Castro's cogent legal arguments calls to mind the use of similar rhetoric by Shiʿi authorities as a means of rejecting well-grounded Sunni logic regarding the permissibility of Scripturist foodstuffs. The ascription of impurity to a group of foreigners justifies the rejection of arguments that are not based on the premise that foreigners are impure.

Capistran is not the only medieval Christian authority who justifies prohibitions against Jewish foodstuffs on the grounds that Jews are impure; we encountered similar notions in the works of Agobard of Lyons. A number of regional laws from the thirteenth through fifteenth centuries, moreover, employ the same logic when forbidding Jews from touching any food in the Christian marketplace, irrespective of who owns that food. Thus, for example, a thirteenth-century statute from Avignon declares that "Jews and prostitutes may not dare to touch with their hands bread or fruit displayed for sale; those who do so must purchase that which they touched or grasped."[37] The rationale underlying these laws is articulated in a ninth-century penitential pseudonimously ascribed to Theodore of Canterbury: "If a Christian takes from the faithless Jews their unleavened bread—or any other food or drink—and participates in their impieties, he shall engage in forty days of penance on bread and water, because it is written, 'For the pure all things are pure but for the defiled and unbelieving nothing is pure' [*Tit.* 1.15], but rather all is profane."[38]

Pseudo-Theodore's prooftext reveals the paradox inherent in arguments like that of Capistran. For Christians, all things are pure; for Jews, who reject the Christian belief that all things are pure, nothing is pure; therefore Christians must avoid Jewish food as impure—despite the fact that for Christians all things are pure! Kenneth Stow captures the irony of these prohibitions: "In expressing horror at the potentially damaging effects of Jewish contact, Christianity was exposing itself as a virtually inverted 'carnal' Judaism," preoccupied by the very concerns about food which Christians claim are distinctively Jewish and thoroughly un-Christian.[39] These prohibitions of food touched by Jews, however "un-Christian" they may appear, are nevertheless the natural corollaries of rhetoric that defines Jews as anti-Christians, the impure antonym to Christian purity. Indeed, such rules constitute an essential means of granting objective, social reality to the notion that Jews are impure and utterly removed from their former state of holiness. In order to establish Jews as anti-Christians on account of their unwarranted concerns about impurity, Christians themselves must be concerned about Jewish impurity and must engage in the very impurity-based avoidance practices which Christians ascribe to the Jews. We observed a similar dynamic at play in Ibn al-Qayyim's insistence that Muslims may not eat certain cuts of meat prepared by Jews so as to demonstrate that the prohibition of such cuts apply to Jews and not to Muslims.

Rhetoric defining Jews and their food as impure has a distinguished pedigree within Latin Christendom stretching back from Capistran through Agobard to the Council of Epaone, and its adherents can plausibly draw support from such figures as Augustine and John Chrysostom as well. Medieval scholars of canon law, however, consistently reject this logic. In the words of Huguccio, an eminent twelfth-century professor, the prohibition of Jewish food "is based not on the impurity of foods but rather on [our] renunciation of and animosity toward the Jewish religion, which is to say that we should not seem to venerate what they treat as sacred. An alternative, and better, explanation is the one offered by the following canon: they distinguish among our foods and avoid them, and for that reason we ought to abstain from their foods."[40] Di Castro, a fellow professor of canon law, embraces this conception of the prohibition of Jewish food and echoes Huguccio in emphasizing that Christians ought not appear to respect such Jewish practices as the avoidance of the hindquarters. At stake in the debate between di Castro and Capistran is not merely the status of meat from an animal that a Jew slaughters yet does not own, but also the underlying rationale for the prohibition of Jewish meat and thus the basic Christian conception of Jews. This conception is crucial to those who perceive Christianity itself as the antithesis of Judaism.

Di Castro and Capistran conceive of the prohibition against Jewish food in fundamentally different ways: according to di Castro, it makes manifest Christian disdain for the Jews and their laws, while Capistran holds that it serves to protect Christians from Jewish impurity. Both, however, embrace the traditional Christian prohibition of Jewish food in general, including the prohibition of hindquarters owned by Jews. Even a jurist sensitive to the idea that the act of distinguishing among foods "is to judaize and sin" cannot imagine condoning Christian consumption of Jewish food: such behavior would blur the essential distinction between Us and Them. These Christian authorities, like their Shiʿi counterparts and, to a lesser degree, Mālikīs and Ibn al-Qayyim, embrace prohibitions against Jewish food because adherence to such laws makes manifest Our conceptions of the relationship between Us and Them. Di Castro no less than Capistran demands that Christians abstain from Jewish food despite the fact that such abstention might reasonably be construed as a quasi-Jewish form of distinguishing among foods.

Christian and Sunni authorities who debate the question, "What constitutes Jewish meat?" employ scholastic discourse about borderline cases as a means of articulating fundamental conceptions regarding Jews. Each of these authorities, moreover, addresses hermeneutical Jews who are constructed in such a way as to support that authority's self-identity and his own understanding of the relationship between Us and Them. For Sunnis, the status of meat that Jewish butchers reject hinges on the proper interpretation of Qur'an 5.5 and related verses, not on Jewish conceptions of their own meat-related practices. Di Castro derives his ownership-based definition of "Jewish food" not from Jewish informants or even from the Old Testament but rather from the application of an interpretive principle about possessive pronouns found in Roman law. Capistran, in response, draws on notions about Jewish impurity taboos expressed in earlier Christian sources, notions that lack any basis in Jewish thought. Jews have no say in defining their own religion.

In a sense, the definition of Judaism is too important to be left to the Jews. The endorsement of restrictions that go against the grain of Christian and Islamic norms and the use of rhetoric regarding sinfulness, heresy, and apostasy attest to the significance Christian and Islamic authorities ascribe to their particular conceptions of the proper relationship between Us and Them. These conceptions, after all, relate directly to fundamental conceptions of Christianity and Islam itself. As Buber observes, "There is no *I* taken in itself": the *I* of the medieval Christian and Islamic self-conception of Us is intimately intertwined with the *It* that is the imagined Jewish Them.

Stated more broadly, medieval Christian and Islamic authorities imagine their own religious tradition at the positive pole of a spectrum of humanity. Ideas about this spectrum and about the proper relationship between the various religious communities ranged along it constitute a significant component of the identity these authorities ascribe to their own communities. We have seen the ways in which these authorities make manifest their idealized social order through discourse about foreign food restrictions related to the Jews. Latin Christian and Sunni authorities, as we shall see, seek to do the same through discourse about the food practices of one another's communities. These authorities ascribe significance, not only to the definition of specific groups of foreigners, but also and perhaps more fundamentally to the very spectrum of humanity within which they construct the identities of these groups.

13

Christians "Adhere to God's Book," but Muslims "Judaize"

Islamic and Christian Classifications of One Another

The Qur'an's prohibition against consuming blood, carrion, pork, and that over which a name other than God's has been invoked came to pose a significant challenge, albeit for very different reasons, to both Sunni and Latin Christian systems for classifying humanity. Latin Christians reject observance of ingredient-based dietary law and regard such behavior as manifesting flagrantly the denial of Christian doctrine. Medieval scholars of canon law imagine that Jews alone persist in distinguishing between permitted and prohibited foodstuffs and perceive adherence to dietary laws as a uniquely Jewish phenomenon: gentiles are supposed to eat all foods, just as Christians do. The fact that Muslims adhere to food restrictions, therefore, poses a challenge to Christian ideas about the distinction between Jews and gentiles: Muslims are gentiles, yet they behave like Jews! Awareness on the part of Islamic authorities that Christian butchers may not adhere to Qur'anic norms when slaughtering animals, in turn, challenges the symbolically significant distinction which Sunni jurists perceive between idolaters and recipients of divine revelations. Christians, as Scripturists, are supposed to observe the basic norms found in the Qur'an, yet Christians behave like idolaters!

Sunni and Christian authorities, however, do not allow troubling data about one another's food practices to unseat the established spectrums along which they place distinct religious communities, and these authorities never consider the possibility that traditional classifications of foreigners might be inadequate or inaccurate. Instead, Sunnis and Christians devote considerable effort to preserving the congruence of their ideas about foreigners and the restrictions that transform these ideas into normative realities. Some redefine traditional rules about food in order to maintain the function of foreign food restrictions as markers of established distinctions among foreigners. Others instead redefine contemporary foreigners as deviants from past practices whose food, although once permissible, is now forbidden.

These acts of redefinition reveal the importance of traditional classificatory systems to Christian and Islamic authorities alike. Indeed, we will find that the different methods by which Christians and Muslims traditionally classify foreigners dictate the different ways in which they interpret information about the religious practices of foreigners. Islamic and Christian discourse about one another's food also reflects a fundamental difference between Sunni and Christian conceptions of foreigners: the former ascribe specific significance to Christianity as well as to Judaism, whereas the latter—even in their discussions of Muslims—are concerned primarily about the Jews. Because foreign food restrictions embody conceptions of the relationships between Us and Them, they shed light on the different roles which foreigners play in the medieval self-definitions of Sunni Islam and Latin Christianity.

SUNNI EFFORTS TO ACCOUNT FOR CHRISTIAN METHODS OF ANIMAL SLAUGHTER

We observed earlier that Shiʿi authorities condemn the willingness of their Sunni counterparts to permit consumption of meat prepared by Jews and, especially, Christians. The trouble with the latter, according to figures like Jaʿfar al-Ṣādiq and pseudo–Ibn Shādhān, is that they invoke Christ, rather than God, when performing the act of animal slaughter. Sunnis also express concern about this Christian manner of animal slaughter, which would seem to render the resulting meat unfit for Muslim consumption on the grounds that the Qurʾan prohibits eating "that over which [a name] other than God's has been invoked" (5.3). The likelihood that a Christian butcher would actually invoke the name of Christ, a practice which to my knowledge is unattested in Christian literature, need not detain us, as Islamic jurists imagined the matter to be a real and pressing concern.[1] Sunni authorities in North Africa and Andalusia also express concern over the fact that Christians neglect to perform the act of animal slaughter required by the Qurʾan, an act in which the animal's blood is drained. This concern is well-founded: we have seen that Augustine rejects the continued authority of the Apostolic Decree's prohibitions against consuming blood and the meat of animals killed by strangulation, and the practice of medieval Christians in the Western Mediterranean region conforms to Augustine's opinion on this subject.

Shiʿi authorities categorically prohibit the consumption of all meat prepared by Christians and are quite happy to declare that Christians, like idolaters, lack an accurate understanding of God and the divine will. For Sunnis, however, the issues raised by Christian methods of animal slaughter are considerably more complicated. According to Sunni authorities, the Qurʾan's permission of meat prepared by Jews and Christians signifies the elevated status of Scripturists over non-Scripturists and expresses the affinity between recipients of God's successive revelations. This affinity, we have seen, contributes to Sunni conceptions of Islam as the ultimate religion. Because of its symbolic significance, more than just the availability of this food to Muslim consumers is at stake in discourse about meat prepared by Christian butchers. The prohibition of such meat would express the notion that Christianity, based though it is on an authentic divine revelation, is equivalent to idolatry and therefore entirely unlike Islam. Such a prohibition would also call into question the very system within which Sunnis classify humanity and define themselves as supreme. Rather than following the lead of their Shi'i counterparts by establishing a binary opposition between Us and Them, Sunnis struggle to preserve both the gradations in their spectrum of humanity and the permissibility of Christian meat that grants normative expression to these gradations. These efforts reflect the importance to Sunni self-definition of the traditional Sunni spectrum of religious traditions, according to which Scripturists are "like Us" in significant ways.

A striking number of early Islamic authorities permit all Christian meat despite the presumption that Christians invoke Christ. Ibn 'Abbās, the preeminent Companion of the Prophet (d. 687/8), finds nothing wrong with such an invocation: he holds that no requirements regarding the invocation of God apply to Scripturists because Qur'an 5.5, among the final Qur'anic verses to be revealed, abrogates earlier verses on that subject. According to the Successor 'Aṭā' b. Abī Rabāḥ (d. 732/3), "God has already permitted [Christian] meat over which [a name] other than God's has been invoked, for God knew in advance that they will say this statement." That is, God knows that Christians invoke the name of Christ when slaughtering animals, so the Qur'an's statement allowing Muslims to eat meat slaughtered by Christians must mean that God permits Christians to use this language of consecration.[2] Among those who accept the statements of Ibn 'Abbās and 'Aṭā' on this subject is Aḥmad b. Muḥammad al-Naḥḥās (d. 950), author of a treatise on abrogating and abrogated verses in the Qur'an. Al-Naḥḥās similarly reports that a number of Companions and Successors explicitly permit meat which Christians slaughter in the name of Christ or "George," presumably St. George Megalomartyros.[3] Certain rules that apply to acts of slaughter performed by Muslims, these authorities declare, simply do not apply to Christian butchers.

Several Mālikī authorities rely on traditions like these to permit the consumption of meat associated with Christian festivals, although we will see below that Mālik himself disapproved.[4] In doing so, these authorities apply the logic of 'Abd al-Wahhāb b. 'Alī al-Baghdādī we encountered in chapter 12: "The permissibility of meat from a slaughtered animal depends on whether its butcher regards it as permitted or prohibited in accordance with his beliefs."[5] Just as Muslims may not consume nonkosher meat prepared by Jewish butchers, they may consume meat prepared by Christian butchers who regard the invocation of Christ as equivalent to the invocation of God. Permissive Islamic authorities go out of their way to affirm to validity of contemporary Christian practice as divinely sanctioned because of the special place Scripturists occupy within the Sunni spectrum of humanity.

The most strident argument for permitting meat over which a Christian has invoked Christ is articulated by Abū Bakr Muḥammad Ibn al-ʿArabī (d. 1148, a Mālikī of no relation to the famous Sufi known by the same patronymic). In the course of taking Sunni insistence on the permissibility of Christian meat to its logical extreme, Ibn al-ʿArabī expresses most clearly the logic that underlies this stance. "God, praised be He, permitted their food even though He knew that they invoke a name other than God's over their slaughter. Nevertheless, greater respect is accorded to them than to idolaters because they adhere to God's Book and cling to the coattails of prophets."[6] Because Christians are Scripturists, God grants them a greater degree of respect than others who revere multiple divine beings; that respect is expressed through the permission of Christian meat. Ibn al-ʿArabī proceeds to offer what he calls "an original statement" on this matter:

> God, praised be He, prohibited meat over which the name of God was not invoked but permitted the food of the People of the Book even though they say that God is Christ son of Mary or that God is one of the Trinity. God is exalted far above their statements! If they do not mention the name of God, praised be He, one may eat of their food, and if they do, your Lord knows what they mention, and if it is something that does not possess divinity, God has already been generous in this case. It is not proper to contradict the command of God, to fail to attend to it, or to treat it metaphorically.[7]

Christians, Ibn al-ʿArabī observes, believed in the Trinity and invoked the name of Christ at the time of the Qur'an's revelation. Despite the manifest falsehood of these beliefs, God chose to overlook the problematic nature of Christian invocations and declared that their meat is permitted for Muslim consumption. One should not dismiss, dispute, or reject God's inscrutable generosity.

Ibn al-ʿArabī, in fact, goes so far as to permit Muslim consumption of almost all meat prepared by Christians, regardless of how the animal was killed, on account of the special status accorded to Christians.

> I have been asked regarding the Christian who twists the neck of a chicken and then cooks it—may it be eaten with him or may one take it from him for food? . . . I say: It may be eaten, because this is his food and the food of his learned and pious authorities,[8] even though this is not proper slaughter according to us. Nevertheless, God, exalted be He, permitted their food without restriction. Everything which they regard as permitted in their religion is permitted for us according to our religion, except for what God, praised be He, has shown to be their lies.[9]

Through this highly atypical response to Latin Christian norms of animal slaughter,[10] Ibn al-ʿArabī affirms the absolute priority of God's permission of Scripturist meat. Unless Christian practices directly contradict Qur'anic norms—Ibn al-ʿArabī may have the consumption of pork or blood in mind—Muslims should not question God's generosity regarding Christian food. Christians, when all is said and done, "adhere to God's Book and cling to the coattails of prophets," and the permission of Christian meat expresses the respect that is consequently due to this group of non-Muslims. Ibn al-ʿArabī imagines Christians as "living letters of scripture" and therefore treats contemporary Christian practices with a greater degree of deference than they would otherwise deserve.

Most Sunni authorities believe that God was not quite so generous in his permission of meat prepared by Christian butchers. These authorities, like their Shiʿi counterparts, express serious concern about the consumption of meat over which a Christian butcher invoked the name of Christ. Sunnis, however, uniformly share with Ibn al-ʿArabī the conviction that God has indeed permitted at least some Christian meat. Those who refuse to interpret traditional rules governing animal slaughter so as to accommodate Christian invocations of Christ instead create distinctions among contemporary Christians so as to preserve the permissibility of at least some acts of Christian animal slaughter. These efforts are motivated by a conviction that foreign food restrictions ought to express the inherent distinction between those who "adhere to God's Book and cling to the coattails of prophets" and other non-Muslims.

The ḥadith collector ʿAbd al-Razzāq b. Hammām al-Ṣanāʿnī (d. 827) reports that Ibn Shihāb al-Zuhrī (d. 742) prohibited consumption of meat over which a Muslim heard a Christian invoke Christ; Ibrāhīm al-Nakhāʿī (d. 714) condemned the consumption of such meat as reprehensible. Both of these Successors, however, explicitly permit eating Christian meat in the absence of incriminating evidence, on the assumption that Christian butchers do not always invoke Christ.[11] Ḥanafī jurists embrace al-Zuhrī's position: Abū Bakr b. Masʿūd al-Kāsānī (d. 1189), for example, prohibits Muslims from eating the meat of animals over which a Christian butcher explicitly has invoked Christ or the Trinity but allows Muslims to eat meat over which Christians have used ambiguous references to God that Muslims can interpret as monotheistic. Al-Kāsānī also permits the consumption of Christian meat when one does not know what form of invocation the butcher employed.[12]

Mālik b. Anas (d. 795) and several subsequent Mālikī authorities condemn consumption of meat over which a Christian invoked Christ or which Christians dedicated in honor their churches or festivals as "reprehensible";[13] Mālik even says such behavior is "extremely reprehensible." No Mālikī, however, goes so far as to declare such behavior to be prohibited outright.[14] Some Ḥanbalī sources indicate that Aḥmad b. Ḥanbal (d. 855) held the same opinion, while others report that he actually prohibited consumption of meat over which the butcher invoked a being other than God, such as Christ or Venus. This prohibition, however, does not extend to all Christian meat.[15] According to the *Kitāb al-umm,* Muḥammad b. Idrīs al-Shāfiʿī (d.

820) excludes meat slaughtered in the name of Christ or any name other than God's from the permission of Christian slaughter, but he too insists that Christians have rituals for slaughter that conform to Qur'anic dictates as well as rituals that do not.[16]

The most comprehensive treatment of the issues raised by Christian butchers who invoke Christ and the most cogent argument for prohibiting consumption of the meat that results from such acts of slaughter appear in the *Aḥkām ahl al-dhimmah* of Ibn Qayyim al-Jawziyyah (d. 1350), whose discussion of Jewish meat we examined in chapter 12. After surveying a variety of earlier opinions on the subject, Ibn al-Qayyim summarizes their disagreement as follows: "Those who permit [the consumption of such meat] say: This is their food, and God has permitted their food to us without qualification even though God, praised be He, already knew that they invoke a name other than His. Those who prohibit say: The Qur'an establishes a clear prohibition of anything over which a name other than God's is invoked, and this encompasses acts of slaughter performed by both idolaters and People of the Book when they invoke a name other than God's."[17]

Ibn al-Qayyim makes clear that the Sunni debate over Christian acts of animal slaughter relates first and foremost to the interpretation of the Qur'an. Does the permission of "the food of those who were given the Book" (Q. 5.5) supersede or constitute an exception to the general prohibition of "that over which a name other than God's has been invoked" (5.3, among others), or is this permission constrained by that general prohibition? Ibn al-Qayyim argues that the general prohibition must trump the specific permission in this case because the consumption of food offered to a being other than God is the most serious dietary offense addressed in the Qur'an, universally singled out for opprobrium within the community of Muslims. The ritual dedication of an animal to other than God, moreover, is an expression of polytheism and therefore cannot possibly be a response to authentic divine instructions, despite what Christians may claim.[18]

Ibn al-Qayyim accounts for the Christian practice of invoking Christ by asserting that those butchers who do so are heretics who deviate from authentic—which is to say, Qur'anic—Christianity by adopting an idolatrous practice. Muslims may not consume meat prepared by such heretics, just as they may not consume meat prepared by apostate Muslims. Ibn al-Qayyim, despite his vehement rejection of Shiʿi arguments for the prohibition of meat prepared by all Jews and Christians, thus effectively endorses the Shiʿi assertion that Christian butchers who invoke Christ lack true knowledge of God and the divine will. By defining butchers who fail to accept Qur'anic norms as "heretics," however, Ibn al-Qayyim preserves the permissibility of meat prepared by orthodox People of the Book, which is to say Jews and Christians who conform to Islamic conceptions of proper Scripturist beliefs.

Whether by exempting Christian butchers from certain rules that govern Muslim butchers or by excluding some Christian butchers from the category of "Christians," Sunni authorities ensure that foreign food restrictions continue to distinguish

Scripturists from other non-Muslims, at least in principle. In doing so, these authorities also demonstrate the importance they ascribe to imagining Christians as being like Us in significant ways: they too, Sunnis insist, adhere to God's Book, revere authentic prophets, and (according to authorities like Ibn al-Qayyim) observe Qur'anic norms regarding food preparation. Sunnis, committed to their traditional system of classifying humanity, are unwilling to sever the link connecting Islam and the Scripturist traditions, Christianity included.

LATIN CHRISTIAN EFFORTS TO ACCOUNT FOR ISLAMIC FOOD RESTRICTIONS

Latin Christian discourse regarding the food practices of Muslims also reflects the significance medieval Christian authorities ascribe to their traditional spectrum of religious traditions. Juxtaposition of this discourse with Sunni statements regarding Christian acts of animal slaughter reveals the implications of the significant differences between Christian and Islamic classificatory systems. Whereas Sunnis classify non-Muslims as Scripturists or non-Scripturists and regard Scripturists as relatively similar to Muslims, Christian authorities classify non-Christians as either Jews or non-Jews and regard Judaism as antithetical to Christianity. Thus, while Sunnis employ the permission of Scripturist acts of animal slaughter as a means of expressing the superiority of Scripturists relative to other non-Muslims, Christians traditionally employ the prohibition of Jewish food as a means of demonstrating through social practice the inferiority of Jews to other non-Christians. Whereas Sunni discourse about Christian meat reflects the significance Sunnis ascribe to Christianity, Christian discourse about the food of Muslims reflects the significance Christians ascribe to *Judaism;* Muslims themselves bear no significance within the traditional Christian system for classifying humanity.[19]

Authorities from the first Christian millennium classify non-Christians as either Jews or gentile pagans, and they collectively employ the permissibility of commensality as a means of expressing the distinction between members of these groups: Christians may eat with the latter but not with the former. Gratian's *Decretum* (ca. 1140), which quickly became the standard textbook of late antique and early medieval law, contains exemplars that reflect this pattern. The *Decretum*'s unit on laws regarding Jews contains both the Council in Trullo's prohibition against eating "the unleavened bread of Jews" and the Council of Agde's prohibition against commensality with Jews on the grounds that "they would judge what we eat with the permission of the Apostle to be impure."[20] Elsewhere, the *Decretum* reproduces an extract from the homilies of John Chrysostom that affirms Paul's permission of commensality with pagans; in another context, it cites an epitome of Augustine's teaching that encourages shared meals with unbelievers as a means of spreading the gospel.[21]

Twelfth-century scholars of Latin canon law, masters of a scholastic form of interpretation that emphasized the harmonization of disparate texts, were quick to notice the distinction between Jews and pagans implicit in these canons. As Rufinus explains in his *Summa decretorum* (published in 1164), the prohibition of commensality "is made specifically regarding Jews, because through the abuse of scripture they subvert faith in Christ in several ways and condemn the food of Christians. Gentiles, however, are not like this, and therefore we are not prohibited from going to their table."[22] Scholars like Rufinus imagine that Jews alone distinguish between permitted and prohibited foodstuffs on account of their embrace of Old Testament norms, and they interpret this behavior as a flagrant rejection of Christian doctrine. Because gentiles do not condemn Christian foods and Christian dietary norms, Christians may eat with gentiles and, indeed, are encouraged to do so as missionaries.

The legal distinction between commensality with pagans and commensality with Jews reflects the tripartite Christian division of humanity and reinforces the Christian perception that Jews are deeply threatening while gentiles are mostly harmless. Twelfth-century canon law scholars promptly extend this pattern to Muslims, whom they call "Saracens" and imagine as adherents of a form of paganism.[23] As Bernard of Pavia explains in his *Summa decretalium* (composed ca. 1191–98), Christians may not eat with Jews on account of Jewish "abuse of scripture and contempt of our food," as attested in the canons promulgated at the Council of Agde and the Council in Trullo, but they may eat with Saracens in accordance with Chrysostom's (and, by extension, Paul's) teachings about shared meals with idolaters.[24] The fact that Muslims in fact condemn certain Christian foods just as Jews do thus poses a significant challenge to Christian ideas about the distinction between Jews and gentiles.

Bernard of Pavia displays no familiarity with statements about Saracens found in the *Summa decretorum* of Huguccio (composed ca. 1188–90), a work that came to have a dramatic impact on canonical discourse about commensality with non-Christians.[25] Huguccio challenges the distinction between Jews and gentiles made by scholars like Rufinus and Bernard.

> With respect to which pagans does [Chrysostom] speak? Nearly all Saracens at the present judaize because they are circumcised and distinguish among foods in accordance with Jewish practices. I say, accordingly, that one ought to abstain from the food of such pagans—that is, those who distinguish among foods—just as from the food of Jews because the same reason for the prohibition, according to [the canon promulgated in Agde], applies to both these and these. [Chrysostom's] canon, however, speaks of those pagans who do not distinguish among foods, whether they are circumcised or not.[26]

Because Saracens "distinguish among foods in accordance with Jewish practices," Huguccio argues, they too are subject to the prohibition against commensality that applies to Jews. In fact, Huguccio's belief that "pagans" now "judaize" leads him to collapse the practical distinction between the categories of non-Christians established by earlier ecclesiastical authorities. Thus, after reviewing traditional arguments explaining why it is worse for a Christian to be enslaved to a Jew than to a pagan, Huguccio dismisses the contemporary relevance of these rationales. "Today, however, one can find nothing teaching that servitude to pagans is different from servitude to Jews, for nearly all contemporary pagans judaize: they are circumcised, they distinguish among foods, and they imitate other Jewish rituals. There ought not be any legal difference between them."[27]

Huguccio imagines Saracens as pagans who have adopted the abhorrent food-related practices traditionally associated with the Jews. The notion that pagans "judaize" is anomalous, as that charge is typically leveled against Christian heretics, but Huguccio's message is clear: all gentiles are susceptible to Judaism's dangerous seductiveness. Implicit in this message is a warning to Christians that the plague of judaizing is real, rampant, and highly contagious. Huguccio's charge that pagans judaize resembles Ibn al-Qayyim's assertion that Christian butchers who invoke Christ are heretics: both authorities account for the difference between Their behavior and Our expectations by asserting that Their practices have become deviant. Ibn al-Qayyim, however, uses the charge of heresy to preserve the permissibility of meat prepared by "orthodox" Christian butchers while Huguccio holds that the practices of "judaizing pagans" call for a wholesale revision of laws that once distinguished Jews from gentiles. Huguccio, unlike his Sunni counterparts, ascribes no significance to the intermediate range of his spectrum for classifying humanity and feels no need to preserve its distinctiveness.

Huguccio's elimination of the practical distinction between Jews and other non-Christians becomes normative among medieval canon law scholars. Precisely because these authorities fear the blurring of boundaries they called judaizing, they are receptive to the conception of Saracens as judaizing pagans when they discover similarities between Islamic and Jewish practices. As a result, these authorities themselves blur the distinction between pagans and Jews by applying the prohibition against commensality to members of both groups, notwithstanding the fact that canonical sources explicitly permit commensality with pagans.

Not all canon law scholars, however, assent to this blurring of distinctions among non-Christians. The anonymous author of *Ecce vicit leo* (second recension, 1210) elects instead to redefine the way in which the commensality prohibition defines Jews as anti-Christians. "It is said that the main point of the prohibition is that Jews distinguish among foods. But according to this we should not eat with pagans! Rather, it is better to say that the reason for this prohibition is that Jews have the Law and by means of it they are able to more easily lead back the hearts of the simple to their dread [rites] if they share meals with them."[28] The author of this commentary affirms the traditional Christian notion that Jews pose a greater threat to uneducated Christians than gentiles because of the fact that Jews revere and observe the Old Testament. He holds that the commensality prohibition ought to express this idea even if pagans now distinguish among foods in the manner of the Jews. Whereas Huguccio maintains the traditional understanding of the rationale behind prohibitions against Jewish food and therefore applies these prohibitions to Jews and "judaizing pagans" alike, *Ecce vicit leo* maintains the traditional distinction between Jewish and gentile food by redefining the purpose of the laws that prohibit Christian consumption of the former. Mālikīs like Ibn al-ʿArabī similarly preserve the distinction between Scripturist and non-Scripturist meat by redefining the scope of Islamic law as it applies to Christian butchers.

The author of *Ecce vicit leo,* like his Sunni counterparts, considers possession of an authentic scripture to be the crucial factor in defining a foreigner's identity. Sunnis, however, regard the affinity between Muslims and Scripturists as a positive attribute calling for a permissive attitude toward Scripturist food while *Ecce vicit leo* considers the affinity between Christians and Jews to constitute the very reason for prohibiting shared meals between the two groups. The author of this work espouses the classical notion that Jews are inferior to other non-Christians, Saracens included, and believes that canon law ought to make manifest this distinction. Indeed, *Ecce vicit leo* holds that Christians should avoid shared meals with Jews even if the latter abandon their distinctive food practices: "We believe that association with them is more distasteful than with gentiles. Since the cause has not ceased, the law's applicability should not cease."[29] Even in the era of the Crusades, when European Christians perceive Muslims as posing a significant military threat, some canon law scholars regard Saracens as less spiritually threatening to Christians than Jews are.[30]

Strikingly, medieval canon law scholars ascribe no significance to Muslims in their own right: their status, and that of their food, depends on whether these "pagans" are seen as being like Jews or unlike Jews. Do Muslims retain their functional status as gentiles because Jews alone "have the Law," or have they become quasi-Jews because "nearly all contemporary pagans judaize"? It is also striking that no participant in medieval scholastic discourse about foreign food restrictions considers the possibility that Muslims are in fact neither "judaizers" nor "pagans." Indeed, several authorities issue strenuous warnings against eating the food which Saracens offer to idols.[31] As Benjamin Z. Kedar has observed, twelfth- and thirteenth-century canon law commentaries display far less familiarity with Islam than do other contemporaneous works of Latin literature.[32] The authors of these commentaries, immersed in the scholastic analysis of sacred texts and conceptual categories, are clearly not interested in actual Muslims. Rather, they focus their attention on imagined Saracens who, as "pagans" who "judaize," constitute a valuable borderline case in discussions about foreign food restrictions precisely because this case clarifies the grounds on which Jews are defined as anti-Christian. These authorities, moreover, seem to have so thoroughly internalized the traditional Christian system of classifying foreigners as either pagans or Jews that they are simply unable to think outside of the traditional categories.

The insistence with which canon law scholars define Muslims as pagans who judaize yields patently ridiculous results. At about the same time that Huguccio penned his commentary, Pope Clement III (r. 1187–91) wrote a letter to the bishop of Livonia (present-day Latvia) permitting Christian missionaries to eat the food served to them by the local pagan population.[33] An extract of this letter appears in the *Decretales*, the authoritative collection of canons compiled by Raymond of Peñafort and published by Pope Gregory IX in 1234.[34] Despite the fact that no Muslims lived in Livonia, commentators on the *Decretales* interpret Clement's letter in light of scholastic discussions about pagans who "distinguish among foods"; as a result, they severely limit the applicability of this canon. Bernard of Parma, author of the *Glossa ordinaria* to the *Decretales* (final recension 1263), goes so far as to declare that Clement's permission has been made moot by changes in pagan food practices. Commensality with pagans, he explains, is only permissible because pagans, unlike Jews, do not distinguish among foods. "Today, however, both these and those distinguish. Therefore, we may not eat in [pagan] homes, nor may they eat in our homes. Even though this [conclusion] is not supported by the words of the law as expressed [in Clement's letter] and in [Chrysostom's teaching], it follows from the law's intent."[35]

Because Bernard and his colleagues place all "pagans" in a single classificatory box, they apply Huguccio's argument for prohibiting commensality with Saracens to all gentiles. In the process, these authorities dismiss the relevance of statements by popes, Church Fathers, and Paul himself, all of whom explicitly permit or even encourage shared meals with gentiles. Pagans, medieval canonists say, have changed, so the law regarding their food must change as well. What remains constant is the spectrum along which Christians classify humanity, a spectrum that ascribes specific and defined identities solely to Christians and to their antitheses, Jews. Canon law scholars feel free to change the laws that apply to pagans in response to new information because Christian conceptions of pagans are of no particular importance and have not been so since about the fourth century. The overarching Christian system for classifying humanity, in contrast, retains its significance; indeed, Christian authorities simply cannot imagine the world in any other fashion.

• • •

Why do Latin Christian authorities go out of their way to prohibit consumption of food associated with Muslims while Sunni authorities go out of their way to permit consumption of meat prepared by Christians? Both dynamics reflect the influence of the traditional spectrums along which medieval religious authorities situate adherents of other religious communities. Ironically, both Sunnis and Christians place one another in the middle of their respective spectrums: Christians are Scripturists, not idolaters, while Muslims are pagans, not Jews. Only Sunnis, however, ascribe positive significance to the intermediate category within their spectrum of humanity: because Scripturists are like Us, meat prepared by Christians must be permitted for Our consumption. Christian authorities, in contrast, ascribe no particular significance to the category of pagan gentiles even as they ascribe great significance to Judaism as anti-Us. Out of concern regarding Jewish food practices and the dangerous phenomenon they call judaizing, most of these authorities opt for defining Muslims as "like Jews" within the context of discourse about foreign food restrictions.

The differences between Christian and Islamic discourse regarding one another's food thus make manifest the differences in their respective systems of classifying humanity. Sunnis ascribe significance to their conceptions of Jews and Christians alike, while Christians ascribe significance to their conception of Jews alone. Jewish authorities, in contrast, ascribe no significance to the conception of any particular group of gentiles so long as the general distinction between Us and Them remains well marked. We should not be surprised, therefore, to discover in our final case study that medieval rabbis go out of their way to justify continued adherence to traditional prohibitions against gentile wine even when they discover that Christians and Muslims, like Jews, do not in fact offer idolatrous wine libations. The boundary-marking function of the prohibition against gentile wine remains important even after the original enactment principle underlying the laws ceases to apply.

14

"Idolaters Who Do Not Engage in Idolatry"

Rabbinic Discourse about Muslims, Christians, and Wine

R. Yosef Karo's *Shulḥan 'Arukh* (published 1565/6), regarded as the final and most definitive of the medieval Rabbinic law codes, contains a curious statement in its discussion of laws regarding foreign wine. In the course of rehearsing the long-standing prohibitions against consuming and deriving benefit both from wine made by gentiles and from Jewish wine touched by gentiles, R. Karo addresses the status of wine prepared or touched by "idolaters who do not engage in idolatry" (*Shulḥan 'Arukh, YD* 124.6). This oxymoronic phrase encapsulates the complex history of medieval Rabbinic efforts to situate Muslims and Christians within a traditional classificatory system that divides humanity into the binary categories of Jews (i.e., monotheists) and gentiles (i.e., idolaters). Even though Jewish authorities acknowledge that Muslims and Christians do not offer idolatrous libations, most continue to regard Them as "idolaters" for practical purposes. Because traditional prohibitions designed to protect Jews against inadvertent involvement in idolatry continue to mark the distinction between Us and Them, they retain some or even all of their force within societies dominated by Islam or Christianity.

This case study, like those we examined in preceding chapters, demonstrates the degree to which medieval discourse about foreign food restrictions reflects and reinforces established conceptions of the relationship between Us and Them. The ideas about Them embedded in traditional systems of classifying humanity are of fundamental importance to Jewish, Christian, and Islamic ideas about Ourselves. For that reason medieval authorities take great pains to preserve these systems even in the face of evidence that real foreigners do not fit comfortably within customary categorical boxes. Unlike their Christian and Islamic counterparts, Jewish authorities do not seek to safeguard specific conceptions of particular groups of foreigners because the Mishnah and Talmuds ascribe no significance to Them in formulating their definition of the Jewish Us. The Sages do, however, insist upon preserving a clear distinction between Us and Them, employing rules about wine as a means of marking gentile otherness and, thus, Jewish distinctiveness. Medieval rabbis, heirs to the Sages, formulate a wide variety of justifications for the continued applicability of foreign wine restrictions despite the high costs sometimes associated with such laws and irrespective of the actual similarities between Jews and their monotheistic neighbors. These similarities, ironically, manifest themselves indirectly through discourse about foreign wine restrictions: rabbis active in the Islamic world conceive of non-Jews in manners that resemble Sunni notions of non-Muslims, while rabbis active in Christian Europe imagine non-Jews in manners that resemble Latin Christian notions of pagans. Rabbis in both regions continue to employ distinctly Jewish styles of thought when discussing foreign food restrictions, but we will see that ideas and modes of thinking prevalent in specific cultural milieus also contribute to this discourse in significant ways.

Before we turn our attention to rabbis active in medieval Islamic and Christian societies, it is worthwhile to return briefly to Sasanid Babylonia, as the Babylonian Talmud constitutes the foundational source for all subsequent discourse regarding foreign wine and thus provides a baseline against which to compare later statements. As we observed in chapters 4 and 5, the Sages divide the world into Jews and non-Jews, and they treat individuals within the latter category as members of an undifferentiated mass of idolaters whose actions affect the legal status of wine but whose own perceptions of these actions are legally irrelevant. If a gentile comes into contact with wine in a legally significant manner, that wine is ipso facto prohibited not only for Jewish consumption but also for Jewish benefit on the presumption that it has been offered in an idolatrous libation. The following incident exemplifies this conception of gentile interaction with wine: "A citron fell into a barrel of [Jewish] wine, and an idolater reached in to retrieve it. R. Ashi said, 'Grab his hand so that he doesn't sprinkle the wine!'" (B. *A.Z.* 59b). R. Ashi's response tells us nothing at all about whether any gentile in Babylonia would have ascribed ritual significance to the act of shaking wine from his hand under these circumstances.[1] Rather, it illustrates the fact that, according to Rabbinic law, a gentile's act of sprinkling wine in this manner triggers the prohibition of the entire container from which that wine was drawn irrespective of the gentile's intentions.

Because of their focus on what gentiles do rather than how gentiles might understand their own behavior, Babylonian Sages rule that even wine touched by a gentile who is in the process of converting to Judaism constitutes libation wine. Shemu'el holds that this prohibition remains in force after conversion, "until such time as idolatry has subsided from their lips"; Rav, in contrast, regards the act of conversion alone to be sufficient. The difference between these authorities seems to be that Shemu'el focuses on the habitualization of gentiles in idolatrous ways whereas

Rav simply focuses on the fact that Rabbinic law defines all gentiles as idolaters. This difference also underlies the opinions of Rav and Shemu'el regarding Jewish wine touched by a newborn gentile: Shemu'el permits Jewish consumption of such wine, as the newborn has not yet become habitualized into idolatry, while Rav forbids consumption of such wine because it was touched by an idolater. Because in this case it is clear that the "idolater" did not intend to touch the wine, however, Rav allows Jews to sell this wine to gentiles instead of discarding it (*A.Z.* 57a–b). The only adult gentile who may intentionally touch wine without rendering it forbidden for Jewish benefit is a "resident alien" (*ger toshav*), a gentile who comes before a Rabbinic court to foreswear idolatry and, according to some authorities, embrace various other Biblical laws. Wine touched by this hypothetical resident alien nevertheless remains off-limits for Jewish consumption, by analogy to the preparer-based prohibitions of other foreign foodstuffs (*A.Z.* 64b).

These borderline cases, among others, exemplify the general Talmudic principle that wine which an ordinary gentile intentionally touches is legally equivalent to wine offered in idolatrous libation. Because idolatry is anathema to Judaism, Jews may not derive benefit from such wine in any manner, much less consume it. The prohibition of gentile wine effectively defines all gentiles as compulsive idolaters; by avoiding that wine entirely, We give expression to this classification of Them, as well as to Our implacable opposition to idolatrous behavior. The cases that appear in the Bavli take this conception of gentiles for granted and explore the intricate implications of this conception within Jewish law without devoting any attention to the mechanics of foreign worship or the nature of foreign religious doctrines. Indeed, the Bavli never addresses the fact that neither Zoroastrianism nor Christianity, the two dominant religions in late antique Babylonia, espouses the kind of ubiquitous libational activity which the Sages discuss. The actual beliefs and practice of so-called "idolaters" are legally irrelevant—until, that is, we turn to post-Talmudic literature.

IMAGINING MUSLIMS AS ANALOGOUS TO NEWBORN IDOLATERS

The geonim, heads of the Rabbinic academies in Babylonia (i.e., Iraq) from the eighth to the eleventh centuries, are the earliest authorities to distinguish between different groups of gentiles with respect to the status of the wine they touch. Geonic responses to queries posed by their followers reveal that some Jews sought to exempt wine touched by Muslims from all Talmudic prohibitions because of the fact that Muslims do not offer wine libations. The geonim, however, defend the continued applicability of these laws, at least in part. In the words of one gaon, "On the subject of leniency regarding the touch of an Ishmaelite gentile and the permission of drinking such wine on the grounds that they do not render wine as offered in libation because they do not offer wine libations in the course of their idolatry: If they did offer libations, such wine would be prohibited for benefit as well [as for consumption]. Simply because they do not offer libations their contact should be less significant than that of a newborn? For that reason, even wine touched by an Ishmaelite is forbidden for consumption."[2] This responsum, whose authorship is ascribed to a variety of geonim, takes the legal relevance of Islam's wine taboo for granted while seeking to limit the implications of that fact. As we observed above, Rav declares that Jews may not consume wine touched by a newborn idolater; surely, this gaon argues, Muslims are no less idolatrous than newborns! Notice that the author of this responsum regards Islam as a form of idolatry even as he acknowledges that wine plays no role in Islamic worship. R. Naḥshon Gaon (d. 879) also argues for maintaining the limited prohibition against consuming wine touched by Muslims despite the fact that they "certainly do not offer wine libations." R. Naḥshon appeals to Talmudic evidence to demonstrate that Muslims, although they do not realize it, are actually idolaters.[3] Both of these geonim construct hermeneutical Muslims on the basis of statements found in the Babylonian Talmud, which these rabbis treat as quasi-scriptural, irrespective of the fact that the Bavli predates the rise of Islam.

Not all early geonim are willing to relax the prohibition against deriving benefit from wine touched by gentiles, Muslim or otherwise. One rabbi rejects any distinction between the wine of Muslims, Christians, and Zoroastrians lest Jews come to think lightly of wine that has been offered in libation or touched by an idolater who does engage in this practice.[4] R. Yehudai Gaon (d. 761), we are told, also refused to allow Jews to derive benefit from wine touched by Muslims. R. Hayya Gaon (or Hai Gaon, d. 1038), in contrast, is quite comfortable declaring that there is nothing wrong with Jewish wine touched by Muslims. "It is clear," he explains, "that wine is not at all associated with their worship and they consider it to be sinful, and therefore we do not hold stringently in this matter and are not concerned about the potential of libation." R. Hayya dismisses the significance of R. Yehudai's ruling to the contrary by explaining that it dates from a time when many Muslims were recent converts from Zoroastrianism who had not yet abandoned their (supposed) ancestral libation practices. Nowadays, however, "they regard one who drinks wine as committing an abomination, and there is no trace of wine in a Muslim's worship." R. Hayya warns, however, that one must remain cautious about Jewish wine falling into Christian hands, "because they do offer wine libations."[5] R. Hayya Gaon, like several of his predecessors, understands the prohibition against deriving benefit from Jewish wine touched by gentiles as stemming directly from concern that idolatrous gentiles are compulsive about offering wine libations, and for that reason he has no qualms about relaxing this aspect of Talmudic restrictions when the idolaters in question are Muslims.

Talmudic authorities hold that, for the purposes of applying the law governing foreign wine, all adult non-Jews aside from the surely hypothetical "resident aliens" are idolaters who offer libations at every opportunity. In doing so, the Sages pay no attention to the actual religious practices of their gentile neighbors. Many geonim accept the classic conception of gentiles as uniformly idolatrous but nevertheless exclude an entire class of actual gentiles from the prohibition against deriving benefit from wine touched by foreigners. They consider Islam's taboo against alcohol to constitute sufficient grounds for allowing Jews to sell wine touched by Muslims; the presence of wine in Christian worship, in contrast, justifies maintaining the traditional prohibitions with respect to wine touched by Christians. There is little reason to presume that Jews living under Islamic rule had greater access to knowledge about the beliefs and practices of their non-Jewish neighbors than did Jews living under Zoroastrian or Christian regimes. Why, then, did many geonim depart from their predecessors by treating their knowledge about a foreign religion as both legally relevant and sufficiently compelling to warrant changes to the law?

The answer, I would suggest, relates to the intellectual context in which the geonim wrote their responsa, a context in which religious differences are ascribed normative significance. Islamic authorities devote considerable attention to "comparative religion," grant legal weight to foreign beliefs and practices, and establish distinctions between different groups of non-Muslims.[6] To cite only the example we observed in chapter 13, Sunni contemporaries of the geonim seek to distinguish "true" Christians, who invoke God when slaughtering animals, from those Christians who instead invoke Christ, and they permit meat prepared by the former while prohibiting meat prepared by the latter. In a culture dominated by Sunni ideas, the legal relevance of information about other religions could be taken for granted as easily as the relevance of information about a law's economic repercussions, data that also plays a role in the pragmatically oriented responsa of the geonim. In this context, moreover, distinctions between varieties of non-Jews pose no risk to the overarching Rabbinic division of humanity into Jews and idolaters. Just as contemporaneous Sunni authorities stretch the category of *Christians* to include those who follow different rituals with respect to animal slaughter, many geonim stretch the category *idolaters* to include those who do not offer wine libations. The redefinition of Muslims as analogous to newborns enables the geonim to apply the laws governing foreign wine differently to different types of "idolaters" while maintaining the traditional dichotomy between Jews and gentiles which these laws reinforce.

DEFINING MUSLIMS AS RESIDENT ALIENS: A GRADATED SPECTRUM OF GENTILES

Talmudic Sages imagine all gentiles to be idolaters and pay no attention to differences within their monolithic category of non-Jews. The geonim agree that all gentiles are idolaters, but they grant legal significance to the fact that Muslims are idolaters who do not offer wine libations while other idolaters, including Christians, continue to engage in this practice. R. Moshe b. Maimon (d. 1204), the great philosopher-jurist known in Rabbinic literature by the acronym Rambam and in Christian and secular literature by the Latinized patronymic Maimonides, ascribes even greater significance to the difference between Muslims and other gentiles: the former, he maintains, are not idolaters at all.[7] In order to accommodate the existence of non-Jewish monotheists within a traditional Rabbinic paradigm, Rambam's discussion of Muslim wine in the *Mishneh Torah* depicts Muslims in a different manner than do geonic responsa.

> The wine of a resident alien—one who accepts seven laws [including the prohibition of idolatry], as we have explained—is prohibited for consumption but permitted for benefit; one may leave [Jewish] wine alone with him but may not store it in his possession. The same applies to all gentiles who do not engage in idolatry, like these Ishmaelites: their wine is prohibited for consumption but permitted for benefit, and so taught all the geonim. Christians, however, are idolaters and their ordinary wine is prohibited for benefit. In all cases regarding this subject [i.e., wine associated with foreigners] in which the wine is prohibited, if the gentile who renders the wine prohibited is an idolater, then the wine is prohibited for benefit; if, however, he is not an idolater, the wine is only prohibited for consumption.[8]

Although Rambam appeals to the authority of the geonim to support his permission of deriving benefit from the wine of Muslims, he actually formulates an entirely new justification for this permission. The geonim imagine Muslims as equivalent to newborn idolaters; Rambam, in contrast, equates Muslims with resident aliens, gentiles who foreswear idolatry and certain fundamentally immoral acts.[9] Wine touched by Muslims differs from wine touched by idolaters because Muslims "do not engage in idolatry," by which Rambam means to say that Muslims neither worship nor believe in idols. The geonim merely acknowledge that Muslims do not employ wine in their liturgy. (Both the geonim and Rambam recognize that, irrespective of the teachings of Islamic authorities, many Muslims do in fact drink wine and other alcoholic beverages.)

By applying the originally hypothetical designation "resident alien" to an entire class of gentiles, Rambam establishes a Talmudic basis for an unprecedented Rabbinic system of classification, one that divides humanity not into monotheistic Jews and idolatrous non-Jews but rather into Jews, idolaters, and non-Jewish monotheists. He employs laws governing foreign wine as a means of externalizing and granting normative significance to this classificatory system: We may derive benefit from wine touched by "resident aliens," including Muslims, but We may not derive benefit from wine touched by idolaters—including Christians[10]—because They are not monotheists. Rambam's innovative interpretation of the Bavli resembles the scriptural exegeses of many other authorities whom we have encountered: a traditional text, viewed through internalized cultural paradigms, takes on a new meaning which, when articulated in normative terms, externalizes a new idea about the relationship between Us and Them (see figure 11, below).

It is no coincidence that Rambam's classificatory system resembles the Sunni division of humanity into Muslims, idolaters, and non-Muslim People of the Book. Rambam, who participated actively in the intellectual life of the Islamic world in which he lived, was quite familiar with this Islamic spectrum and internalized it in his own fashion.[11] Just as Sunni laws regarding foreign meat express the notion that Jews and Christians are like Muslims in a fundamental respect, Rambam's version of the laws regarding foreign wine expresses his conviction that Muslims are like Jews and, for that reason, superior to other non-Jews. Sunnis, however, grant elevated status to non-Muslims on the basis of their receipt of authentic scriptures. Rambam, who regards the Jewish Bible alone as an authentic revelation, instead classifies gentiles on the basis of their monotheistic credentials. Christian theology falls short of Rambam's strict standards, and for that reason Christians fall into Rambam's generic category of idolaters irrespective of their reverence for the Jewish Bible.[12] Only Sunnis, whose classificatory system demands the association of Christians with Jews and Muslims, feel the need to explain away troubling aspects of Christian theology. Implicit in Rambam's relatively complex definition of Them is a proportionally complex definition of Us: Jews are not merely defined by their monotheism but also and more importantly by their adherence to all of the laws which God revealed in the Written and Oral Torah.

Neither Rambam nor his predecessors, I should emphasize, regard laws governing foreign wine as a means of segregating Jews from gentiles or preventing intermarriage; these laws relate exclusively to gentile religious practices or, in the *Mishneh Torah,* to gentile theology.[13] Rambam, building on ideas introduced by the redactors of the Bavli, ascribes a segregative function to other Rabbinic foreign food restrictions: the Sages promulgated these restrictions, he says, "in order to distance [Jews] from gentiles so that Jews will not intermingle with them and ultimately intermarry."[14] Jews, Rambam declares, may not drink wine or other popular alcoholic beverages in majority-gentile settings, even if the alcohol was never touched by a gentile; they may not consume bread baked solely by gentiles, especially when the bread is homemade; and they may not consume foods commonly served to honored guests if those foods require cooking and gentiles alone cooked them. These laws apply with respect to Muslims and idolaters alike: Muslims may be monotheists, but they are not Jews and are therefore unsuitable as marriage partners. Because Rambam establishes the distinction between Jews and Muslims through these laws, he is able to emphasize the similarity of Judaism and Islam by means of the laws governing foreign wine. (We observed earlier that *dhimmī* laws provide similar latitude to Sunni authorities.)

Rambam's conception of a distinction between idolatrous and monotheistic gentiles, the product of a style of thought heavily influenced by Islamic ideas, did not take hold among rabbis living in Christian Europe. Because the Talmud neither distinguishes among gentiles nor grants legal significance to the beliefs of non-Jews, Talmudic scholars who lived outside the Islamic milieu in which such activities are commonplace were not predisposed to accept Rambam's subdivision of gentiles on the basis of their theological doctrines. European rabbis would also have seen little value in Rambam's ruling that Jews may derive benefit from wine associated with Muslims but not from wine associated with Christians. By the time Rambam's work reached the lands of Christendom, moreover, European rabbis had formulated an alternative justification for foreign wine restrictions based on the principle of social segregation, a principle that Rambam does not associate with these laws. To the extent that prohibitions of foreign wine are understood as segregating Jews from gentiles, the theologically oriented distinctions among gentiles that Rambam offers are entirely beside the point.

"BECAUSE OF THEIR DAUGHTERS": RECONSTRUCTING WINE RESTRICTIONS IN CHRISTIAN EUROPE

The authors of geonic responsa and their original recipients all lived within the Islamic world and participated in the same intellectual culture, but copies of these responsa also penetrated into Christian Europe. The geonic equation of contemporary gentiles and newborn idolaters attracted considerable interest among the eleventh- and twelfth-century Talmudic scholars of Ashkenaz, as Jews called the region of northern France and western Germany. Ashkenaz was a major center of European wine production, and Jews participated actively in the wine-centered regional economy as investors, commercial middlemen, and, of course, consumers. The strict prohibition against deriving benefit from wine associated with Christians carried a significant economic cost to Ashkenazic Jews involved in the wine trade, substantially decreased the supply of wine available for Jewish consumption, and necessitated elaborate precautions to ensure that Christian domestic servants did not touch any wine within Jewish households. Adherence to the prohibition of foreign wine also entailed a significant social cost, as Christians were deeply resentful of this Jewish practice. Haym Soloveitchik has offered a masterful account of the ways in which authorities in Ashkenaz treated the subject of wine touched by Christians; the discussion that follows draws on the data Soloveitchik has gathered and analyzed while suggesting a different interpretation of this evidence.[15]

The first Ashkenazic rabbi to address the geonic equation of gentiles and newborns was R. Shelomo Yiṣḥaqi, known by the acronym Rashi (d. 1105). Rashi's grandson, R. Shim'on b. Me'ir ("Rashbam," d. ca. 1174), recounts his grandfather's treatment of this issue as follows:

> Our teacher [i.e., Rashi] discovered in a geonic responsum the opinion that because contemporary gentiles do not know how to offer libations as they do not customarily sprinkle their wine in idolatry, their wine ought to be permitted for the derivation of benefit like that of a newborn. It seemed fitting to our teacher to rely on this [opinion] to permit the derivation of benefit from libation wine given to a Jew [in repayment of a debt] during the harvest season or throughout the year. Such wine should not, however, remain in his possession in barrels so that he might sell it for a higher price, firstly because this might lead to an error [i.e., that the Jew might accidentally consume it]. Even if he stored the wine at a gentile's home, however, such behavior is prohibited for another reason, namely that it shows disrespect toward the words of the Sages and their enactments in that one derives additional benefit from something whose benefit they prohibit. Even though we hold that nowadays it is permitted to derive benefit [from gentile wine] on account of the financial losses that Jews would otherwise suffer, we should not be overly lenient: it is proper to remain as removed from this practice as possible.[16]

Rashi disregards the fact that the responsum to which he apparently refers, cited above, addresses "the touch of an Ishmaelite gentile" in contrast to that of other non-Jews. Unlike rabbis in the Islamic world, those who lived in the lands of Christendom recognized that Christians do not engage in idolatry. Indeed, although Rashi and other rabbis in Ashkenaz continue to refer to wine made by Christians as "libation wine," they take for granted that "the gentiles in our region do not offer idolatrous libations."[17]

Whereas the geonim and Rambam are careful to limit the applicability of their lenient rulings to wine touched by Muslims, rabbis in Ashkenaz, like their Talmudic predecessors, consistently treat all contemporary gentiles alike. One could account for this difference by pointing to the fact that Ashkenazic Jews lived in a society that was uniformly Christian while Jews were not the only non-Muslim minority within Islamic society. This explanation, however, fails to account for the fact that Ashkenazic rabbis seem to willfully overlook the distinctions between Muslims and other gentiles found in the geonic responsa they discuss. Perhaps a better explanation is that rabbis in medieval Christian Europe, in contrast to rabbis in the Islamic world, were culturally predisposed not to make distinctions among gentiles. Talmudic literature, after all, lacks such distinctions, and we have seen that contemporaneous Christian legal scholars also treat all gentiles alike. Just as Christian authorities preserve the uniformity of the category *pagan* even as they adapt their foreign food restrictions upon discovering that contemporary pagans "judaize," Rashi preserves the uniformity of the category *idolaters* even as he embraces the notion that contemporary idolaters "do not offer idolatrous libations" in order to relax certain Talmudic prohibitions.[18] Only within the Islamic world, in which the dominant culture's authorities classify outsiders in multiple categories, do Rabbinic authorities even consider establishing legally significant distinctions among gentiles.

Rashi and fellow Ashkenazic authorities not only expand the class of gentiles to whom geonic leniencies regarding foreign wine apply, they also narrow the scope of these leniencies considerably. Rashi relies on the equation of contemporary gentiles and newborns in order to justify Jewish acceptance of Christian wine in repayment of debts, a leniency which had already gained currency among Ashkenazic authorities despite the fact that no scholar could legitimize this practice, but he prohibits Jews from keeping such wine for any length of time. The geonic responsum that Rashi cites, however, readily justifies far greater leniency with respect to wine touched by gentiles: if the prohibition of benefit does not apply to Christian wine, what is wrong with deriving the most possible benefit from such wine, or deriving benefit from such wine even in circumstances that do not involve the danger of financial loss?

The equation of gentiles and newborns, moreover, readily justifies other leniencies in the laws governing foreign wine which Ashkenazic authorities were unwilling to consider. Recall that the Talmudic authority Shemu'el holds that a Jew may not only sell Jewish wine touched by a newborn gentile but may also consume it. By combining Shemu'el's opinion, which some Ashkenazic authorities accept, with the equation of all contemporary gentiles and newborns, one would effectively eliminate the need to prevent foreign contact with Jewish wine![19] All authorities, moreover, distinguish between Jewish wine which a gentile inadvertently touches and Jewish wine which a gentile inadvertently pours from one vessel to another without direct contact: the former is prohibited for Jewish consumption while the latter is permitted. If all gentile contact with Jewish wine is now deemed to be inadvertent, like that of a newborn, then there is nothing wrong with allowing one's Christian servants to pour Jewish wine. Such a conclusion would eliminate the need for the elaborate precautions Ashkenazic Jews took to ensure that their servants did not engage in such behavior and thus would effect a significant change in daily life.[20]

The Rabbinic virtuosos of Ashkenaz, like contemporaneous scholars of Roman and canon law, excelled in harmonizing disparate texts and fleshing out the logical implications of legal arguments. By applying these techniques to Talmudic discourse about foreign wine restrictions, Ashkenazic authorities were able to shut the floodgates of legal change which the geonic equation of gentiles and newborns threatened to open. These techniques also enabled Ashkenazic rabbis to formulate a new, unassailable rationale for continued adherence to traditional restrictions. R. Yiṣḥaq of Dampierre (Rashi's great-grandson, d. 1198), the greatest of these virtuosos, accomplishes the first of these tasks by disproving the analogy formulated by the geonim. The salient criterion about newborns, R. Yiṣḥaq contends, is not their ignorance regarding libation practices but rather their utter lack of intention when touching wine. Adult gentiles, in contrast, do act with intention when they come into contact with wine, even if that intention has nothing to do with the offering of libations. For that reason one cannot treat adult gentiles as comparable to newborns.[21] R. Yiṣḥaq was unaware of the resident alien analogy employed by Rambam, a contemporary, but we may safely assume that he would have found a way to disprove this analogy as well.

Ashkenazic authorities could have found a way to relax the traditional prohibition against gentile wine despite the flaw in the geonic equation of contemporary gentiles with newborn idolaters. R. Yisha'yah di Trani ("Rid," d. ca. 1250), an Italian rabbi who corresponded with Ashkenazic authorities and employed the same method of Talmudic interpretation, offers one version of the road not taken in Ashkenaz itself. He holds that contemporary gentiles are not analogous to newborn idolaters because the latter grow up to offer libations while the former never do so. Because neither Muslims nor Christians—with the exception of priests standing at the Eucharistic altar—ever offer libations, Rid declares that nowadays gentile contact with Jewish wine ought to be legally meaningless. Rid is careful, however, to clarify that he does not want anyone to act in accordance with this reasoning: by the time he wrote his commentary, it would seem, Ashkenazic authorities had circled the wagons in defense of the prohibition against deriving benefit from wine touched by gentiles who do not engage in idolatry.[22]

Unlike their counterparts in the Islamic world, who redefine contemporary gentiles by extending the scope of Talmudic borderline cases (newborn idolaters, resident aliens), Ashkenazic authorities reconstruct the very rationale that underlies the prohibition of wine touched by foreigners. These rabbis do not insist that Christians are full-fledged idolaters, but instead assert that the religious beliefs and practices of gentiles are beside the point. According to Rashbam, perhaps the earliest authority to formulate this argument, the Sages "enacted a prohibition against the ordinary wine of gentiles 'because of their daughters' [B. *A.Z.* 36b], whereas wine that had actually been offered in idolatrous libations is prohibited by scripture itself. . . . If one says that their ordinary wine was also forbidden out of concern that they might have offered some in an idolatrous libation, [we respond that] such behavior is infrequent and highly unusual, such that there is no need to be concerned about it at all."[23]

Talmudic Sages, the geonim, Rambam, and Rashi all understand the prohibition of foreign wine found in Mishnah *'Avodah Zarah* to relate in some manner to the idolatrous practices or beliefs of non-Jews. Rashbam, in contrast, asserts without precedent that this prohibition is thoroughly social and segregative in its orientation. He draws support for this reinterpretation of the prohibition of foreign wine not from the Bavli's discussion of this prohibition but rather from a stray comment that appears in an entirely different context.[24] Rashbam, like Augustine and the Shi'i authority al-Murtaḍā, employs a statement from one passage of a canonical source to reinterpret another passage that seems to contradict contemporary norms and, in so doing, permanently shifts the way his community understands the

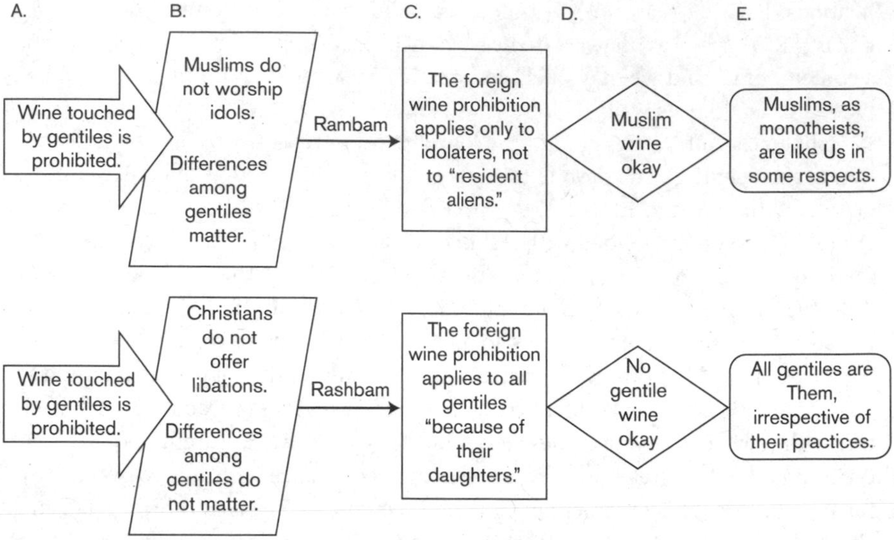

FIGURE 11. THE IMPACT OF TALMUDIC INTERPRETATION: RAMBAM AND RASHBAM ON WINE. (A) Traditional texts and practices (givens), (B) when viewed through internalized cultural paradigms, (C) take on new meanings that, (D) when articulated in normative terms, (E) externalize new ideas about Us and Them.

passages in question (see figure 11). What is distinctive about Rashbam's interpretation, however, is that it does not shift the normative bottom line. To the contrary, Rashbam's interpretation, embraced by all Ashkenazic authorities, successfully preserves in full force the foreign wine restrictions found in the Talmud.

Ashkenazic authorities had at their disposal the legal resources necessary to eliminate a burdensome aspect of Rabbinic foreign wine restrictions, yet they pointedly refrained from doing so and, indeed, went out of their way to justify the continued applicability of these laws. Soloveitchik accounts for this conservatism by positing that Ashkenazic Jews regarded foreign wine as "taboo," by which he means that these Jews exhibit a desire to remain separated from such wine "beyond the degree demanded by the rational considerations of the society itself."[25] According to this theory, Ashkenazic Jews—the general populace no less than their Rabbinic authorities—behaved irrationally with respect to foreign wine because they regarded such wine as especially repugnant. This theory, however, cannot account for the conservatism evident in geonic responsa. These responsa, we have seen, also seek to defend the continued applicability of Talmudic restrictions against the consumption of wine touched by gentiles, yet the geonim express no trace of repugnance toward foreign wine and their petitioners would have been happy to eliminate traditional wine restrictions entirely.

In light of the patterns we have traced in the present study, I would suggest an alternative explanation for Rabbinic conservatism with respect to foreign wine restrictions. The geonim, Ashkenazic authorities, and, in his own way, Rambam all value the traditional laws demanding abstention from foreign wine because these laws function as markers that distinguish Us from Them. Abstention from foreign wine, according to this explanation, is constitutive of Jewish identity not because of anything repugnant or otherwise objectionable about the wine but rather because the act of abstention constructs the boundary separating Jew and gentile. Indeed, this logic appears to underlie the earliest Jewish source that reflects the practice of avoiding foreign wine, *Daniel.* As we observed earlier, this text offers no indication that Daniel's abstention from such wine was motivated by concerns about gentile idolatry. The social significance of foreign wine restrictions was especially strong in medieval Ashkenaz. The importance of these restrictions as a boundary marker and expression of Jewish identity, moreover, could only have increased as Jews came to recognize that Christians, as monotheists, are not as different from Us as We had always imagined Them to be. The justification which Ashkenazic authorities formulate for the continued applicability of traditional foreign wine restrictions gives expression to the important function of these laws as markers of gentile otherness and Jewish distinctiveness. According to this explanation, Ashkenazic rabbis treat the subject of foreign wine rationally even as they make a point of acting against their community's evident social and economic interests.

Ashkenazic authorities, like Ibn al-ʿArabī and the author of *Ecce vicit leo,* redefine the function of a traditional foreign food restriction in order to justify preserving the status quo with respect to its applicability. Rambam, in contrast, is similar to Ibn al-Qayyim and Huguccio in his insistence on revising the contemporary applicability of a traditional foreign food restriction in response to the actual beliefs or practices of foreigners. These approaches are incompatible: Rambam interprets the prohibition against foreign wine in theological terms and distinguishes Muslims from other gentiles, while Ashkenazic authorities interpret this prohibition in social terms and treat all gentiles alike. Rambam and his Ashkenazic counterparts also understand Christianity in fundamentally different ways. Nevertheless, some rabbis of the late Middle Ages sought to reconcile these opinions. R. Shelomo b. Avraham Adret ("Rashba," d. 1310), active in Christian Spain, exemplifies these efforts. Rashba posits that the Sages formulated two separate prohibitions of gentile wine. The first prohibition, intended to segregate Jews and gentiles, forbids consumption of foreign wine "because of their daughters," while the second, promulgated out of concern regarding libations, also forbids the derivation of benefit from such wine. The latter prohibition, Rashba asserts using language borrowed from the *Mishneh Torah,* does not apply to "gentiles who do not engage in idolatry."[26]

Rashba is not the only Rabbinic authority who embraces the "because of their daughters" rationale for the prohibition of foreign wine while allowing Jews to derive benefit from Jewish wine touched by contemporary gentiles on the grounds that idolatry is no longer a concern. Most, however, assert that the prohibition against deriving benefit from such wine remains in force irrespective of the beliefs and practices of contemporary gentiles because concern about their daughters continues unabated. R. Yosef Karo is among these authorities, but he nevertheless incorporates Rashba's more lenient ruling into the *Shulḥan 'Arukh*.[27]

The claim that the Sages promulgated foreign wine restrictions as a means of preventing intermarriage constitutes a significant departure from the discussions of these restrictions found in the Bavli itself, where the concern clearly relates to the idolatrous predilections of gentiles. Indeed, Rashbam's interpretation of the Talmudic prohibition against foreign wine reveals the degree to which Rabbinic conceptions of gentiles changed over the course of a millennium: whereas the Sages are deeply concerned about what they believe to be the ubiquitous gentile practice of offering wine libations, Rashbam regards such behavior to be so infrequent as to merit no concern at all. Reading the Bavli through the lens of his experiences in medieval Ashkenaz, Rashbam ascribes a new meaning to Talmudic foreign wine restrictions.

At the same time, however, Rashbam endorses the Talmud's own conception of gentiles: all gentiles are alike, and their association with wine renders that wine forbidden to Jews irrespective of what the gentiles themselves might think about this association. Precisely because the Ashkenazic interpretation of these laws focuses on gentiles as non-Jews rather than specifically as idolaters, its advocates are the most reluctant to relax the Talmud's severe prohibition against deriving benefit from wine associated with gentiles. After all, gentiles remain non-Jews even if their religious beliefs or practices have changed since Talmudic times. For the same reason, adherents of the Ashkenazic approach to foreign wine restrictions see no need to ascribe significance to gentile behavior, as the geonim are the first to do, much less to advance classificatory systems of unprecedented complexity, as Rambam does. Like the Sages themselves, these medieval authorities hold that there is no significant difference among gentiles and that wine associated with these gentiles is prohibited regardless of how the gentiles themselves may understand that association. R. Yosef Karo, in fact, goes so far as to assert that contemporary gentiles are no different from the gentiles of Talmudic times, as the Christian Eucharist with its offering of wine and bread "is full-fledged idolatry."[28] R. Karo's conception of contemporary gentiles as idolaters may account for the *Shulḥan 'Arukh*'s rewording of Rambam's and Rashba's phrase "gentiles who do not engage in idolatry" as "idolaters who do not engage in idolatry," the oxymoronic phrase with which we began.

We have, in a sense, come full circle in our study of medieval discourse regarding wine associated with Muslims and Christians, as R. Karo's presentation of foreign wine restrictions comes closest to that of the Bavli itself. This return to Talmudic conceptions of gentiles reflects the resilience of scholasticism as a driving force shaping the ways in which religious authorities interpret legal sources, the flexibility of definitions ascribed to hermeneutical foreigners, and, even more so, the power of traditional systems of classification to determine the outcome of contentious legal disputes. With the limited exception of Rambam's *Mishneh Torah,* medieval authorities preserve the binary division of Jew and gentile, brushing away the significance of data that might result in a more complex picture of humanity. From their perspective, the missing details regarding the beliefs and practices of religious foreigners are simply irrelevant. As we have seen, this perspective is common to Christian and Muslim authorities as well as to Jewish authorities: the relevance of information regarding foreigners depends to a considerable degree on the manner in which it relates to preconceived notions about hermeneutical foreigners and the classification of humanity. In all three communities, They constitute what Martin Buber calls an *It,* an object to be defined, classified, and manipulated in accordance with Our needs and desires. Buber observes that "every *It* is bounded by others; *It* exists only through being bounded by others."[29] Jewish, Christian, and Islamic authorities of antiquity and the Middle Ages, we may now add, believe that the meaning of *I*—that is, the self-identity of their own communities—also depends upon the boundaries and *I–It* relationships that exist between Us and Them. Buber understands the *I* of the instrumental *I–It* relationship to be utterly distinct from that of the "*I–Thou*" relationship that exists between two subjects who possess equal agency in self-definition. Our authorities, in contrast, regard these relationships as complementary: they imagine their communities as located at the intersection of temporal *I–It* relationships and the ultimate *I–Thou* relationship, that of humanity and God. As a result, they construct the otherness of religious foreigners in a manner that those foreigners themselves would not recognize.

US AND THEM, *I* AND *IT*, PAST AND PRESENT

This study has explored the ways in which Jewish, Christian, and Islamic authorities define their own *I*s and their own *It*s through the medium of foreign food restrictions. By allowing these authorities to speak for themselves and putting their statements into dialogue with one another, it provides a more nuanced understanding of the ways in which these authorities think and, in particular, the ways in which they imagine both themselves and the broader social order. We are now in a position to answer the question about fences found in Robert Frost's "Mending Wall." The food-fences we have examined in this study "make good neighbors" precisely because they make these neighbors into useful foils. Foreign food restrictions, whether segregative or not, express in thought and through social practice the distinctiveness of Our identity by contrasting Us and Them. The foreigners addressed in discourse about these restrictions are, first and foremost, intellectual constructs, corollaries resulting from the manner in which religious authorities imagine the identity of their own community. The distinct styles in which Jewish, Christian, and

Islamic authorities imagine their own communities and think about foreigners, we have seen, constitute the primary determining factors that shape medieval discourse about foreign food restrictions.

The Jewish, Christian, and Islamic intellectual traditions are by no means uniform in their conceptions of Them or their self-definitions of Us. The case studies we have examined exemplify the internal disputes within medieval communities of scholars over the precise status of food associated with foreigners, disputes that reflect more significant disagreements regarding communal identity. These sharp differences notwithstanding, participants in these disputes are able to debate one another because they accept the same fundamental principles, assumptions, interests, and ideals, just as the narrator of "Mending Wall" and his neighbor are able to construct a shared wall despite their different opinions about its utility. The same cannot be said when one juxtaposes authorities from different religious traditions.

We have seen that Jewish, Christian, and Islamic authorities employ similar scholastic modes of thinking, imagined conceptions of foreigners, and techniques of textual interpretation. These similarities are even greater among authorities who live in a common intellectual culture, whether that of Christian Europe or of the Islamic Near East. We might even say that the intellectual tools with which authorities in these communities construct their identities and their hermeneutical foreigners are the same. The normative walls and cultural towers built by each community, however, differ in significant ways, to the point that joint construction efforts such as the ones depicted in "Mending Wall" or attempted in the Biblical Tower of Babel narrative would have been impossible even if they had been desired. A visitor from one community would recognize many of the construction techniques and even some of the building blocks employed within another community, but would be baffled as to why anyone would build a wall or tower in such a manner and entirely uninterested in following suit. The different kinds of walls constructed by Jews, Christians, and Muslims, their different locations relative to the community's center, and their different functions all reflect the different styles of thought that characterize each religious tradition. These distinct styles of thought, we have seen, reflect distinct styles of imagining Our own community and the broader social order that encompasses both Us and Them.

In order to recognize and appreciate the distinctive styles of thought associated with any given intellectual community, one needs to step outside of that community. Insiders, after all, are wont to take their own presumptions for granted, especially with respect to ideas intertwined with core aspects of their own identity and worldview. Scholars of a single intellectual tradition can also readily take presumptions for granted unless prompted by an external stimulus to do otherwise. By juxtaposing Jewish, Christian, and Islamic sources and analyzing the similarities and differences among them, we are better able both to recognize the common attributes of distinct intellectual traditions and to identify the factors that make each tradition distinctive. This approach has enabled us to develop a more sophisticated understanding of ideas about foreign religious traditions and to better understand the role that these ideas play in the process of religious self-identification. This study thus models a valuable approach to the comparative study of religious communities. It also highlights a significant challenge inherent in contemporary efforts at interreligious dialogue and, perhaps, models an approach to addressing this challenge.

Jewish, Christian, and Islamic authorities of antiquity and the Middle Ages imagine adherents of other religions in accordance with their own preconceptions, paradigms, and visions of the proper social order. Traditional ideas about Us and Them continue to influence religious thought to the present day, even as, in some cases, these ideas have evolved considerably during modern times.[30] Thus, to cite only the most transparent example, during the second half of the twentieth century the Catholic Church officially shifted from imagining Jews as anti-Us to imagining Jews as like Us. What stands unchanged in this substantial about-face, however, is the practice of defining Judaism within a Christian ideological framework in the service of a particular conception of Christianity. Thus, while the Vatican's Commission for Religious Relations with Muslims is housed within the Pontifical Council for Interreligious Dialogue (originally called the Secretariat for Non-Christians), its Commission for Religious Relations with the Jews is housed within the Pontifical Council for Promoting Christian Unity. The traditional Christian system of classifying humanity into Christians, Jews, and gentiles, along with the traditional ascription of particular significance to Jews in the definition of Christian identity, remains intact even as the Catholic Church has repudiated many of its traditional teachings about Jews. The Jews, who clearly benefit from this contemporary reformulation of the relationship, nevertheless remain an *It,* ultimately denied the right of self-definition. Many contemporary Protestants, Muslims, and Jews also draw upon traditional classifications of foreigners without regard for the ways in which these outsiders define themselves. Ideas about Them, rather than the ideas of others about themselves, continue to play an outsized role in interreligious dialogue, contemporary theology, and, of course, the mass media. The result is the inadvertent perpetuation of stereotypes and of mutual misunderstanding, a Babel-like situation in which collaborative construction efforts are severely hobbled, if not doomed to failure.

At the close of chapter 1, we left a priest, a minister, a rabbi, and an imam sitting in a restaurant. Such a cordial interfaith gathering would have been inconceivable until quite recently. The message I would emphasize to clergy and laity committed to interreligious dialogue and constructive collaboration is that we need to pay greater attention to the different ways in which our communities imagine themselves and their respective foreigners. True relationship entails perceiving the other as a *You,* that is, as another *I* with the right to self-definition. Seeing others as others see themselves, however, may require significant changes in the ways we imagine our own distinctive identities, as these identities in their traditional forms rest upon stereotyped definitions of others. As Buber observes, the *I* of the *I–Thou* relationship is quite different from the *I* defined by means of *I–It* relationships. Redefining our respective definitions of ourselves not in terms of traditional conceptions of Us and Them but rather in terms of We and You is among the most important tasks that face contemporary religious authorities and others committed to both tradition and religious pluralism.

NOTES

PREFACE

1. The opening words of Stephen Tournai's *Summa* on the *Decretum*, trans. Somerville and Brasington, *Prefaces*, 194.
2. Freidenreich, "Foreign food."
3. Rosenblum, *Food and identity*.

1. GOOD FENCES MAKE GOOD NEIGHBORS

1. Foster and Anderson, *Medical anthropology*, 268.
2. Throughout this work, I use the term *identity* to refer to the ideas about Us and Them employed by the ancient and medieval scholars whose works I analyze. This term does not function as category of analysis in its own right; as Brubaker and Cooper, "Beyond 'identity,'" demonstrate, "identity" is overly ambiguous as an analytical category and its application by academics tends to reinforce the very concepts which we seek to understand. In effect, I employ *identity* as a synonym for "collective self-definition."
3. Fischler, "Food, self, and identity," 280.
4. See Green, "Otherness within," 49–51; J. Z. Smith, "Differential equations," 232–34.
5. See *Lev.* 11.5, 7, 13 // *Deut.* 14.7–8, 12.
6. Robert K. Merton helpfully distinguishes between "manifest" functions of sociological phenomena, "which are intended and recognized by participants in the system," and those functions that are "latent," which is to say, "neither intended nor recognized" ("Manifest and latent functions," 105). I also follow Merton in limiting my use of the term *function* as a reference to the "observable objective consequences" of laws in contrast to the "subjective dispositions (aims, motives, purposes)" of jurists (78).
7. On Islamic norms governing the consumption of birds of prey, see Cook, "Early Is-

lamic dietary law," 251–52; Cook (258) notes that most Islamic authorities permit the consumption of rock badgers.

8. Foreign food restrictions, which limit Our ability to eat food associated with Them, are distinct from regulations governing Their consumption of Our ritual foods, such as rules about access to the Eucharist or other sacrificial meals. This study does not address laws of the latter type.

9. Lévi-Strauss, *Totemism,* 69.

10. W. R. Smith, *Religion of the Semites,* 247, 257.

11. Grignon, "Commensality and social morphology," 23–24.

12. Douglas, "Deciphering a meal," 249.

13. Lévi-Strauss, *Raw and cooked;* for more condensed expressions of this distinction, see "Culinary triangle"; *The origin of table manners,* 478–79. The third pole of Lévi-Strauss' culinary triangle, the "rotten," constitutes "naturally" transformed food in contrast to the "cultural" transformation called cooking. The "raw," according to Lévi-Strauss, is of neutral valence. The sources examined in this study, however, tend to view both raw and rotten foods as "natural" and contrast them with culturally-mediated prepared ("cooked") foods.

14. Fischler, "Food, self, and identity," 287.

15. I claim no originality in applying Anderson's definition in this manner; among numerous other scholars who do the same, see S. J. D. Cohen, *Beginnings of Jewishness,* 5.

16. B. Anderson, *Imagined communities,* 6, emphasis original.

17. Carr, *Writing on the tablet,* emphasizes the role that education in a canon of traditional texts plays in the enculturation of elites within the ancient Near Eastern and Mediterranean worlds; this role continues well beyond the period of antiquity.

18. Rosenblum, *Food and identity,* 6, emphasis original. I allude here as well to Peter L. Berger's understanding of the three "moments" within the dialectical process of world-building: externalization, objectivation, and internalization (*Sacred canopy,* 4). We will examine the applicability of Berger's theory to foreign food restrictions in greater detail in chapter 12.

19. Abusch, "Hammurabi," 401.

20. Hartog, *Mirror of Herodotus.*

21. Ewald, "Comparative jurisprudence."

22. Ibid., 1947–48.

23. See Ewald, "Comparative jurisprudence," especially 1949–50. I use *intellectual context* instead of Ewald's favored term, *philosophy,* as he understands the latter in an especially broad sense. Although *philosophy* is an adequate term to describe the intellectual context of modern German law, Ewald's primary test case in this essay, it is less applicable in the context of the medieval canon law case which Ewald addresses or the various religious legal traditions which I study.

24. J. Z. Smith, *Drudgery divine,* 51, emphasis original.

25. My use of the lens metaphor—and, indeed, my approach to comparison more broadly—is inspired by Doniger, *The implied spider,* 7–25, who distinguishes between a telescope (focusing on cross-cultural contexts), a microscope (focusing on specific texts), and the naked eye (which sees a text in its cultural context). Also significant in shaping my approach to comparison is the work of Jonathan Z. Smith, especially the essays collected in

Imagining religion and *Relating religion.* For a more detailed description of how comparison may be used to refocus scholarly attention, see Freidenreich, "Comparisons compared," 91–94.

26. In more technical parlance, I employ a form of polythetic taxonomy, in contrast to the familiar monothetic system within which a species must belong to precisely one genus. On the use of taxonomy within religious studies, see J. Z. Smith, "Fences and neighbors."

27. S. J. D. Cohen, *Beginnings of Jewishness,* 341.

28. See ibid., esp. 69–106.

29. Holdrege, *Veda and Torah,* 19–25.

2. MEALS, MEAT, AND THE NATURE OF ISRAEL'S HOLINESS IN THE HEBREW BIBLE

1. I am grateful to Baruch J. Schwartz for sharing this insight.

2. Scholarly convention distinguishes between "Israelites," the community described and addressed by most Biblical texts, and "Jews," reserving the latter term for those who revere the God described in the Hebrew Bible after the sixth-century B.C.E. Babylonian exile.

3. Biblical dietary laws relate exclusively to animal products. This focus is common in many cultures; see Fessler and Navarrette, "Meat is good to taboo," 1–6.

4. The vassal-treaties of Esarhaddon, for example, regard "serving food at table" and "drinking from a cup" as means of establishing treaties; see Wiseman, *Vassal-treaties,* 40.

5. On the political significance of sharing food or refusing to share food, with specific reference to *Genesis* 14, *Judges* 14, and *Deuteronomy* 23.4–7, see Elgavish, "Encounter of Abram and Mechizedek," 499. *Deuteronomy* instructs Israelites to provide food for the *ger* and even to invite the *ger* to celebrate festivals with Israelite families, celebrations that presumably involve shared meals (e.g., 24.19–21, 16.11–14). The *ger* to whom these passages refer, however, may be a displaced Israelite rather than a foreigner; see Olyan, *Rites and rank,* 74–81.

6. On the frequency and function of banquets in *Esther,* see Berlin, *Esther,* xxiv–xxv, 3–4. The composition date of *Esther* is unclear. The range of 400–200 B.C.E. is widely cited among scholars of this book, each of whom shades toward a different point on the range by emphasizing different pieces of evidence. Given the sharp difference between the attitudes toward foreign food expressed in *Esther* and in the first chapter of *Daniel*—which Collins, *Daniel,* 146, dates to the Hellenistic period—I am inclined to support the specifically fourth-century (that is, Persian-period) dating advanced by Berlin, *Esther,* xli–xlii. In the context of this study, however, it is necessary merely to note that the motif of feasting and drinking and the involvement of Jews in these Persian practices is central to the narrative, is found without any significant variations in all ancient versions of the book, and must date from the earliest layer of this text.

7. The Hebrew term I render "food rations," *manot* (here: *menoteha,* literally "her portions"), also appears in *Esther* 9.19, 22, and *Nehemiah* 8.10, 12, where its reference to food is explicit.

8. Berlin, *Esther,* 27.

9. Freedman, "Earliest Bible," 342–43, dates this passage precisely to 561–60 B.C.E.

10. On the complicated issues surrounding the dates of these leaders and the work(s) that bear(s) their names, see Williamson, *Ezra, Nehemiah,* xxi–xliv. Williamson agues that Ezra arrived from Babylonia in 458 B.C.E., Nehemiah in 446; he dates the primary composition of *Ezra/Nehemiah* to around 400.

11. See S. J. D. Cohen, *Beginnings of Jewishness,* 243–44; Hayes, *Gentile impurities,* 27–33.

12. Cassuto, *Exodus,* 444, observes that *Exodus* 34.15–16 contains seven verbs depicting what will happen if the Israelites grant a covenant to the inhabitants of the land; the verb *to eat* falls at the crucial midpoint. Similarly, the verb *to eat* is the fourth of seven verbs describing the events of Shittim in *Numbers* 25.1–3.

13. Note that Jacob, in establishing a covenant with Laban, is careful both to swear only by the God of his father and to personally perform the sacrifice associated with their shared covenant meal (*Gen.* 31.53–54).

14. On the meanings of Biblical and ancient Near Eastern terms for "slaughter" and the sacrificial connotations frequently associated with these terms, see Bergman, Ringgren, and Lang, "Zabhach." See also Bergquist, "Bronze Age sacrificial *koine?*" 29; Hallo, "Origins of the sacrificial cult." More broadly, see Burkert, *Homo necans,* whose relevance to the ancient Near East is affirmed by both Birgquist and Hallo.

15. A compelling argument for the existence of a common precursor to the catalogs of animal species has been made by Meshel, "Lehavdil," 21–24. I am grateful to Naphtali Meshel for sharing this unpublished work, as his "Food for thought," 209–10, presumes this relationship between the two catalogs without providing the supporting argumentation. See also Houston, *Purity and monotheism,* 63–65.

16. Equally effective (and equally absent) would be a statement, "We do not eat the meat of rock badgers because rock badgers metaphorically reflect Their identity." Eilberg-Schwartz, *Savage in Judaism,* 120–26, suggests that such logic underlies Biblical dietary laws, which he claims prohibit consumption of animals frequently used to depict foreign nations (e.g., lions and asses). This aspect of Eilberg-Schwartz's thesis, however, is not compelling because Biblical texts often depict Israelites using the same animal metaphors. See D. C. Kraemer, *Jewish eating,* 19–21.

17. The one possible exception to this generality is the final ("Third") section of *Isaiah,* dated to the sixth or fifth century. Isaiah characterizes Jews disloyal to God as those "who eat the flesh of swine" (65.4) and associates idolatrous Jews with the consumption of such flesh and with the practice of offering pig blood in sacrifice (66.17, 3). Rosenblum, *Food and identity,* 50, concludes from this evidence that "pork is the ultimate metonym for the 'culinary Other' in Israelite/Jewish literature long before the Tannaitic period," i.e., the first centuries of the common era. Isaiah does portray consumption of pork as a thoroughly non-Jewish activity, but he does not indicate that non-Jews regularly engaged in this activity. Isaiah's references to pork consistently appear alongside other taboo foodstuffs: "the broth of foul things" (65.4), the flesh of humans and of dogs (66.3), reptiles and mice (66.17). Archeological studies of Biblical Canaan and Roman Palestine indicate that dogs, reptiles, and mice—to say nothing of human flesh—were not consumed on a regular basis; see Houston, *Purity and monotheism,* 124–80; Grantham, "Zooarchaeological model," 183–201. Only in sources from the Hellenistic era do we begin to find conclusive evidence that pork consumption func-

tions as a marker of the difference between Jews and gentiles; on these sources, see *Food and identity,* 48–58, and, in greater detail, Rosenblum, "'Why do you refuse to eat pork?'"

18. Milgrom, *Leviticus 1–16,* 648, reasonably suggests that the rock badger, a wild animal that lives in craggy regions, is mentioned by name not because its consumption was commonplace but rather because Biblical authors (erroneously) believed it to be one of the few animals that manifests only one of the two criteria associated with permissible quadrupeds. No mention of rock badger remains appears in the archeological studies cited in the previous note.

19. On the place of meat in the diet of ancient Israelites and their neighbors, see Haran, "Ma'akhalim u-mashqa'ot," 4: 543–44, 548–54. Gruber, "Private life," 638, observes that, given the typical sizes of family flocks in the late Bronze Age kingdom of Ugarit, slaughtering more than eight sheep a year for food would effectively wipe out the entire flock. Garnsey, *Food and society,* 16–17, 122–27, similarly emphasizes the limited place of meat in the ancient Mediterranean diet.

20. Houston, *Purity and monotheism,* 177; see also 231–32.

21. Gerstenberger, *Leviticus,* 291, commenting on *Lev.* 20.24b–26 (cited below). See also Houston, *Purity and monotheism,* 13–15; Levine, "Excursus 2." For an argument against the segregationist interpretation similar in some respects to the one that follows, see D. C. Kraemer, *Jewish eating,* 17–19.

22. B. J. Schwartz, "Prohibitions," 43–44. This article is an abridged version of part of the author's dissertation, subsequently published as *Torat ha-qedushah,* 102–20.

23. See Brichto, "On slaughter," 20. Milgrom, *Leviticus 1–16,* 705, observes that the prohibition against consuming blood is the only explicitly universal law in the Torah. Holiness texts, like *Leviticus* 17, consistently use the term *ger* in reference to non-Israelites; see Olyan, *Rites and rank,* 69–74.

24. *Leviticus* 17.13 allows the Israelite and the *ger* to hunt nondomestic animals for food; on the requirement in this chapter that Israelites slaughter domestic animals in a sacrificial context, see below. *Deuteronomy* 12.15–16, 20–25 allows Israelites to perform slaughter in nonsacral contexts; its discussion of animal preparation does not address the issue of animal slaughter performed by non-Israelites.

25. Milgrom, *Leviticus 1–16,* 724; see also Milgrom's graphic depiction of this relationship on p. 722. On the connection between holiness and species-specific dietary restrictions, see also Firmage, "Biblical dietary laws"; Houston, *Purity and monotheism,* 237–43.

26. Interpretations that highlight virtues, ethics, or wholeness and order are offered, respectively, by Eilberg-Schwartz, *Savage in Judaism,* 120–26; Milgrom, *Leviticus 1–16,* 729–31; and Douglas, *Purity and danger,* 53–57.

27. The same may be said with respect to the verse forbidding Israelite consumption of the thigh muscle (*Gen.* 32.33) and those prohibiting the practice of boiling a young goat in its mother's milk (*Exod.* 23.19, 34.26; *Deut.* 14.21); on the latter prohibition, see Haran, "Seething a kid in its mother's milk."

28. On the requirement in *Leviticus* that Israelites offer all sacrificeable animals in sacrifice, see B. J. Schwartz, "'Profane' slaughter." On the applicability to the *ger* of only some of the requirements incumbent upon Israelites, see B. J. Schwartz, *Torat ha-qedushah,* 44–46, esp. n. 11.

29. *Leviticus* 11.39–40 and 17.15, unlike *Deuteronomy,* condone the consumption by non-priestly Israelites of carrion meat from permissible animal species.

30. D. C. Kraemer, *Jewish eating,* 23–24, suggests that the Torah's dietary laws do not seek to segregate Israelites from non-Israelites because virtually all inhabitants of Israelite territories were, by definition, Israelites. On the ethnnic-geographic nature of the term *Jew* (that is, *Judean*) as used in sources from before the mid-second century B.C.E., see S. J. D. Cohen, *Beginnings of Jewishness,* 69–106.

31. For a more detailed discussion of this typology, see Freidenreich, "Holiness and impurity."

32. The term *najāsah* is also used to refer to impurity in general. The clearest summary of the Islamic purity system of which I am aware appears in Gauvain, "Ritual rewards," 341–43. See also M. H. Katz, *Body of text,* who refers to the narrow category of *najāsah* as "substantive impurity."

33. Klawans, *Impurity and sin,* 21–42; Klawans provides a useful survey of the vast literature about ancient Jewish conceptions of impurity on pp. 3–20.

34. There are, however, significant differences between Biblical and Islamic conceptions of impurity; see Maghen, "First blood."

35. Hayes, *Gentile impurities,* 27–32. Sunni authorities do not regard any human being as *najis;* see Maghen, "Close encounters." On Shiʿi notions regarding the intrinsic impurity of non-Muslims, see Freidenreich, "Implications of unbelief."

36. References to impurity in the dietary laws of *Leviticus* 11 and *Deuteronomy* 14 are anomalous within Biblical literature because these texts partially conflate the categories of permitted/prohibited with pure/impure. Because the impurity described in these passages is transmitted by contact (e.g., *Lev.* 11.8 // *Deut.* 14.8), I would argue that these texts address an anomalous instance of circumstantial impurity; Wright, "Spectrum," 165–69, reaches the same conclusion. On this issue, see Klawans, *Impurity and sin,* 31–32; on the relationship between the categories of pure/impure and permitted/prohibited with respect to the dietary laws, see Meshel, "Food for thought."

37. On the relationship between the dichotomous pairs holy/mundane and pure/impure, see Milgrom, *Leviticus 1–16,* 731–32, which also contains the source of inspiration for figure 2.

38. Propp, *Exodus 19–40,* 690, vividly depicts the Israelite sanctuary as a nuclear power plant tended by meticulous technicians who must occasionally mitigate crises of contamination lest disaster result. For a different metaphor depicting the impact of offensive defilement on the sanctuary, see the classic essay by Milgrom, "Israel's sanctuary."

39. Douglas, *Purity and danger,* 35.

3. THE NATURE AND SIGNIFICANCE OF HELLENISTIC JEWISH FOOD PRACTICES

1. Barclay, *Jews in the Mediterranean Diaspora,* 88, defines Hellenism as "the common urban culture in the eastern Mediterranean, founded on the Greek language (the verb *hellenizein* originally meant 'to speak Greek'), typically expressed in certain political and educational institutions and largely maintained by the social elite." Hellenization, Barclay continues,

is cultural engagement with Hellenism, manifesting itself in political, social, linguistic, educational, ideological, religious, and material spheres.

2. S. J. D. Cohen, *Beginnings of Jewishness,* esp. 69–106. Cohen demonstrates that all references to *yehudim* (Hebrew) or *ioudaios* (Greek) prior to the late second century B.C.E. refer to "Judeans" rather than "Jews"; the former is an ethnic-geographic term referring to those associated with a people and its ancestral homeland. I nevertheless employ the term *Jews* throughout this chapter and use *Judean* to refer specifically to Jews living in Judea because the distinction between Judean Jews and other Jews will prove to be an important one.

3. S. J. D. Cohen, *Maccabees to the Mishnah,* 35–37, offers a brief history of the term *Hellenistic Judaism* and demonstrates its proper usage as a chronological indicator rather than as a moniker for a particular type of Judaism. In this context, Cohen suggests that the "Hellenistic" period concludes in the second or first pre-Christian century. For a strong defense of studying early Rabbinic and early Christian sources as manifestations of Hellenistic Judaism (as Cohen himself implicitly does in *Beginnings of Jewishness*), see Boccaccini, *Middle Judaism,* 1–25.

4. With the notable exception of Josephus's works, written in Rome by a former Judean, and the possible exception of *Tobit,* which may derive not from Judea but from neighboring Syria (see note 24), no surviving Jewish sources from other diaspora communities address food restrictions. I use *Judea* in its broad sense as the name of a country, one of whose districts is also named "Judea"; see S. J. D. Cohen, *Beginnings of Jewishness,* 72.

5. *Letter of Aristeas,* 8–9. References to specific passages in this work are to verse numbers.

6. This is precisely the message received by such classical authors as Diodorus Siculus (*Bibliotheca historica* 34/35.1.2), Tacitus (*Historiae* 5.5), and Philostratus (*Vita Apollonii* 5.33), all of whom take umbrage at Jewish refusal to share meals with gentiles. See M. Stern, *Greek and Latin authors,* 1: 182–83; 2: 19, 26; 2: 341.

7. H. Anderson, "3 Maccabees," 510–12, suggests dating this work to the early first century B.C.E.; J. J. Collins, *Between Athens and Jerusalem,* 124–26, prefers to associate it with the Roman period, specifically 24 B.C.E.–41 C.E. For an interpretation of this work in terms of Jewish attitudes toward integration in Hellenistic society, see Barclay, *Jews in the Mediterranean Diaspora,* 195–99.

8. Translations of the *Letter of Aristeas* are by R. J. H. Shutt.

9. Hayes, *Gentile impurities,* 140.

10. *Addition to Esther* F 11. On the dating of the Greek *Esther,* see Moore, *Esther: The additions,* 250–52, who advocates 114–113 B.C.E. See also J. J. Collins, *Between Athens and Jerusalem,* 110–11, who dates the work to 78–77 B.C.E.; a third possibility is 49–48 B.C.E. There are actually two extant versions of the expanded *Esther,* only one of which appears in the Septuagint. Although these texts differ significantly in many respects, they are identical in all passages relevant for this study; references are to the Septuagint's versification.

11. Translation by Moore, *Esther: The additions,* 209, with slight alteration; on the original language and second-century Judean provenance of this passage, see pp. 12–14, 155, 165–67. Emendations to and citations of Septuagintal material are based on the Göttingen (Vandenhoeck and Ruprecht) edition.

12. On the symposium-esque motifs in *Esther,* which ancient audiences would presumably recognize, see Burkert, "Oriental symposia," 14–15.

13. J. J. Collins, *Daniel,* 24–38, 146.

14. The Hebrew word translated as "vegetables" is *zero'im* in *Daniel* 1.12 and *zer'onim* in 1.16. This word, in either form, is unattested elsewhere in Biblical literature; its root means "seed." Ancient translations render the term as either "seeds" or "pulse"; JPS offers "legumes." The translation here follows J. J. Collins, *Daniel,* 128; see also p. 144.

15. Hartman and Di Lella, *Daniel,* 130. J. J. Collins, *Daniel,* 139 n. 109, notes that Athenaeus defines the Greek loan-word *potibazis* as "barley and wheaten bread baked."

16. Support for the assumption that royal rations consist of meat and wine may be found in *Nehemiah* 5.18; I am grateful to Naomi S. Jacobs for drawing my attention to this verse.

17. Such an interpretation is offered by J. J. Collins, *Daniel,* 142–43, among others.

18. Hayes, *Gentile impurities,* 19–22, 47–54; Klawans, "Notions of gentile impurity."

19. D. C. Kraemer, *Jewish eating,* 26, correctly observes that the term *yitga'al* is not a synonym for "impure" (i.e., circumstantially polluted), but I believe he is incorrect to say that the term has no technical meaning and merely conveys a sense of disgust. The Biblical root *g.'.l.,* infrequently attested in the sense of "defile," refers to acts of bloodshed (*Isa.* 59.3, 63.3; *Lam.* 4.14) and to the sacrificial offering of blemished animals (*Mal.* 1.7, 12), transgressions associated with offensive impurity. In *Nehemiah,* the verb refers to those who have defiled their priestly lineage by contracting forbidden marriages with gentiles (*Neh.* 13.29, cf. 7.64 // *Ezra* 2.62). The verb is also used to describe the defiled state of Jerusalem resulting from her disobedience (*Zeph.* 3.1).

20. The connection between the consumption of prohibited foods and the penalties associated with defiling offenses is attested in several earlier sources, including *Leviticus* 7.22–27, 17.10–12; *Ezekiel* 33.25. Daniel is surely not worried about the offensive defilement of the gentile food preparers, as the text of *Daniel* 1 expresses no concern about the behavior of these foreigners and the defilement which the Torah associates with offensive impurity is not contagious in any case.

21. Translations from *First* and *Second Maccabees* are taken from the NRSV, but I have freely emended them on the basis of the Greek original and the translations of Jonathan A. Goldstein. *First Maccabees* was originally written in Hebrew but survives only in its ancient Greek translation; *Second Maccabees* was originally written in Greek. On the dating of these works, see Goldstein, *I Maccabees,* 62–89; Rappaport, *Maqabim 1,* 48–50, 60–61; D. Schwartz, *Maqabim 2,* 13–19.

22. Goldstein, *II Maccabees,* 266.

23. In the same vein, Josephus reports that an Essene expelled from his community "often comes to a most miserable end. For, being bound by their oaths and usages, he is not at liberty to partake of other men's food, and so falls to eating grass and wastes away and dies of starvation" (*Jewish war* 2.143, trans. Thackeray). The Essene oaths to which Josephus refers (but, unfortunately, does not cite) would seem to involve treating the food of non-sectarian Jews as if it were foreign food, prohibited on account of its preparation by outsiders; see note 28 below.

24. On the dating and origin of this work (either Judea or neighboring Syria), see Moore, *Tobit,* 40–43; N. S. Jacobs, "The delicacies were many," 23–24. Jacobs, on pp. 56, 68, suggests

that *Tobit* 1.10–13 is a late addition to the text, citing as support both textual evidence and the fact that most works expressing concern about the food of foreigners date from the time of the Hasmoneans.

25. NRSV translation, slightly revised. Tobit's boastful emphasis of his own righteousness is highlighted by Gruen, *Diaspora*, 148–58. N. S. Jacobs, "The delicacies were many," 50–59, places this passage in the broader context of food references in *Tobit*.

26. For the text of these medieval versions, see Weeks, Gathercole, and Stuckenbruck, *Book of Tobit*, 76–77. Hebrew texts of *Tobit* also employ the verb *ga'al*, used to express Daniel's refusal to become defiled through the consumption of foreign food.

27. *Life of Josephus*, 14, trans. Mason.

28. On sectarian efforts to establish boundaries between their own members and nonsectarian Jews, including restrictions on the food of nonsectarians, see Baumgarten, *Flourishing of Jewish sects*, esp. 7–9, 86–102. Baumgarten makes the compelling argument that sectarians employ the very boundary markers intended to separate Jews from gentiles in order to place Jews who do not belong to the sect in a new category of "outsider" (see note 23). In the process of reapplying foreign food restrictions to fellow Jews, however, many sectarian authorities apparently alter the underlying basis of the original restriction. Indeed, because that restriction is rooted in the non-Jewish identity of the food preparer, sectarians need to create a different, purity-based rationale in order to extend the prohibition to fellow Jews.

29. Qimron and Strugnell, *Miqṣat ma'asei ha-Torah*, 148–50.

30. *Temple Scroll* 63.14–15. Although this text was found at Qumran, its origins are disputed; unlike other sectarian sources, the *Temple Scroll* contains no prohibitions against the food of other Jews.

31. On the determinative role of genealogy in social organization within Sasanian Persia, understood to reflect pre-Hellenistic Iranian structures as well, see Yarshater, *Cambridge history of Iran*, xxxviii–xliii.

32. Isocrates, *Panegyricus* 50, quoted in Hengel, *Judaism and Hellenism*, 64. On the significance of education as a means of elite enculturation in the ancient world, with particular emphasis on the Hellenistic world, see Carr, *Writing on the tablet*.

33. S. Schwartz, *Imperialism*, 27.

34. On the difference between assimilation (i.e., social integration), acculturation (the internalization of language, ideas, and values), and accommodation (the integrative or oppositional use to which acculturaltion is put), see Barclay, *Jews in the Mediterranean Diaspora*, 92–98. On the degree of acculturation manifest among the Hasmoneans, see Gruen, *Heritage and Hellenism*, 1–40.

35. Consider the statement found in Diogenes Laertius's *Lives of Eminent Philosophers* (1.33), according to which Thales (or, some say, Socrates) thanked fortune for the blessing of having been born a Greek and not a barbarian; see Kahn, "On gentiles, slaves, and women." The Jewish embrace of a binary dichotomy between Jews and gentiles is attested explicitly in one of the earliest recorded Jewish blessings (praising God for "not making me a gentile," T. *Berakhot* 6.18) and indirectly by Paul (who challenges its continued relevance in *Gal.* 3.28; see chapter 6). Pre-Hellenistic Biblical texts, in contrast, often distinguish among different non-Jewish peoples; see the conclusion of chapter 5.

36. S. J. D. Cohen, *Beginnings of Jewishness*, 140–74.

37. Douglas, *Natural symbols,* 59–76; Collins, *Daniel,* 146, also appeals to this work in his interpretation of Daniel's food practices.

38. Josephus, *Judean antiquities* 12.119–20. Josephus also cites numerous other decrees by Syrian authorities instructing that Jews have access to their customary foods; see 14.225–27, 259–61.

39. Goodman, "Kosher olive oil," 227–28; Rosenblum, "Kosher olive oil reconsidered," 1–4.

40. Josephus, *Jewish war* 2.591–92; *Life* 74.

41. Goodman, "Kosher olive oil," 240; Goodman further suggests (p. 229) that Josephus takes the taboo against foreign olive oil for granted because it is a part of his own lifestyle.

42. Josephus's romanticized tale of Tobiad exploits appears in *Judean antiquities* 12.160–236; shared meals are recounted in 173–74, 186–89, 210–13. It is noteworthy that the Tobiads (at least while sober) endorse the prohibition against Jewish-gentile sexual intercourse articulated in *Nehemiah* (line 187) without regarding commensality with foreigners as being in any way problematic. Tcherikover, *Hellenistic civilization,* 126–42, relies heavily on this tale in his depiction of those he calls "Hellenizers."

Josephus himself may be another Judean who sees little value in foreign food restrictions. His depictions of Daniel (*Antiquities* 10.90) and the Hasmonean martyrs (12.255, 269; contrast Josephus's source, *1 Macc.* 1.63) contain no reference to abstinence from food associated with gentiles. Josephus's account of the incident in which foreign women seduced Israelites into the worship of Baal-peor (*Antiquities* 4.126–40), which Josephus may have told with the temptations of Hellenistic culture in mind, portrays Biblical dietary restrictions as constituting the essence of Jewish ancestral law. Josephus does not, however, use this opportunity to express the notion that dietary restrictions ought to limit social interaction between Jews and gentiles. On this passage, see van Unnik, "Josephus' account."

43. On the translation and date of this work, see note 21. The Greek term rendered as "forbidden," *koina,* literally means "mundane" and is used occasionally in late Biblical literature (but not in Greek translations of earlier works) to refer to food that is unfit for consumption (e.g., *Rom.* 14.14, discussed in chapter 6). In *Mark* 7.2, the term clearly means "impure" (in the sense of polluted), while in *Acts* 10.14 it appears alongside the Greek word for "impure" and thus presumably carries some supplementary connotation. In *1 Macc.* 1.47, the term refers, alongside pork, to animals unfit for sacrifice, while 1.62 may refer specifically to sacrificial food. The verb rendered "defiled," *mianthōsi,* is often associated with the performance of prohibited, offensive behavior; see, for example, LXX *Lev.* 18.24–30, 11.43–44. The Septuagint, however, occasionally uses forms of the verb *mianein* to refer to circumstantial pollution (e.g., *Lev.* 13); see also *John* 18.28.

44. *Splagchnismon;* see Goldstein, *II Maccabees,* 276; Bergquist, "Bronze Age sacrificial *koine?*" 13–17. The same term is used in *2 Macc.* 7.42.

45. See D. E. Smith, *Symposium to Eucharist,* esp. 30, 67–69. See also Burkert, *Greek religion,* 70–71.

46. *Moses* 1.298; cf. *Special laws* 1.56, *Virtues* 40. Philo also condemns the consumption of food offered to idols in such passages as *Moses* 2.165, 270; *Special laws* 1.21, 316. On Philo's attitudes toward Jewish participation in idolatrous sacrifice, see Barclay, "Who was considered an apostate?" 84–86; Leonhardt, *Jewish worship,* 236–37. An oblique reference to Jewish

abstention from food offered to idols also appears in *Aristeas,* 184, which reports that a Judean priest, rather than one of the king's sacrificial ministers, was invited to offer the prayer that opens the priests' banquet with the king.

47. See 2 *Macc.* 6.18–7.42. This topic is the subject of the entirety of *Fourth Maccabees.* Anderson, "4 Maccabees," 533–34, asserts that *Fourth Maccabees* was probably written between 63 B.C.E. and 70 C.E. and that no more precise date can be offered for the work. Klauck, *4. Makkabäerbuch,* 668–69, however, cites a probable date range of 20–120 C.E. and prefers a date toward the end of the first century. Witherington, "Not so idle thoughts," argues for the late dating of, and Christian influence on, *Fourth Maccabees* based on its use of the term *eidōlothuton,* which otherwise appears solely in Christian literature.

48. This translation is primarily that of VanderKam, *Jubilees,* 131, adapted for increased readability in light of Wintermute, "Jubilees," 98. On the dating of this work, see VanderKam, *Jubilees (Guide),* 21.

49. The dating and provenance of this work are subject to dispute: R. S. Kraemer, *When Aseneth Met Joseph,* 225–44, makes a strong case that the work post-dates the early-second-century demise of the Alexandrian Jewish community.

50. Translation by Burchard, "Joseph and Aseneth."

51. Indeed, the language of this verse closely parallels that of LXX *Gen.* 43.32; see Burchard, *Joseph und Aseneth: Kritisch herausgegeben,* 106–8. No reference to separate seating appears in the depictions of the meal served at Joseph's second visit to Pentephres' home (18.1–5, 11; 20.1–8) or the wedding feast offered by Pharaoh (21.8)

52. Barclay, *Jews in the Mediterranean Diaspora,* 211.

53. Regarding the date and place of composition, see Moore, *Judith,* 67–70. Gruen, *Diaspora,* 162–63, interprets the jumble of chronology and personnel with which *Judith* opens as a deliberate signal of the tale's fictional nature.

54. Translation from Moore, *Judith,* slightly altered.

55. Moore, *Judith,* 218.

56. LSJ, s.v. "opson." As discussed in detail by Davidson, *Courtesans and fishcakes,* 3–35, this term refers generally to the relishes that accompany bread and, in the minds of many Greek writers, to fish in particular. Although it seems unlikely that the author of *Judith* has fish in mind, the present point does not suffer from such an interpretation because most fish is permitted by the Torah and is not generally eaten raw.

57. Barclay, "Who was considered an apostate?" 91–92.

58. For a brief treatment of this subject, see Barclay, *Jews in the Mediterranean Diaspora,* 60–71.

59. Ibid., 1, citing *Moses* 1.278.

60. B. Anderson, *Imagined communities,* 6.

61. The fact that sectarian and nonsectarian sources alike express common sentiments regarding the food of foreigners provides further support for Seth Schwartz's argument that sectarians were in fact part of the Judean mainstream elite; see *Imperialism,* 49.

62. Such is the argument of the great nineteenth-century pioneer of academic Jewish history, Heinrich Graetz, in *Geschichte der Jüden,* 797–810. Graetz asserts that the so-called Eighteen Decrees, which we will examine in chapter 4, were promulgated in 67 C.E. in order to lay the groundwork for the revolt against Rome. This claim has been affirmed by nu-

merous twentieth-century historians, including Weiss, *Dor dor ve-dorshav,* 175–76; Finkelstein, "Life and the law," 143; Hengel, *Zealots,* 203; Urbach, *Sages,* 295–96; and Ben-Shalom, *Beit Shammai.* As the discussion of the Eighteen Decrees in chapter 4 demonstrates, there is no textual basis for this claim.

63. Berger, *Sacred canopy,* 3–19. We will examine the applicability of this theory to foreign food restrictions at greater length in chapter 12.

4. THE FOODSTUFFS OF FOREIGNERS IN EARLY RABBINIC LITERATURE

1. S. J. D. Cohen, "Judaean legal tradition," identifies seven sources of Rabbinic law: (1) scripture, the Torah first and foremost; (2) the legal traditions of the ancient world; (3) the common practice of Jewish society; (4) the realia of Jewish institutions; (5) the teachings of priests; (6) the teachings of pietists and sectarians; and (7) the innovations of the Sages. Foreign food restrictions in the Mishnah and other early Rabbinic literature stem originally from sources 3 and 6; as we will see, these restrictions have also been substantially influenced by source 7.

2. On Rabbinic attitudes toward non-Biblical texts in general, see Kahana, *Sefarim ha-ḥiṣonim,* viii–x. The only apocryphal work cited by name in early Rabbinic literature is *The Wisdom of Ben Sira* (also known as *Ecclesiasticus;* T. *Yadayim* 2.13). The Sages are familiar with the tradition, elaborated upon in *Aristeas,* that Jews translated the Torah into Greek for King Ptolemy (*Mekhilta d'Rabbi Yishmaʿel, Pisḥa* §14), but their list of divergences between the Torah and the Septuagint does not correspond to the text of the latter.

3. On Rabbinic attitudes toward gentiles in general, see Hayes, "'Other' in rabbinic literature"; for a more detailed study focused specifically on tannaitic literature, see Porton, *Goyim.*

4. Cabezón, *Scholasticism,* 4–6; see also the essay by Swarz in this volume.

5. S. J. D. Cohen, "Judaean legal tradition," 134–35; Cohen also employs the term *scholastic* to characterize the mode of thinking manifest in the Mishnah.

6. It used to be commonplace to regard the Tosefta, literally "the supplement," as a supplement to the Mishnah in its present form, but recent scholarship has demonstrated that the relationship between these works is more complicated. On this subject, see Friedman, *Tosefta ʿaṭiqta,* and Hauptman, *Rereading the Mishnah.* Technically speaking, the Aramaic term *Tosefta,* unlike the Hebrew terms *Mishnah* and *Talmud,* contains a built-in direct article; nevertheless, I generally refer in English to "the Tosefta" on the model of "the Mishnah" and "the Talmud."

7. In this text, it seems that an "apostate" (*meshummad*) is one who has rejected aspects of Jewish law (cf. T. *Horayot* 1.5), whereas a "heretic" (*min*) is one who has, according to the speaker, rejected Judaism itself. In some instances, including Tosefta *Ḥullin* 2.20, the term *heretic* evidently refers to Jewish believers in Christ; see note 11 below. On these terms in Rabbinic literature, see S. Stern, *Jewish identity,* 106–12; on the latter, see also Hayes, "'Other' in rabbinic literature," 258–59.

8. The final phrase (*nizbaḥ meʿaleha*), an awkward locution found nowhere else in Rabbinic literature, reflects the author's effort to incorporate a reference to carrion into the literary structure of his interpretation of the Biblical verse.

All translations of the Tosefta are my own, based whenever possible on the unfinished critical edition prepared by Saul Lieberman. For the tractate *'Avodah Zarah,* I use the critical edition prepared by Zeidman, "View of celebrations." Both rely primarily on the text of MS Vienna. For other tractates, including *Sheḥiṭat Ḥullin,* I use the text of MS Vienna found at the Bar-Ilan University Web site (www.biu.ac.il/js/tannaim/ [accessed October 28, 2010]) while consulting the other versions found on that site; the numbers are those found in the Zuckermandel edition. I prepared these translations in consultation with those of Jacob Neusner and his students, published in Neusner, *History of the mishnaic law,* and collected in Neusner, *Tosefta;* I also make use of Zeidman's translation and commentary on Tosefta *'Avodah Zarah.*

9. I am grateful to Jordan D. Rosenblum for this insight regarding the implicit validity of a heretic's act of slaughter. See further Rosenblum, *Food and identity,* 154–58, which discusses, inter alia, an earlier version of the present paragraph.

10. Rosenblum, *Food and identity,* 79–80.

11. *Sheḥitat Ḥullin* 2.21 lists additional prohibitions against interaction with heretics, culminating with a prohibition against turning to heretics for healing. This is followed by a case in which a Sage refused an offer to be healed in the name of Jesus (2.22) and another in which R. Eli'ezer was brought to trial on charges of heresy, an event he ascribes to having been favorably impressed by a tradition ascribed to Jesus (2.24). On Rabbinic attitudes toward "heretics" and the frequent use of this term in reference to Jewish Christ-believers, see P. S. Alexander, "Parting of the ways"; Alexander addresses *Sheḥitat Ḥullin* 2.20–24 on pp. 15–16. See also Boyarin, *Border lines,* 220–22.

12. Green, "Otherness within," 58–59. Similarly, R. Eli'ezer reportedly equated the consumption of bread baked by Samaritans with the consumption of pork (M. *Shevi'it* 8.10); no similar equation with respect to bread baked by gentiles is attested. The practice of adapting restrictions that target "external others" for use against "internal others" is evident in pre-Rabbinic sectarian literature as well; see Baumgarten, *Flourishing of Jewish sects.* (I am indebted to Hayes, "'Other' in rabbinic literature," for the terms *external* and *internal others.*)

13. Westbrook, *Studies,* addresses the use of borderline cases in ancient Near Eastern law, in which such cases illuminate not only the complicated issues they address explicitly but also the principles that apply in ordinary cases; see especially p. 4. Rabbinic literature addresses ordinary cases by articulating legal categories, but the Sages continue to employ borderline cases as a means of fleshing out the nuanced application of these categories. On the existence and function of such cases in the Mishnah, see E. S. Alexander, "Casuistic elements" (on improbable and borderline cases, see esp. 197–200). In chapter 10, we will encounter similar argumentation in Islamic legal sources regarding joint slaughter—and, especially, joint hunting—by Muslims and non-Muslims.

14. This passage is quite terse, and the paraphrase here includes several details not found in the original text. Lieberman, *Tosefet rishonim,* 2: 219, observes that slaughter begun by a gentile and completed by a Jew is *invalid* according to one medieval citation of Tosefta *Sheḥiṭat Ḥullin* 1.2. Neusner, *History of mishnaic law . . . Hullin,* 17, asserts that this alternative reading is consistent with the sense of the Toseftan passage as a whole. On the contrary, I would contend that the reading "valid," found in MSS Vienna, London, and the *editio princeps,* is more consistent, as it produces the precise definition of the act of slaughter described below.

15. This understanding of *Sheḥiṭat Ḥullin* 1.6a as refering to a Jew who accidentally slaughters an animal in the process of flaying it for a gentile follows the interpretation of Lieberman, *Tosefet rishonim,* 2: 219–20. The Tosefta's permission of such accidental slaughter and its unqualified permission of proper slaughter by deaf-mutes or minors differs from the Mishnah's prohibition of the former (M. *Ḥul.* 2.3, based on a very different interpretation of *Deut.* 12.21) and its requirement that slaughter by deaf-mutes and minors be supervised (M. *Ḥul.* 1.1). The Mishnah and the Tosefta also diverge in their remarks about slaughter performed by two people holding the same knife. Both permit such an act, but whereas the Tosefta specifically allows it in cases where one participant is a gentile, the context in which the Mishnah addresses this topic (2.2) implies that both butchers are Jewish.

16. Lévi-Strauss, "Culinary triangle."

17. This translation is based on that of Rosenblum, *Food and identity,* 84.

18. On ancient bread making, see Krauss, *Talmudische Archäologie,* 1: 92–106; Broshi, "Diet," 42–44; Weingarten, "'Magiros,'" 291–97.

19. The version of this list in MS Erfurt concludes "liverwort, boiled water, and parched grain"; cf. B. *A.Z.* 38b.

20. Mishnah *A.Z.* 2.6 contains an explicit prohibition of gentile olive oil and also notes its repeal; see note 24 below.

21. D. C. Kraemer, *Jewish eating,* 60.

22. All translations of the Mishnah are my own, based the Albeck edition and on Rosenthal, *Mishnah 'Avodah Zarah.* David Rosenthal distinguishes between two distinct versions of Mishnah *'Avodah Zarah,* one that circulated in Palestine and one known to Babylonian authorities. Whereas Albeck's text reflects the Babylonian tradition, Rosenthal bases his edition on MS Kaufmann, the primary representative of the Palestinian version. In my translations of this tractate, I rely on the Palestinian tradition but depart from MS Kaufmann when it differs from most Palestinian manuscripts. In preparing my translations, I consulted those of Danby and Neusner. On Mishnah *'Avodah Zarah* 2.6–7, see Steinfeld, "Devarim shel goyim."

23. *Ḥeres adriani* in most manuscripts that preserve the Palestinian text, *hadriani* in the Babylonian Talmud. The Babylonian Talmud (*A.Z.* 32a) explains that this phrase refers to ceramic potsherds soaked in wine and used to flavor other beverages; scholars of classical Greek archeology with whom I have consulted, however, are not familiar with this practice or term. Neusner, *History of mishnaic law . . . Abodah Zarah,* 157, glosses this phrase with the explanation, "Earthenware is assumed to have absorbed wine."

24. Printed editions of the Mishnah and Babylonian Talmud commonly include the parenthetical statement "Rabbi and his court permitted oil" here. As Rosenthal, *Mishnah 'Avodah Zarah,* 166–74, demonstrates, however, this statement constitutes a gloss inserted after the redaction of the text, first in the Palestinian manuscript tradition (where it often appears not after "oil" but rather after "boiled foods") and only during the Middle Ages in the Babylonian manuscript tradition. On the Rabbinic permission of olive oil prepared by gentiles, see Goodman, "Kosher olive oil," 241–43; Rosenblum, "Kosher olive oil."

25. The Babylonian Talmud and, consequently, medieval authorities, treat the prohibition of boiled foods separately from the prohibition of pickled foods likely to contain wine or vinegar; this reading is supported by the Palestinian manuscript tradition, in which the

post-Mishnaic gloss regarding the permission of oil (see the previous note) appears after the term "boiled foods." It seems most probable, however, that the redactor of the Mishnah intended the qualification about wine additives to apply to boiled as well as pickled foods. This is clearly the case in the parallel tradition of Tosefta *'Avodah Zarah* 4.8a, which reads, "One may not derive benefit from gentile pickled and boiled foods which customarily contain wine or vinegar." See Steinfeld, "Devarim shel goyim," 151.

26. Minced fish (*ṭarit ṭerufah*) stands in contrast with unminced fish (*ṭarit she-eino ṭerufah*) in 2.7. Hebrew lexicographers commonly associate the term *ṭarit* with the Greek *thrissa* (LSJ, s.v: "a fish"). *Ṭarit,* however, also refers to what the Greeks called *tarichos:* salted, dried, smoked, or pickled fish, both chopped (*ṭerufah*) and whole (*she-eino ṭerufah*). On *ṭarit* and related terms, see Löw, "Aramäische Fischnamen," 560–62. On *tarichos* (Latin: *salsamentum*) and its production, see Curtis, *Garum,* 6–15.

27. On "brine containing no fish," supplemented by an explanatory gloss in the standard printed edition, see Rosenthal, *Mishnah 'Avodah Zarah,* 240–41.

28. The term for fish paste, *ḥilaq,* is derived from the Latin *allec,* which refers to a sedimentary by-product created while producing the fish-sauce called *garum;* this by-product itself was turned into a kind of fish paste. See Pliny, *Naturalis historia* 31.95; Curtis, *Garum,* 7, 177.

29. The resin extracted from the asafetida plant was one of the most popular spices in the Greco-Roman world and is found in more than half of the recipes in the first century C.E. Latin cookbook of Apicius. Sold in "droplets" or "tears" as well as in other forms, asafetida was often stabilized with various forms of meal, most often bean meal, and sometimes adulterated with a related spice, sagapenum; see Dalby, *Dangerous tastes,* 17, 110–12. The Babylonian Talmud (*A.Z.* 39a) suggests that the problem with asafetida droplets relates to the knife that made the incisions necessary to extract the resin: it may not have been sufficiently cleaned after previously cutting a prohibited foodstuff.

30. Apicius (*De re culinaria* 1.29) provides a recipe for *sal conditum,* evidently the type of salt to which the Mishnah refers, but none of its ingredients would be prohibited under Jewish law. According to the Talmuds (Y. *A.Z.* 2.10, 42a; B. *A.Z.* 39b), spiced salt may contain additives derived from prohibited insects or fish; one Sage reports that his neighbor added lard to spiced salt.

31. The term translated as "honeycombs" (following Danby and Neusner) is unattested elsewhere in early Rabbinic literature and is subject to extensive manuscript variations. Rashi and Albeck interpret this term as referring to clusters of grapes; Even-Shoshan, *Ha-milon he-ḥadash,* s.v. "duvdaniyot," translates it as cherries. Steinfeld, "Devarim shel goyim," 160–62, argues that it refers to honey from wild bees. All of these interpretations are plausible in the context of this mishnah.

32. In MS Kaufmann, *zeitei qelusqah megulgalin.* The last two words are synonyms for round cakes, the latter being a gloss of the former; see Rosenthal, *Mishnah 'Avodah Zarah,* 243–44.

33. MS Kaufmann, unlike the majority of textual witnesses and the parallel statement in Tosefta *'Avodah Zarah* 4.8, ascribes this opinion to R. Yehudah.

34. This interpretation of the laws governing gentile milk is offered by Talmudic Sages; see Y. *A.Z.* 2.8, 41d, and B. *A.Z.* 35b. The alternative, namely that the prohibition against for-

eign milk is preparer-based, is implausible as a Jew only needs to supervise the milking process (and, according to T. *A.Z.* 4.11, may do so from a distance) and does not need to perform the act of milking personally. Milk requires supervision because a glance at raw milk is not sufficient to determine conclusively whether the milk was drawn from a kosher animal. In Mishnah *Nedarim* 6.4, minced fish and fish brine are considered to be sufficiently unrecognizable as "fish" that one who swears off eating fish may still eat them. For that reason, one cannot be sure that the ingredients of these foodstuffs are in fact kosher. See also T. *A.Z.* 4.11.

35. Indeed, the Sages emphasize that gentiles are not subject to any Jewish dietary laws; see Rosenblum, *Food and identity,* 68–73.

36. For a similar interpretation of Mishnah *'Avodah Zarah,* see Hayes, *Gentile impurities,* 141–42. See also S. Stern, *Jewish identity,* 2–4, who uses other works of Rabbinic literature to demonstrate that references to non-Jews often serve "to enhance the identity of the Jews through a dialectical process of contrastive negation."

37. Olive oil, then as now, is best when unadulterated; on the making of bread, see note 18 above. Steinfeld, "Devarim shel goyim," observes that many medieval authorities also recognized that although most items listed in Mishnah *'Avodah Zarah* 2.6 are prohibited "because of [concern regarding] admixture," bread and oil are prohibited "because of their intrinsic nature."

38. According to Tosefta *'Avodah Zarah* 4.8, R. Me'ir and the Sages disagree over whether Hadrianic earthenware and foods which gentiles customarily prepare with wine or vinegar are subject to the prohibition against benefit; the Mishnah, however, distinguishes between the former and the latter.

39. The Mishnah's prohibition of meat prepared by gentiles clearly does not presume that such meat is idolatrous. As the Babylonian Talmud (*Ḥul.* 13a) already observes, this prohibition applies solely to consumption of the meat, whereas Jews may not derive any form of benefit from animals offered in idolatrous sacrifice. R. Eli'ezer holds that gentiles generally intend to slaughter their animals for idolatrous purposes (M. *Ḥul.* 2.7), but his is a dissenting opinion.

40. Dalby, *Food,* s.v. "cheese"; Stol, "Milk, butter, and cheese," 105.

41. In the Babylonian Talmud, R. 'Ula explains R. Yehoshu'a's behavior by asserting that he was following an established Palestinian custom of not revealing the rationale behind new legal decrees in the first year after their promulgation (B. *A.Z.* 35a). R. 'Ula's statement, however, is uncorroborated by any other Talmudic sources and is unconvincing as an interpretation of this mishnah, in which R. Yehoshu'a indeed does try to justify the cheese prohibition.

42. The Bavli, in *Ḥullin* 116b, asserts that the prohibition of carrion-derived rennet in Mishnah *Ḥullin* 8.5 has been abrogated, but cannot find direct proof to support this assertion and relies on indirect argumentation. Citation of Tosefta *Ḥullin* 8.12 would have simplified this discussion considerably, but Babylonian Sages seem not to be familiar with this tradition. For a broader argument that the Bavli is unfamiliar with the Tosefta, see Elman, *Authority and tradition.*

43. Some Talmudic authorities suggest that the prohibition of gentile cheese stems from gentile use of prohibited ingredients such as lard or gentile wine vinegar; see B. *A.Z.* 35b.

44. On the phenomenon of solipsism within rabbinic literature, see S. Stern, *Jewish iden-*

tity, 200–223. Whereas Stern interprets this phenomenon as a quasi-psychological response to the threat of engulfment in the larger non-Jewish culture, I would suggest that this phenomenon relates to the nature of scholasticism as a mode of thinking. See also Porton, *Goyim,* who refers to the Sages as "parochial in their outlook" (285).

45. On the practice of offering wine libations, see D. E. Smith, *Symposium to Eucharist,* 30. On the ubiquity of wine in Palestine and the ancient Mediterranean world, see Broshi, "Wine"; Alcock, *Food in the ancient world,* 92–95.

46. Wine in Mediterranean antiquity was customarily mixed with water; see Dalby, *Food,* s.v. "wine-mixing."

47. Schaefer, "Jews and Gentiles," 338. Schaefer, who proceeds to characterize Mishnah *'Avodah Zarah* 5.5 as resembling "a cops-and-robbers game," makes clear that this observation applies also and especially to the Yerushalmi's tractate *'Avodah Zarah.*

48. S. Schwartz, *Imperialism,* 162–76, argues that the Sages systematically misinterpret the paganism of their surrounding society. I would frame this "misprision," as Schwartz calls it, somewhat differently: the Sages subject manifestations of paganism to their own system of scholastic analysis without concern for the fact that the resulting interpretations bear little relationship to the ideas of gentiles.

49. On the one possible exception to this generalization, T. *A.Z.* 4.6, see the discussion in chapter 5.

50. Philo, *Moses,* 1.278, cited and discussed in chapter 3.

51. This translation is my own, based on the Horowitz edition of *Sifrei.* Both *Sifrei* and *Mekhilta d'Rabbi Shim'on b. Yoḥai* date from approximately the third century. The phrase "Obey me" carries clear sexual overtones.

52. See Porton, *Goyim,* especially pp. 241–43, 256–58. See also Halbertal, "Coexisting with the enemy."

53. Mishnah *Shabbat* 1.4, referring to a series of Sabbath-related restrictions in 1.2–3, states that "these are among the laws" promulgated at the conclave in question. (B. *Sh.* 13b makes the connection between 1.4 and the preceding text explicit; on an incorrect manuscript variant that obscures this connection, see Albeck, *Mishnah,* 2: 406.) The Mishnah proceeds to cite still more Sabbath-related disagreements between the Shammaites and the Hillelites. In total, Mishnah *Shabbat* 1.2–8 contains precisely eighteen Sabbath-related prohibitions, along with an additional prohibition related to circumstantial impurity that is marked as tangential. Tosefta *Shabbat* 1.14–22 shares the Mishnah's understanding of the conclave's subject matter, although it also ascribes impurity-related prohibitions to the conclave's activity. (Impurity-related concerns are similarly the focus of a tradition discussed at length in B. *Sh.* 13b.) It is certainly possible that none of these sources provides an historical account of the conclave in question (if, indeed, the event occurred), but their presence in the Mishnah and the Tosefta weighs heavily against the accuracy of accounts found only in the Talmuds.

54. See chapter 3, note 62.

55. Some medieval sources replace "their cheese" with "their oil"; see Lieberman, *Ha-Yerushalmi kifshuto,* 39–42.

56. All translations of the Yerushalmi are my own, prepared in consultation with Neusner, *Talmud of the Land of Israel.*

57. Confusion of *ḥelqah* and *ḥilaq*, both loanwords, was apparently common in Greek and Latin as well: the cognate Greek and Latin terms *(h)alix* and *(h)alica*, "emmer groats," also refers in some cases to fish paste, properly *(h)al(l)ec* in Latin; see LSJ, s.v. "halix"; *OLD*, s.v. "alica." Rabbinic literature frequently juxtaposes *ḥelqah*, *tragis* (from Greek *tragos*, "spelt," not mentioned in this passage), and *ṭisani* (from *ptisanē*, "peeled barley" or "barley-gruel"). All three foodstuffs are prepared by pounding the grain (B. *Mo'ed Qatan* 13b, cf. M. *Makhshirin* 6.2) in a pot (Y. *Nedarim* 6.2, 39c; cf. B. *Berakhot* 37a, where *ṭisani* is omitted); because of their preparation, they are no longer deemed to be "grain" (T. *Nedarim* 4.3). The addition of pounded and peeled grain to this list is thus unsurprising once one reads *ḥilaq* as *ḥelqah*.

58. Yerushalmi *Shabbat* 1.4, 3c, and *'Avodah Zarah* 2.8, 41d, both reject the sweeping prohibitions of the Eighteen Decrees on account of a tradition similar to the Toseftan statement discussed above. See also the similar discussion in Bavli *'Avodah Zarah* 37b.

59. On the contrasting representation of Jews and gentiles in Rabbinic literature, see S. Stern, *Jewish identity*, 1–50. Stern addresses the different portrayals of Jewish identity in legal and non-legal genres of Rabbinic literature on pp. xxxi–xxxiii.

60. Porton, *Goyim*, 3.

61. This message is encapsulated in the Rabbinic liturgical formula, first attested in the Babylonian Talmud, that praises God for distinguishing "the holy from the mundane, day from night, Israel from the nations . . . " (B. *Pesaḥim* 103b).

62. Adams, *Hitchhiker's guide*, 63; on towels, 27–28.

5. INTERSECTIONS OF TALMUDIC SCHOLASTICISM AND FOREIGN FOOD RESTRICTIONS

1. Steinfeld, "Akhilah 'im ha-goy" (on B. *A.Z.* 8a–b); "Le-heter pat" (35b); "Le-issur shemen" (36a–b); "Gazru 'al pitan" (36b); "Tavshilei goyim" (37b–38a); "Devarim she-nishtanu" (38a); "Kavvanah be-vishul shel goy?" (38a); "Bishul 'al yedei yisrael ve-goy" (38a–b); see also "Devarim shel goyim" (on M. *A.Z.* 2.6–7). These articles, in addition to offering Steinfeld's own valuable insights, provide textual variants and surveys of medieval interpretations for each passage.

2. On the interpretive challenges works of this nature pose to historical scholarship, see S. Schwartz, *Imperialism*, 164–65. On the relationship of these works to one another, conveniently focused on the tractate of most interest in the present context, see Gray, *Talmud in exile*.

3. Cabezón, *Scholasticism*, 5.

4. See Neusner, "Conducting dialectical argument."

5. On the general lack of concern regarding practical law in the Talmuds, especially the Babylonian Talmud, see Tucker, "Literary agendas." Tucker's conclusion emphasizes "the redactors' seeming nonchalance towards practical halakhah [i.e., Jewish law]. Though the world of rabbinic texts is our main source for Jewish law, it often seems that Jewish law, or at least its practical application, was not the primary interest of the final editors of those sources" (405).

6. Gafni, *Yehudei Bavel,* 150.

7. See chapter 4, nn. 29–30, 34.

8. The Bavli treats the Mishnah's reference to "their boiled foods" separately from "their pickled foods when their custom is to add wine or vinegar to them" in order to link its discussion of preparer-based restrictions to the first portion of this Mishnaic clause (B. *A.Z.* 37b–38b, citing M. *A.Z.* 2.6). The redactors of the Bavli may not have actually believed that the Mishnah itself prohibits cooked foods without distinction, however, as their discussion of gentile cooked foods makes no use of the Mishnaic term *shelaqot,* "boiled foods." The Yerushalmi also recognizes a prohibition of gentile cooked foods, albeit only in passing. See Y. *A.Z.* 2.6, 41c, and 2.8, 41d; Y. *Nedarim* 6.1, 39c; Y. *Terumot* 11.1, 47c; see also the statement of R. Manna in the Yerushalmi's discussion of gentile bread, found in multiple essentially identical iterations: Y. *Shevi'it* 8.4, 38a; Y. *Ma'aser Sheni* 1.4, 3c; Y. *Sh.* 1.4, 3c; Y. *A.Z.* 2.8, 41d. In all of these passages, the permissibility of specific gentile foodstuffs is addressed against the backdrop of a general prohibition of gentile cooked food.

9. Y. *Sh.* 1.4, 3c; Y. *A.Z.* 2.8, 41d; see chapter 4, n. 58.

10. B. *A.Z.* 37b. Gray, *Talmud in exile,* 243, identifies this parallel as an instance in which the redactors of the Bavli are familiar with a redacted text of the Yerushalmi, but does not discuss it in any detail. Other such parallels include the discussions of milk and oil (which Gray addresses on pp. 151–52 and 106–16 respectively).

11. Literally, R. Yoḥanan prohibits meats "whose beginning and completion [of cooking] is at the hand of a gentile." One could understand this language to prohibit food whose cooking was started and finished by a gentile even if a Jew was responsible for intermediary stages of the cooking process. Such an interpretation, however, seems unlikely, and for this reason I have chosen to offer a more idiomatic translation. All translations of the Talmud Bavli are my own, prepared in consultation with Jacob Neusner, *Talmud of Babylonia . . . Abodah Zarah.*

12. The significance of R. Yoḥanan's statement regarding partial roasting by a gentile is not immediately apparent. "R. Ḥanan b. Ami [said] that R. Pedat said that R. Yoḥanan said, 'A gentile who singes the head [of an animal]—it is permitted to eat from it, even from its earlobe'" (B. *A.Z.* 38a). The anonymous voice of the Bavli understands this statement to indicate that inadvertant cooking by a gentile (in this case, in the process of removing hairs from the facial skin of an animal) is not legally significant. Steinfeld ("Kavvanah be-vishul shel goy?" 152), however, observes that this interpretation fails to account for R. Yoḥanan's permission of "even" the earlobe, the portion of the head most easily cooked to a state in which it becomes edible. Steinfeld offers a more plausible explanation (156): R. Yoḥanan refers to a case in which a Jew roasts an animal head which a gentile had previously singed, and permits the consumption of the entire head, even that part (the earlobe) that the "cooking" of the gentile may have rendered edible. This position is based on the logic R. Yoḥanan articulates more clearly in his statement about flipped meat.

R. Yoḥanan's second statement regarding partial cooking (the flipped meat comment is the third in this passage) asserts that "any [meat] that is like the food of Ben Derosai does not [fall into the category of] gentile cooked food" (B. *A.Z.* 38b). Ben Derosai, it seems, was an individual who preferred his steak especially rare, on the border of raw; on this figure, see Friedman, "Mi hayah Ben Derosai?" The voice of the Bavli understands this comment to indicate R. Yoḥanan's position that meat cooked by a Jew to the point of being barely edible is sufficiently cooked that its completion by a gentile is legally irrelevant.

13. Y. *A.Z.* 2.8, 41d; cf. Y. *Sh.* 1.4, 3c, and B. *A.Z.* 38a. This translation is based on the analysis offered by Steinfeld, "Tavshilei goyim," 137, 140–41. On the Hellenistic practice of eating cooked relishes with one's bread, especially at fine meals, see Davidson, *Courtesans and fishcakes*, 21.

14. This is the contention of Steinfeld, who argues in "Tavshilei goyim," 139–42, and "Devarim she-nishtanu," 873–76, that Rav has no objection to gentile cooked food per se but rather is concerned solely about prohibited ingredients which might be added to otherwise permitted foods during cooking. This argument, however, fails to account for the language of Rav's statement, which exempts certain types of food from the otherwise prohibited category of "food cooked by gentiles." Rav accepts the legitimacy of this preparer-based category of prohibited foreign food independent of the ingredients these foods contain.

15. See Steinfeld, "Tavshilei goyim," 138.

16. Although this verse is absent from Talmudic discussions of gentile cooking, Rav cites it in a related discussion about the traditional prohibition against gentile oil (B. *A.Z.* 36a). In that context, Rav reads the final word of this verse—*mishtav*, literally, "his drinks"—as referring to two different types of defiling "drink," wine and oil. The Yerushalmi attributes the application of this verse in the context of gentile oil to Rav's student, R. Yehudah (Yudan) (Y. *A.Z.* 2.8, 41d). For a detailed analysis of the Bavli passage on this subject, see Steinfeld, "Le-issur shemen." Steinfeld also links Rav's statements about cooked food to *Dan.* 1.8; see "Tavshilei goyim," 139–40.

17. It seems, however, that this suggestion is offered not by the child but rather by the anonymous, presumably adult, redactor.

18. Y. *A.Z.* 2.3, 41b; B. *A.Z.* 30b–31a. Because all benefit is prohibited, the Bavli (*A.Z.* 62b) prohibits Jews from accepting employment directly associated with *stam yeinam* just as it prohibits employment associated with *yein nesekh*. The Bavli is more lenient regarding the sale of Jewish wine into which gentile wine was inadvertantly mixed when that wine is *stam yeinam*, but the consumption of such wine is still prohibited (74a).

19. We will return to this Talmudic passage in chapter 14. On the use of idolatry as "a defining *metaphor* of non-Jewishness, or even its embodiment," see S. Stern, *Jewish identity*, 139–98 (cited: 196, emphasis in original).

20. In an unrelated context, the Bavli quotes R. Yoḥanan as dismissing the idolatrous credentials of contemporary gentiles: "Gentiles living outside the Land [of Israel] are not truly idolaters; they merely maintain their ancestral practices" (B. *Ḥul.* 13b). Neither R. Yoḥanan nor any other Talmudic authority, however, suggests that the nature of these gentiles has any relevance for the status of their wine. What we see in Talmudic discussions of gentile wine is the staying power of the the Sages' own "ancestral practice" of avoiding all wine touched by gentiles irrespective of what the gentiles actually do with it.

21. The preceding analysis has focused primarily on texts from the Bavli. Schaefer, "Jews and Gentiles," demonstrates that Rabbinic discourse about gentiles in the Yerushalmi similarly fails to engage the realities of non-Jewish religious practices in Greco-Roman Palestine.

22. Neusner, "Stable symbols," 374.

23. B. *A.Z.* 64b–65a; we will discuss this passage in greater detail in chapter 14. The tradition which the Bavli cites was already garbled upon its incorporation into the Talmud, as the redactor feels the need to correct it. The corrected text seems to indicate that the wine of a resident alien is prohibited for Jewish consumption but may be sold, although the text is ambiguous because wine is compared to olive oil, another problematic foodstuff. The equation of the wine of a resident alien and libation wine is ascribed to R. Shim'on who, according to other accounts, permits even the consumption of a resident alien's wine.

24. As we observed in chapter 4, this concern is attested in tannaitic exegetical literature; there is no indication, however, that these texts influenced the discourse of the Bavli.

25. See Geller, "Diet and regimen," 237–40.

26. On the difficulties associated with this passage in the Bavli, see Steinfeld, "Gazru 'al pitan," who argues that the reference to daughters is not original to R. Yiṣḥaq but rather constitutes an addition of the redactor. For an analysis of this passage in light of Rabbinic attitudes toward intermarriage more broadly, see Hayes, *Gentile impurities,* 145–57. We encountered a similar connection between gentile wine and sexual intercourse with gentile women in *Sifrei Bemidbar* §131; see chapter 4.

27. Cases involving wily wine-drinking snakes appear in Y. *A.Z.* 2.3, 41a, and B. *A.Z.* 30a–b. On abstaining from gentile water and alcohol because it was left uncovered, see B. *A.Z.* 30a, 31b; cf. Y. *A.Z.* 2.3, 41a. Similar concerns about gentile milk appear in Y. *A.Z.* 2.8, 41d. R. Pappa (a brewer by profession: B. *Pesaḥim* 113a) and R. Aḥai are evidently not concerned about the physical danger posed by gentile beer.

28. D.C. Kraemer, *Jewish eating,* 69–70. On Rabbinic rhetoric about sex with gentiles more broadly, see Satlow, *Tasting the dish,* 83–118; as Satlow observes, the forms of persuasive rhetoric employed in this context are almost entirely nonlegal in nature.

29. B. *A.Z.* 22b. In a separate discussion of the "original filth" (to reframe Augustine's terminology) found in gentiles, the Bavli indicates that this filth is transmitted to Jews through sexual intercourse with gentiles (B. *Yevamot* 103b). See also Bavli *Shabbat* 146a, in which "original filth" was removed from Israel not at Sinai but rather through the combined righteousness of Abraham, Isaac, and Jacob. Echoing themes found in Alexandrian Jewish literature, Bavli *Shabbat* 145b suggests as an alternative that the filth of gentiles derives from gentile consumption of abhorrent foods rather than from a primordial source. In both variants, the implicit message is that Jews should neither eat the food of foreigners nor sleep with foreign partners. Klawans, *Impurity and sin,* 135, however, carefully distinguishes the "filth" (he translates: "lust") ascribed to gentiles in these passages from notions of offensive (Klawans: "moral") impurity, which the Sages do not ascribe to gentiles.

30. On the portrayal of gentiles as animals in Rabbinic literature, see S. Stern, *Jewish identity,* 33–39.

31. On this passage, including references to parallel sources and manuscript variants, see Hayes, *Between the Babylonian and Palestinian Talmuds,* 159–70; Steinfeld, "Akhilah 'im ha-goy." On the version of unit a that appears in Tosefta *'Avodah Zarah* 4.6, see also Rosenblum, *Food and identity,* 91–95.

32. R. Shim'on b. El'azar's focus specifically on a wedding banquet may reflect the fact that such banquets, unlike other banquets in the Hellenistic world, typically involve the presence of both men and women; see D. E. Smith, *Symposium to Eucharist,* 39–40. As such, Jew-

ish attendance at gentile wedding banquets in particular could yield the results foretold in *Exodus* 34.16.

33. Bavli *Ketubot* 8a; see Steinfeld, "Akhilah 'im ha-goy," 144–45; Hayes, *Between the Babylonian and Palestinian Talmuds,* 163–64.

34. Tucker, "Literary agendas," 13, 16–18.

35. The first of these explanations is offered by Hayes, *Between the Babylonian and Palestinian Talmuds,* 168–69; the others, by Kalmin, *Sage in Jewish society,* 27–60, especially p. 36.

36. As we saw in chapter 4, Mishnah *'Avodah Zarah* 5.5 assumes that Jews and gentiles can drink Jewish wine together in accordance with Rabbinic law, and the Talmuds raise no objections to such behavior when discussing that text (Y. *A.Z.* 5.7, 44d–45a; B. *A.Z.* 69b–70a). A range of *amora'im,* both early and late, Palestinian and Babylonian, discuss whether one may invite a gentile to one's home for a meal on a Sabbath or festival because of issues regarding the preparation of food on these holidays (B. *Beṣah* 21b); the discussion presupposes the permissibility of such a meal on other days. A similar conclusion may be drawn from the stipulation that gentiles do not count toward the liturgical quorum needed for the grace after meals (M. *Berakhot* 7.1; B. *Berakhot* 47b).

I disagree, therefore, with Zvi Arie Steinfeld's argument that the Sages endorsed a general prohibition against commensality with gentiles, an argument based primarily on Bavli *'Avodah Zarah* 8a–b ("Akhilah 'im ha-goy"). Steinfeld is correct that such a prohibition appears in the medieval work *Seder Eliyahu Rabbah,* §9, but I do not believe that one should read this prohibition back into the Talmuds. This prohibition, moreover, is attested only rarely in medieval works; most authorities who do so cite *Eliyahu Rabbah* as the primary basis for this prohibition.

37. In a similarly permissive ruling, Ravina allows the consumption of a pumpkin which a Jew had placed in an oven before a gentile used that oven to harden his knife (B. *A.Z.* 38a), even though the Jew played no role in the cooking process at all.

38. The same discussion of how obfuscation applies to gentile bread appears in Y. *Shevi'it* 8.4, 38a; *Ma'aser Sheni* 1.4, 3c; *Shabbat* 1.4, 3c; *'Avodah Zarah* 2.8, 41d. In the first two cited passages, bread is discussed alongside other "laws based on obfuscation," including the law governing sabbatical year produce (M. *Shevi'it* 8.4). On the *palṭer,* see Rosenfeld and Menirav, *Markets and marketing,* 100–109.

39. Al-Nu'mān, *Da'ā'im al-Islām,* 2: 126, §437.

40. Al-Barqī, *Al-maḥāsin,* 496–97, §601; see also §§596, 600.

41. This translation is based on MS JTS Rab. 15, reprinted in Abramson, *Masekhet 'Avodah Zarah.* Steinfeld, "Le-heter pat," surveys textual variants and offers a somewhat different interpretation of this text.

42. A *se'ah,* in late Biblical times, was about twelve liters. This tradition, however, may be less interested in the quantity of flour than the Biblical resonance of its depiction of the bread: in *Genesis* 18.6, Abraham instructs Sarah to prepare loaves for three distinguished guests out of three *se'ahs* of flour.

43. The pericope concludes by recounting a condemnation of the Sage Aivu for eating gentile bread. On the difficulties associated with the statements about Aivu, see Steinfeld, "Le-heter pat," 338.

44. So Steinfeld, "Le-heter pat," 339–40, who argues that R. Yoḥanan borrowed the

metaphorical use of these terms from the Rabbinic discussion of *Deuteronomy* 22.23–27, a passage that distinguishes between these locations in its discussion of premarital sex that may or may not have been consensual. According to *Sifrei Devarim* §243, the legal status of alleged rape does not actually depend on the geographic location of the act but rather on the presence or absence of those who might have been able to save the alleged victim had she cried out.

45. By placing the second half of R. Yoḥanan's statement where they do, the redactors imply that R. Yoḥanan, like R. Ḥelbo, responds to the statement of R. Yosef. This scenario is implausible: R. Yoḥanan was active in late third-century Palestine while R. Yosef and R. Ḥelbo were active in early fourth-century Babylonia.

46. Green, "Otherness within," 52.

6. THE ROLES OF FOOD IN DEFINING THE CHRIST-BELIEVING COMMUNITY

1. On this process, see, among others, Boyarin, *Border lines.*

2. Taussig, *In the beginning,* esp. ix.

3. See D. E. Smith, *Symposium to Eucharist,* 219–77, as well as the numerous scholars whose work he cites, 221–22. The marginal status of tax collectors is evident in *Matthew* 18.17; as for their Jewish identity, note that *Mark* and *Luke* state that one tax collector is named "Levi."

4. I differ here from scholars such as Esler, *Community and gospel,* 89–93, and Taussig, *In the beginning,* 167–68, who cite *Mark* 7.24–30 to argue that Jesus (or *Mark*) endorses commensality with gentiles. All discussion of food in this passage (and its parallel in *Matt.* 15.21–28) is metaphorical: the gentile woman does not ask for food, she asks for a miraculous healing for her daughter, a healing that Jesus initially refuses to perform by saying, "Let the children be fed first." Although Jesus ultimately does heal the gentile's daughter, the woman does not gain the equal status that commensality implies: indeed, she recognizes this by accepting Jesus' metaphorical equation of gentiles and dogs.

5. As D. E. Smith, *Symposium to Eucharist,* 238, observes, "what is being identified as the historical Jesus at table [in the Gospel narratives] is more likely to be the idealized characterization of Jesus at table that is produced in the early Christian community." The closest the Gospels come to endorsing the sharing of food with gentiles is the parable of the kingdom of heaven in *Matthew* 22.1–14, in which the king, enraged that those invited to his wedding banquet refused to attend, sends his servants out to invite everyone they can find instead. This version of the parable, with its reference to the king burning the city of the invited guests in anger (v. 8; this crucial detail is absent in the *Luke* 14.16–24 version), implies that the original invitees are Jewish and that the masses who attend are gentile. The message of the parable, however, is that gentiles will be called to the kingdom of heaven after the Jews spurn that call, not necessarily that gentiles are welcome to share food with Jews in this world. The reference to the Roman destruction of Jerusalem in 70 C.E. indicates that this version of the parable is relatively late.

6. Indeed, Jesus himself does not question the continued applicability of Biblical dietary laws; statements to the contrary in *Mark* 7.15, 18–19 probably or certainly post-date Jesus. See Räisänen, "Jesus and the food laws."

7. Wilson, *Gentiles and the Gentile mission,* 258.

8. The New Testament contains thirteen letters attributed to Paul, but scholars reject the authenticity of several. All, however, agree that the letters addressing dietary laws or the food of foreigners at length (*Romans, 1 Corinthians, Galatians*) were written by Paul himself.

9. On the term rendered "forbidden," *koina,* see chapter 3, note 43.

10. See Nanos, *Mystery of Romans,* 75–84.

11. Scholars vigorously debate whether or not the term *weak* refers to Jewish Christ-believers. For an argument in favor, see Nanos, *Mystery of Romans,* 85–165. Stowers, *Rereading of Romans,* 317–23, in contrast, contends that "weak" simply means "less mature" and thus does not necessarily refer to a particular subset of the Christ-believing community.

12. Previous generations of New Testament scholars tended to read *1 Corinthians* in light of *Romans* and thus misconstrue Paul's instructions regarding *eidōlothuton,* but that is no longer the norm. On the history of this scholarship, see Fotopoulos, *Food offered to idols,* 4–38.

13. Fotopoulos, *Food offered to idols,* 158–78, emphasizes the attractiveness of Greco-Roman meals, particularly in his introduction and conclusion to this chapter. See also D. E. Smith, *Symposium to Eucharist,* 9–10.

14. On the Greco-Roman banquet, see D. E. Smith, *Symposium to Eucharist,* 13–46.

15. Scholarly consensus once understood this passage as a composite, but its literary unity has been demonstrated by various means. See, among others, Eriksson, *Traditions,* 135–53; Hurd, *Origin of 1 Corinthians,* 131–42; Mitchell, *Rhetoric of reconciliation,* 238–40.

16. For more detailed (and, consequently, more speculative) reconstructions of the Corinthian position, see Sawyer, "Problem," 111; Fee, "*Eidōlothuta* once again," 181; Hurd, *Origin of 1 Corinthians,* 146; Fotopoulos, *Food offered to idols,* 220.

17. I am indebted to Cheung, *Idol food,* 117, for the semisarcastic term "knowers" as a reference to the Corinthian Christ-believers whom Paul debates.

18. Many commentators prefer "consciousness" over the NRSV's "conscience" (from the Latin Vulgate's *conscientia*) as a rendering of the Greek *syneidēsis.* Several explain this term as conveying the meaning of "awareness"; see, among others, Cheung, *Idol food,* 130–33. On the Greek term Paul uses for "defiled," *molunein,* see chapter 3.

19. So Eriksson, *Traditions,* 148–50.

20. On this passage, see Fotopoulos, *Food offered to idols,* 175–77. On the nature and significance of the communal meal in Paul's churches, see D. E. Smith, *Symposium to Eucharist,* 173–217.

21. Scholars debate what proportion of meat available for general consumption—all, most, some—was sacrificial in origin but do not question that this proportion was significant. On archeological evidence regarding the Greco-Roman market and its implications for the interpretation of this verse, see Koch, "'Alles, was *en makellō* . . . '"; Fotopoulos, *Food offered to idols,* 139–42, 156–57.

22. See Fotopoulos, *Food offered to idols,* 162–65; Garnsey, *Food and society,* 128–32; D. E. Smith, *Symposium to Eucharist,* 31–33, 67–85.

23. Al-Mufīd, *Al-muqni'ah,* 580; see chapter 11.

24. Recall that Daniel similarly regards the act of eating the king's food to be defiling even though he does not cast aspersions on that food.

25. *Acts'* portrayal of Paul as supporting the Apostolic Decree finds no support in Paul's

own letters. Paul makes no reference to the decree nor to any prohibition against gentile consumption of blood or strangled meat, and he reports that the only thing asked of him in Jerusalem was to remember the poor (*Gal.* 2.10). Moreover, the incident at Antioch, discussed below, should not have occurred if Paul, Peter, and James all espoused the contents of the decree. It seems prudent, therefore, to treat statements regarding food restrictions in *Acts* and the Pauline letters as independent efforts by early Christ-believing Jews supportive of the gentile mission to address a thorny religious and social issue facing their community.

26. Some versions of the Western text also include a negative form of the Golden Rule, but scholarly consensus is to regard that as a late addition to the text. On the text of the Apostolic Decree in its various forms, see Hurd, *Origin of 1 Corinthians,* 246–50.

27. Van de Sandt and Flusser, *Didache,* 243–53, argue for the authenticity of the Western text; see the list of advocates they cite for both sides of the dispute, p. 244, n. 19.

28. Augustine, *Against Faustus* 32.13, discussed in chapter 11. Church Fathers who interpret the Western version of the Apostolic Decree as prohibiting the consumption of blood include Tertullian (*De pudicitia* 12.4–5, cf. *Apology* 9.13) and Ambrosiaster on *Galatians* 2.2 (Vogels, *Ambrosiastri commentarius,* 3: 18).

29. Simon, "Apostolic Decree," 438; cf. Johnson, *Acts,* 277. By "ceremonial," Simon means that the Decree constitutes "a condensed code of levitical purity" (450). Were Simon to use the purity terminology employed in this study, he would likely argue instead that the Decree prohibits behaviors that result in offensive defilement; his evidence supports such an argument nicely.

30. On the role of circumcision as an identity marker, see S. J. D. Cohen, *Beginnings of Jewishness,* 39–49. On abstention from pork, see Rosenblum, "'Why do you refuse to eat pork?'"

31. For a similar argument, focused specifically on Paul's statements regarding idolatry and sexual immorality, see Sanders, "Paul between Jews and Gentiles."

32. Tosefta *'Avodah Zarah* 8.4–6 addresses seven obligations incumbent upon gentiles, including prohibitions against idolatry, immoral sexual acts, and consuming the meat (and, some say, the blood) of a living animal. We observed in chapter 4 that the Sages exempt gentiles from other aspects of Biblical dietary law, including the prohibition against consuming the blood of a dead animal. We also observed that the Sages treat meat slaughtered by a gentile as forbidden for consumption (because a gentile performed the act of slaughter) but not forbidden for benefit, the degree of prohibition that applies to items associated with idolatry. Aside from the New Testament, no pre-Rabbinic works by Jewish authors address the applicability of Biblical dietary laws to gentiles or subject regulations governing *eidōlothuton* to nuanced analysis.

33. For another treatment of New Testament texts about commensality between Jews and gentiles with an eye to the formation of Christian identity, see Taussig, *In the beginning,* 165–67.

34. "Cephas" (Aramaic *kefa*) and "Peter" (Greek *petros*) both mean "rock," a name Jesus gave to the man born as Simon (*Matt.* 16.18, *John* 1.42). For proof that both epithets refer to the same person, see Allison, "Peter and Cephas."

35. Similar arguments are made by Holmberg, "Jewish versus Christian identity"; Nanos, *Mystery of Romans,* 348–53.

36. For similar arguments, see Brunt, "Paul's attitude," particularly pp. 204–5, and D. E. Smith, *Symposium to Eucharist,* 174–75, 185–87.

37. The different attitudes toward foreign food restrictions ascribed to Peter-Cephas and James in *Galatians* 2 and *Acts* 10–15 cannot be reconciled easily; see note 25. *Acts* 6.1–7 may also allude to tensions regarding the applicability of foreign food restrictions within the Christ-believing community. This passage addresses efforts to resolve a complaint that "Hellenist" widows were being neglected with respect to the daily provision of meals, but does not spell out the nature of that complaint or its resolution. Interpretation of this passage is complicated by lack of clarity in several key terms, inlcuding the meaning of *Hellenists.* For an interpretation arguing for the relevance of this passage in the present context, see Tyson, "Acts 6:1–7."

38. On the gradual acceptance by Peter and his fellows of this new distinction-free conception of the Christ-believing society and of commensality, see Johnson, *Acts,* 186–88; see also Esler, *Community and gospel,* 93–97; Wilson, *Gentiles and the Gentile mission,* 171–78. I am grateful to Asha Kalyani Moorthy for sharing with me her insights into this text.

39. Peter's vision, read independently of its context in *Acts,* appears to indicate that God has abolished ingredient-based dietary restrictions (cf. *Mark* 7.19b). This interpretation is supported by the terminology found in the vision itself. Peter refers the animals he sees as "impure" (*akatharton; Acts* 10.14), but the heavenly voice declares that God has made them pure (*ekatharisen;* v. 15). The adjective *katharos* consistently appears in the Septuagint in the context of passages that relate to circumstantial impurity, including the dietary laws of *Leviticus* 11. Hellenistic Jews, we observed in chapter 3, did not regard gentiles as circumstantially polluted, so Peter's application of the term *akatharton,* "impure," to gentiles in *Acts* 10.28 is forced. On the term rendered "forbidden," *koina,* see chapter 3, note 43.

40. On the significance of table-fellowship in the aftermath of the Apostolic Decree, see Esler, *Community and gospel,* 99–101.

41. *Acts* 27.33–37 is also interpreted as a depiction of commensality by ibid., 101–4.

42. Taussig, *In the beginning,* 167–68, states that *Mark* 8.1–10 depicts Jesus feeding a multitude of gentiles. The location of this feeding and the identity of the beneficiaries, however, are not identified; the parallel account in *Matthew* 15.32–39 makes clear that the miracle occurs in the Galilee and the beneficiaries are Jews (15.29–31), details that make sense in the Markan context as well. It seems unlikely, moreover, that Jesus would have tolerated a crowd of gentiles surrounding him for three days given his efforts to avoid notice in Tyre and his statements to the gentile woman who found him nevertheless (*Mark* 7.24–30).

7. *EIDŌLOTHUTON* AND EARLY CHRISTIAN IDENTITY

1. Origen, *Contra Celsum* 8.29, trans. Chadwick (472).

2. *Barnabas* 10.9, trans. Lightfoot and Harmer, *Apostolic Fathers,* 303. See also *Letter to Diognetus* 4.1–6; Tertullian, *De ieiunio,* 2.4, 15.5, *De monogamia* 5.3; Novatian, *De cibis iudaicis.*

3. See, for example, Augustine's discourse about "Israel according to the flesh," discussed in Robbins, *Prodigal son/elder brother,* 39–41.

4. See Cheung, *Idol food,* 165–295. This survey of early Christian attitudes toward *eidōlothuton* largely, but not completely, supersedes Böckenhoff, *Apostolische Speisegesetz,* which had been the most comprehensive study of early Christian statements regarding dietary laws. For

an English summary of Böckenhoff's work, see Tomson, *Paul and the Jewish law,* 177–86. See also Brunt, "Rejected, ignored, or misunderstood?" 113–24.

5. See, for example, Justin Martyr, *Dialogue with Trypho* 20.1; Tertullian (note 17 below); Clement of Alexandria, *Stromata* 4.15.97.3; Minucius Felix, *Octavius* 30.6; Origen, *Contra Celsum,* 8.30. Additionally, see *Sybilline Oracles* 2.96 and Pseudo-Phocylides' *Sentences* 31, identified as Christian interpolations into earlier texts. Christian refusal to eat blood is also attested in various martyrdom reports (in addition to Tertullian's *Apology,* see, for example, Eusebius, *Ecclesiastical History* 5.1.26) and in the texts of Nag Hammadi (VI,7 65.5–7). See also the secondary literature in the previous note.

6. *Didache* 6.2–3; translation from Cody, "Didache," 8, slightly altered on the basis of the Greek in Rordorf and Tuilier, *Didache,* 168. The date of this work is a matter of scholarly debate.

7. The *Apology* survives in a Syriac translation and a reworked Greek version, both of which appear in the edition by Puderon and Pierre. The editors follow the ancient Christian historian Eusebius in dating this work to 124–25 (32–37). Translations are my own, based on the Syriac, which scholars regard as more faithful to Greek original; the surviving Greek version lacks any reference to food.

8. Marcovich, *Dialogus cum Tryphone;* the translation is my own.

9. See Bagnall and Rives, "A prefect's edict," 85–86.

10. For a convenient historical survey of persecutions related to refusal to sacrifice, see Jones, "Christianity and the cult"; see also de Ste. Croix, "Why were the early Christians persecuted?" Taussig, *In the beginning,* 115–43, offers a broader analysis of Christian meals as a form of resistance to Roman imperial power.

11. *Letters* 10.96, trans. Radice, *Pliny,* 291, emphasis added. The significance of the final clause of this sentence is highlighted (but, in my opinion, misinterpreted) by Zaas and Meany, "Adhuc rarissimus emptor."

12. Bettenson and Maunder, *Documents of the Christian Church,* 14, emphasis added.

13. See, among numerous others, *Martyrium Pionii* 18.1–8.

14. *De lapsis* 15 (citing *Lev.* 7.19–20), trans. Bénvenot, 23. On Cyprian's understanding of the impurity associated with consumption of sacrificial food, see Burns, *Cyprian,* 137–40; Stow, *Jewish dogs,* 11–13.

15. Joannou, *Discipline générale,* 59–62; the translations are my own. Participation in idolatry is addressed in cc. 1–9, 12.

16. See similarly R. Shimʿon b. Elʿazar's prohibition of Jewish participation in gentile wedding banquets (T. *A.Z.* 4.6; B. *A.Z.* 8a), discussed in chapter 5.

17. On the blood prohibition, see Tertullian, *De pudicitia* 12.4–5, *Apology* 9.13; on the prohibition of food offered to idols, see *De corona* 10.4–7, 11.3; *De spectaculis* 13.2–4. Tertullian, familiar with the Apostolic Decree in its Western variant (omitting reference to "strangled meat"), is the first known authority to offer an allegorical reading of its blood prohibition as referring to murder; he nevertheless regards the literal sense of this prohibition as binding.

18. *Apology* 42.1–5; this translation, my own, is based on those of Glover and Daly. Brahmans, according to Strabo (*Geography* 15.1.59), abstain from animal food and live frugally.

19. See G. G. Stroumsa, "Tertullian."

20. See, among others, Clement of Alexandria, *Stromata* 4.15.97.3; Origen, *Contra Celsum* 8.28–30; Novatian, *De cibis iudaicis* (whose last chapter addresses food offered to idols).

21. Food offered to idols is prohibited alongside blood and that which has been strangled at the mid-fourth-century Council of Gangra (c. 2); see also the fourth-century *Pseudo-Clementine homilies* (7.4.2, 7.8.1) and Cyril of Jerusalem's *Catechetical letters* 4.27. I was unable to find any reference to food offered to idols in the discussions of subsequent Eastern councils found in Hefele and Leclercq, *Histoire des conciles;* this work includes the complete text or detailed summaries of all surviving conciliar canons. Examples of canons that prohibit blood and strangled meat yet lack reference to *eidōlothuton* appear in chapter 8.

22. The impact of imperial authority on conceptions of Christianity has been highlighted by studies employing postcolonial methodology, including A. S. Jacobs, *Remains of the Jews.* On the shift in imperial attitudes toward religion that occurred during Theodosius's reign, see S. Schwartz, *Imperialism,* 191–92. Although both of these works focus on Christian attitudes toward Jews, their findings also apply to attitudes regarding other non-Christians.

23. Mommsen and Meyer, *Codex Theodosianus;* English: Pharr, *Theodosian Code.* Laws regarding sacrifice appear in title 16.10, "On pagans, sacrifices, and temples"; eleven of these laws date from the reign of Theodosius I and his successors. (The *Theodosian Code* is named after one of those successors, Theodosius II.)

24. *Theodosian Code* 16.10.23; the earliest reference to "pagans" in the *Code* appears in an edict of Honorius promulgated in 415 (16.10.20).

25. The sixth-century *Justinianic Code* contains only a single law on the subject absent from the *Theodosian Code* (1.11.7, promulgated in 451). Celebrations of the demise of "paganism" within the Roman world among the imperial and ecclesiastical elites were, however, premature; see MacMullen, *Christianizing the Roman Empire,* 74–85; Effros, *Creating community,* 9–11.

26. In a similar vein, c. 78 applies the same punishment to those who commit adultery with a Jew or heretic and fail to confess their sin voluntarily; no canon addresses adultery with other non-Christians.

27. Translations of the canons of the Council of Elvira are based on those of Laeuchli, *Power and sexuality,* 126–35, emended on the basis of Vives, *Concilios Visigóticos,* 1–15.

28. Laeuchli, *Power and sexuality,* 56–59, further observes that the traditional priesthood constituted a power base against which Christian clergy contested when asserting their own authority in societal affairs. Laeuchli demonstrates that the relative severity of punishments prescribed in Elviran canons reflects the relative significance of a given transgression to the bishops and presbyters gathered in Elvira.

29. Latin citations are from the Vulgate, but these terms are attested in many Old Latin texts as well; see the online card catalog of the Vetus Latina Institut, accessible via Brepols Publishers Online, www.brepolis.net.

8. JEWISH FOOD AND THE DEFINITION OF CHRISTIANITY

1. Taylor, *Anti-Judaism,* 139.

2. Vienna, Österreichische Nationalbibliothek, codex 1179, folio 186a. This image offers an allegorical interpretation of *Esther* 1.9–12, in which Queen Vashti refuses to obey King

Ahasuerus's command to leave her own women's banquet and appear before the king and his guests. The allegory equates Vashti with the Jewish community, Ahasuerus with Christ, and Jewish dietary laws with the women's banquet, whose appeal, according to this commentary, is to blame for Vashti's disobedience. On the *Bible moralisée,* see Lipton, *Images of intolerance;* Lipton discusses this specific image on pp. 68–69 and cites evidence that its depiction of kosher slaughter matches those found in medieval Jewish manuscripts.

3. I have omitted from this list the Apostolic Decree's prohibitions against blood and the meat of animals whose blood has not been drained. Medieval Roman Catholics like the author of this *Bible moralisée,* in keeping with Augustine's teachings on this subject, hold that these prohibitions are no longer applicable. I am grateful to Eric Shuler for sharing with me his unpublished work on the medieval history of *Acts* 15.29, presented in part at the 2005 International Congress of Medieval Studies in Kalamazoo, Michigan. See also Böckenhoff, *Speisesatzungen mosaicher Art.* On Augustine's treatment of this subject, see below and in chapter 11.

4. Linder, *Jews in the legal sources,* helpfully collects and translates the vast majority of Greek and Latin Christian legal sources from the early Middle Ages that relate to Jews, including many of the food restrictions discussed below. Early Christian "Jewry law," as the genre is called, addresses such issues as Jewish ownership of Christian slaves, Jewish exercise of public authority, and intermarriage. Most of these laws seek to prevent Jews from assuming a position of social superiority over Christians that does not befit adherents of an inferior religion. Foreign food restrictions, in contrast, are more likely to spell out the reasons for Judaism's inferiority. Translations of such restrictions in this chapter are my own, prepared in consultation with Linder's.

5. Blumenkranz, *Juifs et chrétiens dans le monde occidental,* 106, suggests that canons 26, 36, and 61 (encouraging fasting on the Sabbath, prohibiting images in churches, and prohibiting marriage to one's former wife's sister) are also anti-Jewish in their orientation. These suggestions are plausible but lack supporting evidence.

6. On the translation of Elviran canons, see chapter 7, note 27. Laeuchli, *Power and sexuality,* 132, understands c. 49 as referring to Christian landholders seeking Jewish blessings over their crops. The broader interpretation of this canon suggested in the present translation, however, makes more sense given the subject matter of c. 50 and of *1 Timothy* 4.1–3, to which c. 49 alludes.

7. See Laeuchli, *Power and sexuality,* 81–82.

8. The canon refers to those who "cum Iudaeis cibum sumpserit," while *1 Corinthians* 5.11 instructs believers "cum eiusmodi nec cibum sumere." This reading appears both in the Vulgate text and in many Old Latin versions collected in the online card catalog of Vetus Latina Institut, accessible via Brepols Publishers Online, www.brepolis.net.

9. These translations of *1 Timothy* reflect the language of the Vulgate, a close approximation of the text known to the clerics at Elvira.

10. J. Cohen, *Living letters.* Although the concept behind this formulation, as Lieu, *Image and reality,* observes, is "something of a truism" (1), many scholars have instead interpreted Christian anti-Judaism as a response to a real threat posed by Jews; see Taylor, *Anti-Judaism.* There is insufficient evidence to determine the extent, if any, to which Christians in early-fourth-century Spain actually interacted with Jews or were attracted by Jewish practices.

11. "Chapters which were written from the Orient" (530s), cc. 34–35, in Vööbus, *Synodicon,* 161: 174 (Syriac); cf. Vööbus's English translation, 162: 166. On this document, see Vööbus, *Syrische Kanonessammlungen,* 35: 167–75. The Synod of George I, patriarch of the (Nestorian) Church of the East (676), also condemns Christians who drink wine in Jewish taverns immediately after receiving the Eucharist and imposes sanctions on those who engage in this practice; see Chabot, *Synodicon orientale,* 225 (French trans. 489). Similar prohibitions against commensality with Jews appear in later Syriac collections as well; see, for example, c. 118 in the collection of Isho' bar Nun (d. 828), in Sachau, *Syrische Rechtsbücher,* 2: 170–71.

12. De Clercq, *Concilia Galliae,* 27–28.

13. The first collection containing the canons from Elvira to receive widespread distribution outside of Spain was the seventh-century *Collectio Hispana.* Florus of Lyons, who assembled a fairly comprehensive collection of canons related to Jewish food in the early ninth century, was apparently unaware of the Elviran text; on Florus's collection, see note 48 below.

14. 3 Orléans c. 14 (13), Mâcon c. 15, Clichy c. 13, in de Clercq, *Concilia Galliae,* 120, 226, 294.

15. Vannes c. 12, Agde c. 40, in Munier, *Concilia Galliae,* 154, 210; the version promulgated at Agde appears in Gratian's *Decretum* as C. 28 q. 1 c. 14. The difference in language between these canons reflects the fact that the former council focused exclusively on clerical discipline. On these canons, see Blumenkranz, "Iudaeorum conuiuia," reprinted in *Juifs et chrétiens: Patristique et Moyen Âge.*

16. Linder, *Jews in the legal sources,* 465–82, identifies twelve councils that address Jews (excluding the so-called Council of Rheims, whose canons are virtually identical to those promulgated at the Council of Clichy; scholars question the independent existence of the Rheims gathering). In contrast to the six councils whose canons address commensality, five councils address Jewish ownership of Christian slaves and Jewish exercise of public authority while only four councils treat the subject of intermarriage or other sexual relations between Christians and Jews. Various historians interpret the anticommensality canons as evidence for the widespread presence of Jews in early medieval Gaul and the persistence of close social relations between Jews and their Christian neighbors; see, for example, Blumenkranz, "Anti-Jewish polemics"; Mikat, *Judengesetzgebung,* 23. This interpretation is highly problematic in the absence of other evidence for Jewish settlement in many of these regions of Gaul during the early Middle Ages.

17. A slightly different argument regarding the impurity of Manicheans appears in Augustine's first anti-Manichean treatise, *On the Christian and Manichean ways of life* 2.14.35. There, Augustine uses *Romans* 14.14 to demonstrate that Manicheans become defiled through their consumption of food they believe to be impure. Whereas in that work Manichean defilement results from the failure of Manicheans to adhere stringently to their own impossibly stringent dietary norms, Augustine argues in *Answer to Faustus* that Manichean defilement precedes these norms and, indeed, serves as the impetus for creating them.

18. For a consolidated exposition on the dietary laws, also expressed in the context of anti-Manichean polemic, see *Against Adimantus* 14–15; see also *Sermon* 149.3–5.

19. Augustine himself does not apply his rhetoric regarding Manichean dietary practices to the Jews. The closest Augustine comes to making this connection is in his exposition of

Psalm 126 (LXX 125), in which Jewish dietary practices constitute nothing more than an historical artifact from Old Testament times. Augustine's call for self-purification in this homily is directed against sinful Christians, not Jews. On Augustine's treatment of Jews as hermeneutical constructs rather than contemporary actors, see J. Cohen, *Living letters,* 23–65. On the connection between Augustine's anti-Manichean works, especially *Answer to Faustus,* and his conception of Jews and Judaism more broadly, see also Fredriksen, "Excaecati occulta," and, at greater length, *Augustine and the Jews.*

20. Medieval canon law commentators regularly draw attention to the link between Jewish dietary laws and Jewish attacks against Christian faith; see Freidenreich, "Sharing meals."

21. Augustine, *Sermon* 351.10, trans. Edmund Hill. See also John Chrysostom, *Homilies on Hebrews* 25.3–4. Both of these homilies focus on *1 Corinthians* 5.11, and extracts of each find their way into Gratian's *Decretum.* Chrysostom's words appear in C. 11 q. 3 c. 24; Augustine's sermon is cited directly in C. 2. q. 1 c. 18 and an indirectly (via an epitomized version from the *Glossa ordinaria* to *1 Cor.* 5.10) in C. 23 q. 4 c. 17.

I am aware of only two Christian authorities from the first millennium who articulate prohibitions against commensality with gentiles. In a pair of letters to clerics in Spain, Pope Adrian I (r. 772–95) bemoans the fact that "many who call themselves Catholics carry on public life with Jews and unbaptized pagans, sharing in food and drink alike and also straying into error in several ways while saying that they are not defiled." Adrian calls on those found guilty of these transgressions, among others, to be banished from the community and held in eternal damnation. See Simonsohn, *Apostolic see,* 1: 27–28. Adrian's atypical concern about commensality with pagans and his unusual ascription of defilement to those who engage in such activity likely relate specifically to the fact of Muslim rule in eighth-century Spain. Also exceptional in this regard is the *Corrector,* a penitential by Burchard of Worms incorporated into his *Decretum.* Burchard suggests penance of ten days on bread and water for those who eat "the food of Jews or other pagans" (p. 201r); the penalty for eating food offered to idols is thirty days on this diet (195r–v).

22. The Council of Vannes was the first Catholic council in Brittany. The Council of Agde was the first Catholic council allowed in Arian Visigothic territory and demonstrated the strength of the Catholic faction in the region of Narbonne. The Council of Epaone was called by Sigismund, the first Catholic king of Burgundy. The Third Council of Orléans followed the annexation of Ostrogothic territories into the Catholic Merovingian kingdoms. The remaining pair of commensality-related canons date from later councils that largely restate earlier prohibitions. See Pontal, *Histoire des conciles mérovingiens.*

23. Similarly, see Effros, *Creating community,* 5, 17–18.

24. On the term *judaize,* see Cohen, *Beginnings of Jewishness,* 176–97; Dán, "'Judaizare.'"

25. Visigothic Catholic authorities, unlike their repetitive neighbors to the north, do not promulgate any foreign food restrictions. Just as the *Theodosian Code* prohibits pagan performance of idolatrous sacrifices rather than Christian consumption of its meat, Visigothic ecclesiastical councils and the *Laws of the Visigoths* seek to eradicate Judaism and its practices entirely and therefore contain no prohibitions of commensality with Jews. In addition to their frequent calls for the conversion or expulsion of all Jews, Visigothic authorities prohibit Jews from distinguishing between pure and impure foods (*Laws of the Visigoths* 12.2.8, 12.3.7). These laws reflect the distinctly Visigothic political vision of an exclusively Catholic

kingdom whose monarch was charged with the defense and propagation of Catholic norms. On this vision and the place of Jews within it, see Gonzáles-Salinero, "Catholic anti-Judaism," 126–29; Stocking, *Bishops, councils, and consensus,* 136.

26. Linder, *Jews in the legal sources,* 495–96 (trans. 499). This oath was administered by King Chintila to Jewish converts in Toledo in December 637.

27. Cameron, "Jews and heretics," 350. Note that while Christians blur the distinction between Judaism and polytheism as systems of belief, they do not blur the social distinction between Jews and gentiles.

28. This collection was in circulation by the early fifth century, when it was already associated with Laodicea. Some modern scholars, however, question the historicity of the council, and all agree that the collection consists of two independent units (cc. 1–19, 20–59). See Amann, "Laodicée," 8: 2611–12; Hefele and Leclercq, *Histoire des conciles,* 1: 989–95. Other Laodicean canons regarding food include cc. 24, 27–28, 50, 52–53, 55. Additionally, c. 29 prohibits Christians from judaizing through observance of the Sabbath, while c. 16 enjoins the reading of the Gospels on that day.

29. Joannou, *Discipline générale,* 146.

30. The Canons of the Apostles constitute *Apostolic constitutions* 8.47; for the text and a French translation, see Metzger, *Constitutions apostoliques,* 3: 300–301. Metzger dates these canons to 380 (1: 54–61).

31. Chabot, *Synodicon orientale,* 157–58 (French trans., 417–18).

32. See, for example, the canons of Athanasius of Balad, Patriarch of Antioch, in Nau, "Littérature canonique," 128–29. Vööbus, *Syrische Kanonessammlungen,* 35: 200–202, dates this text to 684–86. On this text, see also Freidenreich, "Muslims in canon law," 91.

33. See chapter 7, note 21.

34. This council, named after the domed hall in which it occurred, is also known as the Quinisext Council because of its subsequent association with the Fifth and Sixth Ecumenical Councils, which did not produce canons of their own. The text of these canons appears in Nedungatt and Featherstone, *Council in Trullo,* 41–186; the translations cited here are Featherstone's.

35. This canon, translated with slight inaccuracies, appears in Gratian's *Decretum* as C. 28 q. 1 c. 13.

36. On Ephrem's anti-Jewish rhetoric, with particular attention to the following hymn, see Shepardson, *Anti-Judaism and Christian orthodoxy.*

37. Ephrem the Syrian, "Hymns on Unleavened Bread" 19, in *Paschahymnen,* 108: 36–37; this partial translation is adapted from that of Shepardson, *Anti-Judaism and Christian orthodoxy,* 32–33.

38. Lamy, *Hymni et sermones,* 2: 399 and 3: 137; see also 3: 165. I am grateful to Adam Becker and Sergey Minov for their assistance in confirming the pseudonimous nature of these sermons.

39. Morin, *Sermones,* 104: 967. Caesarius himself offered a similar sermon against those who would consume food offered to idols; see sermon 54, 103: 235–40. Pseudo-Caesarius evidently does not share Augustine's resistance to the notion that food itself can become impure and accursed.

40. Responsum 3 to Tuma the recluse, in Vööbus, *Synodicon,* 161: 257–58; cf. Vööbus's

translation, 162: 235. (Translations of Jacob's responsa here are my own.) Tuma's question referred solely to wine pressed by Jews, but Jacob chose to answer the question in broader terms; note that all of Jacob's examples are "cooked," not "raw." Jacob freely permits Christians to eat meat from animals slaughtered in nonsacral contexts by pagans; he expresses no concern about defilement that might be communicated to Christians through such behavior because the impurity associated with idolatrous sacrifice does not apply to gentiles themselves. See responsum 17 in the second collection of responsa to Joḥannan Esṭunara found in Vööbus, *Synodicon,* 161: 254; cf. Vööbus's translation, 162: 232. The Catholic *Pseudo-Theodorian penitential* 27.1 (Wasserschleben, *Bussordnungen,* 610–11), cited and discussed in chapter 12, similarly ascribes impurity to all Jewish food while expressing concern solely about gentile food offered in idolatrous sacrifice.

41. Paul W. Harkins translates the title of these sermons, *Logoi kata Ioudaion,* as "Discourses against judaizing Christians" on the grounds that "Chrysostom's primary targets were members of his own congregation who continued to observe the Jewish feasts and fasts." He also notes that the title of these discourses is inconsistent in the manuscript tradition. See Harkins, *Discourses,* x, xxxi, n. 47. Harkins glosses over the fact that Chrysostom's primary method of dissuading Christians from observing Jewish holidays is to attack Jews and Judaism directly. Translations of Chrysostom's *Discourses* are largely those of Harkins, but I have revised them (sometimes to a considerable degree) on the basis of Meeks and Wilken, *Jews and Christians in Antioch,* 85–104, and the Greek original.

42. See Wilken, *John Chrysostom and the Jews.*

43. As Cheung, *Idol food,* 116–17, observes, Chrysostom himself is aware of the rhetorical power of Paul's discussion of food offered to idols, which he addresses in his *Homilies on 1 Corinthians* 20–25.

44. On the nature of this projection, as manifest in anti-Jewish works produced in the mid-seventh-century Eastern Roman Empire, see Olster, *Roman defeat.*

45. The irony of this logic, to which we will return in chapter 12, is explored by Stow, *Jewish dogs.*

46. On Agobard and his anti-Jewish works, see Boshof, *Erzbischof Agobard,* 102–38; J. Cohen, *Living letters,* 123–45.

47. Agobard's depiction of the third-century Saint Hilary, renowned for his efforts to combat Arianism, comes from the *Life of Hilary* by the sixth-century Venantius Fortunatus (3.9). Agobard (§8) also cites the prohibition against Jewish unleavened bread from the Council of Laodicea, conflating it with a Latin prohibition against intermarriage from the Council of Claremont (535, c. 6). This combination suggests that Agobard, like the author of the *Pseudo-Theodorian penitential,* understands the Laodicean canon to prohibit all Jewish food and, moreover, that Agobard understands this prohibition as a means of preventing social and, ultimately, sexual intercourse with Jews. Agobard's source for the canons he cites is the collection compiled by Florus of Lyons; on this work, see Blumenkranz, "Florus de Lyon," 575–76, reprinted in *Juifs et chrétiens: Patristique et Moyen Âge.*

48. Van Acker, *Agobard,* 205. See also Agobard's *On the insolence of the Jews,* p. 193 in van Acker's edition.

49. The cited phrase, inspired by *Matthew* 12.43–45, appears in §20 (van Acker, *Agobard,* 215). The same assertion, with the same prooftext, is made by Chrysostom in *Discourses* 1.6.6–

7. Scholars of the transmission of Greek Christian writings within Latin Christendom, however, do not list Chrysostom's homilies among those that would have been available in Western Europe during Agobard's day.

50. Van Acker, *Agobard*, 208.

51. Ibid., 219. Agobard here employs both *Titus* 1.15 and *Deuteronomy* 28.17, deriving the curses against the granary and storehouses of those who disobey God from a combination of the Vulgate and an alternative translation (§25).

52. Amulo, *Contra Iudaeos* 51; Amulo expresses particular disgust at the practice of using Jewish wine in the eucharistic service. Like Agobard, Amulo declares that "sacrilegious association with Jews—with them and with other heretics—ought to be utterly despised, and their meals ought to be regarded as profane and sacrilegious. Whosoever in whatever way shares with them, [ecclesiastical authorities] assert that he is defiled by their impieties" (§59). Agobard, in his treatise *On the insolence of the Jews,* offers specific justifications for the prohibitions of Jewish meat and wine: Jews sell to Christians meat which they themselves deem unfit for consumption, and they ostentatiously accept an inflated price for the wine they prepare. See van Acker, *Agobard,* 191–95; Cohen, *Living letters,* 127, translates a portion of this treatise, much of which focuses on food-related concerns.

Agobard composed both *Jewish superstitions* and *Insolence of the Jews* in an unsuccessful effort to pursuade the Carolingian emperor Louis the Pious to enforce laws restricting Christian interaction with Jews. Concern regarding Jewish impurity may underlie what is, to my knowledge, the only Carolingian law relating to Jewish food, an edict by Charlemagne ("Capitula de Iudaeis" c. 3, of the year 814) prohibiting Jews from selling wine and produce; see Pertz, *Legum nationum Germanicarum,* 194.

53. J. Cohen, *Living letters,* 127–28; for Cohen's contextualization of Agobard's anti-Jewish works within his broader interests in the proper social order, see pp. 132–45.

54. Douglas, *Purity and danger,* 35. I agree, however, with Douglas's overarching insight that systems of impurity "are used as analogies for expressing a general view of the social order" (3).

55. On Rabbinic discourse that does ascribe impurity of various sorts to gentiles, see Hayes, *Gentile impurities,* 107–92.

56. On the use of impurity rhetoric with respect to the food of non-sectarian Jews in Qumranic literature, see Baumgarten, *Flourishing of Jewish sects,* esp. 7–9, 86–102. Within Rabbinic literature, see T. *Ḥul.* 2.20, cited in chapter 5.

57. See Boyarin, *Border lines,* 202–25.

58. See Stow, *Jewish dogs.*

59. See Freidenreich, "Holiness and impurity."

9. RELATIVIZING COMMUNITIES IN THE QUR'AN

1. The Qur'an refers to "believers" with far greater frequency than "Muslims," and the latter term is absent from the texts we will examine; within the Qur'an, neither term necessarily implies membership in a particular religious community. See further Donner, *Muhammad and the believers.*

2. "Idolaters" is an imprecise translation of the Qur'anic term *mushrikūn,* which refers

not to those who worship man-made objects or even those who believe in the existence of multiple gods but rather those who associate demigod-like partners with God; see Hawting, *Idea of idolatry.* I use this term because of its familiarity and because, in the context of the present study, *mushrikūn* are functionally equivalent to the idolaters addressed by Jewish and Christian authorities. Hawting (esp. pp. 45–66) makes a compelling case that the Qur'an's "idolaters" are a rhetorical construct: no such people existed in the seventh century. The Qur'an, like Christian and Jewish authorities, polemicizes against invented and imagined foreigners for the purpose of advancing its own theological agenda. As a result, the actual beliefs, practices, and even existence of the outsiders are largely irrelevant.

3. The Qur'an, of course, prohibits the consumption not only of certain kinds of meat but also of wine. Its statements on the latter subject—16.67, 2.219, 4.43, and 5.90–91, revealed in that sequence according to Islamic tradition—are not related to the practices of foreigners and consequently play no role in the following discussion.

4. On Qur'anic conceptions of holiness, see Freidenreich, "Holiness and impurity."

5. The distinction between Meccan and Medinan surahs rests not only on Islamic traditions and textual clues regarding the historical circumstances that prompted particular revelations but also on differences in content and style within the Qur'anic text itself. Although the dating of particular surahs is a highly imprecise science, I am aware of no disagreement regarding the periodization of the surahs that address meat-related food restrictions: *Sūrat al-an'ām* (6) and *Al-naḥl* (16) are Meccan, while *Al-baqarah, Āl Imrān, Al-nisā'*, and *Al-mā'idah* (surahs 2–5) are Medinan. On methods of dating the surahs and the results of such efforts, see Robinson, *Discovering the Qur'an,* 60–96.

6. Unlike the Torah and the New Testament, whose dietary laws apply exclusively to Israelites or Christ-believers, Qur'anic norms evidently apply universally. It is for this reason that the Qur'an ridicules idolaters for their ignorance of these norms (6.135–44).

7. The verses are here listed in the sequence of their revelation, according to the scholarship of Theodor Nöldeke and Friedrich Schwally; see Schacht, "Mayta," 924–25. All four versions contain the language found in 16.115. Q. 6.145 supplements this language by defining carrion, blood, and pork as offensively defiling while stating that the act of invoking a name other than God's is sinful. On offensive impurity in the Qur'an, with particular reference to 6.145, see Freidenreich, "Holiness and impurity." Qur'an 2.173 adds to the language of 16.115 a statement that no sin is ascribed to one who is compelled to transgress these prohibitions. The more elaborate version of this text in 5.3 is discussed below.

8. This similarity has not gone unnoticed by scholars; for a different interpretation of its significance, see Simon, "De l'observance rituelle," 84–87.

9. On the ongoing force of the prohibitions against blood and strangled meat in the Eastern Christian tradition, see, for example, cc. 14–15 of what Arthur Vööbus, *Synodicon,* 161: 271 (English: 162: 246) refers to as the "Further canons" of Jacob of Edessa.

10. On *maytah,* see M. H. Katz, *Body of text,* 20; Schacht, "Mayta."

11. On the relationship between Qur'anic food restrictions and both Arab and Eastern Christian practices, see Rodinson, "Ghidhā'." Various Christian sources refer to communities of "heretics" that abstain from pork: see Arthur Vööbus, *Didascalia,* 179: 230–31 (English 180: 213); Pines, *Jewish Christians,* 10, 25–26. See also Philonenko, "Le Décret apostolique," who uses the Qur'an as evidence for Christian abstention from pork.

12. On the term *ẓālim,* wrongdoer, see Izutsu, *Ethico-religious concepts,* 164–72.

13. On these prohibitions as understood in subsequent Sunni discourse, and on the relationship between the prohibitions found in the Qur'an and those found in Biblical and Rabbinic literature, see Maghen, *After hardship cometh ease,* 123–60. The interpretation of Biblical dietary laws as punishment for the guilt of the Jews is attested in Christian anti-Jewish polemic as well, including the fourth-century Syriac writer Aphrahat's *Demonstration* 15.2–3.

14. This verse apparently alludes to the prohibition of the thigh muscle found in *Genesis* 32.33, after Jacob's injury when wrestling the angel. On this verse and its subsequent interpretation, see Maghen, *After hardship cometh ease,* 102–22.

15. On this passage and its relationship to Christian traditions about the Lord's Supper and Eucharist, see Comerro, "La nouvelle alliance," 305–8; Cuypers, *Banquet,* 397–440; Radscheit, "Table." The title of the surah reflects the fact that the word *al-mā'idah,* a term that originally may have referred specifically to the eucharistic altar, appears only in this passage; the fact that this word encapsulates the theme I seek to highlight within the surah is most likely coincidental.

16. Michel Cuypers suggests that the rhetoric of the opening passage of *Sūrat al-mā'idah,* which we will examine below, echoes the rhetoric found in *Deuteronomy:* "These convergences . . . make Muhammad appear as *a new Moses,* giving *a new legislation* linked to the founding *covenant of a new people*" (*Banquet,* 85–87, emphasis original).

17. On this polemic and its function in legitimizing the nascent religion of Islam, see Comerro, "La nouvelle alliance."

18. On the relationship between the restrictions found at the beginning and near the conclusion of *Sūrat al-mā'idah,* see Cuypers, *Banquet,* 455–57; Robinson, "Hands outstretched." On vv. 1–5, see also *Banquet,* 61–123.

19. See the references in note 10 above.

20. M. H. Katz, *Body of text,* 33–36, 40–41, 43; Katz, however, dismisses the significance of the eschatological allusion she observes. Cuypers, *Banquet,* 85–87, offers a similar interpretation of the significance of the term *today.*

21. In addition to these verses, the Qur'an associates this word with the manna and quail which God provided to the Children of Israel (2.57, 7.160, 20.80–81) and the food and drink which God gave the Children of Adam (7.31–32). There is no indication in these or other verses that the meaning of this term is restricted to specific types of foodstuffs. See, however, classic Shi'i interpretations of Q. 5.5, discussed in chapter 11.

22. Friedmann, *Tolerance and coercion,* 161.

23. Newby, *History of the Jews of Arabia,* 83. A similar interpretation of subsequent Sunni traditions and statements regarding the food of Jews and Christians is offered by Tsafrir, "Attitude of Sunnī Islam."

24. Friedmann, *Tolerance and coercion,* 191. The reference in Q. 5.3 to the "perfection of your religion" is traditionally understood to indicate that verses 1–5, if not the entirety of *Sūrat al-mā'idah,* were revealed at the conclusion of Muḥammad's life, during the Farewell Address he delivered in Medina prior to his final pilgrimage to Mecca; see, for example, al-Wāḥidī, *Asbāb al-nuzūl,* 126–27.

25. We observed in chapters 7–8 that Elviran canons about intermarriage (cc. 15–17)

were also more precise in their classification of non-Christians than that council's foreign food restriction (c. 50). In both cases, it seems that marriage regulations are better suited to nuance than dietary regulations.

26. See the tradition about the "Abrahamic" Zayd b. ʿAmr b. Nufayl in Ibn Hishām, *Sīrat al-Nabī*, 1: 228; Guillaume, *Life of Muhammad*, 99. On the history of this tradition, see Kister, "ʻA bag of meat,'" reprinted in *Studies in Jāhiliyya;* and Rubin, *Eye of the beholder*, 77–81.

27. The requirement to drain an animal's blood at the time of slaughter, we have seen, is found in both the Torah and the New Testament and was reaffirmed without hesitation by both Rabbinic and Eastern Christian authorities. Among the latter, see c. 67 of the Council in Trullo and cc. 13–15 of the "Further canons of Jacob of Edessa," in Vööbus, *Synodicon*, 161: 271, 162: 246; see further Böckenhoff, *Speisesatzungen mosaicher Art*, 37–49.

Rabbinic literature testifies to a requirement that God be invoked, in the form of a blessing, at the time of slaughter (T. *Berakhot* 6.1). The only Eastern Christian source addressing the requirements of slaughter of which I am aware is the *Ktābā d-hudāye* (or *Nomocanon*) of the Syrian Orthodox Gregorius Barhebraeus (d. 1286). Barhebraeus requires butchers—who must be Christian—to slaughter "in the name of the living God" (*bshem elāhā ḥayā*; *Nomocanon*, 461). Although this work reflects significant Islamic influence, its discussion of the laws of slaughter clearly draws on distinctively Christian sources and may well reflect traditional Christian practice in this regard; see Freidenreich, "Fusion cooking."

10. SUNNI DISCOURSE ON NON-MUSLIM ACTS OF ANIMAL SLAUGHTER

1. *Ṣaḥīḥ al-Bukhārī*, 1: 82–83, §393.

2. See Kimber, "Qibla."

3. I am indebted for the term *Scripturist* to Neal Robinson, who employs it in passing in "Hands outstretched," 2. I find this term more mellifluous than *Scriptuary*, the translation employed in Friedmann, *Tolerance and coercion*.

4. In fact, this term originally refers solely to a single Zoroastrian priestly caste; see Morony, s.v. "Madjūs." Muslims, however, freely apply the term *Magians* not only to all Zoroastrians but also to non-Zoroastrian peoples, including the Vikings; see Melvinger, s.v. "al-Madjūs." Islamic authorities, moreover, intentionally apply the laws governing Magians to peoples known not to be Zoroastrian, including Hindus; see Friedmann, "Temple of Multān," and *Tolerance and coercion*, 78–80. In effect, therefore, the term *Magian* functions in Islamic legal discourse like the term *gentile* does in Jewish and Christian sources.

5. On this subject, see also García Sanjuán, "Alimentos de los *Ḏimmíes*," which is especially strong on Andalusian sources.

6. On the expansion of the category of *ahl al-dhimmah* beyond Jews and Christians, see Friedmann, *Tolerance and coercion*, 72–86. For a synopsis of the laws imposed upon *dhimmīs*, see Freidenreich, "Christians in Sunni law"; for comprehensive treatment, see Fattal, *Statut légal*.

7. I am indebted to Nurit Tsafrir for this distinction, which appears in her master's thesis, "Yaḥas ha-halakhah," 2.

8. Mālikī and Ḥanbalī opinions regarding the blood-money owed to the relatives of a murder victim quantify the relative similarity and dissimilarity of non-Muslims to Muslims:

Jews and Christians are literally worth one-third or one-half the value of Muslims, whereas Zoroastrians are worth one-fifteenth that value. See Friedmann, *Tolerance and coercion,* 48.

9. I depart here from my standard translation of *mushrikūn* as "idolaters," instead employing "polytheists," because of al-Ṭabarī's specific reference to worshippers of images and statues. Neither captures the precise meaning of the Arabic term; see chapter 9, note 2.

10. *Tafsīr al-Ṭabarī* on Q. 5.5, 9: 572–73 and 577–79, §§11236–51.

11. *Ṣaḥīḥ al-Bukhārī,* 3: 1150, §5566; cf. *Tafsīr al-Ṭabarī* 9: 578–79, §§11248, 11253. Other attestations of this equation in ninth-century works include ʿAbd al-Razzāq, *Al-muṣannaf,* 6: 119, §10182; Muqātil b. Sulaymān, *Tafsīr,* 167, 250.

12. See, among others, al-Jaṣṣāṣ, *Aḥkām al-Qurʾān,* 2: 322; al-Qurṭubī, *Jāmiʿ,* 6: 79; al-Rāzī, *Tafsīr,* 11: 146.

13. Ibn Hishām, *Sīrat al-Nabī,* 3: 450–51 (English: Guillaume, *Life of Muhammad,* 516). See also Fishbein, *Victory of Islam,* 123–24.

14. This tradition appears in five of the most authoritative collections, always with the same early chain of Basran transmitters: *Ṣaḥīḥ al-Bukhārī* 2: 615, §3189; *Ṣaḥīḥ Muslim* 2: 771–72, §§4704–6; *Sunan Abī Dāʾūd* 2: 463, §2704; *Sunan al-Nasāʾī* 2: 727, §4452; *Sunan al-Dārimī* 3: 1624–25, §2542.

15. Ibn Hishām, *Sīrat al-Nabī,* 3: 452–53; this translation is based on Guillaume, *Life of Muhammad,* 516.

16. We will explore exceptions to this general rule in chapters 12 and 13.

17. See chapter 9, note 26.

18. Ben Shemesh, *Abū Yūsuf's Kitāb al-kharāj,* 88, slightly modified. See also the edition of al-Bannā, 265, which contains a longer and more awkward version of the same statement.

19. See, for example, the Ḥanbalī jurist Ibn Qudāmah, *Al-mughnī,* 9: 392–93, §7757, who cites Ibn Ḥanbal. See also al-Zamakhsharī, *Al-kashshāf,* on Q. 5.5, 1: 595; al-Zamakhsharī (d. 1144), who affirms a ḥadith allowing a sick Muslim to instruct a Magian to slaughter meat properly on his behalf, condemns Abū Thawr for permitting such behavior to a healthy Muslim.

To my knowledge, the only Sunni other than Abū Thawr who permits Magian meat is ʿAlī b. Aḥmad Ibn Ḥazm (d. 1064), whose legal opinions are frequently at odds with the Sunni mainstream. Ibn Ḥazm, *Al-muḥallā,* 6: 146, §1059, contends that Muḥammad's acceptance of the *jizyah* from Magians demonstrates that their food is no different than that of Jews and Christians; he dismisses the significance of Abū Yūsuf's tradition to the contrary on the grounds that its transmission is unsound. Ibn Ḥazm's opinion is acknowledged as a legitimate minority viewpoint by Ibn Rushd (Averroës), *Bidāyat al-mujtahid,* 1: 464 (English: *Distinguished jurist's primer,* 1: 546).

20. See Maghen, *After hardship cometh ease.*

21. Al-Shaybānī, *Siyyar* §146–49, in al-Sarakhsī, *Sharḥ al-siyar,* 1: 147–48; see also Ibn Qudāmah, *Al-mughnī,* 9: 393–94, §7759. On the Zoroastrian practice of murmuring, see *Dādestān ī dēnīg,* 39.15–17, p. 169. Al-Sarakhsī (d. 1090) questions the reliability of al-Shaybānī's source regarding the bread of "blacks," but does so based on concern that the bread might have been prepared in vessels that previously contained pork or wine rather than because the bread was made by a foreigner.

22. See, among others, ʿAbd al-Razzāq, *Al-muṣannaf,* 4: 469, §§8495–96; 6: 108–9, §§10152–55; Ibn Abī Shaybah, *Al-muṣannaf,* 5: 547–49, §§1–14; al-Bayhaqī, *Al-sunan,* 9: 253. Fish are not subject to the requirements of proper slaughter in Islamic law.

23. Regarding these estimates and the evidence on which they are based, see Morony, "Age of conversions."

24. On the place of scholastic modes of thinking within Islamic legal discourse, see Makdisi, *Rise of colleges,* esp. 105–52.

25. For a comprehensive study of Islamic laws regarding animal slaughter and hunting, see Gräf, *Jagdbeute und Schlachttier.*

26. Al-Kāsānī, *Badāʾiʿ al-sanāʾiʿ,* 5: 46. Most jurists apply the logic expressed by al-Kāsānī. An exception is Mālik b. Anas (d. 795), who reportedly prohibits game killed by Scripturists on the basis of the Qur'anic dictum permitting "game that your hand or your lances catch" (Q. 5.94): "your," he asserts, refers solely to Muslims. (We encountered a similarly narrow reading of *Deuteronomy* 12.21 by Rabbinic Sages in T. *Ḥullin* 1.1.) Some of Mālik's disciples accept this prohibition while others reject it; see Saḥnūn, *Al-mudawwanah,* 2: 631. For an extensive discussion of the issue, see Ibn Rushd al-Jadd, *Fatāwā,* 1: 561–67; Ibn Rushd (grandfather of the famous philosopher, d. 1126) seems to favor the permission of Jewish and Christian hunting. Mālik's unusual opinion is cited and criticized by a variety of non-Mālikī, jurists, including Ibn Qudāmah, *Al-mughnī,* 9: 390, §7751.

27. Al-Ghazālī, *Al-wajīz* (literally: "the concise book [of Shāfiʿī law]"), printed in al-Rāfiʿī, *Al-ʿazīz: sharḥ al-wajīz,* 12: 3. The following summary draws on the commentary by ʿAbd al-Karīm b. Muḥammad al-Rāfiʿī (d. 1226), which appears on pp. 3–6, and on al-Ghazālī's more expansive *Al-wasīṭ,* 7: 102.

28. To my knowledge, the first Imāmī to discuss joint hunting in detail is Muḥammad b. al-Ḥasan al-Ṭūsī (*Al-mabsūṭ,* 6: 258, 261–62; *Al-khilāf,* 6: 12, 19–20, §§7, 18–20). The nature of the discussion in the latter work makes clear that al-Ṭūsī (d. 1066/7) is inspired by the detailed and highly theoretical discussions about hunting taking place in Sunni circles and that he regards himself as a participant in these scholastic debates. Among Shiʿis to discuss joint hunting, al-Ṭūsī is preceded by the Zaydī al-Nāṭiq bi-'l-Ḥaqq Yaḥyā b. al-Ḥusayn (d. 1032/3); see note 32 below.

29. This principle is attested in Mālik, *Al-muwaṭṭa',* 176, post-§1060, and al-Shāfiʿī, *Al-umm,* 3: 593, 606, as well as in works by members of the Mālikī and Shāfiʿī schools; see also the works by the Imāmī authority al-Ṭūsī cited in the previous note. Some early traditions, in contrast, prohibit game killed by Magian dogs without consideration of who sends them; see, for example, *Sunan al-Tirmidhī,* 1: 397, §1539.

30. This issue is addressed in various Ḥanafī works, including *Mukhtaṣar al-Ṭaḥāwī,* 297. It is also discussed by the Ḥanbalī jurists Abū al-Barakāt, *Al-muḥarrar,* 193, and al-Kalwadhānī, *Al-hidāyah,* 2: 154, among others.

31. This position, articulated by al-Ṭūsī, *Mabsūṭ,* 6: 258, is cited in numerous Imāmī sources and appears as well in the Zaydī work cited in the following note; see also the Ḥanbalī al-Kalwadhānī, *Al-hidāyah,* 2: 154.

32. Al-Nāṭiq, *Taḥrīr,* 2: 488.

33. Aḥmad b. al-Ḥusayn Abū Shujāʿ (d. post-1106), *Kitāb al-taqrīb,* printed in Ibn Qāsim

al-Ghazzī, *Fatḥ al-qarīb,* 83; the cited statement constitutes the entirety of this work's discussion of the subject. The *Taqrīb,* in part because of its brevity, became very popular within Shāfiʿī circles and is the subject of numerous commentaries, Ibn Qāsim's among them.

34. Sunnis and Shiʿis alike make clear that the permissibility of meat prepared by "all Muslims" encompasses women as well as men but excludes mentally incompetent butchers, namely young children and those who are insane or intoxicated.

35. On the subject of mixed non-Muslim marriages and the offspring of such relationships, see Friedmann, *Tolerance and coercion,* 174–75.

36. Saḥnūn, *Al-mudawwanah,* 2: 631–32; al-Qurṭubī, *Jāmiʿ,* on Q. 5.5, 6: 80.

37. See, for example, al-Māwardī, *Al-ḥāwī al-kabīr,* 15: 24–25, who also offers a detailed discussion and refutation of the Ḥanafī position. Al-Ghazālī's *Al-wajīz* merely states both Shāfiʿī alternatives.

38. Al-Kāsānī, *Badāʾiʿ al-sanāʾiʿ,* 5: 46; see also al-Ṭaḥāwī, *Ikhtilāf,* 70–71, by a Ḥanafī who surveys the opinions of the various schools.

39. Al-Ṭūsī, *Al-khilāf,* 6: 20, §20.

40. De Blois, "Sabians."

41. On Islamic conceptions of the Sabians more broadly, see McAuliffe, "Exegetical identification."

42. *Mukhtaṣar al-Taḥāwī,* 297; cf. al-Kāsānī, *Badāʾiʿ al-sanāʾiʿ,* 5: 46.

43. Al-Zamakhsharī, *Al-kashshāf,* 1: 595.

44. Sabians as Jews: Ibn Abī Mūsā, *Al-irshād,* 379; Sabians as Christians: al-Nawawī, *Rawḍat al-ṭālibīn,* 5: 476.

45. The first of these opinions is expressed by the Mālikīs Ibn Abī Zayd, *Al-nawādir,* 366; and Ibn Juzayy, *Qawānīn,* 201; the second appears both in *Al-nawādir* (4: 352) and in *Tafsīr al-Ṭabarī,* on Q. 2.62, 2: 146, §§1104–6.

46. The historical existence of the Samaritans does not imply that Sunni authorities knew much about them. These authorities differ regarding whether the Samaritan religion is merely a type of Judaism or whether Samaritanism constitutes an independent religion lacking a recognized scripture; those who hold the latter position, unsurprisingly, regard Samaritan animal slaughter as invalid. Permissive opinions may be found in ʿAbd al-Razzāq, *Al-muṣannaf,* 4: 487, §8576 (citing ʿUmar b. ʿAbd al-ʿAzīz); Ibn Abī Zayd, *Al-nawādir,* 4: 366; Ibn Abī Mūsā, *Al-irshād,* 378; al-Nawawī, *Rawḍat al-ṭālibīn,* 5: 476. Restrictive opinions ascribed to various authorities appear in al-Ṭaḥāwī, *Ikhtilāf,* 70.

47. On the Banū Taghlib, see Lecker, "Tribes," 34–47. See also Tsafrir, "Yaḥas ha-halakhah," 16–29. In this unpublished thesis, Tsafrir argues that the traditions focused specifically on the Banū Taghlib, as opposed to "Arab Christians," are early. These traditions reflect both the concerns of Iraqi authorities regarding this powerful tribe and the influence of anti-Monophysite Christians affiliated with the Church of the East, which was dominant in Sasanid Iraq and became so again under ʿAbbāsid rule. Tsafrir dates the traditions referring to Arab Christians in general to a later stage of legal development and regards the statements that understand traditions about the Banū Taghlib as referring to all Arab Christians to be an even later misunderstanding. On legal attitudes regarding Arab Christians, see Friedmann, *Tolerance and coercion,* 60–67.

48. *Tafsīr al-Ṭabarī* 9: 575–76, §§11230–34; cf. ʿAbd al-Razzāq, *Al-muṣannaf,* 4: 485–86,

§8570. According to some sources (including al-Ṭabarī §11233), ʿAlī flatly prohibits meat prepared by Christian Arabs; according to others (including al-Ṭabarī §11234 and ʿAbd al-Razzāq §8570), he considers such meat to be reprehensible, but not forbidden. See also the statement found in the *Majmūʿ al-fiqh* of Zayd b. ʿAlī, discussed in chapter 11.

49. Al-Shāfiʿī, *Al-umm,* 3: 604–5, §§1382–83. Cf. Abū Yūsuf, *Kharāj,* ed. Bannā, 250, in which ʿUmar declares that Taghlibīs "are an Arab people, not from the People of the Book" and instructs his tax collector to treat them severely; this tradition is absent from the translation by Ben-Shemesh.

50. *Tafsīr al-Ṭabarī* 9: 573–75, §§11220–29; cf. ʿAbd al-Razzāq, *Al-muṣannaf,* 4: 486–87, §§8571–75; al-Shāfiʿī, *Al-umm,* 3: 605, §1384.

51. Contradicting the argument presented here, an anomalous tradition cited by al-Ṭabarī (9: 576, §11235) asserts: "You may not eat meat slaughtered by an Arab Christian, nor meat slaughtered by an Armenian Christian." Perhaps the author of this tradition regards Armenians as latecomers to Christianity—after all, Armenians are not Greeks or Romans, let alone descendants of the Children of Israel—and extends to them the rationale he presumes underlies the prohibition of Arab Christian meat. This tradition is also problematic because it is ascribed to Ibn ʿAbbās, a frequent proponent of permitting Arab Christian meat (see, in *Tafsīr al-Ṭabarī* alone, 9: 573–74, §§11220, 11221, 11228).

52. Al-Shāfiʿī, *Al-umm,* 3: 605.

53. *Tafsīr al-Ṭabarī,* on Q. 5.5, 9: 573–77. Al-Ṭabarī attributes to al-Shāfiʿī a more radical stance, namely that "those who were given the Book" refers exclusively to the biological descendants of the original recipients of the Torah and the Gospels to the exclusion of all converts. This opinion, which makes better exegetical sense but fails to capture the underlying issue that seems to bother al-Shāfiʿī, is attributed by al-Shāfiʿī to the Successor ʿAṭāʾ b. Abī Rabāḥ (d. 732/3) in *Al-umm,* 6: 18.

54. For statements representative, respectively, of the Ḥanafī, Ḥanbalī, and Mālikī schools, see al-Jaṣṣāṣ, *Aḥkām al-Qurʾān,* 2: 222–23; Ibn Taymiyyah, *Majmūʿ fatāwā Ibn Taymiyyah,* 35: 212–33; al-Qurṭubī, *Jāmiʿ,* on Q. 5.5, 6: 80.

55. See Little, "Ḥaram documents," 257–60.

56. Al-Nawawī, *Rawḍat al-ṭālibīn,* 5: 474–75.

11. THE TARGETS OF SHIʿI FOREIGN FOOD RESTRICTIONS

1. The third branch of Shiʿi law, Ismāʿīlī law, revolves around the works of a single jurist, al-Nuʿmān b. Muḥammad (d. 974), who served as chief jurist of the Fātimid empire. As we will see, the ideas expressed by al-Ṭūsī develop after al-Nuʿmān's lifetime.

2. Al-Ṭūsī, *Al-nihāyah,* 582, 589.

3. For this reason, Sunnis are instructed to wash the dishes of non-Muslims before use. Some authorities also worry that foods prepared by non-Muslims in such dishes might themselves contain prohibited ingredients. See, among others, *Ṣaḥīḥ al-Bukhārī* 2: 1148, §5554; Ibn Abī Zayd, *Al-nawādir,* 366.

4. This status has unfortunate consequences for Jews and Christians in modern Iran; see Maghen, "Strangers and brothers," 188–89.

5. For a detailed treatment of the evolution of the classical Shiʿi position on this subject,

see Freidenreich, "Implications of unbelief." On early Sunni attitudes toward the impurity of non-Muslims, see M. H. Katz, *Body of text,* 157–67. On classical Sunni and Shiʿi conceptions of non-Muslim impurity, see Maghen, "Strangers and brothers."

6. Zayd b. ʿAlī, *Majmūʿ al-fiqh,* §526 (in Griffini, *Corpus iuris,* 141–42); on the nature and date of the *Majmūʿ al-fiqh,* see Griffini's introduction and Madelung, *Imam al-Qāsim,* 54–57. See also Zayd's *Tafsīr gharīb al-Qurʾān,* 126 (on Q. 5.5).

7. Aḥmad b. ʿĪsā (d. 861/2), *Raʾb al-ṣadʿ,* 2: 1604, addresses the impurity which idolaters and Magians transmit to the fish they touch but indicates that Jews and Christians do not have such an effect upon fish; Aḥmad also distinguishes between Scripturist and non-Scripturist acts of animal slaughter. Zayd b. ʿAlī indicates that idolaters are impure (*Majmūʿ al-fiqh* 13, §55) but consistently distinguishes Jews and Christians from idolaters.

8. Muʾayyad bi-'llah, *Al-tajrīd,* 341.

9. Al-Qāsim b. Ibrāhīm, *Masāʾil al-Qāsim* §128, in *Majmūʿ kutub wa-rasāʾil,* 2: 599. See also al-Hādī, *Al-aḥkām,* 2: 291.

10. Traditions about animal slaughter performed by non-Muslims, most of which are attributed to Jaʿfar al-Ṣādiq, may be found in al-Kulaynī, *Al-kāfī,* 6: 238–41, §§1–17; Ibn Bābawayh, *Al-faqīh,* 3: 210–11, §§971–75; al-Ṭūsī, *Tahdhīb,* 9: 63–71, §§266–99; al-Ṭūsī, *Al-istibṣār,* 4: 81–87, §§299–331. Cited traditions are *Al-kāfī* §§1–2; cf. §16.

11. Ibn Bābawayh, *Al-faqīh,* 3: 210, §971; in the following ḥadith, Jaʿfar goes so far as to permit Muslims to accept meat from a Christian who invokes the name of Christ because "by Christ, they mean God, exalted be He." See also al-Kulaynī, *Al-kāfī* 6: 240–41, §14. Contradictions among traditions associated with Jaʿfar are commonplace in Imāmī legal literature; see Hodgson, "D̲jaʿfar al-Ṣādiq," 375.

12. This verse is cited by Muḥammad al-Bāqir, the fifth Imām, in Ibn Bābawayh, *Al-faqīh* 3: 210, §973.

13. Al-Nuʿmān, *Al-iqtiṣār,* 78; Ibn Bābawayh, *Al-muqniʿ wa-'l-hidāyah,* p. 140 of *Al-muqniʿ* and pp. 79–80 of *Al-hidāyah.*

14. Analysis of Shiʿi discourse about marriage with non-Muslims and the employment of non-Muslim wetnurses reveals that the Shiʿi spectrum of humanity is not truly binary: the status of Scripturists is elevated slightly over that of other non-Muslims. The status of Scripturists in Shiʿi law, however, is far inferior to their status in Sunni law. Thus, for example, whereas many Sunni authorities hold that the blood-money due to the family of a Jewish or Christian murder victim is one half or one third the amount due if the victim is a Muslim, Shiʿi authorities rule that the blood-money for a Jew or Christian is only one-fifteenth the standard amount. See Freidenreich, "Christians in Shiʿi law."

15. Al-Kulaynī, *Al-kāfī,* 6: 241, §15.

16. Ibn Shādhān, *Al-īḍāḥ,* 207–9. I am grateful to Etan Kohlberg for drawing to my attention the Persian-language work of Pāktačī, "Ibn Shādhān," 4: 52, who, Kohlberg informs me, documents the pseudonimous nature of this attribution.

17. Indeed, some Sunni authorities do just that, although most condemn this form of invocation or forbid outright consumption of the resulting meat. We will examine this issue in chapter 13.

18. Muʾayyad bi-'llah, *Sharḥ al-tajrīd,* 6: 208–10; among Zaydī authorities, see also al-Nāṭiq bi-'l-Ḥaqq, *Al-taḥrīr,* 2: 487, 490, 492.

19. Al-Mufīd, *Taḥrīm,* 24; I am grateful to Michael Cook for drawing my attention to this work. See also al-Mufīd, *Al-muqni'ah,* 579–81.

20. Al-Murtaḍā, *Al-intiṣār,* 189.

21. Al-Ṭūsī, *Tahdhīb* 9: 70–71; *Al-istibṣār* 4: 76–77.

22. On Sunnis who manifest hostility toward the Imams (*al-nāṣiba*) and Shi'i laws regarding such apostates, see Kohlberg, "Non-Imāmī Muslims"; "Development," 77; both are reprinted in *Belief and law.* Prohibitions of animal slaughter performed by *nāṣibīs* appear in al-Mufīd, *Al-muqni'ah,* 579–80; al-Ṭūsī, *Al-nihāyah,* 582; and subsequent systematic works of Shi'i law.

23. Al-Mufīd, *Taḥrīm,* 31–32; al-Ṭūsī, *Tahdhīb,* 9: 70–71; *Al-istibṣār,* 4: 76–77. On the Shi'i concept of dissimulation, see Stewart, "*Taqiyyah* as Performance."

24. On the distinction between the purity status of Scripturists and Magians in early Shi'i sources, see note 7 above. Aḥmad b. Muḥammad al-Barqī (d. ca. 893/4), compiler of the earliest and most comprehensive collection of Imāmī ḥadiths on this subject, preserves traditions that refer exclusively to the impurity of Magians and those that also refer to the impurity of Jews and Christians, as well as traditions that express different notions regarding the implications of such impurity; see *Al-maḥāsin,* 452–55, §§369–80. To my knowledge, al-Mufīd is the latest authority who holds that non-Muslim impurity is not communicable to foodstuffs; this opinion is implicit in statements about non-Muslim foodstuffs found in *Al-muqni'ah* 580–82. For further documentation and more detailed discussion, see Freidenreich, "Implications of unbelief."

25. This shift within Sunni thought reflects the influence of Muḥammad b. Idrīs al-Shāfi'ī (d. 819/20), whose insistence upon the purity of all human beings is discussed by M. H. Katz, *Body of text,* 164–71; see also Maghen, "Strangers and brothers," 221–22. I am unaware of information that can establish a genealogical relationship between the antithetical Sunni and Shi'i ideas on this subject.

26. Kohlberg, "Non-Imāmī Muslims," 100, 104.

27. Al-Murtaḍā, *Al-intiṣār,* 193, 10–11.

28. See also al-Ṭūsī's comments on Q. 5.5 and 9.28 (in this edition, 9.29) in *Al-tibyān,* 6: 445–46, 10: 200–201. Among later Imāmī works of law, see, for example, Ibn Idrīs al-Ḥillī, *Al-sarā'ir,* 3: 122. Zaydī adoption of this position regarding the impurity of non-Muslims and their food is articulated clearly by Aḥmad b. Yaḥyā Ibn al-Murtaḍā (d. 1437), *Baḥr al-zakhkhār,* 1: 12–13, who associates this position solely with his Zaydī predecessors. On the classical Shi'i conception of non-Muslim impurity, see Maghen, "Strangers and brothers," 179–94.

29. Similarities between Shi'i Islam and Judaism were perceived by medieval observers as well; see Bar-Asher, "Meqom ha-Yahadut"; Wasserstrom, *Between Muslim and Jew,* 94–119. The Shi'i system of classifying humanity is not quite binary; see note 14 above.

30. We observed in chapter 8 that Christian authorities also make use of anti-Jewish rhetoric in their polemics against so-called Christian heretics. There are no surviving indications, however, that "heretical" Christians adopted a different stance regarding Jews and their food than did the orthodox. In chapter 1, I remarked in passing on the decision by some American supporters of the 2003 Iraq War to abstain from "French" foods. Those who engaged in this practice sought not only to express their displeasure toward the more reluctant govern-

ment of France but also and more importantly to distinguish themselves from American opponents of the invasion who, by implication, were "French" and thus not truly American.

31. W. C. Smith, *What is Scripture?* 18.

32. *Tafsīr al-Qummī,* 1: 191. Al-Qummī proceeds to offer a different objection to the permission of meat, reminiscent of Latin Christian anti-Jewish restrictions: "By God! They do not regard your meat as permitted—how can you regard their meat as permitted?" In his commentary on Q. 6.121, al-Qummī glosses "that over which the name of God was not mentioned" as "meat slaughtered by Jews and Christians and that which was slaughtered outside of Islam." See also *Tafsīr al-ʿAyyāshī,* 1: 324–25, §§36–37 (on Q. 5.5).

33. Al-Kulaynī, *Al-kāfī,* 6: 240–41, §§10, 17 (both "grains and the like"); 263, §§1–2 (both "grains"); 264, §6 ("grains and legumes"); Ibn Bābawayh, *Al-faqīh,* 3: 219, §§1012 ("grains"), 1013 ("lentils, chickpeas, and the like"); see also *Tafsīr al-ʿAyyāshī,* cited in the previous note.

34. Ibn Shādhān, *Al-īḍāḥ,* 207.

35. Al-Mufīd, *Al-muqniʿah,* 580; *Taḥrīm,* 26.

36. Al-Murtaḍā, *Al-intiṣār,* 193, 10–11.

37. The late ninth- or early tenth-century exegetes al-Qummī and al-ʿAyyāshī, both of whom take a stand against the permissibility of non-Muslim meat in their commentaries on Q. 5.5 (see note 32 above), devote no attention in their commentaries to 9.28, presumably because they have nothing to say about this verse. Although a number of ḥadiths report that the Imams directly addressed such verses as Q. 5.5, 6.118, and 6.121, Imāmī collections contain no reports that cite 9.28. (The verse is cited twice in al-Ṭūsī's *Tahdhīb,* 1: 223 and 262, but in both cases the citation appears in a statement by al-Ṭūsī himself.) Al-Nuʿmān, *Daʿāʾim al-Islām,* 1: 149, preserves a ḥadith in which ʿAlī cites Q. 9.28 as evidence that Jews, Christians, Sabians, and Magians may not enter mosques, but this tradition does not interpret the portion of this verse referring to impurity. This Ismāʿīlī collection is the only work from before the time of al-Murtaḍā to cite Q. 9.28, according to a full-text search of Noor Digital Library.

38. Articulations of the common assumption appear, for example, in Goldziher, *Introduction,* 213; Maghen, "Strangers and brothers," 179–81. For further discussion, see Freidenreich, "Implications of unbelief."

39. Fredriksen, "Divine justice," 44.

40. Augustine, *Answer to Faustus,* 32.13, trans. Roland Teske.

41. This is not to say that Augustine dismisses the importance of this last taboo. Quite the contrary: he prohibits consuming food known to have been offered to an idol even if one is dying of hunger and no other food is available; see *Letters* 46–47, as well as *De bono coniugiali* 16.18 and *Sermon* 149.3. In the present context, however, Augustine bends over backwards to reconcile the Apostolic Decree with his own principle that no food is impure; he supports this principle by appeal to the scriptural dictum, "for the pure, all things are pure" (*Tit.* 1.15).

42. Cook, "Magian cheese," 450.

43. Al-Bayhaqī, *Al-sunan,* 10: 6.

44. Ibn Ḥanbal, *Al-musnad,* 4: 267, §2755.

45. In addition to the Sunni traditions cited in Cook, "Magian cheese," 455–56, see Ibn Abī Shaybah, *Al-muṣannaf,* 5: 552–54, §§7, 9–11, 13. Al-Jaṣṣāṣ, *Aḥkām al-Qurʾān,* 1: 119–20,

reports that the early Ḥanafī authorities Abū Yūsuf, al-Shaybānī, and Sufyān al-Thawrī regard the consumption of rennet derived from carrion to be reprehensible, although Abū Ḥanīfah himself maintains that such rennet is permitted; al-Jaṣṣāṣ cites several traditions to support the permissive opinion, including two cited below. Cook (454–55) also cites the early Ibāḍī authority Jābir b. Zayd as prohibiting Magian cheese and requiring that rennet be derived from a properly slaughtered animal. On the Zaydī sources Cook cites on p. 454, see note 48 below.

46. Mālik prohibits cheese made by Magians and idolaters on the grounds that it contains carrion-derived rennet, according to the *Mustakhrajah* of al-ʿUṭbī; see Ibn Rushd al-Jadd, *Al-bayān,* 3: 271, 283. Cook, who cites a similar tradition in the *Muwaṭṭaʾ* of Ibn Ziyād (p. 456), regards it as exceptional. Numerous Mālikī authorities, however, adhere to the prohibition of Magian cheese. These include Ibn Rushd al-Jadd; Ibn Abī Zayd, *Al-nawādir,* 366; and al-Qurṭubī, *Jāmiʿ,* on Q. 5.5, 6: 60. Ibn Juzayy declares that such cheese renders impure the seller, the purchaser, and the scale on which it is weighed; see *Qawānīn,* 201.

The Andalusian Ẓāhirī ʿAlī b. Aḥmad Ibn Ḥazm (d. 1064), who on this matter holds in accordance with his Mālikī neighbors, explains that because the curdling effect rennet has on cheese is evident, anything containing rennet from carrion, even in a tiny proportion, is prohibited for Muslim consumption; see *Al-muḥallā,* 6:101, §1019. This rationale for the prohibition of foreign cheese is also offered by a fellow Andalusian, R. Moshe b. Maimon (d. 1204; *Mishneh Torah, M.A.* 3.13; cf. B. *A.Z.* 35a).

47. Al-Hādī, *Al-aḥkām,* 2: 311.

48. Muʾayyad bi-ʾllah, *Sharḥ al-tajrīd,* 6: 232. See also *Al-tajrīd,* 345, in which Muʾayyad bi-ʾllah reports that al-Hādī prohibited both cheese and clarified butter without explaining either prohibition. Cook, "Magian cheese," 454, cites later Zaydī jurists who also prohibit foreign cheese; I have not had access to their works, which are available only in manuscript form. Cook states that these jurists prohibit foreign cheese not because of its rennet but rather because of concerns about the impurity of non-Muslims and their foodstuffs. He notes that his sources juxtapose the prohibition of cheese and clarified butter, the second of which is not made with rennet. Al-Hādī and Muʾayyad bi-ʾllāh also discourage the consumption of foreign butter on the grounds of its polluted status, and similarly juxtapose statements about butter and cheese. They are careful, however, to state explicitly that the concern about cheese relates to the rennet it contains rather than (or, perhaps, in addition to) its polluted state.

49. Al-Barqī, *Al-maḥāsin,* 695–97, §§596, 600–601 (citation from §600).

50. Ibn Abī Shaybah, *Al-muṣannaf,* 5: 542, §2; 5: 544, §22.

51. ʿAbd al-Razzāq, *Al-muṣannaf,* 4: 539, §8784. The attribution to ʿUmar b. al-Khaṭṭāb here must be inferred, as this specific tradition refers to the speaker with a pronoun. The previous tradition cites ʿUmar, however, as does a similar tradition (4: 539–40, §8787), in which the caliph declares that cheese is nothing more than milk. ʿUmar's lenient position regarding Magian cheese is also attested by al-Bayhaqī (*Al-sunan,* 10: 6).

52. Ibn Bābawayh, *Al-faqīh,* 3: 216, §1006, 219, §1011; al-Ṭūsī, *Tahdhīb,* 9: 75–77, §§54–60; *Al-istibṣār,* 4: 89–90, §§339, 340, 343. These traditions make clear that the specified animal parts—even the hair of a pig (*Tahdhīb* §55)!—are not intrinsically impure and may be used in conjunction with food. Various sources require a specific manner for obtaining feathers from carrion and stipulate that eggs retrieved from dead birds must be intact. Al-Ṭūsī

(*Tahdhīb* §60, *Al-istibṣār* §340) cites a tradition prohibiting milk milked from the udder of a dead sheep, but questions its legitimacy.

53. *Sunan al-Tirmidhī,* 1: 460–6, §1830; al-Jaṣṣāṣ, *Aḥkām al-Qur'ān,* 1: 121; al-Bayhaqī, *Al-sunan,* 9: 320; see also ʿAbd al-Razzāq, *Al-muṣannaf,* 4: 533–34, §8765, where the statement is not attributed to the Prophet. Different concerns apparently underlie the questions about these foodstuffs. Clarified butter, addressed in various legal sources, is a prepared foodstuff that may be made in a vessel containing traces of prohibited ingredients. Animal pelts are acquired through slaughter or hunting. Cheese is both a prepared foodstuff and a product of animal slaughter, although from other traditions it seems that the latter factor is the primary concern.

54. ʿAbd al-Razzāq, *Al-muṣannaf,* 4: 539, §8785; see also §8786. The principle that ignorance is bliss appears in Sunni discussions of other foodstuffs of unknown provenance as well. *Ṣaḥīḥ al-Bukhārī* 3: 1150, §5565, reports that the Prophet, asked about meat prepared by a butcher who may or may not have invoked God, instructed his interlocutors to mention God's name themselves and then eat. As we will see in chapter 13, Ibrāhīm al-Nakhāʿī condemns as reprehensible the consumption of meat sacrificed in the name of Christ, but raises no objection if one does not know that this form of consecration was employed. Mālik, however, regards such willful ignorance to have been legitimate only in the early days of Islam, and objects to the continued application of this manner of addressing problematic food; see *Al-muwaṭṭa',* 174, §1045 (English trans. p. 221).

55. Al-Barqī, *Al-maḥāsin,* 495, §597; in the version of this statement known to the Ismāʿīlī jurist al-Nuʿmān (*Da'ā'im* 2: 126, §437), the Imam refers specifically to cheese prepared by non-Muslims with rennet derived from carrion.

56. Al-Bayhaqī, *Al-sunan,* 10: 7; al-Barqī, *Al-maḥāsin,* 496, §598; see also Ibn Bābawayh, *Al-muqniʿ,* 185.

57. Al-Kulaynī, *Al-kāfī,* 6: 339, §2.

58. Al-Barqī, *Al-maḥāsin,* 495–97, §§596, 601; Ibn Bābawayh, *Al-faqīh,* 3: 216, §1002.

59. This logic, however, also works in reverse: because the milk would not become cheese without rennet, the presence of rennet is by definition evident; see note 46 above.

60. Ibn Ḥanbal, *Al-musnad,* 4: 287, §2755; cf. 3: 345, §2080.

61. ʿAbd al-Razzāq, *Al-muṣannaf,* 4: 538–39, §§8781–83; 4: 540, §8788; 4: 542, §8795. Many of the traditions cited in Ibn Abī Shaybah, *Al-muṣannaf,* 5: 552–54, refer to this practice as well. (On the invocation of God over all food, see 5: 265–66.) See also *Sunan Abī Dā'ūd,* 2: 645, §3821, in which the Prophet calls for a knife, mentions God's name, and then proceeds to cut the cheese; it is unclear in this tradition whether the act of cutting is associated with the ritual of invoking God's name. In Shiʿi literature, see al-Barqī, *Al-maḥāsin,* 496, §599.

62. Cook, "Magian cheese," 462–66.

63. Nedungatt and Featherstone, *Council in Trullo,* 137–38; this translation of c. 56 is by Featherstone.

64. Rabbinic arguments for the permissibility of foods made with bones from improperly slaughtered animals, a subject of considerable dispute, are unrelated to those that appear in discussions of rennet from such animals. For one such argument, citing many of the major sources on this subject, see Klein, "Gelatin."

65. Al-Ṭūsī, *Tahdhīb,* 9: 75, §319; the attribution of this tradition is ambiguous.

12. THE IMPLICATIONS OF MEDIEVAL ISLAMIC AND CHRISTIAN DEBATES

1. Berger, *Sacred canopy,* 3–19. Berger speaks primarily of "society," a specific aspect of culture, but it is clear that he understands his observations about society to apply to all aspects of culture.

2. Figures 4, 5, 9, and 11 offer another depiction of the cycle of objectivation, internalization, and externalization.

3. Buber, *I and Thou,* 3–4.

4. Maghen, *After hardship cometh ease.*

5. The hermeneutical focus of Mālikī discourse about Jewish meat is especially evident in Mālikī discussions about game hunted by Scripturists; see chapter 10, note 26.

6. This statement, quoted from Ibn Ḥabīb's *Wāḍiḥah,* appears in Ibn Abī Zayd, *Al-nawādir,* 4: 367; a similar citation appears in the *Risālah* of Ibn ʿAbd al-Raʾūf (ca. 12th. c.), reprinted and translated in Melville and Ubaydli, *Christians and Moors,* 112–15.

7. The Mālikī jurist Ibn Lubābah (d. 926), in contrast, permits Muslims to purchase *al-ṭarīf* from Jewish butchers; see García Sanjuán, "Alimentos de los Ḍimmíes," 127–28, 134.

8. Ibn Abī Zayd, *Al-nawādir,* 4: 368, citing Abū Bakr b. al-ʿAlāʾ. Ibn Abī Zayd al-Qayrawānī (d. 996) understands this logic to account for Mālik's statement that consumption of such fatty portions is permitted but reprehensible (but cf. the following note). Ibn Abī Zayd himself also regards such behavior to be reprehensible; see Ibn Abī Zayd, *Risālah,* 158.

9. ʿAbd al-Wahhāb b. ʿAlī al-Baghdādī, *Al-ishrāf,* 2: 922, §1852; ʿAbd al-Wahhāb ascribes this logic to Mālik who, he reports, either prohibits the consumption of fatty portions or regards such behavior as reprehensible. In *ʿUyūn al-Majālis,* 2: 986, §691, ʿAbd al-Wahhāb reports that Mālik personally declares consumption of the fatty portions to be reprehensible while his disciples Ibn al-Qāsim and Ashhab prohibit this behavior. ʿAbd al-Wahhāb, a Mālikī himself, contrasts his school's position with that of Abū Ḥanīfah and al-Shāfiʿī, who permit the fatty portions outright on the grounds that Jewish opinions about the permissibility of various cuts of meat are meaningless to Muslims.

10. The difference of opinion regarding the status of fatty portions also manifests itself in Mālikī discussions of meat from an animal which Jews reject as *al-ṭarīf.* Saḥnūn (d. 855), *Al-mudawwanah,* 2: 641–42, the earliest Islamic authority to address the case of lung defects, reports that Mālik originally permitted such meat but later repeatedly declared its consumption to be reprehensible, whereas Ibn al-Qāsim (d. 806), Mālik's most prominent disciple, prohibits its consumption outright. Ibn Abī Zayd, *Al-nawādir,* 4: 365, 367, like Mālik, holds that Muslim consumption of meat from animals with lung defects slaughtered by Jews is reprehensible, but he reports that Mālik's disciples Ashhab, Ibn Wahb, and Muḥammad b. ʿAbd al-Ḥakam permit such behavior without reservation. See also Ibn Rushd al-Jadd, *Al-bayān,* 3: 366–68.

11. See J. Cohen, *Living letters,* 2.

12. The Bible requires that quadrupeds have split hoofs (that is, "divided toes"), but does not apply this or any other explicit criterion to birds. The Rabbinic criteria for determining the permissibility of birds are the presence of an extra toe, a crop, and a gizzard which can be separated from the surrounding muscle, to the exclusion of birds of prey (M. *Ḥul.* 3.6). Geese meet this standard and the rabbis take their permissibility for granted (see, for ex-

ample, M. *Ḥul.* 12.1). Some Karaite authorities prohibit consumption of all birds not explicitly permitted in the Bible, including geese, but Ibn Ḥabīb clearly does not have this practice in mind as these Karaites prohibit eating chicken as well. On Karaite opinions regarding the permissibility of fowl, see Lasker, "Science in the Karaite communities." On the relationship—and lack thereof—between Jewish dietary regulations and Islamic conceptions of Jewish dietary regulations with respect to both undivided toes and prohibited fatty portions, see Maghen, *After hardship cometh ease,* 146–60.

13. Ibn Ḥazm, *Al-iḥkām,* 722–23; this translation is based on that of Adang, "Ibn Ḥazm's criticism," 6–7. Adang observes that Ibn Ḥazm here employs an argument used in the anti-Rabbanite polemics of Karaite Jews.

14. Ibn Ḥazm, *Al-muḥallā,* 6: 143–44.

15. Ibn Ḥazm dismisses the normative value of Jewish and Christian scriptures in various other works as well; see Perlmann, "Andalusian authors," 271–80, reprinted in Chazan, *Medieval Jewish life,* 149–58. On Ibn Ḥazm's ideas about the abrogation of the Torah, see Adang, *Muslim writers,* 216–22.

16. Ibn Ḥazm, *Al-muḥallā,* 6: 143–44; for a more extensive discussion of this passage, see Adang, "Ibn Ḥazm's criticism," 4–6.

17. Ibn Ḥazm, *Al-muḥallā,* 6: 145. Ibn Ḥazm's argument on this subject was sufficiently persuasive to sway both Muḥammad b. Aḥmad Ibn Rushd the grandfather and his identically named grandson, better known in the West as Averroës; see, by the former, *Al-bayān,* 3: 366–68; by the latter, *Bidāyat al-mujtahid,* 1: 463 (English: *Distinguished jurist's primer,* 1: 546). Sunni jurists uniformly hold that men and women alike are fit to perform the act of animal slaughter.

18. See, for example, al-Māwardī, *Al-ḥāwī al-kabīr,* 15: 24; al-Ghazāli in al-Rāfiʿī, *Al-ʿazīz: sharḥ al-wajīz,* 12: 5; Ibn Kathīr, *Tafsīr,* 2: 501–3; for a synopsis of early Sunni opinions on the subject, see also al-Ṭaḥāwī, *Ikhtilāf,* 73–74.

19. Ibn al-Qayyim's discipleship cannot account for his opinions as a fellow disciple, Ismāʿīl b. ʿUmar Ibn Kathīr (d. 1373), permits all problematic Jewish meat in passing; see the previous note. For a more detailed study of Ibn al-Qayyim's discussion of this subject, along with a summary of Ibn Taymiyyah's discussion of related matters, see Freidenreich, "Five questions."

20. Ibn Qayyim al-Jawziyyah, *Aḥkām ahl al-dhimmah,* 1: 256–57; Ibn al-Qayyim addresses the second of these points in greater detail on pp. 260–63. Ibn al-Qayyim is not the first Ḥanbalī to prohibit such meat when prepared by Jews, and he is quick to emphasize that he follows in the footsteps of Ibn Abī Mūsā al-Hāshimī, *Al-irshād,* 378.

21. See note 12 above.

22. Ibn al-Qayyim, *Aḥkām,* 1: 267. Ibn al-Qayyim's knowledge of the Torah's treatment of this subject derives from Samau'al al-Maghribī, *Ifḥām al-yahūd,* 71–85 (Arabic), 64–70 (English). Ibn al-Qayyim also notes that in this case the butcher slaughters the animal believing it to be permitted, whereas a Jewish butcher who slaughters a camel knows from the outset that his act of slaughter is invalid.

23. Ibn al-Qayyim, *Aḥkām,* 1: 257–67. Ibn al-Qayyim quotes and responds to the passages of Ibn Ḥazm's *Al-muḥallā* discussed above.

24. Maghen, *After hardship cometh ease.*

25. Ibn al-Qayyim, *Aḥkām,* 1: 263–64, has great difficulty accounting for the tradition regarding Muḥammad's nonchalant attitude toward the sack of fat ʿAbd Allāh b. Mughaffal obtained during the Battle of Khaybar (see chapter 10). He suggests that ʿAbd Allāh was going to do something with the fat other than eat it, or perhaps that he was starving and wished to eat the fat out of necessity, or that what really interested ʿAbd Allāh was the sack itself. Ibn al-Qayyim even entertains the possibility that the fat came from animals that Muslims slaughtered, although he acknowledges the unlikeliness of this possibility: the sack came from inside the Jewish fortress which the Muslims were besieging. Ibn al-Qayyim's favored hypothesis is that the sack contained fat only from the portions of animals that Jews are permitted to eat. It seems clear that these interpretations are eisegetical rather than exegetical.

26. The text of these competing legal opinions, accompanied by an introduction, appears in Angiolini, "'Cibus iudaei.'" For a discussion of these texts which interprets them differently, see Stow, *Jewish dogs,* 153–56.

27. Toaff, *Love, work, and death,* 61–68. Concern about Christian consumption of the meat of animals slaughtered by Jews is also attested in France and Spain; see Jordan, "Meat market of Béziers"; Nirenberg, *Communities of violence,* 169–72; Stouff, *Ravitaillement,* 143–50.

28. Di Castro refers here to in Trullo (692), c. 11, and Agde (506), c. 40, as they appear in Gratian's *Decretum,* C. 28 q. 1 cc. 13–14.

29. Angiolini, "'Cibus iudaei,'" 109.

30. See the letter by Innocent III to the Count of Nevers (1208), edited and translated by Grayzel, *Church and the Jews, 1198–1254,* 126–27. On this and other documents forbidding the sale of meat by Jewish butchers to Christian consumers, see Jordan, "Meat market of Béziers."

31. Angiolini, "'Cibus iudaei,'" 109. Di Castro supports his interpretation of the possessive pronoun through a citation of Roman law (*Digest* 34.2.10).

32. Angiolini, "'Cibus iudaei,'" 110.

33. On the term *judaize,* see the references in chapter 8, note 24.

34. For an extensive treatment of the symbolism associated with Christian consumption of foods Jews refuse, as reflected in attitudes toward pork consumption, see Fabre-Vassas, *Singular beast.*

35. Given the secular interests di Castro's responsum advances, Capistran may well be correct in his assessment of its underlying motivation. Unlike many of the other authorities whose opinions we have examined in this chapter, however, Capistran does not accuse di Castro of apostasy or heresy. This difference may reflect Capistran's deference toward the professor he addresses as "most brilliant and most worthy teacher, father, and master."

36. Angiolini, "'Cibus iudaei,'" 111. It is probably no coincidence that Capistran singles out for special condemnation Christian consumption of Jewish meat and wine, the two foodstuffs which medieval Jews absolutely insisted on refusing when prepared by Christians. On the latter, see chapter 14.

37. See Kriegel, "Le Juif comme intouchable," 327; Coulet, "'Juif intouchable,'" 210. Many of the laws discussed by Kriegel and Coulet, along with numerous other medieval prohibitions of food associated with Jews, appear in Grayzel, *Church and the Jews, 1198–1254;* see 72, nn. 138–39 and documents 4, 18, 37, and 41. Fully half the twenty-six provincial councils

whose anti-Jewish canons are surveyed by Grayzel and Stow in *Church and the Jews, 1254–1314,* prohibit Jewish foodstuffs or commensality with Jews: see numbers 5–8, 11–12, 15–17, 19–20, 24, 26, and see also papal document no. 50.

38. *Pseudo-Theodorian penitential* 27.1, in Wasserschleben, *Bussordnungen,* 610–11.

39. Stow, *Jewish dogs,* 153.

40. Huguccio, *Summa decretorum,* C. 28 q. 1 c. 13, referring to the following canon in the *Decretum* (Agde, c. 40). On the attitudes of canon law scholars toward the prohibition of Jewish food, see Freidenreich, "Sharing meals"; a transcription of the cited statement by Huguccio, drawn from an unpublished manuscript, appears at 56, n. 29, of this essay. See also chapter 13.

13. ISLAMIC AND CHRISTIAN CLASSIFICATIONS OF ONE ANOTHER

1. It is quite possible that Islamic concern about Christian invocations of Christ over slaughter stems from the imagination of Islamic authorities rather than from information about Christian behavior: just as Muslims invoke God when slaughtering animals, Christians might well invoke Christ on account of their false theology. On Christian acts of animal slaughter, see chapter 9, note 27. The suspicion that Muslim jurists are preoccupied with an imagined concern inspired by Qur'anic hermeneutics is only enhanced by the occasional authority who addresses not only Christian invocations of Christ but also Jewish invocations of Ezra; see, for example, al-Qurṭubī, *Jāmiʿ,* on Q. 5.5, 6: 78. The latter concern undoubtedly stems from familiarity with Q. 9.30 ("The Jews say Ezra is the son of God, while the Christians say Christ is the son of God") rather than with actual Jewish slaughter practices, and the former may as well. The tenor of Sunni discussions regarding Christian slaughter practices, moreover, is generally abstract and scholastic in its nature and can best be read as an effort to work out legal nuances by reference to purely hypothetical circumstances.

2. Ibn ʿAbbās on the abrogating force of Q. 5.5: Abū Dāʾūd, *Sunan,* 2: 485, §2819; see also ʿAbd al-Razzāq, *Al-muṣannaf,* 6: 118, §§10177–78. ʿAṭāʾ: 6: 119, §10184; cf. 6: 118, §10180. ʿAṭāʾ is consistent in his lack of regard for what a monotheistic butcher says while slaughtering: in another tradition cited by ʿAbd al-Razzāq (4: 481, §8547), he permits meat over which a Muslim invokes Satan.

3. Al-Naḥḥās, *Al-nāsikh wa-'l-mansūkh,* on Q. 5.5, 363–64, referring to *jirjis.* The authorities to whom he ascribes this position are al-Qāsim b. Mukhaymarah, Rabīʿah, al-Shaʿbī, Abū al-Dardāʾ, and ʿIbādah b. al-Ṣāmit. Al-Naḥḥās reports that ʿAlī b. Abī Ṭālib, ʿĀʾishah, Ibn ʿUmar, Ṭāwūs, and al-Ḥasan prohibited meat over which a Scripturist is known to have invoked a being other than God and that Mālik condemned but did not prohibit such behavior.

Sharf, "Animal sacrifice," 449, reprinted in *Jews and other minorities,* cites evidence that Armenians sacrificed rams on St. George's Day. On St. George Megalomartyros in Islamic thought, see Newby, *Making of the last prophet,* 231–41.

4. The *Mustakhrajah* of al-Uṭbī ascribes permissive opinions to ʿĪsā and Ibn Wahb; see Ibn Rushd al-Jadd, *Al-bayān,* 3: 272, 378. See also al-Qurṭubī, *Jāmiʿ,* on Q. 5.5, 6: 78–79; al-Qurṭubī (d. 1273) appears to rely on al-Naḥḥās for his prooftexts and on Ibn al-ʿArabī (discussed below) for his arguments.

5. ʿAbd al-Wahhāb, *Al-ishrāf*, 2: 922, §1852.

6. Ibn al-ʿArabī, *Aḥkām al-Qurʾān*, on Q. 5.5, 2: 552.

7. Ibid. See also Ibn al-ʿArabī, *Al-nāsikh*, 2: 194–95.

8. *Aḥbārihi wa-ruhbānihi*, an allusion to Q. 9.31's reference to "rabbis and monks." Ibn al-ʿArabī may use the former term in reference to priests, but the logic of his argument applies equally to all Scripturists so Ibn al-ʿArabī may in fact have Jewish authorities in mind.

9. Ibn al-ʿArabī, *Aḥkām al-Qurʾān*, on Q. 5.5, 2: 554; on this passage, see also García Sanjuán, "Alimentos de los *Dimmíes*," 118–19. Whereas concern about the invocation of Christ over animal slaughter may be a product of Islamic imagination, the scenario Ibn al-ʿArabī addresses here is a real one in the Western Mediterranean, where Christians followed Augustine's teachings and rejected the literal authority of the regulations about animal slaughter found in the Apostolic Decree. Augustine, in fact, cites the slaughter of birds without draining their blood as his example of a practice both unobjectionable and widespread among Christians (*Answer to Faustus*, 32.13).

10. More typical is the following statement, attributed to Mālik by Ibn Abī Zayd al-Qayrawānī: "The meat of a [Scripturist] butcher, whether from among the *dhimmī*s or not, may be eaten unless he is one of those whose practice is to eat carrion" (*Al-nawādir*, 4: 365). (It seems unlikely that Mālik actually addressed this scenario, particular to Latin Christian practice, as no other early authority from Medina or other Near Eastern locales makes reference to it.) See also Ibn Ḥazm, *Al-muḥallā*, 6: 144. On the modern reception of Ibn al-ʿArabī's ruling, see Masud, "Food and the notion of purity."

11. Al-Zuhrī: ʿAbd al-Razzāq, *Al-muṣannaf*, 6: 121, §10190. Ibrāhīm: 6: 119, §10185; cf. Abū Yūsuf, *Al-āthār*, 239, §1059. ʿAbd al-Razzāq also reports that the pious caliph ʿUmar b. ʿAbd al-ʿAzīz (r. 717–20) took the proactive step of appointing Muslims to supervise Christian butchers in Syria to prevent them from consecrating their meat to any but God alone (6: 119, §10186; cf. 4: 88, §8581).

12. Al-Kāsānī, *Badāʾiʿ al-sanāʾiʿ*, 5: 46; see also al-Ṭaḥāwī, *Ikhtilāf*, 69; al-Zaylaʿī, *Tabyīn al-ḥaqāʾiq*, 6: 449.

13. On the continued practice of ritual sacrifice among Christians, see Burkert, *Homo necans*, 8–9; Sharf, "Animal sacrifice."

14. Saḥnūn, *Al-mudawwanah*, 2: 631. Among the earliest Mālikī sources, see also the *Wāḍiḥah* of ʿAbd al-Mālik Ibn Ḥabīb (d. 852/3), as cited in both Ibn Abī Zayd, *Al-nawādir*, 365; and Ibn ʿAbd al-Raʾūf, "Risālah," 95. See also the *Mustakhrajah* of Ibn Ḥabīb's contemporary, Muḥammad al-Uṭbī, published in Ibn Rushd al-Jadd, *Al-bayān*, 3: 272, 276. See also the discussion in García Sanjuán, "Alimentos de los *Dimmíes*," 129–32.

15. See, among others, Ibn Abī Mūsā al-Hāshimī, *Al-irshād*, 378; Ibn Qudāmah, *Al-mughnī*, 9: 391–92, §7755.

16. Al-Shāfiʿī, *Al-umm*, 3: 603–4.

17. Ibn Qayyim al-Jawziyyah, *Aḥkām ahl al-dhimmah*, 1: 253.

18. Ibid., 1: 249–56. For a more extensive treatment of Ibn al-Qayyim's discussion of this subject matter, see Freidenreich, "Five questions."

19. For a more detailed treatment of this discourse, including transcriptions of the sources discussed below but lacking the insight found in this sentence, see Freidenreich, "Sharing meals."

20. *Decretum,* C. 28 q. 1 cc. 13–14, citing in Trullo (692), c. 11, and Agde (506), c. 40. The former, as a translation of the Greek original, differs slightly from the version cited in chapter 8; the latter is effectively identical to the version cited in that chapter.

21. Chrysostom: C. 11 q. 3 c. 24, citing a translation of John Chrysostom's *Homilies on Hebrews,* 25.3–4. Augustine: C. 23 q. 4 c. 17, citing the *Glossa ordinaria* to *1 Cor.* 5.10, 12. This text is based on Augustine's *Sermon* 351.10; a direct citation of that passage appears in the *Decretum* as C. 2 q. 1 c. 18.

22. Rufinus, *Summa decretorum,* 317, commenting on C. 11 q. 3 c. 24. Rufinus is the first medieval scholar of canon law to notice the distinction between canons about shared meals with Jews and those addressing shared meals with gentiles, and his explanation for this phenomenon gained widespread acceptance. The dates of canonists and their works may be found in a variety of sources, sometimes conflicting; I have relied on Hartmann and Pennington, *Bio-bibliographical guide.*

23. Indeed, the terms *pagan* and *Saracen* are interchangeable in many texts of medieval canon law; see, for example, *Summa "Elegantius",* 189. The various references to Muslims we encountered in chapter 8 also portray them as idolatrous gentiles. Bernard of Pavia, *Summa decretalium,* 210, explains that "Saracens" are so named on account of Abraham's wife Sarah, even though they descend from his maidservant Hagar; this etymology is commonly accepted among medieval Latin canonists. See Kedar, "*De iudeis et sarracenis,*" reprinted in *Franks in the Levant.*

24. Bernard of Pavia, *Summa decretalium,* 211.

25. On this jurist, among the most influential commentators on the *Decretum,* see Müller, *Huguccio.*

26. Huguccio, *Summa decretorum,* on C. 11 q. 3 c. 24; for a transcription of this text, presently available only in manuscript, see Freidenreich, "Sharing meals," 59, n. 37.

27. Huguccio, *Summa decretorum,* D. 54 c. 13; see Pakter, *Medieval canon law and the Jews,* 120, n. 109. Note the interchangeability of *pagan* and *Saracen* in this passage and the one cited above.

28. *Ecce vicit leo,* on C. 11 q. 3 c. 24; see Freidenreich, "Sharing meals," 62, n. 41. See p. 54 of that article for further examples of arguments that possession of the Old Testament makes Jews especially threatening to Christians.

29. *Ecce vicit leo,* C. 28 q. 1 c. 14, s.v. inferiores esse inciperiat; see Freidenreich, "Sharing meals," 62 n. 42.

30. See Freidenreich, "Muslims in Western canon law."

31. See Freidenreich, "Sharing meals," 67, 70.

32. Kedar, "*De iudeis et sarracenis,*" 212–13.

33. This permission is hardly innovative; it can be found in early Christian sources, in the *Decretum,* and in the teachings of mid-twelfth century canonists. The more radical concession in this letter, and perhaps the real reason for the bishop of Livonia's petitions, is Clement's indulgence to the Baltic Crusade that clerics who wish to leave their posts to become missionaries may do so. For further details about Clement's letter, see Freidenreich, "Sharing meals," 50, n. 17.

34. *Decretales,* 5.6.10. The same extract from Clement's letter appears in the *Compilatio secunda* of John of Wales (compiled ca. 1210–12; this canon is *2 Comp.* 5.4.4). It is striking

that Clement's letter is the only canon about genuine pagans to appear in the sections of the *Compilatio secunda* and *Decretales* labeled "On Jews, Saracens, and their servants." This location may indicate that John and Raymond already understood Clement's words as relating to Muslims.

35. Bernard of Parma, *Glossa ordinaria* to *Decretales* 5.6.10. On this comment and its relationship to those of earlier commentators, see Freidenreich, "Sharing meals," 74–75. Several of Bernard's contemporaries, including Bartholomew of Brescia, Pope Innocent IV (Sinibaldo dei Fieschi), Geoffrey of Trani, and Hostiensis (Henry of Susa) argue instead that Clement offered an exception to the general prohibition of commensality with pagans: missionaries with papal authorization may engage in such otherwise prohibited behavior. Their statements are all discussed in "Sharing meals."

14. RABBINIC DISCOURSE ABOUT MUSLIMS, CHRISTIANS, AND WINE

1. Soloveitchik, *Yayin bi-yemei ha-beynayim,* 12, 109, is thus mistaken in his use of this example to demonstrate that gentiles in Sasanid Babylonia in fact offered libations at every available opportunity.

2. Miller, *Halakhot pesuqot,* 22, §25. *Halakhot pesuqot* attributes this statement to R. Kohen Ṣedeq Gaon (d. 848), but Miller notes that other sources ascribe the same words to other authorities.

3. R. Abraham b. Isaac, *Eshkol,* 2:77–78. R. Naḥshon's prooftext, B. *A.Z.* 11b, lists a shrine in Arabia as one of five permanent sites of idolatrous worship.

4. Miller, *Halakhot pesuqot,* 21, §21; Miller attributes this responsum to R. Naṭronai Gaon, but Brody, *Teshuvot Rav Naṭronai,* 444, dismisses the validity of this attribution.

5. R. Abraham b. Isaac, *Eshkol,* 2:74.

6. On the phenomenon of "comparative religion" in medieval Islamic thought, see Wasserstrom, *Between Muslim and Jew,* 136–64.

7. For an especially clear statement to this effect, see responsum 448 in Blau, *Teshuvot ha-Rambam,* 725–28, written to the convert ʿOvadyah (English: Twersky, *Maimonides reader,* 475–76).

8. Rambam (Maimonides), *Mishneh Torah, M.A.* 11.7–8. Rambam's definition of the resident alien appears in *Hilkhot ʿAvodah Zarah* 10.6. For a more detailed treatment of Rambam's conception of Islam as manifest in his discussion of wine associated with Muslims, see Freidenreich, "Fusion cooking." Among other discussions of this passage and its relationship to Maimonidean attitudes regarding Islam, see Novak, "Treatment of Islam," 236–37; Schlossberg, "Yaḥaso shel ha-Rambam," 42–45.

9. Rambam acknowledges the geonic analogy between Muslims and newborns in a responsum on the subject, indicating that this analogy was cited by the petitioner; see Blau, *Teshuvot ha-Rambam,* 515–16, §269. On the basis of his statement in the *Mishneh Torah,* however, it would seem that Rambam himself cannot accept the logic that underlies geonic opinions. Given his theory that monotheism reflects a higher stage of human development than idolatry, Rambam may even have found the equation of Muslims with newborns to be offensive. On that theory, see S. Stroumsa, *Maimonides in his world,* 84–124.

10. Rambam condemns Christians as idolatrous on account of their belief in the divin-

ity of Christ. See his commentary on M. *A.Z.* 1.3 in Fiqsler, *'Avodah Zarah 'im perush ha-Rambam,* 8; see also *Mishneh Torah, A.Z.* 9.4.

11. Rambam's system of classifying humanity most closely resembles that of the Almohads, under whose rule Rambam lived during his formative years; see Freidenreich, "Fusion cooking." I am grateful to Sarah Stroumsa for alerting me to this similarity. On Rambam's familiarity with Almohad thought, with Islamic methods of classifying foreigners, and with Islamic thought more broadly, see S. Stroumsa, *Maimonides in his world.*

12. Because Christians share the Jewish scripture, however, Rambam regards scriptural disputations with Christians to be constructive; he holds that such disputations with Muslims are futile. See Blau, *Teshuvot ha-Rambam,* 284–85, §149.

13. See Soloveitchik, *Yeinam,* 137–38, who adds that early Ashkenazic authorities also drew no connection between the prohibition of foreign wine and concern about intermarriage.

14. *Mishneh Torah, M.A.* 17.9; discussion of these prohibitions, partially summarized below, extends through 17.26.

15. Soloveitchik, *Yeinam;* see especially 128–42. See also *Yayin bi-yemei ha-beynayim.*

16. Soloveitchik, *Yeinam,* 56–57, based on *Or zaru'a, A.Z.* §220, and manuscript evidence. Soloveitchik cites Rashi's own, much briefer, statement regarding this discovery on p. 55.

17. *Teshuvot Rashi* §58, cited in Soloveitchik, *Yeinam,* 51–52; "Can halakhic texts," 157. See also the opening statement on libation wine in *Sefer ha-oreh,* cited and discussed in *Yeinam,* 41–43. The fact that gentiles, in the words of Rashi and Rashbam, "do not know how to offer libations" is unsurprising, seeing as the legal definition of proper wine libations is a product of Rabbinic imagination. Soloveitchik, *Yeinam,* 55, n. 41, identifies only one Ashkenazic authority who expresses concern that Christians in fact do offer wine libations, and his concerns are based on reports of behavior in Russia rather than on the observed behavior of local Christians.

18. I depart here from the opinion of Jacob Katz, who holds that "Christians were exempted from the category of idolaters and given a special status" by medieval Ashkenazic rabbis (*Exclusiveness and tolerance,* 25). The evidence which Katz adduces points not toward the placement of Christians in a special category of gentiles but rather toward a willingness to relax various prohibitions regarding interactions with gentiles in general and thus interactions with Christians in particular.

19. Among the authorities who reportedly accepted Shemu'el's opinion on this subject is Rabbenu Tam (R. Jacob of Ramerupt, d. 1171); *Tosafot, A.Z.* 57b, s.v. "le-apoqei," contains an account of R. Yiṣḥaq of Dampierre's observation regarding the implications of this opinion, which Rabbenu Tam quickly disavowed. On this text, see Soloveitchik, *Yeinam,* 104–8.

20. See Soloveitchik, *Yeinam,* 122–23.

21. *Tosafot, A.Z.* 57b, s.v. "le-apoqei," discussed in Soloveitchik, *Yeinam,* 123–25. Soloveitchik describes this argument as "one of the classic distinctions that, once it is established, one stands amazed by the fact that earlier authorities failed to notice it."

22. R. Yisha'yah di Trani, *Tosefot Rid,* on B. *A.Z.* 57a, s.v. "ṭinoq ben yomo."

23. R. Moshe b. Naḥman, *Ḥiddushei ha-Ramban, A.Z.* 36b, s.v. "ve-'al yeinan"; a similar statement appears without attribution in *Tosafot, A.Z.* 29b, s.v., "yayin minalan." R. Moshe b. Naḥman (Ramban, or Nahmanides, d. ca. 1270) cites this explanation in the name of "R. Shemu'el"; a survey of references in Ramban's work to "R. Shemu'el" makes clear that the au-

thority in question is Rashbam, R. Shemu'el b. Me'ir. Ramban, however, lived a century after Rashbam, and no earlier source ascribes this opinion to him; for that reason, Soloveitchik (*Yeinam,* 152) minimizes the significance of this passage. I ascribe this opinion to Rashbam rather than to an anonymous Ashkenazic rabbi purely for the sake of convenience.

24. Soloveitchik, *Yeinam,* 137–40.

25. Ibid., 16.

26. R. Shelomo b. Avraham Adret, *Torat ha-bayit: ʿArokh* §5.1 (2: 401–3); see also *Qaṣar* §5 (2: 406) and *Ḥiddushei ha-Rashba, A.Z.* 64b (p. 158). In *She'elot u-teshuvot,* 4: 107, Rashba forcefully asserts that the prohibition against wine touched by Muslims remains in force; if Rashba is being consistent, he refers in this context solely to the prohibition against consuming such wine. On the implications of Rashba's misreading of the *Mishneh Torah,* see Freidenreich, "Fusion cooking."

27. The lenient position, prefaced with the qualifier "one might say" and followed by an exhortation toward stringency, appears at the conclusion of the printed text of Tosafot, B. *A.Z.* 57b, s.v. "le-apoqei." Supporters of the restrictive opinion include R. Moshe b. Naḥman (*Ḥiddushei ha-Ramban, A.Z.* 36b, s.v. "ve-ʿal yeinan"); R. Asher b. Yeḥi'el (d. 1327, *Tosefot ha-Rosh, A.Z.* 4.7); R. Yom Ṭov b. Avraham Ishbili (d. 1330, *Ḥiddushei ha-Riṭba, A.Z.* 29b, s.v. "yayin minalan"); and R. Ya'aqov b. Asher (d. 1340, *Arbaʿah ṭurim, YD* 123; see also R. Yosef Karo's *Beit Yosef* on this passage). These authorities explain that the unusual severity of the wine prohibition—which extends to the derivation of benefit even though other segregationist foreign food restrictions apply solely to consumption—results from the fact that the Sages wished to avoid confusion about the status of wine offered in idolatrous libations.

28. *Beit Yosef, YD* 123.1. R. Karo supports his claim by citing Rambam's declaration that Christians are idolaters; although he quotes the entirety of Rambam's statement contrasting Muslims and Christians, R. Karo ignores the fact that Rambam himself distinguishes at least some contemporary gentiles from their Talmudic predecessors.

29. Buber, *I and Thou,* 4.

30. Discourse about foreign food restrictions continues to function as an effective barometer with which to measure these changes, many of which reflect the impact of dynamics particular to modernity. I look forward to devoting future studies to foreigners and their food in modern times.

WORKS CITED

Primary sources for which I consulted the standard printed edition (e.g., the Vilna edition of the Babylonian Talmud) are not listed below.

ʿAbd al-Razzāq b. Hammām al-Ṣanʿānī. *Al-muṣannaf.* Edited by Ḥabīb al-Raḥmān al-Aʿẓamī. 11 vols. Beirut: Maktab al-Islāmī, 1983.

ʿAbd al-Wahhāb b. ʿAlī al-Baghdādī. *Al-ishrāf ʿala nukat masāʾil al-khilāf.* 2 vols. Beirut: Dār Ibn Ḥazm, 1999.

———. *ʿUyūn al-majālis.* Edited by Imbāy Ibn Kība Kāh. 5 vols. Riyadh, Saudi Arabia: Al-Rushd, 2000.

Abraham b. Isaac of Narbonne, R. *Sefer ha-eshkol.* Edited by Chanokh Albeck and Shalom Albeck. 2 vols. Jerusalem: Reuven Mass, 1934–38.

Abramson, Shraga, ed. *Masekhet ʿAvodah Zarah: Ketav yad Bet ha-Midrash la-Rabbanim be-New York.* New York: Jewish Theological Seminary of America, 1957.

Abū al-Barakāt, Majd al-Dīn. *Al-muḥarrar fī al-fiqh ʿalā madhhab al-Imām Aḥmad b. Ḥanbal.* 2 vols. Cairo: Al-Sunnah al-Muḥammadiyyah, 1950.

Abū Dāʾūd Sulaymān b. al-Ashʿath al-Sijistānī. *Sunan Abī Dāʾūd.* 2 vols. Vaduz, Liechtenstein: Jamʿiyyat al-Maknaz al-Islāmī, 2000.

Abū Yūsuf, Yaʿqūb b. Ibrāhīm. *Kitāb al-āthār.* Beirut: Dār al-Kutub al-ʿIlmiyyah, 1978.

———. *Kitāb al-kharāj.* Edited by Muḥammad Ibrāhīm al-Bannā. N.p.: Dār al-Iṣlāḥ li-l-Ṭabʿ wa-ʾl-Nashr wa-ʾl-Tawzīʿ, 1981.

Abusch, Tzvi. S.v. "Hammurabi." In *The HarperCollins Bible dictionary,* edited by Paul J. Achtemeier, 400–401. San Francisco: HarperSanFrancisco, 1996.

Acker, Leonardo van, ed. *Agobardi Lugdunensis: Opera omnia.* Corpus Christianorum, Continuatio Mediaevalis. Turnhout, Belgium: Brepols, 1981.

Adams, Douglas. *The hitchhiker's guide to the galaxy.* London: Pan, 1979.

Adang, Camilla. "Ibn Ḥazm's criticism of some 'Judaizing' tendencies among the Mâlikites."

In *Medieval and modern perspectives on Muslim-Jewish relations,* edited by Ronald L. Nettler, 1–16. Luxembourg: Harwood, 1995.

———. *Muslim writers on Judaism and the Hebrew Bible: From Ibn Rabban to Ibn Ḥazm.* Leiden, Netherlands: Brill, 1996.

Adret, R. Shelomo b. Avraham. *Ḥiddushei ha-Rashba ʿal masekhet ʿAvodah Zarah.* Edited by Yehudah Leib Zaks. Jerusalem: Mosad ha-Rav Kook, 1966.

———. *She'elot u-teshuvot ha-Rashba.* 7 vols. Jerusalem: Or ha-Mizraḥ, 1997.

———. *Torat ha-bayit ha-arokh ve-ha-qaṣar.* Edited by Moshe ha-Kohen Baron. 2 vols. Jerusalem: Mosad ha-Rav Kook, 1995.

Aḥmad b. ʿĪsā. *Ra'b al-ṣadʿ: Amālī Aḥmad b. ʿĪsā.* Edited by ʿAlī b. Ismāʿīl al-Ṣanʿānī. 3 vols. Beirut: Dār al-Nafā'is, 1990.

Alcock, Joan P. *Food in the ancient world.* Westport, Conn.: Greenwood, 2006.

Alexander, Elizabeth Shanks. "Casuistic elements in mishnaic law: Examples from M. Shevuʿot." *Jewish studies quarterly* 10 (2003): 189–243.

Alexander, Philip S. "'The parting of the ways' from the perspective of Rabbinic Judaism." In *Jews and Christians: The parting of the ways,* A.D. 70 to 135, edited by James D. G. Dunn, 1–25. Tübingen, Germany: Siebeck, 1992.

Allison, Dale C., Jr. "Peter and Cephas: One and the same." *Journal of biblical literature* 111 (1992): 489–95.

Amann, Émile. S.v. "Laodicée (Concile de)." In *Dictionnaire de théologie catholique,* edited by A. Vacant and E. Mangenot, 8: 2611–15. Paris: Letouzey, 1899–1950.

Amulo. *Contra Iudaeos.* In *Patrologia latina,* edited by J.-P. Migne, 116: 141–84. Paris: 1844–1904.

Anderson, Benedict. *Imagined communities: Reflections on the origin and spread of nationalism.* Rev. ed. London: Verso, 1991.

Anderson, H., trans. "3 Maccabees." In *The Old Testament pseudepigrapha, vol. 2,* edited by James H. Charlesworth, 509–30. Garden City, N.Y.: Doubleday, 1985.

———. "4 Maccabees." In *The Old Testament pseudepigrapha, vol. 2,* edited by James H. Charlesworth, 531–64. Garden City, N.Y.: Doubleday, 1985.

Angiolini, Hélène. "'Cibus iudaei': Un 'consilium' quasi inedito di Angelo di Castro sulla macellazione con rito ebraico e una 'reprobatio' di san Giovanni da Capestrano." In *La storia degli ebrei nell'Italia medievale: Tra filologia e metodologia,* edited by Maria Giuseppina Muzzarelli and Giacomo Todescini, 102–14. Bologna: Istituto per i beni artistici culturali naturali della Regione Emilia-Romagna, 1990.

Arberry, A. J., trans. *The Koran interpreted.* London: Allen and Udwin, 1955.

Aristides. *Apologie.* Edited by Bernard Puderon and Marie-Joseph Pierre. Sources Chrétiennes. Paris: Éditions du Cerf, 2003.

Augustine. *Answer to Faustus, a Manichean.* Translated by Roland Teske. Hyde Park, N.Y.: New City, 2007.

———. *Contra Faustum.* Edited by Joseph Zycha. Corpus Scriptorum Ecclesiasticorum Latinorum. Vienna: Tempsky, 1891.

———. *Sermons 341–400.* Translated by Edmund Hill. Hyde Park, N.Y.: New City, 1995.

ʿAyyāshī, Muḥammad b. Masʿūd al-. *Tafsīr al-ʿAyyāshī.* 2 vols. Beirut: Mu'assassat al-Aʿlamī, 1991.

Bagnall, Roger S., and James B. Rives. "A prefect's edict mentioning sacrifice." In *Archiv für*

Religionsgeschichte, vol. 2.1, edited by Jan Assman, Fritz Graf, Tomo Holscher, Ludwig Koenen, and John Scheid, 77–86. Munich: Saur, 2000.

Bar-Asher, Meir M. "'Al meqom ha-Yahadut ve-ha-Yehudim be-sifrut ha-datit shel ha-Shi'ah ha-qedumah." *Pe'amim* 61 (1994): 16–36.

Barclay, John M. G. *Jews in the Mediterranean Diaspora: From Alexander to Trajan (323 B.C.E.–117 C.E.).* Berkeley: University of California Press, 1996.

———. "Who was considered an apostate in the Jewish Diaspora?" In *Tolerance and intolerance in early Judaism and Christianity,* edited by Graham N. Stanton and Guy G. Stroumsa, 80–98. Cambridge: Cambridge University Press, 1998.

Barhebraeus, Gregorius. *Nomocanon.* Edited by Paul Bedjan. Paris: Harrassowitz, 1898.

Barqī, Aḥmad b. Muḥammad al-. *Al-maḥāsin.* Edited by Jalāl al-Dīn al-Ḥusaynī. Tehran: Dār al-Kitāb al-Islāmiyyah, 1951.

Baumgarten, Albert I. *The flourishing of Jewish sects in the Macabean era: An interpretation.* Leiden, Netherlands: Brill, 1997.

Bayhaqī, Aḥmad b. al-Ḥusayn al-. *Al-sunan al-kubrā.* 11 vols. Hyderabad, India: Majlis Dā'irat al-Ma'ārif al-Niẓāmiyyah, 1937.

Ben-Shalom, Yisrael. *Beit Shammai u-ma'avaq ha-qana'im neged Romi.* Jerusalem: Yad Yiṣḥaq Ben-Ṣevi, 1993.

Ben Shemesh, Aharon. *Abū Yūsuf's Kitāb al-Kharāj.* Leiden, Netherlands: Brill, 1969.

Berger, Peter L. *The sacred canopy: Elements of a sociological theory of religion.* Garden City, N.Y.: Doubleday, 1967.

Bergman, Jan, Helmer Ringgren, and Bernhard Lang. "Zabhach." In *Theological dictionary of the Old Testament,* edited by C. Johannes Botterweck and Helmer Ringgren, translated by David E. Green, 4: 8–29. Grand Rapids, Mich.: Eerdmans, 1980.

Bergquist, Birgitta. "Bronze Age sacrificial *koine* in the Eastern Mediterranean? A study of animal sacrifice in the Ancient Near East." In *Ritual and sacrifice in the Ancient Near East: Proceedings of the international conference organized by the Katholieke Universiteit Leuven from the 17th to the 20th of April 1991,* edited by Jan Quaegebeur. Louvain, Belgium: Peeters, 1993.

Berlin, Adele. *The JPS Bible commentary: Esther.* Philadelphia: Jewish Publication Society, 2001.

Bernard of Pavia. *Summa decretalium.* Edited by Ernst Adolph Theodor Laspeyres. 1860. Repr., Graz, Austria: Akademische Druck- und Verlagsanstalt, 1956.

Bettenson, Henry, and Chris Maunder, eds. *Documents of the Christian Church.* 3rd ed. Oxford: Oxford University Press, 1999.

Blau, Joshua, ed. *Teshuvot ha-Rambam.* 3 vols. Jerusalem: Meqiṣe Nirdamim, 1957.

Blois, François de. "The 'Sabians' (Ṣābi'ūn) in pre-Islamic Arabia." *Acta Orientalia* 56 (1995): 39–61.

Blumenkranz, Bernhard. "Anti-Jewish polemics and legislation in the Middle Ages: Literary fiction or reality?" *Journal of Jewish studies* 15 (1965): 125–40.

———. "Deux compilations canoniques de Florus de Lyon et l'action antijuive d'Agobard." *Révue historique de droit français et étrangers* 33 (1955): 227–54, 560–82.

———. "'Iudaeorum conuiuia', à propos du Concile de Vannes (465), c. 12." In *Études d'histoire du droit canonique dédiées à Gabriel Le Bras,* 2: 1055–58. Paris: Sirey, 1965.

———. *Juifs et chrétiens dans le monde occidental: 430–1096.* Paris: Mouton, 1960.
———. *Juifs et chrétiens: Patristique et Moyen Âge.* London: Variorum, 1977.
Boccaccini, Gabriele. *Middle Judaism: Jewish thought, 300 B.C.E. to 200 C.E.* Minneapolis: Fortress, 1991.
Boshof, Egon. *Erzbischof Agobard von Lyon: Leben und Werk.* Cologne: Böhlau, 1969.
Böckenhoff, Karl. *Das apostolische Speisegesetz in den ersten fünf Jahrhunderten.* Paderborn, Germany: Schöningh, 1903.
———. *Speisesatzungen mosaicher Art in mittelalterlichen Kirchenrechtsquellen des Morgen- und Abendlandes.* Münster, Germany: Aschendorffschen Buchhandlung, 1907.
Boyarin, Daniel. *Border lines: The partition of Judaeo-Christianity.* Philadelphia: University of Pennsylvania Press, 2004.
Brichto, Herbert Chanan. "On slaughter and sacrifice, blood and atonement." *Hebrew Union College annual* 47 (1976): 19–55.
Brody, Robert. *Teshuvot Rav Naṭronai bar Hila'i Ga'on.* 2 vols. Jerusalem: Mekhon Ofeq, 1994.
Broshi, Magen. "The diet of Palestine in the Roman period: Introductory notes." *Israel Museum journal* 5 (1986): 41–56.
———. "Wine in ancient Palestine: Introductory notes." *Israel Museum journal* 3 (1984): 21–42.
Brubaker, Rogers, and Frederick Cooper. "Beyond 'identity.'" *Theory and society* 29 (2000): 1–47.
Brunt, John Carlton. "Paul's attitude toward and treatment of problems involving dietary practice: A case study in Pauline ethics." Ph.D. diss., Atlanta: Emory University, 1978.
———. "Rejected, ignored, or misunderstood? The fate of Paul's approach to the problem of food offered to idols in early Christianity." *New Testament studies* 31 (1983): 113–24.
Buber, Martin. *I and Thou.* 2nd ed. Translated by Ronald Gregor Smith. New York: Scribner, 1958.
Bukhārī, Muḥammad b. Ismāʿīl al-. *Ṣaḥīḥ al-Bukhārī.* 3 vols. Vaduz, Liechtenstein: Jamʿiyyat al-Maknaz al-Islāmī, 2000.
Burchard, Christoph. "Joseph and Aseneth." In *The Old Testament pseudepigrapha, vol. 2,* edited by James H. Charlesworth, 177–248. Garden City, N.Y.: Doubleday, 1985.
———. *Joseph und Aseneth: Kritisch herausgegeben.* Leiden, Netherlands: Brill, 2003.
Burchard of Worms. *Decretorum Libri XX.* 1548. Repr., Aalen, Germany: Scientia, 1992.
Burkert, Walter. *Greek religion: Archaic and classical.* Translated by John Raffan. Oxford: Blackwell, 1985.
———. *Homo necans: The anthropology of ancient Greek sacrificial ritual and myth.* Translated by Peter Bing. Berkeley: University of California Press, 1983.
———. "Oriental symposia: Contrasts and parallels." In *Dining in a classical context,* edited by William J. Slater, 7–24. Ann Arbor: University of Michigan Press, 1991.
Burns, J. Patout, Jr. *Cyprian the bishop.* London: Routledge, 2002.
Cabezón, José Ignacio, ed. *Scholasticism: Cross-cultural and comparative perspectives,* 1–17. Albany: State University of New York Press, 1998.
Cameron, Averil. "Jews and heretics: A category error." In *The ways that never parted: Jews and Christians in late antiquity and the early Middle Ages,* edited by Adam H. Becker and Annette Yoshiko Reed, 345–60. Tübingen, Germany: Siebeck, 2003.

Carr, David M. *Writing on the tablet of the heart: Origins of scripture and literature.* Oxford: Oxford University Press, 2005.

Cassuto, Umberto. *A commentary on the Book of Exodus.* Translated by Israel Abrahams. Jerusalem: Magnes, 1967.

Chabot, J. B. *Synodicon orientale.* Paris: Klincksieck, 1902.

Chazan, Robert, ed. *Medieval Jewish life: Studies from the Proceedings of the American academy for Jewish research.* New York: Ktav, 1976.

Cheung, Alex T. *Idol food in Corinth: Jewish background and Pauline legacy.* Sheffield, England: Sheffield Academic Press, 1999.

Chrysostom, John. *Logoi kata Iudaion.* In *Patrologia graeca.* edited by J.-P. Migne, 48: 843–61. Paris: 1844–1904.

Clercq, Charles de. *Concilia Galliae, A. 511–A. 695.* Corpus Christianorum, Series Latina. Turnhout, Belgium: Brepols, 1963.

Cody, Aelred. "The *Didache:* An English translation." In *The* Didache *in context: Essays on its text, history and transmission,* edited by Clayton N. Jefford, 3–14. Leiden, Netherlands: Brill, 1995.

Cohen, Jeremy. *Living letters of the Law: Ideas of the Jew in medieval Christianity.* Berkeley: University of California Press, 1999.

Cohen, Shaye J. D. *The beginnings of Jewishness: Boundaries, varieties, uncertainties.* Berkeley: University of California Press, 1999.

———. *From the Maccabees to the Mishnah.* Philadelphia: Westminster, 1987.

———. "The Judaean legal tradition and the *halakhah* of the Mishnah." In *The Cambridge companion to the Talmud and rabbinic literature,* edited by Charlotte E. Fonrobert and Martin S. Jaffee, 121–43. Cambridge: Cambridge University Press, 2007.

Collins, John J. *Between Athens and Jerusalem: Jewish identity in the Hellenistic diaspora.* 2nd ed. Grand Rapids, Mich.: Eerdmans, 2000.

———. *Daniel: A commentary on the Book of Daniel.* Hermeneia. Minneapolis: Fortress, 1993.

Comerro, Viviane. "La nouvelle alliance dans la sourate al-Mā'ida." *Arabica* 48 (2001): 285–314.

Cook, Michael. "Early Islamic dietary law." *Jerusalem studies in Arabic and Islam* 7 (1986): 217–77.

———. "Magian cheese: An archaic problem in Islamic law." *Bulletin of the School of Oriental and African studies* 47 (1984): 449–67.

Coulet, Noël. "'Juif intouchable' et interdits alimentaires." In *Exclus et systèmes d'exclusion dans la littérature et la civilisation médiévales,* 207–21. Aix-en-Provençe, France: C.U.E.R. M.A., 1978.

Curtis, Robert I. *Garum and salsamenta: Production and commerce in materia medica.* Leiden, Netherlands: Brill, 1991.

Cuypers, Michel. *The banquet: A reading of the fifth sura of the Qur'an.* Miami: Convivium, 2009.

Cyprian. *"De lapsis" and "De ecclesiae catholicae unitate."* Translated by Maurice Bévenot. Oxford: Clarendon, 1971.

Dādestān ī dēnīg. Edited by Mahmoud Jaafari-Dehagui. Paris: Association pour l'avancement des études iraniennes, 1998.

Dalby, Andrew. *Dangerous tastes: The story of spices.* Berkeley: University of California Press, 2000.
———. *Food in the ancient world from A to Z.* London: Routledge, 2003.
Dán, Róbert. "'Judaizare': The career of a term." In *Antitrinitarianism in the second half of the 16th century,* edited by Róbert Dán and Antal Pirnát, 25–34. Budapest: Akadémiai Kiadó, 1982.
Danby, Herbert, trans. *The Mishnah.* London: Oxford University Press, 1933.
Dārimī, ʿAbd Allāh b. ʿAbd al-Raḥmān al-. *Musnad al-Dārimī al-maʿruf bi-Sunan al-Dārimī.* 4 vols. Riyadh, Saudi Arabia: Dār al-Mughnī, 2000.
Davidson, James N. *Courtesans and fishcakes: The consuming passions of classical Athens.* New York: St. Martin's Press, 1997.
Dawood, N. J., trans. *The Koran: With a parallel Arabic text.* New York: Viking, 1990.
Decretales D. Gregorii Papae IX . . . una cum glossis. . . . Venice: n.p., 1604.
Decretalium collectiones. Edited by Emil Friedberg. 1881. Leipzig, Germany: Tauchnitz, 1959.
Decretum magistri Gratiani. Edited by Emil Friedberg. 1879. Leipzig, Germany: Tauchnitz, 1959.
Doniger, Wendy. *The implied spider: Politics and theology in myth.* New York: Columbia University Press, 1998.
Donner, Fred M. *Muhammad and the believers: At the origins of Islam.* Cambridge, Mass.: Belknap, 2010.
Douglas, Mary. "Deciphering a meal." In *Implicit meanings: Essays in anthropology,* 249–75. London: Routledge and Kegan Paul, 1975.
———. *Natural symbols: Explorations in cosmology.* New York: Pantheon, 1970.
———. *Purity and danger: An analysis of concepts of pollution and taboo.* New York: Praeger, 1966.
Effros, Bonnie. *Creating community with food and drink in Merovingian Gaul.* New York: Palgrave Macmillan, 2002.
Eilberg-Schwartz, Howard. *The savage in Judaism: An anthropology of Israelite religion and ancient Judaism.* Bloomington: Indiana University Press, 1990.
Elgavish, David. "The encounter of Abram and Melchizedek King of Salem: A covenant establishing ceremony." In *Studies in the Book of Genesis: Literature, redaction and history,* edited by André Wénin, 495–508. Louvain, Belgium: Leuven University Press, 2001.
Elman, Yaakov. *Authority and tradition: Toseftan baraitot in talmudic Babylonia.* Hoboken, N.J.: Ktav, 1994.
Ephrem the Syrian. *Des Heiligen Ephraem des Syrers Paschahymnen.* Edited by Edmund Beck. Corpus Scriptorum Christianorm Orientalium, Scriptores Syri, vols. 108–9. Louvain, Belgium: Secrétariat du Corpus SCO, 1964.
Eriksson, Anders. *Traditions as rhetorical proof: Pauline argumentation in 1 Corinthians.* Stockholm: Almqvist and Wiksell, 1998.
Esler, Philip Francis. *Community and gospel in Luke–Acts: The social and political motivations of Lucan theology.* Cambridge: Cambridge University Press, 1987.
Even-Shoshan, Avraham. *Ha-milon he-ḥadash.* Jerusalem: Qiryat Sefer, 1966–70.
Ewald, William. "Comparative jurisprudence (I): What was it like to try a rat?" *University of Pennsylvania law review* 143 (1995): 1889–2149.

Fabre-Vassas, Claudine. *The singular beast: Jews, Christians, and the pig.* Translated by Carol Volk. New York: Columbia University Press, 1997.

Fakhry, Majid, trans. *An interpretation of the Qur'an: English translation of the meanings, a bilingual edition.* New York: New York University Press, 2002.

Fattal, Antoine. *Le statut légal des non-Musulmans en pays d'Islam.* Beirut: Imprimerie Catholique, 1958.

Fee, Gordon D. "*Eidōlothuta* once again: 1 Corinthians 8–10." *Biblica* 61 (1980): 179–97.

Fessler, Daniel M. T., and Carlos David Navarrette. "Meat is good to taboo: Dietary proscriptions as a product of the interaction of psychological mechanisms and social processes." *Journal of cognition and culture* 3 (2003): 1–41.

Finkelstein, Louis. "Life and the law: A study in Jewish adjustments." *Menorah journal* 24 (1936): 131–43.

Fiqsler, Deror. *Masekhet 'Avodah Zarah 'im perush ha-Rambam: Mahadurah mevo'eret.* Jerusalem: Ma'aliyot, 2002.

Firmage, Edwin. "The biblical dietary laws and the concept of holiness." In *Studies in the Pentateuch,* edited by J. A. Emerton, 177–208. Leiden, Netherlands: Brill, 1990.

Fischler, Claude. "Food, self, and identity." *Social science information* 27 (1988): 275–92.

Fishbein, Michael, trans. *The History of al-Ṭabarī.* Vol. 8, *The victory of Islam.* Albany: State University of New York Press, 1997.

Foster, George M., and Barbara Gallatin Anderson. *Medical anthropology.* New York: Wiley, 1978.

Fotopoulos, John. *Food offered to idols in Roman Corinth.* Tübingen, Germany: Siebeck, 2003.

Fredriksen, Paula. *Augustine and the Jews: A Christian defense of Jews and Judaism.* New York: Doubleday, 2008.

———. "Divine justice and human freedom: Augustine on Jews and Judaism, 392–398." In *From witness to witchcraft: Jews and Judaism in medieval Christian thought,* edited by Jeremy Cohen, 29–54. Wiesbaden, Germany: Harrassowitz, 1996.

———. "*Excaecati occulta justitia Dei:* Augustine on Jews and Judaism." *Journal of early Christian studies* 3 (1995): 299–324.

Freedman, David Noel. "The earliest Bible." In *Divine commitment and human obligation: Selected writings of David Noel Freedman,* edited by John R. Huddlestun, 1: 341–49. Grand Rapids, Mich.: Eerdmans, 1997.

Freidenreich, David M. "Christians in early and classical Shi'i law." In *Christian–Muslim relations: A bibliographical history,* edited by David Thomas et al., 3: 27–40. Leiden, Netherlands: Brill, 2011.

———. "Christians in early and classical Sunni law." In *Christian–Muslim relations: A bibliographical history,* edited by David Thomas et al., 1: 83–98. Leiden, Netherlands: Brill, 2009.

———. "Comparisons compared: A methodological survey of comparisons of religion from 'A magic dwells' to *A magic still dwells.*" *Method and theory in the study of religion* 16 (2004): 80–104.

———. "Five questions about non-Muslim meat: Toward a new appreciation of Ibn Qayyim al-Ǧawziyyah's contribution to Islamic law." In *A scholar in the shadow: Essays in the legal and theological thought of Ibn Qayyim al-Ǧawziyyah,* edited by Caterina Bori and Livnat Holtzman. *Oriente moderno* 90, no. 1 (2010): 43–64.

———. "Foreign food: A comparatively-enriched analysis of Jewish, Christian, and Islamic law." Ph.D. diss., Columbia University, 2006.

———. "Fusion cooking in an Islamic milieu: Jewish and Christian jurists on food associated with foreigners." In *Border crossings: Interreligious interaction and the exchange of ideas in the Islamic Middle Ages,* edited by David M. Freidenreich and Miriam Goldstein, chap. 10. Philadelphia: University of Pennsylvania Press, 2011.

———. "Holiness and impurity in the Torah and the Quran: Differences within a common typology." *Comparative Islamic studies* (forthcoming).

———. "The implications of unbelief: Tracing the emergence of distinctively Shiʿi notions regarding the food and impurity of non-Muslims." *Islamic law and society* 18 (2011): 53–84.

———. "Muslims in canon law, ca. 650–1000." In *Christian–Muslim relations: A bibliographical history,* edited by David Thomas et al., 1: 99–114. Leiden, Netherlands: Brill, 2009.

———. "Muslims in Western canon law, 1000–1500." In *Christian–Muslim relations: A bibliographical history,* edited by David Thomas et al., 3: 41–68. Leiden, Netherlands: Brill, 2011.

———. "Sharing meals with non-Christians in canon law commentaries, circa 1160–1260: A case study in legal development." *Medieval encounters* 14 (2008): 41–77.

Friedman, Shamma Yehudah. "Mi hayah Ben Derosai?" *Sidra* 14 (1998): 77–91.

———. *Tosefta ʿaṭiqta: Masekhet Pesaḥ Rishon.* Ramat Gan, Israel: Bar-Ilan University Press, 2002.

Friedmann, Yohanan. "The temple of Multān: A note on early Muslim attitudes to idolatry." *Israel Oriental studies* 2 (1972): 176–82.

———. *Tolerance and coercion in Islam: Interfaith relations in the Muslim tradition.* Cambridge: Cambridge University Press, 2003.

Frost, Robert. "Mending wall." Reprinted in *Collected poems, prose, and plays,* 39–40. New York: Library of America, 1995.

Gafni, Isaiah. *Yehudei Bavel bi-tequfat ha-Talmud: Ḥayyei ha-ḥevrah ve-ha-ruaḥ.* Jerusalem: Shazar, 1990.

García Sanjuán, Alejandro. "El consumo de alimentos de los *Ḏimmíes* en el Islam medieval: Prescripciones jurídicas y práctica social." *Historia, instituciones, documentos* 29 (2002): 109–46.

Garnsey, Peter. *Food and society in classical antiquity.* Cambridge: Cambridge University Press, 1999.

Gauvain, Richard. "Ritual rewards: A consideration of three recent approaches to Sunni purity law." *Islamic law and society* 12 (2005): 333–93.

Geller, Markham J. "Diet and regimen in the Babylonian Talmud." In *Food and identity in the ancient world,* edited by Cristiano Grottanelli and Lucio Milano, 217–42. Padua, Italy: S.A.R.G.O.N., 2004.

Gerstenberger, Erhard S. *Leviticus: A commentary.* Translated by Douglas W. Stott. Old Testment library. Louisville, Ky.: Westminster John Knox, 1996.

Ghazālī, Muḥammad b. Muḥammad al-. *Al-wasīṭ fī al-madhāhib*. Edited by Aḥmad Maḥmūd Ibrāhīm. 7 vols. Cairo: Dār al-Salām, 1997.

Goldstein, Jonathan A. *I Maccabees: A new translation with introduction and commentary.* Anchor Bible. Garden City, N.Y.: Doubleday, 1976.

———. *II Maccabees: A new translation with introduction and commentary.* Anchor Bible. Garden City, N.Y.: Doubleday, 1983.

Goldziher, Ignaz. *Introduction to Islamic theology and law.* Translated by Andreas Hamori and Ruth Hamori. Princeton, N.J.: Princeton University Press, 1981.

Gonzáles-Salinero, Raúl. "Catholic anti-Judaism in Visigothic Spain." In *The Visigoths: Studies in culture and society,* edited by Alberto Fereiro, 123–50. Leiden, Netherlands: Brill, 1999.

Goodman, Martin. "Kosher olive oil in antiquity." In *A tribute to Geza Vermes: Essays on Jewish and Christian literature and history,* edited by Philip R. Davies and Richard T. White, 227–46. Sheffield, England: JSOT, 1990.

Graetz, Heinrich. *Geschichte der Jüden von den Ältesten Zeiten bis auf die Gegenwart.* Vol. 3. 1863. Repr., Leipzig, Germany: Leiner, 1906.

Gräf, Erwin. *Jagdbeute und Schlachttier im islamischen Recht: eine Untersuchung zur Entwicklung der islamischen Jurisprudenz.* Bonn, Germany: Selbstverlag des Orientalischen Seminars der Universität Bonn, 1959.

Grantham, Billy J. "A zooarchaeological model for the study of ethnic complexity at Sepphoris." Ph.D. diss., Northwestern University, 1996.

Gray, Alyssa M. *A Talmud in exile: The influence of Yerushalmi Avodah Zarah on the formation of Bavli Avodah Zarah.* Providence, R.I.: Brown Judaic Studies, 2005.

Grayzel, Solomon. *The Church and the Jews in the XIIIth century: A study of their relations during the years 1198–1254, based on the papal letters and the conciliar decress of the period.* Philadelphia: Dropsie College, 1933.

———. *The Church and the Jews in the XIIIth century, vol. II: 1254–1314.* Edited by Kenneth R. Stow. New York: Jewish Theological Seminary of America, 1989.

Green, William Scott. "Otherness within: Towards a theory of difference in Rabbinic Judaism." In *"To see ourselves as others see us": Christians, Jews, "others" in late antiquity,* edited by Jacob Neusner and Ernest S. Frerichs, 49–69. Chico, Calif.: Scholars Press, 1985.

Griffini, Eugenio, ed. *"Corpus iuris" di Zaid ibn ʿAli.* Milan: Ulrico Hoepli, 1919.

Grignon, Claude. "Commensality and social morphology: An essay of typology." In *Food, drink, and identity: Cooking, eating, and drinking in Europe since the Middle Ages,* edited by Peter Scholliers, 23–33. Oxford: Berg, 2001.

Gruber, Mayer I. "Private life in ancient Israel." In *Civilizations of the ancient Near East,* edited by Jack M. Sasson, 633–48. New York: Scribner's, 1995.

Gruen, Erich S. *Diaspora: Jews amidst Greeks and Romans.* Cambridge, Mass.: Harvard University Press, 2002.

———. *Heritage and Hellenism: The reinvention of Jewish tradition.* Berkeley: University of California Press, 1998.

Guillaume, Alfred, trans. *The Life of Muhammad: A translation of Isḥāq's Sīrat Rasūl Allāh.* Oxford: Oxford University Press, 1955.

Hādī ilā al-Ḥaqq Yaḥyā b. al-Ḥusayn, al-. *Kitāb al-aḥkām fī bayān al-ḥalāl wa-'l-ḥarām.* Edited by ʿAlī b. Aḥmad b. Abī Ḥarīṣah. 2 vols. Sana, Yemen: Maktabat al-Yaman al-kubrā, 1990.

Halbertal, Moshe. “Coexisting with the enemy: Jews and pagans in the Mishnah.” In *Tolerance and intolerance in early Judaism and Christianity,* edited by Graham N. Stanton and Guy G. Stroumsa, 159–72. Cambridge: Cambridge University Press, 1998.

Hallo, William W. “The origins of the sacrifical cult: New evidence from Mesopotamia and Israel.” In *Ancient Israelite religion: Essays in honor of Frank Moore Cross,* edited by Patrick D. Miller, Jr., Paul D. Hanson, and S. Dean McBride, 3–13. Philadelphia: Fortress, 1987.

Haran, Menaḥem. S.v. “Ma'akhalim u-mashqa'ot.” In *Encyclopaedia miqra'it,* 4: 543–58. Jerusalem: Bialik, 1962.

———. “Seething a kid in its mother's milk.” *Journal of Jewish studies* 30 (1979): 23–35.

Harkins, Paul W., trans. *John Chrysostom: Discourses against judaizing Christians.* Fathers of the Church. Washington, D.C.: Catholic University of America Press, 1979.

Hartman, Louis F., and Alexander A. Di Lella. *The Book of Daniel: A new translation with introduction and commentary.* Anchor Bible. New York: Doubleday, 1978.

Hartmann, Wilfried, and Kenneth Pennington. “Bio-bibliographical guide of canonists, 1140–1500.” Catholic University of America, Kenneth Pennington's page, http://faculty.cua.edu/Pennington/biobibl.htm.

Hartog, François. *The mirror of Herodotus: The representation of the other in the writing of history.* Translated by Janet Lloyd. Berkeley: University of California Press, 1988.

Hauptman, Judith. *Rereading the Mishnah: A new approach to ancient texts.* Tübingen, Germany: Siebeck, 2005.

Hawting, G. R. *The idea of idolatry and the emergence of Islam: From polemic to history.* Cambridge: Cambridge University Press, 1999.

Hayes, Christine Elizabeth. *Between the Babylonian and Palestinian Talmuds: Accounting for halakhic differences in selected sugyot from Tractate Avodah Zarah.* New York: Oxford University Press, 1997.

———. *Gentile impurities and Jewish identities: Intermarriage and conversion from the Bible to the Talmud.* New York: Oxford University Press, 2002.

———. “The 'other' in rabbinic literature.” In *The Cambridge companion to the Talmud and rabbinic literature,* edited by Charlotte E. Fonrobert and Martin S. Jaffee, 243–69. Cambridge: Cambridge University Press, 2007.

Hefele, Carl Joseph, and H. Leclercq. *Histoire des conciles.* 11 vols. Paris, 1907. Repr., Hildesheim, Germany: Olms, 1973.

Hengel, Martin. *Judaism and Hellenism: Studies in their encounter in Palestine during the early Hellenistic period.* Translated by John Bowden. Philadelphia: Fortress, 1974.

———. *The Zealots: Investigations into the Jewish freedom movement in the period from Herod I until 70 A.D.* Translated by David Smith. Edinburgh, Scotland: Clark, 1989.

Hodgson, Marshall G. S. S.v. “D̲ja'far al-Ṣādiq.” In *Encyclopaedia of Islam,* new ed., 2: 374–75. Leiden, Netherlands: Brill, 1960–2004.

Holdrege, Barbara A. *Veda and Torah: Transcdending the textuality of scripture.* Albany: State University of New York Press, 1996.

Holmberg, Bengt. “Jewish versus Christian identity in the early Church?” *Revue biblique* 105 (1998): 397–425.

Houston, Walter. *Purity and monotheism: Clean and unclean animals in biblical law.* Sheffield, England: JSOT, 1993.

Hurd, John Coolidge, Jr. *The Origin of 1 Corinthians*. Macon, Ga.: Mercer University Press, 1983.

Ibn ʿAbd al-Raʾūf. "Risālah." In *Documents arabes inédits sur la vie sociale et économique en occident musulman au moyen âge*. Vol. 1, *Trois traités hispaniques de ḥisba*, edited by E. Lévi-Provençal, 67–116. Cairo: L'Institut Français d'Archéologie Orientale, 1955.

Ibn Abī Mūsā al-Hāshimī, Muḥammad b. Aḥmad. *Al-irshād ilā sabīl al-rashād*. Edited by ʿAbd Allāh b. ʿAbd al-Muḥsin al-Turkī. Beirut: Al-Risālah, 1998.

Ibn Abī Shaybah, ʿAbd Allāh b. Muḥammad. *Al-muṣannaf fī al-aḥādīth wa-'l-āthār*. Edited by Saʿīd al-Laḥḥām. 9 vols. Beirut: Dār al-Fikr, 1989.

Ibn Abī Zayd al-Qayrawānī, Abū Muḥammad ʿAbd Allāh. *Al-nawādir wa-'l-ziyādāt ʿalā mā fī al-mudawwanah wa-ghayrihā min al-ummahāt*. Edited by ʿAbd al-Fattāḥ Muḥammad al-Ḥulw. 15 vols. Beirut: Dār al-Gharb al-Islāmī, 1999.

———. *Risâla*. Edited by Léon Bercher. Algiers, Algeria: Editions Populaires de l'Armée, 1968.

Ibn al-ʿArabī, Abū Bakr Muḥammad. *Aḥkām al-Qurʾān*. Edited by ʿAli Muḥammad al-Bajāwī. 4 vols. Cairo: Dār Iḥyāʾ al-Kutub al-ʿArabiyyah, ʿĪsā al-Bābī al-Ḥalabī wa-Shurakāʾuhu, 1957.

———. *Al-nāsikh waʾl-mansūkh fī al-Qurʾān al-karīm*. Edited by ʿAbd al-Kabir al-ʿAlawī al-Mudghirī. 2 vols. Rabat, Morocco: Al-Mamlakah al-Maghribiyah, Wizārat al-Awqāf wa-'l-Shuʾūn al-Islamiyyah, 1988.

Ibn al-Murtaḍā, Aḥmad b. Yaḥyā. *Al-baḥr al-zakhkhār al-jāmiʿ li-madhāhib ʿulamāʾ al-amṣār*. 6 vols. 1947–49. Repr., Sana, Yemen: Dār al-Ḥikma al-Yamāniyya, 1988.

Ibn Bābawayh al-Qummī, Muḥammad b. ʿAlī. *Man lā yaḥḍuruhu al-faqīh*. Edited by Ḥasan al-Mūsawī al-Kharsān. 4 vols. Tehran: Dār al-Kutub al-Islāmiyyah, 1970.

———. *Al-muqniʿ wa-'l-hidāyah*. Qom, Iran: Al-Maṭbūʿāt al-Dīniyyah, 1957.

Ibn Ḥanbal, Aḥmad b. Muḥammad. *Al-musnad*. Edited by Aḥmad Muḥammad Shākir. 20 vols. [Cairo?]: Dār al-Maʿārif, 1949–90.

Ibn Ḥazm, ʿAlī b. Aḥmad. *Al-iḥkām fī uṣūl al-aḥkām*. Edited by Aḥmad Shākir. 8 vols. Cairo: Al-ʿĀṣimah, 1968.

———. *Al-muḥallā bi-'l-āthār*. Edited by ʿAbd al-Ghaffār Sulaymān al-Bindārī. 12 vols. Beirut: Dār al-Kutub al-ʿIlmiyyah, 1988.

Ibn Hishām, ʿAbd al-Malik. *Sīrat al-Nabī*. Edited by Muḥammad Khalīl Harrās. 4 vols. Cairo: Al-Jumhūriyyah, 1971.

Ibn Idrīs al-Ḥillī, Abū Jaʿfar Muḥammad b. Manṣūr. *Al-sarāʾir*. 3 vols. Qom, Iran: Al-Nashr al-Islāmī, 1991.

Ibn Juzayy, Muḥammad b. Aḥmad. *Qawānīn al-aḥkām al-sharʿiyyah wa-masaʾil al-furūʿ al-fiqhiyyah*. Beirut: Dār al-ʿIlm li-l-Malāyīn, 1968.

Ibn Kathīr, Ismāʿīl b. ʿUmar. *Tafsīr al-Qurʾān al-ʿaẓīm*. 7 vols. Beirut: Dār al-Andalus li-l-Ṭibāʿah wa-'l-Nashr, 1966.

Ibn Qāsim al-Ghazzī, Muḥammad. *Fatḥ al-qarīb al-mujīb fī sharḥ alfāẓ al-Taqrīb*. Beirut: Al-Zuʿbī, 1979.

Ibn Qayyim al-Jawziyyah, Muḥammad b. Abī Bakr. *Aḥkām ahl al-dhimmah*. Edited by Ṣubḥī al-Ṣāliḥ. 2 vols. 1961. Beirut: Dār al-ʿIlm li-l-Malāyīn, 1981.

Ibn Qudāmah, Muwaffaq al-Dīn ʿAbd Allāh b. Aḥmad. *Al-mughnī*. Edited by Ṭāhā Muḥammad al-Zaynī. 10 vols. Cairo: Al-Qāhirah, 1968–70.

Ibn Rushd (Averroës), Abū al-Walīd Muḥammad. *Bidāyat al-mujtahid wa-nihāyat al-muqtaṣid.* Edited by Haytham Khalīfah Ṭaʿīmī. 2 vols. Sidon, Lebanon: Al-ʿAṣriyyah, 2002.

———. *The distinguished jurist's primer.* Translated by Imran Ahsan Khan Nyazee. 2 vols. Reading, England: Garnet, 2002.

Ibn Rushd al-Jadd, Abū al-Walīd Muḥammad. *Al-bayān wa-'l-taḥṣīl wa-'l-sharḥ wa-'l-tajhīh wa-'l-taʿlīf fī masā'il al-Mustakhrajah.* Edited by Muḥammad al-Ḥajjī. 20 vols. Beirut: Dār al-Gharb al-Islāmī, 1984–87.

———. *Fatāwā Ibn Rushd.* Edited by al-Mukhtār b. al-Ṭāhir al-Talīlī. 3 vols. Beirut: Dār al-Gharb al-Islāmī, 1987.

Ibn Shādhān, Abū Muḥammad al-Faḍl. *Al-īḍāḥ.* Tehran: Maṭbaʿat Jāmiʿat Ṭihrān, 1972.

Ibn Taymiyyah, Aḥmad b. ʿAbd al-Ḥalīm. *Majmūʿ fatāwā Shaykh al-Islām Aḥmad Ibn Taymiyyah.* Edited by ʿAbd al-Raḥmān b. Muḥammad b. Qāsim. 37 vols. Rabat, Morocco: Al-Maʿārif, 1980.

Izutsu, Toshihiko. *Ethico-religious concepts in the Qur'ān.* 1966. Montreal: McGill–Queen's University Press, 2002.

Jacobs, Andrew S. *Remains of the Jews: The Holy Land and Christian empire in late antiquity.* Stanford, Calif.: Stanford University Press, 2004.

Jacobs, Naomi S. "'And I saw that the delicacies were many': A commentary on food and eating in the Book of Tobit." Ph.D. diss., Durham University, 2007.

Jaṣṣāṣ, Aḥmad b. ʿAlī al-. *Aḥkām al-Qur'ān.* 3 vols. Istanbul: Dār al-Khilāfah al-ʿAliyyah, 1917–20.

Joannou, Périclès-Pierre, ed. *Discipline générale antique (IVe–IXe s.).* Vol. 1, pt. 2, *Les canons des Synodes particuliers.* Grottaferrata (Rome): Italo-Orientale "S. Nilo." 1962.

Johnson, Luke Timothy. *The Acts of the Apostles.* Sacra Pagina. Collegeville, Minn.: Liturgical Press, 1992.

Jones, Donald L. "Christianity and the Roman imperial cult." In *Aufstieg und Niedergang der Römischen Welt* II 23.2, edited by Wolfgang Haase, 1023–54. Berlin: De Gruyter, 1980.

Jordan, William C. "Problems of the meat market of Béziers, 1240–1247: A question of anti-Semitism." *Révue des études juives* 135 (1976): 31–49.

Josephus. *The Jewish war, books I–III.* Translated by H. St. J. Thackeray. Loeb Classical Library. Cambridge, Mass.: Harvard University Press, 1976.

———. *Life of Josephus.* Translated by Steve Mason. Flavius Josephus: Translation and commentary. Leiden, Netherlands: Brill, 2000.

Kahana, Avraham. *Ha-sefarim ha-ḥiṣonim la-Torah, la-Nevi'im, la-Ketuvim, u-she'ar sefarim ḥiṣonim.* 2nd ed. Tel Aviv: Massada, 1956.

Kahn, Yoel H. "On gentiles, slaves, and women: The blessings 'who did not make me'; Historical survey." In *My people's prayer book: Traditional prayers, modern commentaries.* Vol. 5, *Birkhot Hashachar,* edited by Lawrence A. Hoffman, 17–27. Woodstock, Vt.: Jewish Lights, 2001.

Kalmin, Richard. *The sage in Jewish society of late antiquity.* New York: Routledge, 1999.

Kalwadhānī, Maḥfūẓ b. Aḥmad b. al-Ḥasan al-. *Al-hidāyah fī furūʿ al-fiqh al-Ḥanbalī.* Edited by Muḥammad Ḥasan Ismāʿīl. 2 vols. Beirut: Dār al-Kutub al-ʿIlmiyyah, 2002.

Kāsānī, Abū Bakr b. Masʿūd al-. *Badā'iʿ al-sanā'iʿ fī tartīb al-sharā'iʿ.* 7 vols. Beirut: Dār al-Kitāb al-ʿArabī, 1974.

Katz, Jacob. *Exclusiveness and tolerance: Studies in Jewish-Gentile relations in medieval and modern times.* Oxford: Oxford University Press, 1961.

Katz, Marion Holmes. *Body of text: The emergence of the Sunni law of ritual purity.* Albany: State University of New York Press, 2002.

Kedar, Benjamin Z. "*De iudeis et sarracenis:* On the categorization of Muslims in medieval canon law." In *Studia in honorem eminentissimi cardinalis Alphonsi M. Stickler,* edited by R. I. Castillo Lara, 207–13. Rome: Libreria Ateneo Salesiano, 1992.

———. *Franks in the Levant, 11th to 14th centuries.* Aldershot, England: Ashgate, 1993.

Kimber, Richard. S.v. "Qibla." In *Encyclopaedia of the Qur'an,* edited by Jane Dammen McAullife, 4: 325–28. Leiden, Netherlands: Brill, 2004.

Kister, M. J. "'A bag of meat': A study of an early *ḥadith.*" *Bulletin of the School of Oriental and African studies* 33 (1970): 267–75.

———. *Studies in Jāhiliyya and early Islam.* London: Variorum, 1980.

Klauck, Hans-Josef. *4. Makkabäerbuch.* Gütersloh, Germany: Mohn, 1989.

Klawans, Jonathan. *Impurity and sin in ancient Judaism.* Oxford: Oxford University Press, 2000.

———. "Notions of gentile impurity in ancient Judaism." *AJS review* 20 (1995): 285–312.

Klein, Isaac. "The kashrut of gelatin." In *Responsa and halakhic studies,* 59–74. New York: Ktav, 1975.

Koch, Dietrich-Alex. "'Alles, was *en makellō* verkauft wird, eßt . . .': Die *macella* von Pompeji, Gerasa und Korinth und ihre Bedeutung für die Auslegung von 1Kor 10,25." *Zeitschrift für die Neutestamentliche Wissenshcaft* 90 (1999): 194–219.

Kohlberg, Etan. *Belief and law in Imāmī Shī'ism.* Aldershot, England: Variorum, 1991.

———. "The development of the Imāmī Shī'ī doctrine of *jihād.*" *Zeitschrift der Deutschen Morgenländischen Gesellschaft* 126 (1976): 64–86.

———. "Non-Imāmī Muslims in Imāmī fiqh." *Jerusalem studies in Arabic and Islam* 6 (1985): 99–105.

Kraemer, David C. *Jewish eating and identity through the ages.* London: Routledge, 2007.

Kraemer, Ross Shepard. *When Aseneth met Joseph: A late antique tale of the Biblical patriarch and his Egyptian wife, reconsidered.* New York: Oxford University Press, 1998.

Krauss, Samuel. *Talmudische Archäologie.* 3 vols. 1910. Hildesheim, Germany: Olms, 1966.

Kriegel, Maurice. "Un trait de psychologie sociale dans les Pays Méditerranéens du Bas Moyen Âge: Le Juif comme intouchable." *Annales, économies, sociétés, civilisations* 31 (1976): 326–30.

Kulaynī, Abū Ja'far Muḥammad b. Ya'qūb al-. *Al-kāfī.* Edited by 'Alī Akbar al-Ghaffarī. 8 vols. Beirut: Dār al-Adwā', 1985.

Laeuchli, Samuel. *Power and sexuality: The emergence of canon law at the Synod of Elvira.* Philadelphia: Temple University Press, 1972.

Lamy, Thomas Joseph, ed. *Sancti Ephraem Syri hymni et sermones.* 4 vols. Malines, Belgium: Dessain, 1886.

Lasker, Daniel J. "Science in the Karaite communities." In *Science in medieval Jewish cultures,* edited by Gad Freudenthal, chap. 20. Cambridge: Cambridge University Press, 2011.

Lecker, Michael. "Tribes in pre- and early Islamic Arabia." In *People, tribes, and society in Arabia around the time of Muḥammad,* XI 1–106. Aldershot, England: Ashgate, 2005.

Leonhardt, Jutta. *Jewish worship in Philo of Alexandria.* Tübingen, Germany: Siebeck, 2001.
Letter of Aristeas. Translated by R. J. H. Shutt. In *The Old Testament pseudepigrapha,* edited by James H. Charlesworth, 2: 7–34. Garden City, N.Y.: Doubleday, 1985.
Levine, Baruch A. "Excursus 2: The meaning of the dietary laws." In *The JPS Torah commentary: Leviticus,* 243–49. Philadelphia: Jewish Publication Society, 1989.
Lévi-Strauss, Claude. "The culinary triangle." *Partisan review* 33 (1966): 586–95.
———. *The origin of table manners.* New York: Harper and Row, 1978.
———. *The raw and the cooked.* Translated by John Weightman and Doreen Weightman. London: Harper and Row and Jonathan Cape, 1969.
———. *Totemism.* Translated by Rodney Needham. Boston: Beacon, 1963.
Liddell, Henry George, Robert Scott, and Henry Stuart Jones. *A Greek-English lexicon.* Oxford: Clarendon, 1968.
Lieberman, Saul. *Ha-Yerushalmi kifshuto.* Vol. 1. Jerusalem: Darom, 1935.
———. *Tosefet rishonim.* 4 vols. 1937. New York: Jewish Theological Seminary of America, 1999.
Lieu, Judith. *Image and reality: The Jews in the world of the Christians in the second century.* Edinburgh, Scotland: Clark, 1996.
Lightfoot, J. B., and J. R. Harmer, eds. *The Apostolic Fathers: Greek texts and English translations of their writings.* 2nd ed. Revised by Michael W. Holmes. Grand Rapids, Mich.: Baker Book House, 1992.
Linder, Amnon, ed. *The Jews in the legal sources of the early Middle Ages.* Detroit: Wayne State University Press, 1997.
Lipton, Sara. *Images of intolerance: The representation of Jews and Judaism in the* Bible moralisée. Berkeley: University of California Press, 1999.
Little, Donald P. "Ḥaram documents related to the Jews of late fourteenth century Jerusalem." *Journal of Semitic studies* 30 (1985): 227–64.
Löw, Immanuel. "Aramäische Fischnamen." In *Orientalische Studien Theodor Nöldeke zum siebzigsten Geburtstag gewidmet von Freunden und Schülern,* edited by Carl Bezold, 1: 549–70. Gieszen, Germany: Töpelmann, 1906.
MacMullen, Ramsay. *Christianizing the Roman Empire.* New Haven, Conn.: Yale University Press, 1984.
Madelung, Wilferd. *Der Imam al-Qāsim b. Ibrāhīm und die Glaubenslehre der Zaiditen.* Berlin: De Gruyter, 1965.
Maghen, Ze'ev. *After hardship cometh ease: The Jews as backdrop for Muslim moderation.* Berlin: De Gruyter, 2006.
———. "Close encounters: Some preliminary observations on the transmission of impurity in early Sunni jurisprudence." *Islamic law and society* 6 (1999): 348–92.
———. "First blood: Purity, edibility, and the independence of Islamic jurisprudence." *Islam* 81 (2004): 49–95.
———. "Strangers and brothers: The ritual status of unbelievers in Islamic jurisprudence." *Medieval encounters* 12 (2006): 173–223.
Makdisi, George. *The rise of colleges: Institutions of learning in Islam and the West.* Edinburgh, Scotland: University of Edinburgh Press, 1981.
Mālik b. Anas. *Al-muwaṭṭa'.* Vaduz, Liechtenstein: Jam'iyyat al-Maknaz al-Islāmī, 2000.

———. *Al-muwaṭṭa'*. Translated by 'A'isha 'Abdarahman at-Tarjumana and Ya'qub Johnson. Norwich, England: Diwan, 1982.
Marcovich, Miroslav, ed. *Iustini Martyris Dialogus cum Tryphone*. Berlin: De Gruyter, 1997.
Masud, Muhammad Khalid. "Food and the notion of purity in the *fatāwā* literature." In *Alimentacion de las culturas Islamicas*, edited by Manuela Marín and David Waines, 89–110. Madrid: Agencia Español de Cooperación Internacional, 1994.
Māwardī, 'Alī b. Muḥammad al-. *Al-ḥāwī al-kabīr fī fiqh madhhab al-Imām al-Shāfi'ī wa-huwa sharḥ Mukhtaṣar al-Muzanī*. Edited by 'Ālī Muḥammad Mu'awwaḍ and 'Ādil Aḥmad 'Abd al-Mawjūd. 18 vols. Beirut: Dār al-Kutub al-'Ilmiyyah, 1994.
McAuliffe, Jane Dammen. "Exegetical identification of the Sabi'un." *Muslim world* 72 (1982): 95–106.
Meeks, Wayne A., and Robert L. Wilken. *Jews and Christians in Antioch in the first four centuries of the common era*. Missoula, Mont.: Scholars Press, 1978.
Melville, Charles, and Ahmad Ubaydli. *Christians and Moors in Spain*. Vol. 3, *Arabic sources (711–1501)*. Warminster, England: Aris and Phillips, 1992.
Melvinger, Arne. S.v. "al-Madjūs." In *Encyclopaedia of Islam*, new ed., 5: 1118–21. Leiden, Netherlands: Brill, 1960–2004.
Merton, Robert K. "Manifest and latent functions." In *Social theory and social structure*, enlarged ed., 73–138. New York: Free Press, 1968.
Meshel, Naphtali S. "Food for thought: Systems of categorization in Leviticus 11." *Harvard theological review* 101 (2008): 203–29.
———. "Lehavdil: 'Iyyun be-shiṭat sivvug ha-ṭame' ve-ha-ṭahor, ha-issur ve-ha-mutar be-Sefer Kohanim." M.A. thesis, Hebrew University, 2004.
Metzger, Marcel, ed. *Les constitutions apostoliques*. 3 vols. Sources chrétiennes. Paris: Cerf, 1987.
Mikat, Paul. *Die Judengesetzgebung der merowingisch-fränkischen Konzilien*. Opladen, Germany: Westdeutscher, 1995.
Milgrom, Jacob. "Israel's sanctuary: The Priestly 'Picture of Dorian Gray.'" *Revue biblique* 83 (1976): 390–99.
———. *Leviticus 1–16: A new translation with introduction and commntary*. Anchor Bible. New York: Doubleday, 1991.
Miller, Joel, ed. *Halakhot pesuqot min ha-geonim*. 1893. Repr., New York: Menorah, 1957.
Mitchell, Margaret M. *Paul and the rhetoric of reconciliation: An exegetical investigation of the language and composition of 1 Corinthians*. Tübingen, Germany: Siebeck, 1991.
Mommsen, Theodor, and Paul M. Meyer, eds. *Theodosiani libri XVI cum Constitutionibus Sirmondianis [Codex Theodosianus]*. 1905. Repr., Berlin: Weidmann, 1954.
Moore, Carey A. *Daniel, Esther and Jeremiah: The additions; A new translation with introduction and commentary*. Anchor Bible. New York: Doubleday, 1977.
———. *Judith: A new translation with introduction and commentary*. Anchor Bible. New York: Doubleday, 1985.
———. *Tobit: A new translation with introduction and commentary*. Anchor Bible. New York: Doubleday, 1996.
Morin, Germain, ed. *Sancti Caesarii Arelatensis sermones*. Corpus Christianorum, Series Latina, vols. 103–104. Turnhout, Belgium: Brepols, 1953.

Morony, Michael G. "The age of conversions: A reassessment." In *Conversion and continuity: Indigenous Christian communities in Islamic lands, eighth to eighteenth centuries*, edited by Michael Gervers and Ramzi Jibran Bikhazi, 135–50. Toronto: Pontifical Institute of Mediaeval Studies, 1990.

———. S.v. "Madjūs." In *Encyclopaedia of Islam*, new ed., 5: 1110–18. Leiden, Netherlands: Brill, 1960–2004.

Moshe b. Naḥman, R. *Ḥiddushei ha-Ramban le-masekhet 'Avodah Zarah*. Edited by Ḥayyim Dov Shevel. Jerusalem: Mekhon ha-Talmud ha-Yisraeli ha-Shalem, 1970.

Mu'ayyad bi-'llah Aḥmad b. al-Ḥusayn. *Sharḥ al-Tajrīd fī fiqh al-Zaydiyyah*. 6 vols. Damascus: Dār Usāmah, 1985.

———. *Al-tajrīd fī fiqh al-imāmayn al-a'ẓamayn al-Qāsim b. Ibrāhīm wa-ḥafīẓuhu al-Imām al-Hādī Yaḥyā b. al-Ḥusayn*. Amman: Mu'assasat al-Imām Zayd b. 'Alī al-Thaqāfiyyah, 2002.

Mufīd, Muḥammad b. Muḥammad al-. *Al-muqni'ah*. Qom, Iran: Al-Nashr al-Islāmī, 1990.

———. *Taḥrīm dhabā'iḥ ahl al-kitāb*. Muṣannafāt al-Shaykh al-Mufīd, vol. 43. Qom, Iran: Al-Mu'tamar al-'Ālamī li-Alfiyyat al-Shaykh al-Mufīd, 1992.

Munier, Charles. *Concilia Galliae, A. 314–A. 506*. Corpus Christianorum, Series Latina. Turnhout, Belgium: Brepols, 1963.

Muqātil b. Sulaymān. *Kitāb tafsīr al-khams mi'at āyah min al-Qur'ān*. Edited by Isaiah Goldfeld. Shefaram, Israel: Dār al-Mashriq, 1980.

Murtaḍā, 'Alī b. al-Ḥusayn al-. *Al-intiṣār*. Beirut: Dār al-Aḍwā', 1985.

Muslim b. al-Ḥajjāj al-Qushayrī. *Ṣaḥīḥ Muslim*. 2 vols. Vaduz, Liechtenstein: Jam'iyyat al-Maknaz al-Islāmī, 2000.

Müller, Wolfgang P. *Huguccio: The life, works, and thought of a twelfth-century jurist*. Washington, D.C.: Catholic University of America Press, 1994.

Naḥḥās, Aḥmad b. Muḥammad al-. *Al-nāsikh wa-'l-mansūkh*. Kuwait City: Al-Falāḥ, 1988.

Nanos, Mark D. *The mystery of Romans: The Jewish context of Paul's letter*. Minneapolis: Fortress, 1996.

Nasā'ī, Aḥmad b. Shu'ayb al-. *Sunan al-Nasā'ī*. 2 vols. Vaduz, Liechtenstein: Jam'iyyat al-Maknaz al-Islāmī, 2000.

Nāṭiq bi-'l-Ḥaqq Yaḥyā b. al-Ḥusayn, al-. *Kitāb al-taḥrīr*. Edited by Muḥammad Yaḥyā Sālim 'Azzān. 2 vols. Sana, Yemen: Badr, 1997.

Nau, François. "Littérature canonique syriaque inédiete." *Revue de l'Orient chrétien*, 2nd ser., vol. 4 (1909): 1–49, 113–30.

Nawawī, Yaḥyā b. Sharaf al-. *Rawḍat al-ṭālibīn*. Edited by 'Ādil Aḥmad 'Abd al-Mawjūd and 'Alī Muḥammad Mu'awwaḍ. 8 vols. Beirut: Dār al-Kutub al-'Ilmiyyah, 2006.

Nedungatt, George, and Michael Featherstone, eds. *The Council in Trullo revisited*. Rome: Pontificio Istituto Orientale, 1995.

Neusner, Jacob. "Conducting dialectical argument in the Talmud." In *The intellectual foundations of Christian and Jewish discourse: The philosophy of religious argument*, by Jacob Neusner and Bruce Chilton, 47–69. London: Routledge, 1997.

———. *A history of the mishnaic law of Damages*. Vol. 4, *Shebuot, Eduyot, Abodah Zarah, Abot, Horayot*. Leiden, Netherlands: Brill, 1985.

———. *A history of the mishnaic law of Holy Things.* Vol. 3, *Hullin, Bekhorot.* Leiden, Netherlands: Brill, 1979.
———. *A history of the mishnaic law.* 43 vols. Leiden, Netherlands: Brill, 1974–86.
———, trans. *The Mishnah: A new translation.* New Haven, Conn.: Yale University Press, 1988.
———. "Stable symbols in a shifting society: The delusion of the monolithic gentile in documents of late fourth-century Judaism." In *"To see ourselves as others see us": Christians, Jews, "others" in late antiquity,* edited by Jacob Neusner and Ernest S. Frerichs, 373–96. Chico, Calif.: Scholars Press, 1985.
———. *The Talmud of Babylonia: An academic commentary; XXV, Bavli tractate Abodah Zarah.* Atlanta: Scholars Press, 1995.
———, ed. *The Talmud of the Land of Israel: A preliminary translation and explanation.* 35 vols. Chicago: University of Chicago Press, 1982–94.
———, trans. *The Tosefta.* Peabody, Mass.: Hendrickson, 2002.
Newby, Gordon Darnell. *A history of the Jews of Arabia: From ancient times to their eclipse under Islam.* Columbia: University of South Carolina Press, 1988.
———. *The making of the last prophet: A reconstruction of the earliest biography of Muhammad.* Columbia: University of South Carolina Press, 1989.
Nirenberg, David. *Communities of violence: Persecution of minorities in the Middle Ages.* Princeton, N.J.: Princeton University Press, 1996.
Noor digital library: Jāmiʿ fiqh ahl al-bayt. Version 1.2. Qom, Iran: Computer Research Center of Islamic Sciences, 2006.
Novak, David. "The treatment of Islam and Muslims in the legal writings of Maimonides." In *Studies in Islamic and Judaic traditions,* edited by William M. Brinner and Stephen D. Ricks, 233–50. Atlanta: Scholars Press, 1986.
Nuʿmān b. Muḥammad, Abū Ḥanīfah al-. *Daʿāʾim al-Islām.* Edited by Asaf Ali Asghar Fyzee. 2 vols. 1951. Repr., Beirut: Dār al-Adwāʾ, 1991.
———. *Al-iqtiṣār.* Beirut: Dār al-Adwāʾ, 1996.
Olster, David M. *Roman defeat, Christian response, and the literary construction of the Jew.* Philadelphia: University of Pennsylvania Press, 1994.
Olyan, Saul M. *Rites and rank: Hierarchy in biblical representations of cult.* Princeton, N.J.: Princeton University Press, 2000.
Origen. *Contra Celsum.* Translated by Henry Chadwick. Cambridge: Cambridge University Press, 1965.
Oxford Latin dictionary. Oxford: Clarendon, 1968.
Pāktačī, Aḥmad. "Ibn Shādhān." In *Dāʾirat al-maʿārif-i buzurg-i Islāmī,* edited by Kāẓim Mūsavī Bujnūrdī, 4: 52. Tehran: Markaz-i Dāʾirat al-maʿārif-i Buzurg-i Islāmī, 1990.
Pakter, Walter. *Medieval canon law and the Jews.* Ebelsbach, Germany: Gremer, 1988.
Paret, Rudi, trans. *Der Koran.* Stuttgart: Kohlhammer, 1966.
Perlmann, Moshe. "Eleventh-century Andalusian authors on the Jews of Granada." *Proceedings of the American academy for Jewish research* 18 (1948–49): 269–90.
Pertz, George Heinrich, ed. *Legum nationum Germanicarum.* Monumenta Germaniae historica. 1835. Repr., Stuttgart: Hiersemann-Krauss, 1965.

Pharr, Clyde, trans. *The Theodosian Code and Novels and the Sirmondian Constitutions.* Princeton, N.J.: Princeton University Press, 1952.

Philonenko, Marc. "Le Décret apostolique et les interdits alimentaires du Coran." *Révue d'histoire et de philosophie religieuses* 47 (1967): 165–72.

Pines, Shlomo. *The Jewish Christians of the early centuries of Christianity according to a new source.* Jerusalem: Israel Academy of Sciences and Humanities, 1966.

Pontal, Odette. *Histoire des conciles mérovingiens.* Paris: Éditions du Cerf; Institut de la recherche et de histoire des textes (CNRS), 1989.

Porton, Gary G. *Goyim: Gentiles and Israelites in Mishnah-Tosefta.* Atlanta: Scholars Press, 1988.

Propp, William H. C. *Exodus 19–40.* Anchor Bible. New York: Doubleday, 2006.

Qāsim ibn Ibrāhīm, al-. *Majmū' kutub wa-rasā'il al-Imām al-Qāsim b. Ibrāhīm al-Rassī.* Edited by 'Abd al-Karīm Aḥmad Jadabān. 2 vols. Sana, Yemen: Dār al-Ḥikmah al-Yamāniyyah, 2001.

Qimron, Elisha, and John Strugnell. *Miqṣat ma'asei ha-Torah.* Discoveries in the Judean Desert. Oxford: Clarendon, 1994.

Qummī, 'Alī b. Ibrāhīm al-. *Tafsīr al-Qummī.* Edited by Ṭayyib al-Mūsawī al-Jazā'irī. 2 vols. Beirut: Dār al-Surūr, 1991.

Qurṭubī, Muḥammad b. Aḥmad al-. *Al-jāmi' li-aḥkām al-Qur'ān.* Edited by Muḥammad Ibrāhīm al-Ḥifnāwī. 22 vols. Cairo: Dār al-Ḥadīth, 1994.

Radice, Betty, trans. *Pliny Letters and Panegyricus II.* Loeb Classical Library. Cambridge, Mass.: Harvard University Press, 1975.

Radscheit, Matthias. S.v. "Table." In *Encyclopaedia of the Qur'ān,* edited by Jane Dammen Mcauliffe, 5: 188–91. Leiden, Netherlands: Brill, 2006.

Rāfi'ī, 'Abd al-Karīm b. Muḥammad al-. *Al-'azīz: sharḥ al-Wajīz.* Edited by 'Alī Muḥammad Mu'awwaḍ and 'Ādil Aḥmad 'Abd al-Mawjūd. 14 vols. Beirut: Dār al-Kutub al-'Ilmiyyah, 1997.

Räisänen, Heikki. "Jesus and the food laws: Reflections on Mark 7.15." *Journal for the study of the New Testament* 16 (1982): 79–100.

Rambam (Maimonides). *Mishneh Torah.* 12 vols. Jerusalem: Shabse Frankel, 1975.

Rappaport, Uriel. *Sefer Maqabim 1: Mavo, tirgum, u-ferush.* Jerusalem: Yad Yiṣḥaq Ben-Ṣevi, 2004.

Rāzī, Fakhr al-Dīn Muḥammad b. 'Umar al-. *Al-tafsīr al-kabīr.* 32 vols. Tehran: Shirkat Ṣaḥāfī Nawīn, 1980.

Robbins, Jill. *Prodigal son/elder brother: Interpretation and alterity in Augustine, Petrarch, Kafka, Levinas.* Chicago: University of Chicago Press, 1991.

Robinson, Neal. *Discovering the Qur'an: A contemporary approach to a veiled text.* London: SCM, 1996.

———. "Hands outstretched: Towards a re-reading of *Sūrat al-Mā'ida.*" *Journal of Qur'ānic studies* 3 (2001): 1–19.

Rodinson, Maxime. S.v. "Ghidhā'." In *Encyclopaedia of Islam,* new ed., 2: 1057–72. Leiden, Netherlands: Brill, 1960–2004.

Rordorf, Willy, and André Tuilier, eds. *La doctrine des douze apôtres (Didachè).* Paris: Éditions du Cerf, 1978.

Rosenblum, Jordan D. *Food and identity in early Rabbinic Judaism.* Cambridge: Cambridge University Press, 2010.

———. "Kosher olive oil in antiquity reconsidered." *Journal for the study of Judaism* 40 (2009): 1–10.

———. "'Why do you refuse to eat pork?' Jews, food, and identity in Roman Palestine." *Jewish quarterly review* 100 (2010): 95–110.

Rosenfeld, Ben-Zion, and Joseph Menirav. *Markets and marketing in Roman Palestine.* Translated by Chava Cassel. Leiden, Netherlands: Brill, 2005.

Rosenthal, David. "Mishnah 'Avodah Zarah: Mahadurah biqurtit be-ṣeruf mavo." Ph.D. diss., Hebrew University, 1981.

Rubin, Uri. *The eye of the beholder: The life of Muhammad as viewed by the early Muslims; A textual analysis.* Princeton, N.J.: Darwin, 1995.

Rufinus. *Summa decretorum.* Edited by Heinrich Singer. 1902. Repr., Aalen, Germany: Scientia, 1963.

Sachau, Eduard, ed. *Syrische Rechtsbücher.* 3 vols. Berlin: Reimer, 1907–14.

Saḥnūn, 'Abd al-Salām b. Sa'īd. *Al-mudawwanah al-kubrā.* Edited by Ḥamdī al-Damardāsh Muḥammad. 9 vols. Mecca: Nizār Muṣṭafā al-Bāz, 1999.

Samau'al al-Maghribī. *Ifḥām al-yahūd: Silencing the Jews.* Edited by Moshe Perlmann. New York: American Academy for Jewish Research, 1964.

Sanders, Jack T. "Paul between Jews and Gentiles in Corinth." *Journal for the study of the New Testament* 65 (1997): 67–83.

Sandt, Huub van de, and David Flusser. *The Didache: Its Jewish sources and its place in early Judaism and Christianity.* Assen, Netherlands: Van Gorcum, 2002.

Sarakhsī, Muḥammad b. Aḥmad al-. *Sharḥ Kitāb al-siyar al-kabīr li-Muḥammad b. al-Ḥasan al-Shaybānī.* Edited by Ṣalāḥ al-Dīn al-Munajjid. 5 vols. Cairo: Ma'had al-Makhṭūṭāt, 1971.

Satlow, Michael L. *Tasting the dish: Rabbinic rhetorics of sexuality.* Atlanta: Scholars Press, 1995.

Sawyer, William Thomas. "The problem of meat sacrificed to idols in the Corinthian Church." Ph.D. diss., Southern Baptist Theological Seminary, 1968.

Schacht, Joseph. S.v. "Mayta." In *Encyclopaedia of Islam,* new ed., 6: 924–26. Leiden, Netherlands: Brill, 1960–2004.

Schaefer, Peter. "Jews and Gentiles in Yerushalmi Avoda Zarah." In *The Talmud Yerushalmi and Graeco-Roman culture,* edited by Peter Schaefer, 3: 335–52. Tübingen, Germany: Siebeck, 2002.

Schlossberg, Eliezer. "Yaḥaso shel ha-Rambam el ha-Islam." *Pe'amim* 42 (1990): 38–60.

Schwartz, Baruch J. "'Profane' slaughter and the integrity of the Priestly Code." *Hebrew Union College annual* 67 (1996): 15–42.

———. "The prohibitions concerning the 'eating' of blood in Leviticus 17." In *Priesthood and cult in ancient Israel,* edited by Gary A. Anderson and Saul M. Olyan, 34–66. Sheffield, England: JSOT, 1991.

———. *Torat ha-qedushah: 'Iyyunim be-ḥuqah ha-kohanit she-ba-Torah.* Jerusalem: Magnes, 1999.

Schwartz, Daniel. *Sefer Maqabim 2: Mavo, tirgum, u-ferush.* Jerusalem: Yad Yiṣḥaq Ben-Ṣevi, 2004.

Schwartz, Seth. *Imperialism and Jewish society, 200 B.C.E.–640 C.E.* Princeton, N.J.: Princeton University Press, 2001.

Septuaginta: Vetus Testamentum Graecum auctoritate Societatis Litterarum Gottingensis editum. Göttingen, Germany: Vandenhoeck and Ruprecht, 1931–93.

Shāfiʿī, Muḥammad b. Idrīs al-. *Kitāb al-umm.* Edited by Rifʿat Fawzī ʿAbd al-Muṭṭalib. 11 vols. El Mansoura, Egypt: Dār al-Wafāʾ li-l-Ṭibāʿah wa-ʾl-Nashr wa-ʾl-Tawzīʿ, 2001.

Sharf, Andrew. "Animal sacrifice in the Armenian Church." *Revue des études arméniennes* 16 (1982): 418–49.

———. *Jews and other minorities in Byzantium.* Ramat Gan, Israel: Bar-Ilan University Press, 1995.

Shepardson, Christine. *Anti-Judaism and Christian orthodoxy: Ephrem's hymns in fourth-century Syria.* Washington, D.C.: Catholic University of America Press, 2008.

Shishah sidrei Mishnah. Edited by Ḥanokh Albeck. Jerusalem: Bialik, 1952–59.

Sifrei de-ve Rav. Edited by Ḥayim Sha'ul Horowitz. Jerusalem: Wahrman, 1966.

Simon, Marcel. "The Apostolic Decree and its setting in the ancient Church." *Bulletin of the John Rylands library* 52 (1970): 437–60.

———. "De l'observance rituelle à l'ascèse: Recherches sur le Décret Apostolique." *Revue de l'histoire des religions* 193 (1978): 27–104.

Simonsohn, Shlomo. *The apostolic see and the Jews.* 8 vols. Toronto: Pontifical Institute of Mediaeval Studies, 1988–91.

Smith, Dennis E. *From symposium to Eucharist: The banquet in the early Christian world.* Minneapolis: Fortress, 2003.

Smith, Jonathan Z. "Differential equations: On constructing the other." In *Relating religion: Essays in the study of religion,* 230–50. Chicago: University of Chicago Press, 2004.

———. *Drudgery divine: On the comparison of early Christianities and the religions of late antiquity.* Chicago: University of Chicago Press, 1990.

———. "Fences and neighbors: Some contours of early Judaism." In *Imagining religion: From Babylon to Jonestown,* 1–18. Chicago: University of Chicago Press, 1982.

———. *Imagining religion: From Babylon to Jonestown.* Chicago: University of Chicago Press, 1982.

———. *Relating religion: Essays in the study of religion.* Chicago: University of Chicago Press, 2004.

Smith, William Robertson. *Lectures on the religion of the Semites: The fundamental institutions.* New York: Appleton, 1889.

Smith, Wilfred Cantwell. *What is Scripture? A comparative approach.* Minneapolis: Fortress, 1993.

Soloveitchik, Haym. "Can halakhic texts talk history?" *AJS Review* 3 (1978): 152–96.

———. *Ha-yayin bi-yemei ha-beynayim: Yein nesekh: Perek be-toledot ha-halakhah be-Ashkenaz.* Jerusalem: Shazar, 2008.

———. *Yeinam: Saḥar be-yeinam shel goyim ʿal gilgulah shel halakhah be-ʿolam ha-maʿaseh.* Tel Aviv: ʿAlma, 2003.

Somerville, Robert, and Bruce Brasington. *Prefaces to canon law books in Latin Christianity: Selected translations, 500–1245.* New Haven, Conn.: Yale University Press, 1998.

Ste. Croix, G. E. M. de. "Why were the early Christians persecuted?" *Past and present* 26 (1963): 6–38.

Steinfeld, Zvi Arie. "Bishul ʿal yedei yisrael ve-goy, ve-ʿal ha-minhag lehashlikh qeisam latanur." *Sidra* 14 (1998): 101–30.

———. "Devarim shel goyim ha-assurim ve-ha-mutarim be-akhilah." *Sinai* 86 (1980): 149–66.

———. "Gazru ʿal pitan mishum shamnan ve-ʿal shamnan mishum yeinan." *Sinai* 87 (1980): 273–81.

———. "Ha-im yesh ṣorekh be-kavvanah be-vishul shel goy? Hanaḥot ha-stamma leʿumat mashmaʿutan ha-meqorit shel ha-memrot." *Sidra* 13 (1997): 147–57.

———. "Le-dinam shel devarim she-nishtanu ʿal yedei goyim." *Sinai* 100 (1987): 866–81.

———. "Le-heter pat shel goyim." *Universitat Bar-Ilan: Sefer ha-shanah le-madaʿei ha-yahadut ve-ha-ruaḥ* 26–27 (1995): 321–41.

———. "Le-issur akhilah ʿim ha-goy." *Sidra* 5 (1989): 131–48.

———. "Le-issur shemen shel goyim." *Tarbiẓ* 49 (1980): 264–77.

———. "Le-mashmaʿo shel ha-issur ʿal tavshilei goyim." *Sidra* 2 (1986): 125–43.

Stern, Menahem. *Greek and Latin authors on Jews and Judaism.* 2 vols. Jerusalem: Israel Academy of Sciences and Humanities, 1976.

Stern, Sacha. *Jewish identity in early rabbinic writings.* Leiden, Netherlands: Brill, 1994.

Stewart, Devin J. "*Taqiyyah* as Performance: The Travels of Baha' al-Din al-ʿAmili in the Ottoman Empire (991–93/1583–85)." In *Law and Society in Islam,* 1–70. Princeton, N.J.: Wiener, 1996.

Stocking, Rachel L. *Bishops, councils, and consensus in the Visigothic kingdom, 589–633.* Ann Arbor: University of Michigan Press, 2000.

Stol, Marten. "Milk, butter, and cheese." *Bulletin on Sumerian agriculture* 7 (1993): 99–113.

Stouff, Louis. *Ravitaillement et alimentation en Provence aux XIVe et XVe siècles.* Paris: Mouton, 1970.

Stow, Kenneth R. *Jewish dogs: An image and its interpreters; Continuity in the Catholic-Jewish encounter.* Stanford, Calif.: Stanford University Press, 2006.

Stowers, Stanley K. *A rereading of Romans: Justice, Jews, and gentiles.* New Haven, Conn.: Yale University Press, 1994.

Stroumsa, Guy G. "Tertullian and the limits of tolerance." In *Tolerance and intolerance in early Judaism and Christianity,* edited by Graham N. Stanton and Guy G. Stroumsa, 173–84. Cambridge: Cambridge University Press, 1998.

Stroumsa, Sarah. *Maimonides in his world: Portrait of a Mediterranean thinker.* Princeton, N.J.: Princeton University Press, 2009.

Summa "Elegantius in iure diuino" seu Coloniensis. Edited by Gerard Fransen and Stephan Kuttner. Vol. 2. Vatican City: Biblioteca Apostolica Vaticana, 1978.

Swarz, Michael D. "Scholasticism as a comparative category and the study of Judaism." In *Scholasticism: Cross-cultural and comparative perspectives,* edited by José Ignacio Cabezón, 91–114. Albany: State University of New York Press, 1998.

Ṭabarī, Abū Jaʿfar b. Jarīr al-. *Jāmiʿ al-bayān ʿan taʾwīl āy al-Qurʾān [Tafsīr al-Ṭabarī].* Edited by Maḥmūd Muḥammad Shākir and Aḥmad Muḥammad Shākir. Cairo: Dār al-Maʿārif, 1961.

Ṭaḥāwī, Aḥmad b. Muḥammad al-. *Ikhtilāf al-fuqahā'*. Edited by Muḥammad Ṣaghīr Ḥasan al-Ma'ṣūmī. Islamabad, Pakistan: Ma'had al-Abḥāth al-Islāmiyyah, 1971.

———. *Mukhtaṣar al-Taḥāwī*. Edited by Abū al-Wafā' al-Afghānī. Hyderabad, India: Lajnat Iḥyā' al-Kutun al-Nu'māniyyah, 1951.

Taussig, Hal. *In the beginning was the meal: social experimentation and early Christian identity.* Minneapolis: Fortress, 2009.

Taylor, Miriam S. *Anti-Judaism and early Christian identity: A critique of the scholarly consensus.* Leiden, Netherlands: Brill, 1995.

Tcherikover, Victor. *Hellenistic civilization and the Jews.* Philadelphia: Jewish Publication Society, 1959.

Tertullian. "Apology." Translated by Emily Joseph Daly. In *Tertullian: Apologetical works, and Minucius Felix: Octavius,* 3–126. New York: Fathers of the Church, 1950.

———. *Apology.* Translated by T. R. Glover. Loeb Classical Library. Cambridge, Mass.: Harvard University Press, 1953.

Tirmidhī, Muḥammad b. 'Isā al-. *Sunan al-Tirmidhī.* 2 vols. Vaduz, Liechtenstein: Jam'iyyat al-Maknaz al-Islāmī, 2000.

Toaff, Ariel. *Love, work, and death: Jewish life in medieval Umbria.* Translated by Judith Landry. London: Littman Library of Jewish Civilization, 1998.

Tomson, Peter J. *Paul and the Jewish law: Halakha in the letters of the Apostle to the Gentiles.* Assen, Netherlands: Van Gorcum, 1990.

Tosefta. Edited by Saul Lieberman. 1955–88. Repr., New York: Jewish Theological Seminary of America Press, 1995.

———. Edited by Moses Samuel Zuckermandel. 1881. Repr., Jerusalem: Wahrman, 1970.

Tsafrir, Nurit. "The attitude of Sunnī Islam toward Jews and Christians as reflected in some legal issues." *Al-Qanṭara* 26 (2005): 317–36.

———. "Yaḥas ha-halakhah ha-muslemit kelapei datot aḥerot: 'Inyanei sheḥiṭah ve-nisu'in." Master's thesis, Hebrew University, 1988.

Tucker, Ethan M. "Literary agendas and legal conclusions: The contributions of rabbinic editors to the laws of forbidden mixtures." Ph.D. diss., Jewish Theological Seminary of America, 2006.

Ṭūsī, Muḥammad b. al-Ḥasan al-. *Al-istibṣār fī-mā ikhtalafa min al-akhbār.* Edited by Ḥasan al-Mūsawī al-Kharsān. 4 vols. Tehran: Dār al-Kutub al-Islāmiyyah, 1970.

———. *Al-khilāf.* 6 vols. Qom, Iran: Al-Nashr al-Islāmī, 1987–96.

———. *Al-mabsūṭ fī fiqh al-imāmiyyah.* Edited by Muḥammad Taqī al-Kashfī and Muḥammad al-Bāqir al-Bahbūdī. 8 vols. Tehran: Al-Maktabah al-Murtaḍawiyyah li-Iḥyā' al-Āthār al-Ja'fariyyah, 1967–72.

———. *Al-nihāyah fī mujarrad al-fiqh wa-'l-fatāwā.* Beirut: Dār al-Kitāb al-'Arabī, 1980.

———. *Tahdhīb al-aḥkām.* Edited by Ḥasan al-Mūsawī al-Khūrasān. 10 vols. Najaf, Iraq: Maṭba'at al-Nu'mān, 1959.

———. *Al-tibyān fī tafsīr al-Qur'ān.* 10 vols. Najaf, Iraq: Al-'Ilmiyyah, 1957–63.

Twersky, Isadore, ed. *A Maimonides reader.* New York: Behrman, 1972.

Tyson, Joseph B. "Acts 6:1–7 and dietary regulations in early Christianity." *Perspectives in religious studies* 10 (1983): 145–61.

Unnik, Willem Cornelis van. "Josephus' account of the story of Israel's sin with alien women in the country of Midian (Num. 25:1 ff.)." In *Travels in the world of the Old Testament: Studies presented to Professor M. A. Beek on the occasion of his 65th birthday,* edited by M. S. H. G. Heerma van Voss, Ph. H. J. Houwink ten Cate, and N. A. van Uchelen, 241–61. Assen, Netherlands: Van Gorcum, 1974.

Urbach, Ephraim E. *The Sages: Their concepts and beliefs.* Translated by Israel Abrahams. Jerusalem: Magnes, 1975.

VanderKam, James C. *The Book of Jubilees.* Guides to Apocrypha and Pseudepigrapha. Sheffield, England: Sheffield Academic Press, 2001.

———, trans. *The Book of Jubilees.* Corpus Scriptorum Christianorm Orientalium. Louvain, Belgium: Peeters, 1989.

Vives, José, ed. *Concilios Visigóticos e Hispano-Romanos.* Barcelona: Consejo Superior de Investigaciones Científicas, 1963.

Vogels, Henry Joseph, ed. *Ambrosiastri qui dicitur commentarius in Epistulas Paulinas.* Corpus Scriptorum Ecclesiasticorum Latinorum. Vienna: Hoelder-Pichler-Tempsky, 1968–69.

Vööbus, Arthur, ed. *The Didascalia Apostolorum in Syriac.* Corpus Scriptorum Christianorum Orientalium, Scriptores Syri, vols. 175–76, 179–80. Louvain, Belgium: Sécretariat du Corpus SCO, 1979.

———, ed. *The Synodicon in the West Syrian tradition.* Corpus Scriptorum Christianorum Orientalium, Scriptores Syri, vols. 161–64. Louvain, Belgium: Secrétariat du Corpus SCO, 1975.

———. *Syrische Kanonessammlungen: Ein Beitrag zur Quellenkunde.* Louvain, Belgium: Secrétariat du Corpus SCO, 1970.

Wāḥidī al-Nīsābūrī, ʿAlī b. Aḥmad al-. *Asbāb al-nuzūl.* Cairo: Al-Ḥalabī, 1968.

Wasserschleben, F. W. H. *Die Bussordnungen der abendländischen Kirche.* Halle, Germany: Graeger, 1851.

Wasserstrom, Steven M. *Between Muslim and Jew: The problem of symbiosis under early Islam.* Princeton, N.J.: Princeton University Press, 1995.

Weeks, Stuart, Simon Gathercole, and Loren Stuckenbruck, eds. *The Book of Tobit: Texts from the principal ancient and medieval traditions.* Berlin: De Gruyter, 2004.

Weingarten, Susan. "'Magiros,' 'naḥtom,' and women at home: cooks in the Talmud." *Journal of Jewish studies* 56 (2005): 285–97.

Weiss, Isaac Hirsch. *Dor dor ve-dorshav.* Vol. 1. Vilna, Lithuania: Rom, 1904.

Westbrook, Raymond. *Studies in biblical and cuneiform law.* Paris: Gabalda, 1988.

Wilken, Robert L. *John Chrysostom and the Jews: Rhetoric and reality in the late 4th century.* Berkeley: University of California Press, 1983.

Williamson, Hugh G. M. *Ezra, Nehemiah.* Word Biblical Commentary. Waco, Tex.: Word Books, 1985.

Wilson, Stephen G. *The Gentiles and the Gentile mission in Luke-Acts.* Cambridge: Cambridge University Press, 1973.

Wintermute, O. S. "Jubilees." In *The Old Testament pseudepigrapha,* edited by James H. Charlesworth, 2: 35–142. New York: Doubleday, 1985.

Wiseman, Donald J. *The vassal-treaties of Esarhaddon.* London: British School of Archaeology in Iraq, 1958.

Witherington, Ben, III. "Not so idle thoughts about *eidolothuton*." *Tyndale bulletin* 44 (1993): 237–54.

Wright, David P. "The spectrum of priestly impurity." In *Priesthood and cult in ancient Israel,* edited by Gary A. Anderson and Saul M. Olyan, 150–81. Sheffield, England: JSOT, 1991.

Yarshater, Ehsan, ed. *The Cambridge history of Iran.* Vol. 3, pt. 1, *The Seleucid, Parthian and Sasanian periods.* Cambridge: Cambridge University Press, 1983.

Yisha'yah di Trani. R. *Tosefot Rid.* Jerusalem: Yerid ha-Sefarim, 1995.

Yom Ṭov b. Avraham Ishbili, R. *Ḥiddushei ha-Riṭba: masekhet 'Avodah Zarah.* Edited by Moshe Goldstein. Jerusalem: Mosad ha-Rav Kook, 1978.

Zaas, Peter, and Mary Meany. " . . . Adhuc rarissimus emptor: A final stage of early Christian kashrut." *Jewish Law Association studies* 10 (2000): 265–75.

Zamakhsharī, Maḥmūd b. 'Umar al-. *Al-kashshāf 'an ḥaqā'iq al-tanzīl wa-'uyūn al-aqāwīl fī wujūh al-ta'wīl.* 4 vols. Cairo: Al-Bābī al-Ḥalabī, 1966–68.

Zayd b. 'Alī. *Tafsīr al-shahīd Zayd b. 'Alī, al-musammā bi-Tafsīr gharīb al-Qur'ān.* Edited by Ḥasan Muḥammad Taqī al-Ḥākim. Beirut: Al-Dār al-'Ālamiyyah, 1992.

Zayla'ī, 'Uthmān b. 'Alī al-. *Tabyīn al-ḥaqā'iq.* Beirut: Dār al-Kutub al-'Ilmiyyah, 2000.

Zeidman, Reena. "A view of celebrations in early Judaism: Tosefta Avodah Zarah [Idolatry]." Ph.D. diss., University of Toronto, 1992.

INDEX OF SOURCES

This index provides references to citations and discussions of specific passages in the Hebrew Bible, Rabbinic literature, the New Testament, the Qur'an, and collections of ḥadith. References to general discussions of these works and to citations of other primary sources appear in the general index, often under the author's name.

RABBINIC LITERATURE

Mishnah

GENERAL INDEX

TEXT
10/12.5 Minion Pro
DISPLAY
Minion Pro
COMPOSITOR
Integrated Composition Systems
PRINTER AND BINDER
Sheridan Books, Inc.